Alternative Validation Strategies

THE PROFESSIONAL PRACTICE SERIES

The Professional Practice Series is sponsored by the Society for Industrial and Organizational Psychology (SIOP). The series was launched in 1988 to provide industrial/organizational psychologists, organizational scientists and practitioners, human resource professionals, managers, executives, and those interested in organizational behavior and performance with volumes that are insightful, current, informative, and relevant to organizational practice. The volumes in the Professional Practice Series are guided by five tenets designed to enhance future organizational practice:

1. Focus on practice, but grounded in science
2. Translate organizational science into practice by generating guidelines, principles, and lessons learned that can shape and guide practice
3. Showcase the application of industrial/organizational psychology to solve problems
4. Document and demonstrate best industrial and organizational-based practices
5. Stimulate research needed to guide future organizational practice

The volumes seek to inform those interested in practice with guidance, insights, and advice on how to apply the concepts, findings, methods, and tools derived from industrial/organizational psychology to solve human-related organizational problems.

Previous Professional Practice Series volumes include:

Published by Jossey-Bass

Customer Service Delivery
Lawrence Fogli, Editor

Employment Discrimination Litigation
Frank J. Landy, Editor

The Brave New World of eHR
Hal G. Gueutal, Dianna L. Stone, Editors

Improving Learning Transfer in Organizations
Elwood F. Holton III, Timothy T. Baldwin, Editors

Resizing the Organization
Kenneth P. De Meuse, Mitchell Lee Marks, Editors

Implementing Organizational Interventions
Jerry W. Hedge, Elaine D. Pulakos, Editors

Organization Development
Janine Waclawski, Allan H. Church, Editors

Creating, Implementing, and Managing Effective Training and Development
Kurt Kraiger, Editor

The 21st Century Executive
Rob Silzer, Editor

Managing Selection in Changing Organizations
Jerard F. Kehoe, Editor

Evolving Practices in Human Resource Management
Allen I. Kraut, Abraham K. Korman, Editors

Individual Psychological Assessment
Richard Jeanneret, Rob Silzer, Editors

Performance Appraisal
James W. Smither, Editor

Organizational Surveys
Allen I. Kraut, Editor

Employees, Careers, and Job Creation
Manuel London, Editor

Published by Guilford Press

Diagnosis for Organizational Change
Ann Howard and Associates

Human Dilemmas in Work Organizations
Abraham K. Korman and Associates

Diversity in the Workplace
Susan E. Jackson and Associates

Working with Organizations and Their People
Douglas W. Bray and Associates

Alternative Validation Strategies

JB JOSSEY-BASS

Alternative Validation Strategies

Developing New and Leveraging Existing Validity Evidence

S. Morton McPhail, Editor

Foreword by Allan H. Church
and Janine Waclawski

BICENTENNIAL
1807
WILEY
2007
BICENTENNIAL

John Wiley & Sons, Inc.

Published by Jossey-Bass
A Wiley Imprint
989 Market Street, San Francisco, CA 94103-1741   www.josseybass.com

Jossey-Bass books and products are available through most bookstores. To contact Jossey-
Bass directly call our Customer Care Department within the U.S. at 800-956-7739, outside
the U.S. at 317-572-3986, or fax 317-572-4002.

Jossey-Bass also publishes its books in a variety of electronic formats. Some content that
appears in print may not be available in electronic books.

Library of Congress Cataloging-in-Publication Data

Alternative validation strategies : developing new and leveraging existing validity evidence
/ S. Morton McPhail, editor ; foreword by Allan H. Church and Janine Waclawski.
    p. cm. – (Professional practice series)
  Includes index.
  ISBN-13: 978-0-7879-8242-3 (cloth)
  ISBN-10: 0-7879-8242-3 (cloth)
  1. Employee selection. 2. Employment tests. 3. Prediction of occupational success.
I. McPhail, S. Morton.
  HF5549.5.S38A45 2007
  658.3'112–dc22

                                                    2006033436

Printed in the United States of America
FIRST EDITION
HB Printing   10 9 8 7 6 5 4 3 2 1

Contents

Foreword

We are pleased to offer this volume as our second contribution as co-editors of the SIOP Professional Practice Series. This book touches on a topic that is essential to every practicing I/O psychologist: specifically, making sure that we develop and implement selection tools in organizations that effectively put the right people in the right jobs. Although a seemingly simple task to the average hiring manager (whose typical criterion measure is something akin to "did I like the person in the interview?"), the process of ensuring that we have valid, credible, and defensible measures for selection and placement can actually be very challenging at times. This is particularly true when practitioners are presented with business scenarios and challenges (such as small samples or the need for immediate turnaround of results) that do not lend themselves well to more traditional methodologies.

Moreover, as Mort McPhail points out in Chapter One, this realm of practice reflects an applied science existing in a political context, so the I/O practitioner is on occasion placed in a position to justify (that is, "prove") or document rather than actually design an appropriate and effective selection process with the appropriate measures and controls in place. All of this requires that we as practitioners have a firm understanding of an appropriate set of alternative validation strategies to meet the various needs of our clients. As Mort notes, it is all a question of ensuring that an appropriate degree of rigor is embedded in the process.

Given these challenges, and as reflected in our goals for the Professional Practice series, we are very pleased to see this volume explore the balance between science and practice in this area. Mort and his colleagues have done an excellent job of framing up the very practical issues that practitioners face in developing and applying valid selection tools. Further, the volume comprises chapters that, when taken as a whole, contain a nice blend of the theoretical and the practical. In effect, there is something for everyone. The novice and the expert, the academic and the practitioner, the I and the O all will find relevant content in this book. In addition, the contributors included here are leaders in the field; all speak from experience and with authority on the topic at hand. We fully expect practitioners who peruse this volume to come away with a number of new ideas and approaches to the whole concept of validation.

We would like to thank Mort for all of his efforts in planning and preparing this volume, and we thank the highly accomplished group of authors he has assembled for their contributions. We hope you will find this volume as compelling and useful as we do.

August 2006

Janine Waclawski
Allan H. Church
Series Editors

Preface

After wandering down some dark dead-end alleys, most industrial and organizational psychologists have finally agreed that validity is a unitary concept subject to scientific hypothesis testing. It is not an attribute of a particular selection procedure, and it does not come in types or stamp albums. Rather, validity "is a property of the inferences drawn from test scores" (Guion & Highhouse, 2006, p. 134).

This conceptualization is captured in both the *Standards for Educational and Psychological Testing* (American Educational Association, 1999) and the *Principles for the Validation and Use of Personnel Selection Procedures* (Society for Industrial and Organizational Psychology, 2003). Consistent with this consensus view, the extent and nature of evidence that is relevant and appropriate for evaluating the hypothesized inferences based on test scores is both broad and varied. Such evidence has often been predicated on the statistical relationship of the scores with job-relevant criteria. But the capacity to conduct the necessary research to obtain data to test those relationships may be limited by an array of factors that make it impracticable, expensive, even impossible. There are, however, alternative research approaches available that offer practitioners viable ways to meaningfully and rigorously assess the validity of inferences proposed from selection and other measures.

The chapters that follow capture the state of the science regarding the alternative validation strategies considered. They also address the very real and even vexing practical problems faced by practitioners, as they are challenged to be both creative in development and evaluation of selection procedures and compliant with relevant legal and professional guidelines and principles. In this volume, by tying the strategies discussed to the *Uniform Guidelines on Employee Selection Procedures* (Equal Employment Opportunity Commission, Civil Service Commission, Department of Labor, &

Department of Justice, 1978), the *Principles*, and the *Standards*, and by providing examples and procedures, we seek to inform and lead practice into fruitful application of the strategies in appropriate situations.

In these chapters, the authors present a variety of alternative paths for developing evidence regarding the validity of selection procedures. These paths fall into two broad (and often overlapping) categories: (1) application of existing evidence to new or different situations and (2) development of new evidence bearing on the validity (and legal defensibility) of selection procedures. In no case, however, are these procedures and methods to be confused with shortcuts that offer an "easy out" for researchers. These methods may allow for the development of relevant evidence in situations for which traditional criterion evidence is either unavailable or unobtainable or for which programmatic construct research is impracticable. However, the effort necessary to use them and the rigor with which they must be applied must nonetheless be compatible with the importance of the application to which the results will be put and the implications of the inferences that will be drawn.

Part One: Applying Existing Validity Evidence

After a brief overview of the conceptual issues that have surrounded validation, Chapter One outlines some of the constraints on traditional criterion-related validation research in organizations. Chapters Two through Six deal with methods for leveraging existing validation evidence to additional settings and situations.

Transportation of validation results. The use of validity information from a study in another location or even for related jobs is specifically included as an available strategy in the *Uniform Guidelines*. Doing so has long been recognized as a viable means to leverage the cost and difficulty of conducting criterion-related studies. Since 1978, the concept has been expanded in a number of ways. In Chapter Two, Wade Gibson and Julie Caplinger address the specific requirements imposed by the *Uniform Guidelines*, with particular emphasis on the central difficulties of defining and measuring job similarity.

Job component validation. The term *job component validity* (JCV) was first coined by McCormick (1959) to describe an inference of test validity based on the empirical relationships between test constructs and job analytic data, based on what came to be called the *gravitational hypothesis.* The methodology was operationalized using Position Analysis Questionnaire (PAQ) job dimensions to predict means, variances, validities, and specific test battery inclusion for the tests of the General Aptitude Test Battery (GATB). Subsequent research linked the predictions to commercially available tests. More recently, research on the Occupational Information Network (O*NET) has expanded this concept into new areas, including personality measures. In Chapter Three, Cal Hoffman, Boris Rashkovksy, and Erika D'Egidio discuss this history and theoretical development as well as the practical applications of the method, including its use and success in litigation.

Synthetic validation. As originally conceived, *synthetic validation* referred to the building up of evidence for test validity by combining judgments or data about linkages among job elements, test constructs, and performance constructs. Subsequently, the term has been used to refer to various methods of combining or constructing evidence to support the validity of test measures and constructs. In Chapter Four, Jeff Johnson explores current uses of synthetic validation procedures, with a focus on new methodologies, extensions to fairness analyses, and recommended best practices. He also examines the larger issue of how this concept underlies other methodological approaches.

Meta-analysis and validity generalization. The powerful mathematical methods underlying meta-analysis have revolutionized the development of broad knowledge in the field of I/O psychology. The increased scope of understanding and the ability to bring together large amounts of information into a coherent picture have provided a basis for more general statements about the prediction of performance. However, there remains a gap between what we know scientifically and what we are able to do in practice. In Chapter Five, Mike McDaniel focuses on practical ways to use available research data to develop defensible evidence to support test use. He reviews both the literature and the litigation history of validity generalization to provide practical means by which the method may be used to develop and document evidence supporting selection procedures, avoiding past mistakes, and capitalizing on the state of the science to inform and direct practice.

Generalizing personality-based validity evidence. Bringing together aspects of transportability, synthetic, and meta-analytic approaches, in Chapter Six Joyce Hogan, Scott Davies, and Bob Hogan extend the scope of these methods to the domain of personality characteristics for selection. To some extent this chapter describes execution of a multifaceted construct validation strategy. The authors describe as part of their approach the development and use of instrumentation specifically designed to obtain job analysis data related to this domain. This method appears to have most immediate application for broad-based personal variables such as personality factors, but in principle it might be extendable to other personal variables. Linking these data to an existing database, the authors describe the multiple strands of evidence that they assemble to support the selection inferences from a personality test.

Part Two: Developing New Evidence for Validity

Beyond applying existing evidence, Chapters Seven through Nine address methods of research designed to investigate new evidence to support test score inferences.

Consortium studies. The *Uniform Guidelines* specifically mention and even encourage test users to engage in cooperative studies with other users to increase the viability of empirical research, especially when sample sizes are limited within a single organization. Such cooperative studies reduce the costs and the personnel burdens for individual employers. However, they impose a number of unique problems of their own, such as coordinating data collection efforts and ensuring commonality of jobs, and the introduction of organizational variables as uncontrolled error variance. In Chapter Seven, Nancy Tippins and Bill Macey address both theoretical and practical advantages and point to the substantial difficulties associated with doing validation research in consortia and strategies for addressing them.

Content validity for broader constructs. The *Uniform Guidelines* specifically restrict the use of content validation for supporting some constructs such as judgment or conscientiousness. The *Uni-*

form Guidelines are frequently interpreted as limiting use of the content approach to observable work behaviors, perhaps even to work samples or simulations. On the other hand, a broader understanding of content validation tends in some cases to verge on a deeper, almost construct, interpretation. Certainly, the limits of content validation have been expanded and even tested as researchers and practitioners have sought to reduce the risks of validation research. In Chapter Eight, Damian Stelly and Harold Goldstein examine the limits and practical use of content validation strategies for a variety of constructs and applications. They discuss such concerns as what constitutes operationalizing work behaviors, appropriate sampling from the job domain, and low-fidelity simulations with appropriate recommendations for practice.

Practical construct validation. The *Uniform Guidelines* specifically include construct validity as an acceptable strategy for demonstrating job relatedness, though the agencies seemed to do so with considerable trepidation. As I discuss in Chapter One, construct validation may be viewed as the essence of validity to which other strategies contribute evidence, but doing so greatly complicates the scientific process of test validation. Seldom has any method describing itself as construct validation been used to document or defend a selection procedure in actual practice. In Chapter Nine, Tim Landon and Rich Arvey address the various sources and research strategies that can be meaningfully integrated to form an epistemological whole on which a selection procedure or even an entire selection strategy might be based and supported. They point to advances in research and analytical methodologies that support this integration and offer examples of their use in applied settings.

Part Three: Implementation

In many cases the alternate strategies just described will not yield empirical data to inform the setting of cut scores. Although the *Principles* indicate that linearity is a reasonable assumption for most selection procedure predictions, making rank order selection viable, there are many situations in which other approaches to implementation may have substantial practical value. Moreover, the *Uniform Guidelines* require a reasonable showing of this assumption to support rank order selection in the presence of disparate impact.

Additionally, the process of combining selection measures into composites will be complicated under some of the strategies.

Implementation based on alternate validation procedures: ranking, cut scores, banding, and compensatory models. With these issues in mind, in Chapter Ten Lorin Mueller, Dwayne Norris, and Scott Oppler have provided practitioners with guidance about the use of judgmental and other implementation procedures for selection procedures for which validity evidence is based on alternate procedures.

Part Four: Where Do We Go from Here?

Although any declaration of the "death of the job" is undoubtedly premature, there are certainly a number of identifiable trends affecting work, as we have known it. Issues affecting the stability of job-task clusters such as contingent work, job rotation, shared jobs, and task-responsive jobs are more prevalent in the workplace today than ever before. Team-based work, matrix organizations, and virtual work groups also are changing the nature of what we have traditionally labeled *jobs*. Finally, globalization has changed the specific competency requirements of some jobs and broadened the concepts of contextual job performance to include cultural issues. All of these changes are likely to have implications for how validation research can be and is accomplished. Some of them may make traditional empirical analyses impractical or impossible to conduct.

Changing work and the future of validation. In Chapter Eleven, Frank Landy has outlined how trends such as those mentioned above may interact with the scientific process of determining whether the selection processes we use are in fact valid and reliable predictors of future success in organizations. He explores the implications of these developments for research and practice.

Summary

By focusing attention on the appropriate application of these strategies in various situations, together with the constraints that may accompany them, practitioners will find assistance in identifying the best solutions for the specific problems they encounter. As appropriate, the chapters identify the strengths and weaknesses of the strategy under consideration. Researchers may well be able to examine the disadvantages or weaknesses (which may, in fact, lie in a paucity of research on the method itself) to develop empirical data in response to the concerns identified.

Acknowledgments

It is with deep appreciation that I acknowledge the time and effort of such a highly qualified group of authors in their contributions to this volume. They devoted many hours and endured multiple iterations of edits and increasing time pressures as it took shape. Without their willingness to share their professional expertise, practical experience, and valuable time, this book would not have been possible. Special thanks go to Damian Stelly, Julie Caplinger, and Nancy Tippins for lending their editorial skills to review the first chapter. Thanks also go to my colleagues, especially Dick Jeanneret, who picked up the work load as I took time to work on this project. In addition, recognition goes to Rene Miller for her diligent literature searches and to Donna Roberts for reading my cryptic notations and preparing the final manuscripts. Finally, I would like to thank Janine Waclawski and Allan Church, the editors of the Professional Practice Series, and the editorial staff at Jossey-Bass for shepherding me through the arcane and complex world of publishing.

References

American Educational Research Association, American Psychological Association, & National Council on Measurement in Education. (1999). *Standards for educational and psychological testing*. Washington, DC: American Psychological Association.

Equal Employment Opportunity Commission, Civil Service Commission, Department of Labor, & Department of Justice. (1978). *Uniform guidelines on employee selection procedures. Federal Register, 43*(166), 38295–38309.

Guion, R. M., & Highhouse, S. (2006). Essentials of Personnel Assessment and Selection. Mahwah, NJ: Lawrence Erlbaum Associates, Publishers.

McCormick, E. J. (1959). The development of processes for indirect or synthetic validity: III. Application of job analysis to indirect validity. A symposium. *Personnel Psychology, 12*, 402–413.

Society for Industrial and Organizational Psychology. (2003). *Principles for the validation and use of personnel selection procedures*. Bowling Green, OH: Society for Industrial and Organizational Psychology.

The Authors

S. Morton McPhail, Ph.D., is a senior vice president and managing principal with Valtera Corporation (formerly Jeanneret & Associates). Since earning his doctorate at Colorado State University, he has served as a consultant for more than twenty-eight years to a wide variety of public and private sector clients on issues ranging from selection, training and development, and performance assessment to termination. He has served as an expert in litigation involving such diverse issues as job analysis, test development and validation, violence in the workplace, equal employment opportunity, and compensation. Dr. McPhail is currently involved in developing promotional and selection processes for a variety of private sector clients for jobs ranging from entry-level clerical and plant operations to managerial and technical positions. In addition, he is involved in research and development of selection, promotion, and performance management procedures for several public safety entities. He has published in professional journals, made numerous presentations at professional meetings, and currently serves on the editorial board for *Personnel Psychology*. Dr. McPhail is a licensed psychologist and serves as adjunct faculty for both the University of Houston and Rice University.

Wade M. Gibson, Ph.D., received his doctorate in industrial psychology from Bowling Green State University in 1989. He has fifteen years of experience in the consulting and test publishing industry, where he has designed, developed, and validated published and proprietary employment tests and has consulted with organizations to implement and support employee selection procedures. Dr. Gibson has provided litigation support and expert witness testimony in matters involving validation and employment statistics. He has published in numerous scholarly journals on various testing issues and is a regular speaker at professional conferences, addressing topics ranging from technical psychometrics to testing and the law. He is presently president of W. M. Gibson & Associates, where he helps organizations develop, validate, and implement effective employee selection programs. Dr. Gibson is a member of the American Psychological Association and of the Society for Industrial and Organizational Psychology.

Julie A. Caplinger, M.A., is a senior consultant with Valtera Corporation (formerly Jeanneret & Associates) in Houston, Texas. She has designed systems to transport validation evidence in a variety of settings, including the design and implementation of standardized job similarity processes for many clients. She manages projects involving test validation research, client-specific selection tool development, multirater feedback surveys, job classification and compensation structures, performance management tools, and other organizational systems in both the public and private sectors. Ms. Caplinger also conducts individual assessments for clients in various industries for both selection and development purposes. She has experience developing and delivering training classes for clients on human resource processes. Ms. Caplinger holds a master's degree in industrial and organizational psychology and human resource management from Appalachian State University in North Carolina. She is an associate member of the Society for Industrial and Organizational Psychology and the American Psychological Association and is a licensed psychological associate in the State of Texas.

Calvin C. Hoffman, Ph.D., earned his doctorate in industrial and organizational psychology from the University of Nebraska in 1984. The majority of his professional experience has been in the private sector, where he has been involved in conducting a variety of interventions, including job analysis, job evaluation, job family development, selection system design and validation, management assessment and development programs, customer satisfaction research, and HR system redesign. He has published on a variety of topics including job analysis, test validation, utility analysis, and job component validation. He has also consulted extensively with both public and private sector organizations. Dr. Hoffman is currently a civilian employee with the Los Angeles County Sheriff's Department, a member of the editorial board of *Personnel Psychology,* and an adjunct faculty member of Alliant International University.

Boris Rashkovsky, Ph.D., is an organizational development specialist at City of Hope National Medical Center. He is responsible for developing and providing consulting services in organizational surveys, leadership development, performance management, and competency development. He is experienced in managing the entire gamut of activities for employee engagement and organizational effectiveness. Dr. Rashkovsky has designed and led departmental, pulse, business unit, customer, and organization wide survey initiatives. He also specializes in performance management and culture formation. His dissertation focused on extending the Job Component Validity model to include personality predictors. Dr. Rashkovsky received his doctorate in industrial and organizational psychology from Alliant International University, Los Angeles.

Erika L. D'Egidio, Ph.D., is director of talent management at Bristol-Myers Squibb. She is responsible for partnering with the business to design systems, processes, and programs focused on the identification, selection, development, and retention of talent within the organization. She has been with Bristol-Myers Squibb since March 2004. Prior to joining Bristol-Myers Squibb, Dr. D'Egidio worked nine years with Jeanneret & Associates (now Valtera Corporation), a consulting firm based in Houston, Texas. Her work at Jeanneret & Associates focused on designing and validating selection systems, providing advice and counsel to clients about human resource processes, and litigation support regarding a variety of employment issues. She received her master's and doctoral degrees in industrial and organizational psychology from the University of Houston and her bachelor's degree in psychology from the University of Texas.

Jeff W. Johnson, Ph.D., is a senior staff scientist at Personnel Decisions Research Institutes, where he has directed many applied organizational research projects for a variety of government and private sector clients. His primary research interests are in the areas of personnel selection, performance measurement, research methods, and statistics. He has particular expertise in quantitative analysis, with expertise in a variety of statistical and psychometric techniques. Dr. Johnson developed relative weight analysis, which determines the relative importance of correlated predictors in a regression equation, and synthetic differential prediction analysis, which increases the power of differential prediction analysis by applying synthetic validity techniques. His research has been published in academic journals such as the *Journal of Applied Psychology, Personnel Psychology,* and *Multivariate Behavioral Research.* He is an associate editor of *Personnel Psychology* and is on the editorial board of *Human Performance.* Dr. Johnson received his doctorate in industrial and organizational psychology from the University of Minnesota.

Michael A. McDaniel, Ph.D., received his doctorate in industrial and organizational psychology at George Washington University in 1986. He is a professor of management at Virginia Commonwealth University and president of Work Skills First, a human resource consulting firm. Dr. McDaniel is nationally recognized for his research and practice in personnel selection system development and validation. He has published in several major journals, including the *Academy of Management Journal,* the *Journal of Applied Psychology,* and *Personnel Psychology.* He is a member of the Academy of Management and a fellow of the Society of Industrial and Organizational Psychology and the American Psychological Society. His current research interests include situational judgment tests, applications of meta-analysis to I/O psychology, publication bias, and demographic differences in the workplace.

Joyce Hogan, Ph.D., is vice president of Hogan Assessment Systems, a corporation specializing in test publishing and organizational consulting. Dr. Hogan received her doctorate from the University of Maryland. She was a research scientist at the Johns Hopkins University and professor of psychology at the University of Tulsa. Her research includes job analysis and test development as well as validating personality-based selection systems for private and public sector organizations. She is recognized nationally as an expert in human performance and in 1991 was named a fellow of the American Psychological Association. Among her scholarly publications are chapters that appear in the *Handbook of Industrial and Organizational Psychology* (2nd ed.) and the *Handbook of Personality Psychology*. Dr. Hogan edited the book *Business and Industry Testing* and the journal *Human Performance,* a quarterly publication of scholarly articles on performance measurement and evaluation. Currently, she serves on the editorial boards of the *Journal of Applied Psychology, Human Performance,* and the *International Journal of Selection and Assessment.*

Scott Davies, Ph.D., is an applied psychologist with more than twenty years of measurement research and consulting experience in a variety of industries. His work in the private sector has included selection projects, goal setting, performance measurement, job analysis, process design, workplace intervention, and shift work scheduling. Additionally, he has worked with local, state, and federal government agencies in the areas of litigation support, policy analysis, program evaluation, organizational research, and strategic planning. In his recent position as director of research and development for Hogan Assessment Systems, Dr. Davies directed job analysis projects, validation research, item banking, test maintenance, and assessment development. Previously, he was a senior research scientist at the American Institutes for Research in Washington, D.C. Currently Dr. Davies is adjunct professor at the University of Tulsa and lead psychometrician for Pearson, Inc. He has published or presented more than fifty papers on his research. Dr. Davies received his master's and doctoral degrees in industrial and organizational psychology from the Ohio State University.

Robert Hogan, Ph.D., president of Hogan Assessment Systems, is recognized as an international authority on personality assessment, leadership, and organizational effectiveness. Dr. Hogan was McFarlin Professor and chair of the Department of Psychology at the University of Tulsa for fourteen years. Prior to that, he was professor of psychology and social relations at the Johns Hopkins University. He has received a number of research and teaching awards, and is the editor of the *Handbook of Personality Psychology* and author of the Hogan Personality Inventory. Dr. Hogan received his doctorate from the University of California, Berkeley, specializing in personality assessment. Dr. Hogan is the author of more than three hundred journal articles, chapters, and books. He is widely credited with demonstrating how careful attention to personality factors can influence organizational effectiveness in a variety of areas—ranging from organizational climate and leadership to selection and effective team performance. Dr. Hogan is a fellow of the American Psychological Association and the Society for Industrial and Organizational Psychology.

Nancy T. Tippins, Ph.D., is currently senior vice president and managing principal for the Selection Practice Group of Valtera Corporation (formerly Personnel Research Associates) where she is responsible for the development and execution of firm strategies related to employee selection and assessment. She has extensive experience in the development and validation of selection tests for all levels of management and hourly employees as well as in designing leadership development programs, including the development of assessment programs for executive development and the identification of high-potential employees. Dr. Tippins has been active in professional affairs and the Society for Industrial and Organizational Psychology. She is a past president of SIOP and a fellow of SIOP and the American Psychological Association. Dr. Tippins received her master's and doctoral degrees in industrial and organizational psychology from the Georgia Institute of Technology. She also holds a master of education degree in counseling and psychological services from Georgia State University and an undergraduate degree in history from Agnes Scott College.

William H. Macey, Ph.D., is CEO of Valtera Corporation (formerly Personnel Research Associates) and has thirty years' experience in consulting with organizations in various facets of assessment and organizational diagnostics. Dr. Macey is a fellow and a past president of the Society for Industrial and Organizational Psychology and a previous member of the editorial board of *Personnel Psychology*. He received his doctorate from Loyola University, Chicago, in 1975.

Damian J. Stelly, Ph.D., is a senior consultant with Valtera Corporation (formerly Jeanneret & Associates). Prior to joining Valtera, he worked as an internal consultant in private industry for

Anheuser-Busch Companies and the J.C. Penney Company. In his ten years of experience as an internal and external consultant, Dr. Stelly has managed a broad range of projects, including the development of employee selection and placement systems, employee survey programs, organizational development initiatives, and employee training and development programs. He has extensive experience conducting validation research and implementing employee selection programs in litigious contexts, under conditions of intense scrutiny. Dr. Stelly has presented and/or published research on several topics including content validation, setting cut scores, and leadership. He is a member of the American Psychological Association and the Society for Industrial and Organizational Psychology. Dr. Stelly holds a bachelor's degree in psychology from Louisiana State University and received both his master's and doctoral degrees in industrial and organizational psychology from the University of Missouri–St. Louis. He is a licensed psychologist in Texas.

Harold W. Goldstein, Ph.D., is associate professor in the industrial and organizational psychology program at Baruch College, the City University of New York. He received his doctorate in 1993 from the University of Maryland at College Park. His primary research interests and consulting work focus on leadership assessment and managerial development, the formation of organizational culture, and the impact of personnel selection practices on resulting racial differences. His work has been published in numerous journals including the *Journal of Applied Psychology* and *Personnel Psychology*. Dr. Goldstein also serves as an expert for the U.S. Department of Justice on the application of legal issues in personnel selection processes.

Timothy E. Landon, Ph.D., is a faculty member and director of graduate programs at the School of Management, University of Michigan-Dearborn. He received his undergraduate and M.B.A. degrees from Kansas State University and his doctorate in human resource management in 1994 from the University of Minnesota. His areas of interest are graduate business education, employee selection and testing, evaluation of fairness in testing, employee turnover, and free-agent employees.

Richard D. Arvey, Ph.D., is currently a professor at the National University of Singapore. He received his doctorate from the University of Minnesota. Previously he held positions at the Universities of Tennessee, Houston, and Minnesota. His research has ranged across many areas, from conducting studies on employment testing, bias, and discrimination in selection to studies on the genetic components of job satisfaction and leadership. He was awarded the Career Achievement Award from the Academy of Management in 2006.

Lorin Mueller, Ph.D., received his bachelor's degree in psychology from the University of Texas at Austin in 1995, and both his master's degree and doctoral degrees in industrial and organizational psychology from the University of Houston in 1999 and 2002, respectively. In 2000, he joined the American Institutes for Research (AIR) in Washington, D.C., where he currently works as a senior research scientist. Since joining AIR, he has worked in such diverse areas as employment litigation, disability determination and the capacity to perform future work, validation, program evaluation, high-stakes testing, and educational measurement. Dr. Mueller has presented and published work in the areas of the assessment of individuals with disabilities, alternative methods for setting cut scores, and statistical issues in employment discrimination analyses. He is a member of the Society for Industrial and Organizational Psychology and the American Psychological Association, and an associate member of the American Bar Association. He serves as an adjunct faculty member at George Mason University, where he has taught graduate-level multivariate statistics.

Dwayne Norris, Ph.D., joined the American Institutes for Research (AIR) in Washington, D.C., in 1996 and is currently a principal research scientist in AIR's Workforce Research and Analysis group. Since joining AIR, he has engaged in numerous applied research and consulting projects in such diverse areas as personnel selection, certification and licensing, job and occupational analysis, work performance management, validation research, and organizational and attitude assessment. Dr. Norris has presented and published work in the areas of job analysis, competency modeling, validation, selection, and job satisfaction. He is a member of the

Society for Industrial and Organizational Psychology, the American Psychological Association, and the Society of Human Resource Management. He received his doctorate in industrial and organizational psychology from Virginia Tech in 1996.

Scott Oppler, Ph.D., received his doctorate in industrial and organizational psychology from the University of Minnesota in 1990 and joined the American Institutes for Research (AIR) at their headquarters in Washington, D.C. As chief methodologist for AIR's Applied Behavioral and Social Sciences division, Dr. Oppler works with staff on a variety of projects, providing direction on a wide range of measurement and methodological issues. During the past seventeen years, he has conducted research on the validity and other psychometric characteristics of such instruments as the Medical College Admissions Test for the Association of American Medical Colleges, the Armed Services Vocational Aptitude Battery for the Department of Defense, the General Aptitude Test Battery for the U.S. Department of Labor, and the SAT I for the College Board. Dr. Oppler is the author or coauthor of more than fifty journal articles, book chapters, or conference presentations concerning the measurement or prediction of human abilities, achievement, or performance.

Frank J. Landy, Ph.D., received his doctorate from Bowling Green University in 1969 and spent the following twenty-four years at Penn State, retiring as an emeritus professor in 1993. During his academic career, Dr. Landy wrote extensively—in textbooks, chapters, and articles—on the topic of validity, most notably the article "Stamp Collecting versus Science," which appeared in *American Psychologist* in 1986. During his career at Penn State, Dr. Landy was an active consultant and expert witness on topics related to validation. Since 1993, he has directed a litigation support practice and has had many occasions to address the topic of validation in that role. Recently, in collaboration with Jeff Conte, he has completed new editions of his I/O textbooks (Landy & Conte, 2004; Landy & Conte, 2007), in which he noted that work in the twenty-first century was very different from what it had been previously, suggesting that the concept of validity and validation procedures needed to be revisited. His chapter in this volume is based on that observation.

Alternative Validation Strategies

CHAPTER 1

Development of Validation Evidence

S. Morton McPhail, Valtera Corporation

The owner of a small restaurant chain with three locations employs five food servers at each location. As repeat business in the neighborhoods near her restaurants is vital to her success, she is concerned about the level of customer service being provided by her current employees. She has two openings to fill and wants to do a better job of selecting people who will display the cordial, attentive, helpful behaviors she believes are so crucial to her business' success.

At a large petrochemical processing facility, many of the maintenance mechanics were hired at about the same time and will reach retirement age in the next year or so. Although the plant is quite large, the company has been contracting increasing amounts of the maintenance work. Currently, there are thirty maintenance mechanics, thirty plant electricians, five machinists, and twenty-five pipefitters employed at the facility. The plant superintendent recognizes that when the company hires replacements for the mechanics, it will be hiring at the journey- level, but he wants to make sure that the new employees will be able to learn the plant's equipment and become effective quickly. His own experience suggests that mechanical aptitude will be an important selection requirement. He has told the human resources manager to implement use of such a measure for the upcoming round of hiring.

A large manufacturer of food products anticipates a need to hire plant operators in the near future. The company has a dozen plants scattered across the United States, but there are fewer than thirty operators at any single facility. The company is seeking to migrate to team-based operations, and Human Resources has determined that strong interpersonal skills have been important factors in the success of a pilot of the team-based model.

An aluminum manufacturer is preparing to hire workers at a new, state-of-the-art rolling mill. The "greenfield" plant incorporates new technology and work techniques that are unlike those used at any other such facility in the world. The company will need to hire some three hundred workers into multicraft, multiskilled positions before the plant is operational to ensure that training can be completed prior to initial startup. The human resource director anticipates that because of the desirability of the working conditions and the reputation of the company, there will be over six thousand applicants.

A public safety agency has a long and troubled history of dealing with representatives of the employees' bargaining unit. There is a significant level of mistrust among the employees concerning management's intentions. Anticipating a need to select and hire new employees from among a very large applicant pool, the agency (which has faced substantial litigation in the past) wants to be sure that the selection measures comply with legal requirements. However, despite sincere reassurances, employees are reluctant to participate in experimental testing, and supervisors are hesitant to make meaningful evaluations of subordinates based on the defined performance criteria.

Many practitioners will recognize these or similar situations. These scenarios include large and small organizations in both manufacturing and service and in both the public and private sectors. They include concerns about both cognitive and noncognitive individual differences. They represent many of the issues that make the selection problems faced by organizations distinct and unique, yet in some ways similar. In what way, then, are these scenarios similar? Is there a common theme here? Despite their apparent differences, the underlying dilemma these situations present for selection research is the same. Given the constraints inherent in practical applications and field research, how are we to develop evidence supporting the interpretations of the selection measures we use in these and many other diverse, yet similar situations? This volume offers some answers to this dilemma.

As the epistemological character of what validity means in the selection context has matured, the nature of the research necessary to evaluate it as a basis for the use of, and reliance on, selection procedures has become both more varied and conceptually complex. This complexity both raises constraints and offers opportunities. On the one hand, we have come to understand that straightforward correlational approaches sometimes are simply not available to us and in many instances raise questions of scientific feasibility and veracity. On the other hand, a broadened understanding of validity as evidence-based hypothesis testing offers an array of strategies for seeking and obtaining relevant evidence. Before exploring issues (some of which are illustrated by the opening scenarios) that constrain and complicate validation research, I begin by examining the concept of validity and validation itself. Subsequent chapters examine alternatives for obtaining and evaluating evidence bearing on the question of validity.

The Evolving Conception of Validation

Early selection research focused on what has come to be called *dust bowl empiricism*. Far from addressing the underlying questions of why a particular measure or assessment provides meaningful information about future job behaviors, most researchers were satisfied to demonstrate that a functional relationship existed between the test measure and performance indicators (Schmitt & Landy, 1993); that is, the empirical finding was considered sufficient to sustain the inferences made on the basis of the test scores.

From 1950 to 1954 the American Psychological Association (APA) undertook to codify requirements for technical justification and publication of tests, culminating in the Technical Recommendations for Psychological Tests and Diagnostic Techniques (APA, 1954). These recommendations became the basis for the *Standards for Educational and Psychological Testing,* now in its fifth version (American Educational Research Association, American Psychological Association, & National Council on Measurement in Education, 1999). In its recommendations, the APA Committee on Psychological Tests in 1954 identified four categories of validation evidence: predictive, concurrent (which became lumped with predictive as criterion validation), content, and construct (a category subsequently explicated by Cronbach & Meehl, 1955). These categories came to be widely discussed as "types" of validity, and some effort was made to define the situations and purposes for which each provided meaningful evidence of validity (see Landy, 1986).

Initially, there was some confusion about what was meant by the term *construct validity*. However, seminal articles by Cronbach and Meehl (1955) and Campbell and Fiske (1959) were instrumental in clarifying the meaning of the concept and providing research methodologies to evaluate the extent to which a test demonstrated this "type" of validity. Key concepts such as the nomological network (the consistent web of theoretical and empirical relationships into which a construct systematically fits) (Cronbach & Meehl, 1955) and convergent and discriminant validity and multitrait, multi-method matrices (Campbell & Fiske, 1959) were introduced and ultimately adopted widely in the field of psychology.

The tripartite validity typology provided a convenient way for psychologists to discuss how one would go about the scientific process of providing evidence to support a proposed interpretation of a test score. But the "law of unintended consequences" was lurking in the unexplored woods of civil rights litigation. With the passage of the Civil Rights Act of 1964 and the creation of the Equal Employment Opportunity Commission (EEOC), tests would be subjected to new and intense scrutiny as being potential barriers to equal opportunities for groups now protected under law from discrimination. The EEOC's original *Guidelines on Employee Testing Procedures* (1966) and *Guidelines on Employee Selection Procedures* (1970) borrowed from the *Standards* and for the first time incorporated technical testing standards into governmental regulations. By 1978, with the adoption of the *Uniform Guidelines on Employee Selection Procedures* (Equal Employment Opportunity Commission, Civil Service Commission, Department of Labor, & Department of Justice, 1978) by the federal equal employment enforcement agencies, the "trinitarian" (Guion, 1980) conception of validity was firmly enshrined in both regulatory rules and case law.

Thinking about the meaning of validity and validation continued to evolve. It had never been the intent of those who conceived of validation as falling into three categories to limit the concept to these types. Guion (1980), following Loevinger (1957), pointed out that this conception was unacceptably limiting. Landy (1986) as well as others (such as Cronbach, 1971, and Messick, 1988) reframed the issues by firmly placing validation as a scientific process in the mainstream of hypothesis testing. Validation, Landy argued, is directed toward justifying the inferences drawn about people based on a test score. Thus, to the extent that the inference we are seeking to make is that job performance is a function of the knowledge, skills, abilities, and other characteristics (KSAOs) reflected in a test score, we are engaged in the process of accumulating evidence to test the hypothesis of the existence of a functional relationship against the null of no relationship. Thus, even if the goal is to draw inferences about future job performance, "it does not necessarily follow that criterion-related validation strategies are the only means for documenting the soundness of those inferences" (p. 1187). Landy concluded that psychologists must reject the artificial distinction made in the *Uniform Guidelines* between behavior and mental process and instead begin thinking of validation research as hypothesis testing. As scientists, psychologists are trained to conduct research to test just such hypotheses.

In a retrospective article, Guion (1987) made note of a number of trends that he had observed in validation research. He reviewed changes in predictors, criteria, data collection methods, and validity and validation. In discussing changes in the conception of validation, he made a very pragmatic distinction between job-relatedness and construct validity, noting that "[a] variable that reliably predicts a job-related criterion is job related, even when one does not know what it measures. Validity of measurement is a psychometric question; it requires, in contrast, a clear idea of the construct being measured . . ." (Guion, 1987, p. 212). This distinction is of particular importance for practitioners who often lack the resources and opportunity to apply the rigorous, programmatic research implied by Messick's (1988, 1989) more scientifically orthodox discussions of validity.

In a symposium paper subsequently published in Wainer and Braun (1988), Messick offered what may be the most quoted definition of validity in the unified perspective (author's emphasis):

> Validity is an overall evaluative judgment, founded on empirical evidence and theoretical rationales, of the *adequacy* and *appropriateness* of *inferences* and *actions* based on test scores. (p. 33)

He argued that three issues were foundational to the concept of validity: (a) "interpretability, relevance, and utility of scores," (b) "import or value implications of scores for action," and (c) "functional worth of scores in terms of social consequences of their use" (p. 33). As an aside, it should be noted that this final point did not go unchallenged, and the concept of "consequential validity" has met with considerable debate, with cogent arguments being made both supporting and attacking it (see Shepard, 1993, 1997; Lees-Haley, 1996; Zimiles, 1996; Linn, 1997; Mehrens, 1997; and Popham, 1997).

Messick (1989) decried what he described as the "disjunction between validity conception and validation practice" (p. 34). He argued that "construct-related evidence undergirds not only construct-based inferences but content- and criterion-based inferences as well" (p. 40), setting a standard for validation research that seems to require a programmatic approach to validation. Like Landy (1986), Messick (1988) viewed validation as a fundamentally scientific endeavor:

> Test validation in the construct framework is integrated with hypothesis testing and with all of the philosophical and empirical means by which scientific theories are evaluated. Thus, construct validation embraces all of the statistical, experimental, rational, and rhetorical methods of marshaling evidence to support the inference that observed consistency in test performance has circumscribed meaning. (p. 41)

In a similar vein at the same symposium, Angoff (1988) made it clear that ". . . construct validity as conceived by Cronbach and Meehl cannot be expressed as a single coefficient. Construct validation is a process, not a procedure; and it requires many lines of evidence, not all of them quantitative" (p. 26).

This viewpoint had, of course, always been at the heart of the notion of construct validity but was obscured by the more easily understood tripartite typology, which in applied practice led to the notion of the need to make a choice between types of validity or appropriateness of a particular strategy. But as the unitary conception tied to the scientific process was being reasserted more and more strongly, the fly in the ointment continued to be the codification of the threesome into the *Uniform Guidelines,* a fact that was not going to change any time soon.

In a subsequent chapter in Linn (1989) (and in a later paper in *American Psychologist* [Messick, 1995]), Messick expanded on this position and furthered his theme of the importance of taking into account the social impacts of testing in considering the validity of tests. He asserted that the justification for testing could be divided into two facets: evidential and consequential. The consequential facet (or basis)

> . . . of test interpretation is the appraisal of the value implications of the construct label, of the theory underlying test interpretations, and of the ideologies in which the theory is embedded. . . . [V]alue implications are not ancillary but, rather, integral to score meaning. (p. 20)

In that seminal chapter, Messick (1989) traced the philosophical history of validity contrasting and integrating the "verifiability" requirements of logical positivism (Ayer, 1935/1946/1952) and the "falsification" principle of Popper (1935/1959/2002). In a subsequent, essentially philosophical, analysis, Markus (1998) described this integration (as had Messick) in terms of a Hegelian synthesis. In making these arguments, Messick noted that the early development of concepts of construct validity owes much to the positivist position. The notion of the development of a verifiable nomological network as a basis for claims of construct validity arose from this same tradition. He cited Cronbach (1989) (in press at the time) as stating: "it was pretentious to dress up our immature science in the positivist language; and it was self-defeating to say . . . that a construct not a part of a nomological network is not scientifically admissible" (Messick, 1989, p. 23).

With Messick's (1989) chapter, the unitary conception of validity was firmly established. In that same year, Schmitt (1989) similarly defined construct validity as "the degree to which certain explanatory psychological concepts or constructs account for performance on a test" (p. 332). He argued for greater attention to such validity in both tests and performance indices. He then proceeded to review literature demonstrating a variety of means by which evidence relevant to the validity of a purported measure of a construct could be developed.

Binning and Barrett (1989) reinforced the unitary conceptualization of validity. They expanded Nunnally's (1978) model of critical linkages in validation by articulating and distinguishing relationships among the elements of the logical system composed of the inferences that underlie the unitary concept of validity. They extended the concept of construct validity to the performance domain and emphasized the role of job analysis as an integral part of the validation process. Concluding with a call for "experimenting organizations," they recommended a process of "formative evaluation," which they defined as implying "the successive approximation of desired organizational systems, built through a series of trials in which failures are considered as informative as successes" (p. 490).

Kane (1992) presented the case for an "argument-based approach to validity" in which the plausibility of a test score interpretation depends on the existence of evidence supporting "various lines of argument in specific contexts, the plausibility of assumptions, and the impact of weak arguments on the overall plausibility" (p. 528) of the proposed interpretation. Such arguments may be theory-driven, but it is not necessary that they be so. This approach extended the "hypothesis testing" paradigm to better identify and specify what hypotheses (regarding the argument itself, its cohesiveness, and its underlying assumptions) need to be tested to support the inferences required by the interpretation.

Arvey (1992) sought to clarify conceptual and research issues involving construct validation. He defined construct validity as "providing, acquiring, developing, or otherwise establishing information or data to decision makers that an operational measure does indeed reflect the construct that is thought to underlie the measure" (p. 61). With this definition, he conceptualized construct validation as a special case of model building and testing in which "there is a reliance on both empirical data and analytic methods and rational deductive logic to confirm the model" (p. 65). One might note here some similarities to the argument-based approach proposed by Kane (1992). Arvey proposed a number of practical research methods that might be thought of as construct validation procedures for how one could go about developing evidence for test validity. Landon and Arvey (2006) revisit and extend this discussion in this volume.

Contemporaneously, Geisinger (1992) traced the history of validation thinking and identified ten ways that the concept of validity has changed (loosely paraphrased):

1. From emphasis on the test *to* emphasis on evidence to support specific inferences from the test
2. From atheoretical *to* primarily theory-based
3. From grand nomological networks *to* "micromodels"
4. From behavioral criteria *to* limited scope theories
5. From focus on the test developer as arbiter of validity *to* users and decision makers as responsible for the validity of test use
6. From the tripartite view—with construct validation as equal to (or even slightly less than) criterion-related validation—*to* a view of construct-related validation as incorporating other evidential bases for evaluating validity
7. From the (perhaps still ongoing) debate about content validity as a form of validation *to* content relevance and content coverage as important evidential bases for construct validation
8. From concurrent and predictive validity *to* criterion-related validation as an aid to applied decision making instead of formal validation
9. From situation specificity *to* validity generalization
10. From single validation analyses *to* meta-analyses and structural equation modeling

In a volume of the Frontiers series, Schmitt and Landy (1993) recapped the development of the concept of validation as testing the inferences required by the Nunnally (1978) model, which had been further articulated by Binning & Barrett (1989), arguing for all validation research to be theory/construct grounded. They examined "construct-relevant research" as it occurs in the selection context, pointing to the centrality of job analysis (as had Binning and Barrett, 1989) as part of the evidential basis for validation. They further considered research requirements for both criteria (long overlooked) and predictor constructs (of various kinds) with emphasis on the theoretical linkages between predictors and the performance domain. They concluded with a discussion of alternate methods of validation—all of which are considered in greater depth in this volume.

Continuing the theme he had broached earlier (Guion, 1987), Guion (1998) differentiated between "psychometric validity," referring to "[i]nterpretive inferences [that] describe characteristics revealed by the measurement procedure itself" (p. 237), and "job relatedness," which are "[r]elational inferences interpret[ing] scores in terms of different but correlated characteristics" (p. 237). He then described four bases of evidence that bear on the "*evaluation* [emphasis in original] of tests and test uses" (p. 239): (1) test development, (2) reliability, (3) patterns of correlates, and (4) outcomes.

From 1993 to 1999, representatives from the American Educational Research Association (AERA), the American Psychological Association (APA), and the National Council of Measurement in Education (NCME) served on a joint committee to review and revise the 1985 *Standards for Educational and Psychological Testing*. The resulting *Standards* (American Psychological Association, 1999) continued the precedent set by the 1985 version of referring to "types of validity evidence" rather than to "types of validity." The language in the discussion of validity evidence continued to reject the tripartite view: "Validity is a unitary concept. It is the degree to which all the accumulated evidence supports the intended interpretation of test scores for the proposed purpose" (p. 11). The section goes on to discuss different sources of validity evidence that resemble Guion's (1998) outline, including evidence based on (1) test content, (2) response processes, (3) internal structure, (4) relations to other variables, and (5) consequences of testing.

Over the two-year period from 2000 to 2001, a task force appointed by the president of the Society for Industrial and Organizational Psychology (SIOP) worked to review and revise the third edition of *Principles for the Validation and Use of Personnel Selection Procedures* (Society for Industrial and Organizational Psychology, 1985). The task force was charged to review and update the 1985 *Principles* to ensure that they continued to reflect the state-of-the-science in I/O psychology and to make them consistent with the then recently issued *Standards*. Their work resulted in the fourth edition of the *Principles* adopted by SIOP and APA in 2003. The 2003 *Principles* continued to endorse the unitary concept of validity, embracing and quoting the definition adopted by the *Standards* regarding accumulation of evidence supporting test interpretations. The *Principles* elaborated on this definition as follows:

> Because validation involves the accumulation of evidence to provide a sound scientific basis for the proposed score interpretations,

it is the interpretation of these scores required by the proposed uses that are evaluated, not the selection procedure itself. (p. 4)

The subsequent discussion went on to specifically reject the tripartite view of validity and to adopt the unitary concept as stated in the *Standards*. To this end, the *Principles* explicitly addressed the issue of types of evidential bases for supporting validity:

> . . . even when different strategies are employed for gathering validation evidence, the inference to be supported is that scores on a selection procedure can be used to predict subsequent work behaviors or outcomes. Professional judgment should guide the decisions regarding the sources of evidence that can best support the intended interpretation and use. (p. 5)

Thus, our current conceptualization of the nature and purpose of validation has matured and changed. Validation is seen as embracing both science ("scientific basis") and practice ("can be used to predict").

The Scientist-Practitioner Dilemma

With this background, we come to a dilemma that we face today. As scientist-practitioners, we find ourselves serving two purposes having different goals. On the one hand, we are engaged in theory building that involves hypothesis testing, as Landy (1986), Messick (1989), and Binning and Barrett (1989) described. On the other, we are engaged in application and demonstration of job relatedness that often has a different standard of success.

Theory Building

The philosophy of science underwent a number of substantial developments in the twentieth century. A philosophical position associated with the Vienna circle of philosophers in the 1920s and 1930s became known as logical positivism and reached its apogee in the work of Ayer (1935/1946/1952). In the purest form of logical positivism, the positivists argued that propositions had to be verifiable and verified through empirical evidence in order to have status as meaningful (Messick, 1989; Ayer, 1935/1946/1952). This position met with substantial reaction, especially from Karl Popper

(1935/1959/2002), who argued for a principle of falsification (Cohen, 1994/1997; Thornton, 2005) rather than verification.

Following Popper, as Hubley and Zumbo (1996) put it, "The essential logic of construct validation is disconfirmatory. That is, one is trying to show that alternative or competing inferences do not destroy the intended interpretation" (p. 211). It is not possible to assert the verification of a statement of validity with certainty, but it is possible to assert that empirical data contradict it.

The rationale for falsification as the basis for statistical inference lies in Ockham's Razor (Rindskopf, 1997), which states that "entities are not to be multiplied beyond necessity" (Blackburn, 1996); that is, the most parsimonious explanation for an observation is likely to be the best explanation. Thus, we hypothesize no effect or no relationship (the simplest theory) until that theory is falsified by the reliable observation of an effect different from that simplest theory, and we are thus obliged to accept the existence of a more complicated explanation.

Theory building, then, becomes a process of postulates subjected to "test to failure." No statement or theory can be fully proven; rather, it must be viewed as not yet rejected as false (Messick, 1989; Popper, 1935/1959/2002). No fault attaches to the assertion of a theoretical position that is falsified; rather, falsification itself is viewed as a step on the path to better, more accurate understanding. Indeed, theories that are not subject to falsification do not have the status of scientific theories at all. Failure to sustain our predicted theoretical outcomes is not failure, but progress to a new and better theory.

Application and Demonstration

In actual practice, however, we are seldom asked by organizations to evaluate data from a falsification viewpoint; that is, we are asked to "validate" selection procedures, not to falsify the null hypothesis. We are asked to demonstrate—or even, in some cases, just to document—the validity of those procedures. Indeed, in the legal arena we are often asked to prove the validity of our tests, and it is cold comfort on cross-examination that the most we can say is that the data are incompatible with a zero relationship. To some extent the process appears at least akin to validating a parking receipt or, as Landy (1986) put it, "stamp collecting."

The Challenge

Is what we do in practice, then, science? Messick (1988) noted this conflict somewhat obliquely in a comment about applied science: "Moreover, the practical use of measurements for decision making and action is or ought to be *applied* [emphasis in original] science, recognizing that applied science always occurs in a political context" (p. 43).

It would seem that the answer to this question depends on the rigor (both operational and intellectual) that we bring to the endeavor. To the extent that we use the methods of science to reduce the chance that we will be self-deluded into false conclusions based on what we *want* to be the case rather than what *is*, we can lay claim to the rubric of science. However, to the extent that we simply misuse the trappings of science to support our self-serving (or even heartfelt) conclusions, we are charlatans putting on airs.

The following chapters do not address the traditional trinitarian sources of validation evidence. They do not discuss issues of criterion studies or content validation of work samples or simulations. The chapters in this volume deal with the practical realities of validation research. For example, Chapter Nine, "Practical Construct Validation for Personnel Selection," deals only tangentially with tying test measures into the nomological network; it chiefly addresses concrete methods and techniques for evaluating the inferences implied by the use of a selection measure to predict future performance. In most cases, the evidential methods described in this volume are appropriate for situations like the vignettes at the beginning of this chapter in which traditional (in particular, criterion-related) validation research is not possible or practical; however, they are also evidential bases in their own right. Viewed from Binning and Barrett's (1989) model of inferential requirements, each of these strategies can be considered part of the larger scientific process of validation: adding bit by bit to our knowledge, testing hypotheses, reforming our models, and testing them yet again—in short, conducting "formative evaluation" (Binning & Barrett, 1989). Some of the strategies offer small steps (such as extending existing knowledge into new spaces), others offer broader information (such as may be gained from assembling large samples in consortia), but all of them can be seen as contributing in some way to the validity evidential base. Moreover, these strategies offer recommendations for conducting the relevant research in ways that can stand up to professional scrutiny and comply with regulatory requirements.

Practical Constraints

There are a variety of practical constraints that affect the research that I/O psychologists conduct in organizations. Some of these constraints will impact any selection research done in organizations, from job analysis to criterion validation, including some of the alternatives presented in the following chapters. Most, however, are particularly relevant to criterion-related and some construct (for example, experimental) research designs. Many of these constraints lead to effects addressed by Campbell and Stanley (1963) and Cook and Campbell (1979), such as threats to internal or external validity; others, however, may preclude or limit the conduct of the research itself. A number of these constraints are illustrated in the vignettes that opened this chapter.

For ease of presentation, I have organized these constraints into five categories. In the discussions that follow I have described each category and provided examples of the kinds of constraints implied. However, it should be clear that the categories are not necessarily mutually exclusive and, further, that this discussion is by no means an exhaustive compendium of all of the practical constraints faced by researchers in applied settings.

Scientific

A number of the constraining factors are somewhat technical in nature. I have termed them *scientific* constraints because they raise questions about the veracity of conclusions reached from the research that is conducted. At the top of this list is our inability (or perhaps unwillingness) to articulate "strong" hypotheses, thus failing to ask questions of sufficient relevance to the types of inferences of greatest interest. This point has been made by many, but possibly none more cogently and pointedly than Cohen (1994/1997). By failing to specify our hypotheses correctly (both in terms of the contingent probabilities and the comparative effect sizes), our hypothesis testing becomes weak, constraining the conclusions we may legitimately draw from them. For a more in-depth examination of this issue see Harlow, Mulaik, and Steiger (1997).

Perhaps most ubiquitous among the scientific concerns is that of sample availability. Schmidt and Hunter (1998) pointed out that investigations of distributions of correlations have identified small sample size as a major source of error, resulting in what Guion (1987) earlier recognized as "far fewer situations where local validation studies are considered feasible" (p. 206). Other authors (such as Messick, 1989) have suggested that small sample validation studies actually provide less—and less reliable—information than that available from meta-analytic research, a view adopted in part (albeit with substantial caveat) by the *Principles*. Sackett and Arvey (1993) addressed issues of selection in situations that provide only small samples. Some of the methodologies that they discussed are included in this volume, with considerable expansion. Their conclusion about the value of conducting limited research in such settings is worth noting. They sought "to frame the issue as one of incremental improvements over the haphazard selection done in many organizations" (Sackett & Arvey, 1993, p. 445). This same theme is reflected in many of the chapters to follow with a continued emphasis on the need for careful rigor, which is, if anything, greater when seeking "incremental improvements" in the absence of substantial datasets.

Size, however, is only one of the constraints faced when we consider samples for our research. Indeed, especially with respect to concurrent validation research, even the mere existence of appropriate samples is often problematic. For example, long-tenured, highly selected workforces are certainly not ideal for generalizing to the applicant pool expected for future job openings, but those may be the only employees available for data collection. Moreover, it is often the case that the in-place workforce lacks sufficient demographic diversity to allow for meaningful evaluation of subgroup differences or test fairness. Certainly other designs (such as longitudinal studies) could address some of these issues, but as is discussed in the following passages, few employers are prepared to invest the time and resources necessary for such analyses.

A related but different issue involves the predicate for virtually all of our statistical models: random selection and assignment. If scientific research is to be able to attribute causal effects, then our research designs must allow rejection of a null hypothesis, leaving us with a known alternative. Absent meaningfully large samples selected at random, we are left with either the need to control for a great many additional variables or the existence of a great many alternative hypotheses that could account for the observed result. In applied research, seldom do researchers have sufficient control over samples to meet this criterion. Employees may refuse to participate or may abandon their participation for any of a long list of reasons, ranging from hostility toward the employing organization to fear of revealing some negative information about themselves. Research participants may not be available for data collection when we need them for a variety of reasons, such as operational demands, illness, or simply vacation time. More often than not, we are constrained to work with the sample that is available.

Finally, I would note, though somewhat in passing, what has long been termed the *criterion problem*. Binning and Barrett (1989) make the point that "*a job performance domain is a construct* [emphasis in original]" (p. 480), though we often give too little attention to the development of measures of it for the purposes of validation research (Schmitt & Landy, 1993). Guion (1987) has commented that he wished he could discern a movement away from the use of supervisory ratings as criteria, but he could not. I suspect that most industrial and organizational psychologists would acknowledge the many problems associated with this most common of criteria. Their continued use, however, is almost certain for three reasons: (1) there are many jobs for which it is extremely difficult, if not impossible, to identify relevant objective performance measures at the individual employee level, (2) the costs and practical problems associated with obtaining such criteria can be virtually insurmountable, and (3) objective measures sometimes suffer from psychometric issues that render them inappropriate for use as criteria. So, it seems likely that we will continue to use the flawed, but available, evaluations of individuals by supervisors.

Business

Although I have treated business issues as constraints on our research, it is important that we not forget that among the reasons we seek to improve selection into organizations is to achieve improvements in productivity. Organization leaders rightly ask, "How will doing this research improve our competitive position or further our mission?" It is thus incumbent upon us to respond to organizations' needs to show relevance and utility for the research we propose. Our failure to do so may constrain both the nature and the extent of what we will be allowed to do.

It is essential never to underestimate the implications of costs and budgets on the research we propose and conduct for organizations. Smaller organizations and those in businesses with lower profit margins must be concerned about every dollar expended. In larger, very profitable organizations, it is easy to fall into the trap of comparing the cost of selection research to the organization's revenues or what it spends on product research, but these are seldom the comparisons that matter. In actuality, the costs of research tend to be viewed relative to the discretionary budgets allocated to human resource functions, which are usually much smaller. Public sector organizations are far from immune to these pressures; indeed, by law most are required to engage in competitive bidding that emphasizes costs along with technical competence. Even when researchers conduct analyses to demonstrate the utility of selection programs, these analyses are often presented after the research is complete to justify the implementation of a testing program. In other words, we seldom conduct and present utility arguments (even when we have the data) as part of our proposals to justify conducting the research in advance, and even when we do, these are frequently dismissed as not credible.

And the costs for the research we do can be high. One example is the cost for data collection alone. It is cost prohibitive for many organizations to collect data from a number of far-flung but sparsely staffed facilities. Moreover, for all organizations, data collection usually means lost productivity due to employees' absence from their jobs or additional costs incurred for overtime. This issue accounts in some substantial part for both the small sample sizes that are obtained and the tendency of many researchers to resort to samples of convenience.

As scientists, we are in no position to make promises or guarantees regarding the outcome of our research, and even the most carefully conducted validation study may not produce the desired results. Moreover, in order to gain acceptance for this complex and expensive undertaking, all too often the arguments for conducting validation research lean heavily on legal liability, rather than on the intrinsic value of the knowledge to be gained.

As the world economy has become ever more competitive, many businesses (and public sector entities) have adopted the spirit of NASA's one-time mantra of "faster, better, cheaper." It is up to us, then, to offer both (1) better explanations of the need for and value of the research we need to conduct to investigate the validity of our selection procedures and (2) creative and substantive alternative strategies for developing and leveraging this evidence.

The fact that organizations will not sit still or even slow down while I/O psychologists conduct selection research means that that research may be constrained by ongoing events. Changes in the business environment at the macro-economic level may change both budgets and the perceived need for selection of new employees at all. The research that was viewed as valuable and necessary previously may become the cost-saving budget cut in a surprisingly short time frame. Mergers, acquisitions, sales, and purchases of businesses may make the research moot or cast doubt on its continued relevance or applicability.

The research that is acceptable or even allowed may be limited or changed by the intervention of third-party influences, including bargaining units and the general public (typically as represented by the media). It is not usually the case that union contracts place pre-employment selection under their purview (though some may). However, research that involves the participation of bargaining unit members (to provide job analysis information, serve as SMEs, or respond to surveys or tests) will require the cooperation (or at least nonresistance) of union leadership. If the measures to be researched are for promotion or certification, one can expect substantial involvement by these leaders and, in some cases, considerable resistance. Such resistance may change the level of cooperation of participants, change their psychological set while participating, alter the composition of the available sample, and possibly render the research infeasible. Engaging in validation research under the pressure of public scrutiny (and political oversight in the public sector) can have equally daunting effects. Certainly, no flaw in the research—even if unavoidable—will go unnoticed, and failure to produce "good" results (that is, significant correlations, low subgroup differences, and so on) will be attributed to failures of the research or even of the researcher. Finally, the external influence of ongoing or pending litigation (or enforcement agency actions) may make organization leaders reluctant to pursue research. In some cases, the existence of previous litigation may impose specific or general constraints on the nature, type, and expectations for validation research.

A final "business" issue lies in a bias that human resource work is basically pretty easy stuff. This bias has two implications. First, it leads to a tendency to assume the veracity of personal theories of selection. Successful managers and business leaders have histories of making reasonably good decisions, and they often develop idiosyncratic models for how best to select the people they need for their organizations. These personal theories account in part for the endurance and ubiquity of traditional unstructured interviews despite years of research demonstrating their flaws. It is because of such theories, too, that managers so often cannot (or choose not to) understand our "unreasonable" need to conduct validation research when it is obvious to them that the test must be measuring things important to the job (such as mechanical or mathematical ability). Second, the bias about the simplicity of human resource functions leads managers to a belief that they, too, are experts in this area of the business. From their perspective, we are making it harder than it needs to be and dressing it up in unnecessary complexity and jargon. This bias may result in business leaders being susceptible to each new fad in testing that shows up on the Internet. It also accounts for their questioning our research demands: you don't need a sample that big; surely the fifty people in our main plant will be more than sufficient.

Legal

In discussing business constraints, I mentioned litigation in passing. These issues have, however, become ever more prominent for I/O practitioners. As I noted previously, the existence of ongoing litigation or investigations may make business leaders reluctant to undertake or continue validation research. In addition, organizations may enter into agreements with enforcement agencies or have conditions imposed on them by courts that constrain their selection practices and limit the alternatives that they may consider.

More commonly, however, it is not the actuality of legal or enforcement action that impacts validation research in organizations.

Rather, it is concerns about the risk of such events, often advanced or supported by internal or external counsel, that impact our research opportunities and methods. The actual risks of litigation are a function of (1) the extent of exposure (in terms of amount of use of a selection procedure and the level of disparate impact resulting from that use) and (2) the extent to which there is evidence supporting its use (defensibility) (McPhail, 2005). Organizations and their legal counsel may impose requirements for either that cannot be achieved given the constraints imposed by the situation. In these situations, alternative and supplementary evidentiary sources may be necessary to meet the criteria.

Temporal

The business world moves quickly, and, more and more, the public sector world does so as well. Elapsed time for completion of validation research can become a serious concern for researchers. From the business perspective, there is a need for results to be available quickly. If business leaders are convinced that there is competitive advantage in improving selection, delay in realizing that advantage may be perceived as a business loss. Further, validation research is often not undertaken until there is an urgent "felt need," thus increasing the pressure to take "short cuts" to complete the research in as short a time as possible. Research that takes an extended period of time may fall from a priority to a nonessential; it may lose its sponsor or its budget; and it may lose its relevance to a crucial event—such as a plant opening, a new acquisition, or a hiring window—from which the felt need originally grew.

Another aspect of time constraint is availability of time from internal resources, especially employees to serve as contributors or participants in the validation research. As noted earlier, this can be a cost issue, but beyond the costs, leaner organizations have fewer employees available and the impact of their absence from their jobs is greater. This constraint applies to an even greater extent to those supervisors who have increasing numbers of employees within their spans of control.

Organizational cycles also may impose significant time constraints in terms of both operational dynamics and availability of employees. For example, plant maintenance shutdowns, seasonal work variability, and financial cycles may all impact an organization's willingness and ability to support and participate in validation research.

Organizational and Logistical

A long list of organizational and logistical issues arises to constrain research efforts. Of particular importance is the primacy of operational need. We cannot demand access to research participants in conflict with business goals, safety requirements, or time urgent organizational activities (such as provision of emergency services or completion of required maintenance activities).

As noted previously, validation research requires the active cooperation and participation of employees. Their fear of organizational consequences from the use of test and performance data in ways inimical to their best interests (whether justified or not) can have at least three effects: (1) nonrandom, nonrepresentative samples, (2) smaller samples, and (3) undetectably bad data (or increased error variance) from inattention or intentional undermining of the research. Finally, organizational structure, operating procedures, and schedules may impose situational constraints that preclude standard scientific research designs.

Alternative Strategies

Despite the organizational advantages (aside from the scientific value) that accrue from accurate information about the usefulness and job-relatedness of selection procedures, in many cases, employers engage in validation research solely to comply with legal obligations. The result has too often been hurriedly conducted, small-sample research barely sufficient to meet those minimum requirements imposed by the *Uniform Guidelines*. Because of resource constraints, many employers turn to tests misleadingly advertised as being "pre-validated," "EEOC approved," or "self-validating," or to selection procedures of questionable utility.

I/O psychology has offered a number of alternative strategies that may provide time and cost advantages and in some cases may improve on the accuracy of results obtained from small, limited samples. These alternatives are not widely known, and in some cases they are misapplied or applied in inappropriate situations. The objective of this volume is to present these alternative strategies in sufficient detail and with appropriate cautions to allow practitioners greater access to their meaningful application.

Conclusion

When faced with situations like those described at the beginning of this chapter, too often I/O psychology has responded to organizations' requests for selection by saying, "No, you can't do that," rather than "Here is what we can do in this situation." Frequently, when faced with the inevitable contingencies of organizational reality (trade-offs in budgets, available personnel, and competing human resource objectives), decision makers have come to believe that I/O psychologists are insensitive to their needs. This volume provides practitioners with viable alternatives that allow them to address in a professionally acceptable manner a broader array of problems with a more sophisticated set of tools.

References

American Educational Research Association, American Psychological Association, & National Council on Measurement in Education. (1999). *Standards for educational and psychological testing.* Washington, DC: American Education Research Association.

American Psychological Association. (1954). *Technical recommendations for psychological tests and diagnostic techniques.* Washington, DC: APA.

Angoff, W. H. (1988). Validity: An evolving concept. In H. Wainer & H. I. Braun (Eds.), *Test validity* (pp. 33–45). Mahwah, NJ: Erlbaum.

Arvey, R. D. (1992). Constructs and construct validation: Definitions and issues. *Human Performance, 5*(1 & 2), 59–69.

Arvey, R. D., & Faley, R. H. (1988). *Fairness in selecting employees* (2nd ed.). Reading, MA: Addison-Wesley.

Ayer, A. J. (1935/1946/1952). *Language, truth and logic.* New York: Dover.

Binning, J. F., & Barrett, G. V. (1989). Validity of personnel decisions: A conceptual analysis of the inferential and evidential bases. *Journal of Applied Psychology, 74*(3), 478–494.

Blackburn, S. (1996). *Oxford dictionary of philosophy.* New York: Oxford University Press.

Campbell, D. T., & Fiske, D. W. (1959). Convergent and discriminant validation by the multitrait-multimethod matrix. *Psychological Bulletin, 56,* 81–105.

Campbell, D. T., & Stanley, J. C. (1963). *Experimental and quasi-experimental designs for research.* Chicago: Rand McNally & Company. (Reprinted from *Handbook of research on teaching,* by the American Educational Research Association, 1963.)

Cohen, J. (1994/1997). The earth is round (p< .05). In L. L. Harlow, S. A. Mulaik, & J. H. Steiger (Eds.), *What if there were no significance tests?* (pp. 21–35). Mahwah, NJ: Erlbaum. (Reprinted from The earth is round (p< .05), J. Cohen, 1994, *American Psychologist, 49*(12), pp. 997–1003.)

Cook, T. D., & Campbell, D. T. (1979). *Quasi-experimentation: Design and analysis issues for field settings.* Chicago: Rand McNally.

Cronbach, L. J. (1971). Test validation. In R. L. Thorndike (Ed.), *Educational measurement* (2nd ed., pp. 443–507). Washington, DC: American Council on Education.

Cronbach, L. J. (1989). Construct validation after thirty years. In R. L. Linn (Ed.), *Intelligence: Measurement, theory, and public policy* (proceedings of a symposium in honor of Lloyd G. Humphreys). Urbana, IL: University of Illinois Press.

Cronbach, L. J., & Meehl, P. E. (1955). Construct validity in psychological tests. *Psychological Bulletin, 52*(4), 281–302.

Equal Employment Opportunity Commission. (1966). *Guidelines on employee testing procedures.* Washington, DC: Equal Employment Opportunity Commission.

Equal Employment Opportunity Commission. (1970). *Guidelines on employee selection procedures. Federal Register, 35*(149), 12333–12336.

Equal Employment Opportunity Commission, Civil Service Commission, Department of Labor, & Department of Justice. (1978). *Uniform guidelines on employee selection procedures. Federal Register, 43*(166), 38295–38309.

Geisinger, K. F. (1992). The metamorphosis of test validation. *Educational Psychologist, 27*(2), 197–222.

Guion, R. M. (1980). On trinitarian doctrines of validity. *Professional Psychology, 11*(3), 385–398.

Guion, R. M. (1987). Changing views for personnel selection research. *Personnel Psychology, 40,* 199–213.

Guion, R. M. (1998). *Assessment, measurement, and prediction for personnel decisions.* Mahwah, NJ: Erlbaum.

Harlow, L. L., Mulaik, S. A., & Steiger, J. H. (Eds.). (1997). *What if there were no significance tests?* Mahwah, NJ: Erlbaum.

Hubley, A. M., & Zumbo, B. D. (1996). A dialectic on validity: Where we have been and where we are going. *The Journal of General Psychology, 123*(3), 207–215.

Kane, M. T. (1992). An argument-based approach to validity. *Psychological Bulletin, 112*(3), 527–535.

Landon, T. E., & Arvey, R. D. (2006). Practical construct validation for personnel selection. In S. M. McPhail (Ed.), *Alternative validation strategies: Developing new and leveraging existing validity evidence* (pp. xx–xx). San Francisco: Jossey-Bass.

Landy, F. J. (1986). Stamp collecting versus science: Validation as hypothesis testing. *American Psychologist, 41*(11), 1183–1192.

Lees-Haley, P. R. (1996). Alice in validityland, or the dangerous consequences of consequential validity. *American Psychologist, 51*(9), 981–983.

Linn, R. L. (1997). Evaluating the validity of assessments: The consequences of use. *Educational Measurement: Issues and Practice,* 14–16.

Loevinger, J. (1957). Objective tests as instruments of psychological theory. *Psychological Reports, 3,* 635–694.

Markus, K. A. (1998). Science, measurement, and validity: Is completion of Samuel Messick's synthesis possible? *Social Indicators Research, 45,* 7–34.

McCormick, E. J. (1959). The development of processes for indirect or synthetic validity: III. Application of job analysis to indirect validity. A symposium. *Personnel Psychology, 12,* 402–413.

McPhail, S. M. (2005). Auditing selection processes: Application of a risk assessment model. *The Psychologist-Manager Journal, 8*(2), 205–221.

Mehrens, W. A. (1997). The consequences of consequential validity. *Educational Measurement: Issues and Practice,* Summer, 16–18.

Messick, S. (1988). The once and future issues of validity: Assessing the meaning and consequences of measurement. In H. Wainer & H. I. Braun (Eds.), *Test validity* (pp. 33–45). Mahwah, NJ: Erlbaum.

Messick, S. (1989). Validity. In R. L. Linn (Ed.), *Educational measurement* (3rd ed., pp. 13–103). New York: American Council on Education.

Messick, S. (1995). Validity of psychological assessment: Validation of inferences from persons' responses and performance as scientific inquiry into score meaning. *American Psychologist, 50*(9), 741–749.

Nunnally, J. C. (1978). *Psychometric theory* (2nd ed.). New York: McGraw-Hill.

Popham, W. J. (1997). Consequential Validity: Right concern—Wrong concept. *Educational Measurement: Issues and Practice,* Summer, 9–13.

Popper, K. (1935/1959/2002). *Logic of scientific discovery* (15th ed.). New York: Taylor & Francis.

Rindskopf, D. M. (1997). Testing "small," not null, hypotheses: Classical and Bayesian approaches. In L. L. Harlow, S. A. Mulaik, & J. H. Steiger (Eds.). *What if there were no significance tests?* (pp. 319–332). Mahwah, NJ: Erlbaum.

Sackett, P. R., & Arvey, R. D. (1993). Selection in small *N* settings. In N. Schmitt & W. C. Borman (Eds.), *Personnel selection in organizations* (pp. 418–447). San Francisco: Jossey-Bass.

Schmidt, F. L., & Hunter, J. E. (1998). The validity and utility of selection methods in personnel psychology: Practical and theoretical implications of 85 years of research findings. *Psychological Bulletin, 124*(2), 262–274.

Schmitt, N. (1989). Construct validity in personnel selection. In B. J. Fallon, H. P. Pfister, & J. Brebner (Eds.), *Advances in industrial organizational psychology* (pp. 331–341). New York: Elsevier Science.

Schmitt, N., & Landy, F. J. (1993). The concept of validity. In N. Schmitt & W. C. Borman (Eds.), *Personnel selection in organizations* (pp. 275–309). San Francisco: Jossey-Bass.

Shepard, L. A. (1993). Evaluating test validity. *Review of Research in Education, 19*, 405–450.

Shepard, L. A. (1997). The centrality of test use and consequences for test validity. *Educational Measurement: Issues and Practice,* Summer, 5–8, 13, 24.

Society for Industrial and Organizational Psychology (2003*). Principles for the validation and use of personnel selection procedures.* Bowling Green, OH: Society for Industrial and Organizational Psychology.

Thornton, S. (2005). Karl Popper. In E. N. Zalta (Ed.), *The Stanford encyclopedia of philosophy* (Summer 2005 ed.). Retrieved from http://plato.stanford.edu/archives/sum2005/entries/popper/>

Wainer, H., & Braun, H. I. (Eds.). (1988). *Test validity.* Mahwah, NJ: Erlbaum.

Zimiles, H. (1996). Rethinking the validity of psychological assessment. *American Psychologist, 51*(9), 980–981.

PART 1

Applying Existing Validity Evidence

CHAPTER 2

Transportation of Validation Results

Wade M. Gibson and
Julie A. Caplinger

Theoretical Development

Transportability and transported validity are common labels that have been ascribed to a validation strategy sanctioned in the *Uniform Guidelines* (Equal Employment Opportunity Commission, Civil Service Commission, Department of Labor, & Department of Justice, 1978), Section 7B. This section allows for validity evidence to be borrowed from one setting and applied to another. In this sense, validity is "transported" to a new setting, giving rise to the commonly used name. As described in this chapter, the process of transporting validity entails formally extending empirical, criterion-related validation evidence obtained in one setting by applying it to similar jobs in another setting, where no empirical validation research has been conducted.

Transportability is distinguishable from other validation strategies described in this book, in that it did not derive from a theory or body of research in validation, nor do the strategies for establishing it follow a strong professional consensus developed from integrated theory or research. Instead, formal statements of transported validity have tended to follow explicit requirements articulated in the

Uniform Guidelines, and in this sense the *Uniform Guidelines* have provided controlling language that has driven validation practice in this area. Because it is fundamental to the validation strategy itself, an understanding of Transportability must come from examination of the relevant *Uniform Guidelines* language.

Section 7B of the *Uniform Guidelines* provides the basis for establishing transported validity through the following language:

> Criterion-related validity studies conducted by one test user, or described in test manuals and the professional literature, will be considered acceptable for use by another user when the following requirements are met:
>
> Validity evidence. Evidence from the available studies meeting the standards of section 14B of this part clearly demonstrates that the selection procedure is valid;
>
> Job similarity. The incumbents in the user's job and the incumbents in the job or group of jobs on which the validity study was conducted perform substantially the same major work behaviors, as shown by appropriate job analyses both on the job or group of jobs on which the validity study was performed and on the job for which the selection procedure is to be used; and
>
> Fairness evidence. The studies include a study of test fairness for each race, sex, and ethnic group which constitutes a significant factor in the borrowing user's relevant labor market for the job or jobs in question. If the studies under consideration satisfy paragraphs (1) and (2) of this section but do not contain an investigation of test fairness, and it is not technically feasible for the borrowing user to conduct an internal study of test fairness, the borrowing user may utilize the study until studies conducted elsewhere meeting the requirements of these guidelines show test unfairness, or until such time as it becomes technically feasible to conduct an internal study of test fairness and the results of that study can be acted upon. Users obtaining selection procedures from publishers should consider, as one factor in the decision to purchase a particular selection procedure, the availability of evidence concerning test fairness. (Sect. 7.B.)

A fourth condition for transporting validity is provided in Section 7D of the *Uniform Guidelines.* It states:

> If there are variables in the other studies which are likely to affect validity significantly, the user may not rely upon such studies, but will be expected either to conduct an internal validity study or to comply with section 6 of this part. (Sect. 7.D.)

Thus, three requirements for transporting validity entail establishing: (1) criterion-related validity evidence from one setting that satisfies *Uniform Guidelines* requirements for documenting validity; (2) evidence from job analysis of the similarity between the job(s) from the original validation study and the job(s) in the setting to which validity will be transported; and (3) fairness evidence, where available or technically feasible to obtain, or until unfairness is demonstrated elsewhere. A final condition is that there must not be variables in the borrower's situation that would likely change the validity results.

A closer examination of each of the four elements of transportability is useful for better understanding it. The four conditions vary in clarity and in importance, and, as discussed throughout this chapter, the second one, job similarity, has been the subject of the greatest range of interpretation.

The first requirement, validity evidence, is a critical element of transportability but is relatively straightforward: "Evidence from the available studies meeting the standards of section 14B of this part clearly demonstrates that the selection procedure is valid." The research techniques and *Uniform Guidelines* requirements for conducting criterion-related validation studies are well understood by industrial psychologists. Use of the word "clearly" in the *Uniform Guidelines* statement suggests that the original validity evidence should be persuasive; that there should be no doubt that validity has been demonstrated. Although it is obviously open to interpretation, many practitioners have concluded that issues such as sample size, quality and comprehensiveness of criteria, timeliness, and the magnitude of computed validity should all be carefully considered when contemplating a transportability approach (Tippins, McPhail, Hoffman, & Gibson, 1999). An extremely cautious interpretation may be a belief that the quality and comprehensiveness of the borrowed validity study (source study) should be as good as or better than that which would be possible if original criterion-related validation research were to be conducted in the setting to which validity will be transported (target setting). This interpretation is not supported by specific language in the *Uniform Guidelines*. At a minimum, however, the *Uniform Guidelines* language makes clear that the borrowed validity evidence shall be subjected to the scrutiny of requirements in Section 14B, and suggests that the original inference of validity—that from the source study—should be clearly supported.

The third requirement, fairness evidence, might be better described as a strong suggestion, because the second sentence of that requirement excuses users from demonstrating it. It states,

> If the studies under consideration satisfy paragraphs (1) and (2) of this section but do not contain an investigation of test fairness, and it is not technically feasible for the borrowing user to conduct an internal study of test fairness, the borrowing user may utilize the study until studies conducted elsewhere meeting the requirements of these guidelines show test unfairness, or until such time as it becomes technically feasible to conduct an internal study of test fairness and the results of that study can be acted upon.

A study of test fairness requires data from a criterion-related validation study, with adequate sample sizes for each of the studied groups (such as gender, racial, ethnic) to support the appropriate analyses. By definition, without local criterion-related validation research in the borrowing user's setting, fairness studies are not feasible. Unless a local criterion-related validation study is conducted, fairness studies remain unfeasible. Thus, only in the case of an affirmative finding of test unfairness, established elsewhere based on research on the selection procedure of interest, will the requirement of researching fairness be a barrier to transportability. Of course, if the original validation research includes a study of fairness, then the "requirement" will have already been met. If it does not, the borrowing user need only satisfy the final sentence of Section 7B:

> Users obtaining selection procedures from publishers should consider, as one factor in the decision to purchase a particular selection procedure, the availability of evidence concerning test fairness.

This sentence most certainly applies to all borrowed validity evidence, not just to that borrowed from test publishers, but in any case, it appears to be a very modest requirement and would seem to be met easily. (Section 7 of the *Uniform Guidelines* begins with the statement, "Users may, under certain circumstances, support the use of selection procedures by validity studies conducted by other users or conducted by test publishers or distributors and described in test manuals." This introductory sentence suggests, as has been common in practice, that users may borrow validity evidence from any number of sources, not just test publishers. Presumably, borrowing users should consider availability of research on test fairness regardless of the source from which they are borrowing.)

Whether intended or not, the *Uniform Guidelines* language, placing no absolute requirement of studies of fairness on transportability, was prescient of professional consensus in industrial psychology. As described later in this chapter, fairness of ability tests—those most likely to result in adverse impact and to require validation in accordance with the *Uniform Guidelines*—has been well established for the major demographic groups (Society for Industrial and Organizational Psychology, 2003).

The fourth "requirement" provides that there must not be differences in variables that are likely to impact validity results. This condition is explained further in the *Uniform Guidelines* Question and Answer section, in Question # 66, which in pertinent part states,

> Q. Under what circumstances can a selection procedure be supported (on other than an interim basis) by a criterion-related validity study done elsewhere?
> A. A validity study done elsewhere may provide sufficient evidence if four conditions are met . . .
> 4. Proper account is taken of variables which might affect the applicability of the study in the new setting, such as performance standards, work methods, representativeness of the sample in terms of experience or other relevant factors, and the currency of the study.

It is interesting to note that neither Section 7 nor the Questions and Answers describe this fourth condition as a "requirement." Nor is the term *evidence* used to describe what is probative in establishing that the condition has been met. This fourth condition was set apart from the three requirements of Section 7B, and the language used to describe it both is general and appears to be less rigorous. Based on these differences, many practitioners have concluded that this fourth condition requires little documentation above and beyond that required to satisfy their own professional judgment that such variables do not threaten an inference of transported validity.

The second requirement, job similarity, is the crux of transportability. The *Uniform Guidelines* state,

> The incumbents in the user's job and the incumbents in the job or group of jobs on which the validity study was conducted perform substantially the same major work behaviors, as shown by appropriate job analyses both on the job or group of jobs on which the validity study was performed and on the job for which the selection procedure is to be used.

The plain language requires that job analysis in both settings establish that the source and target jobs entail "substantially the same major work behaviors." Thus, it appears job similarity is to be judged on the basis of work behaviors, as opposed to required personal characteristics such as knowledge, skills, abilities, and other characteristics (KSAOs). This interpretation appears to be reinforced by the definition of *work behavior* provided in Section 16Y of the *Uniform Guidelines*, which states:

> Work behavior. An activity performed to achieve the objectives of the job. Work behaviors involve observable (physical) components and unobservable (mental) components. A work behavior consists of the performance of one or more tasks. Knowledges, skills, and abilities are not behaviors, although they may be applied in work behaviors.

Some practitioners, however, view a firm distinction between behaviors and KSAOs as artificial. For example, the KSAO "ability to communicate orally" is manifestly behavioral, and in any regard, it may be written in explicit behavioral terms by rephrasing it to "communicates orally" or "communicating orally." Further, many practitioners believe that to the extent that they are distinguishable, a showing of job similarity on the basis of required, measurable KSAOs is more directly relevant to a judgment of transported validity than is one based on common behaviors or tasks. Certainly, it can be argued that there are fewer inferences in a KSAO approach than there are in one based on common work behaviors. Much of what is interesting and challenging in transportability research and practice, as discussed throughout this chapter, entails exploration of job similarity and various proposed methods for evaluating and documenting it.

Transportability versus Traditional Approaches to Validity

Although transportability, as it is discussed in this chapter, derives from *Uniform Guidelines* language establishing it, transportability obviously is connected to other standard concepts of validity. It is used to extend a cornerstone approach—criterion-related validity—to unstudied jobs. At its core, transported validity requires an inference that differences between research settings have not disturbed or undermined validity. In this regard, it is connected closely to the concept of validity generalization (VG), the conclusion that validity generalizes across common situational variables that may differ from one setting to another. If meta-analysis and VG are conceptualized as the body of research and techniques used to understand the threats to generalized validity, then transportability is obviously related to them. Techniques for establishing validity through meta-analysis and validity generalization are covered elsewhere in this book.

Throughout this chapter we will attempt to distinguish between the two approaches, to the extent possible. Transportability, in this chapter, will be defined on the basis of *Uniform Guidelines* requirements for establishing it. Thus, whether the term can be interpreted more broadly or applied to a broader array of procedures is moot for our purpose. This distinction may seem false because conclusions from validity generalization research—namely those relating to the potential for moderators to limit generalizations of research conducted remotely to other settings—are profoundly important to transporting validity. One of the authors has conceptualized establishing transportability as a carefully played game of documentation, in which a rulebook, the *Uniform Guidelines* (and perhaps developed case law related to it), is referenced and followed closely, but in which independent professional judgment, beyond *Uniform Guidelines* requirements, is required and used to make decisions. This professional judgment is properly impacted by developed professional consensus regarding research in meta-analysis and validity generalization as well as other issues regarding moderators of validity. Certainly, the body of research associated with validity generalization entails much of the developed thought that should guide professional judgment in this area. Thus, when judging whether evidence of job similarity is sufficient to warrant transporting validity, the practitioner must consider two standards: (1) whether existing evidence is sufficient to conform with *Uniform Guidelines* requirements (one standard), and (2) whether the existing data and other relevant information actually support an inference of validity (another standard). Successful transportability efforts occur when the application at hand is thoroughly understood and all information and data relevant to an inference of validity support an affirmative conclusion under both standards.

Acknowledging a distinction between *Uniform Guidelines* requirements and professional judgment used to transport or generalize validity is not meant to undermine practitioners who might wish to blur the two or acknowledge they are strongly connected. Ideally, the standards of judgment would be the same, and indeed, when they were published, the *Uniform Guidelines* and professional consensus were better aligned. Thirty years ago there was relatively little appreciation for the effects of sampling error and other artifacts on computed validity coefficients, and situational specificity was presumed to account for varied results among validity studies. This point illustrates how the two standards can yield different conclusions today. The 1978 *Uniform Guidelines* were shaped by the zeitgeist of the time and are still intact; however, situational specificity, at least for ability tests, has been largely disconfirmed. Hence, there are common situations in which informed professional judgment would support an inference of transported or generalized validity, yet *Uniform Guidelines* requirements based on available data for transportability may be unmet. This issue is obvious to practitioners and illustrates the two standards. However, an opposite situation is feasible as well. Suggested procedures described in this chapter, if followed blindly without thought or inappropriately manipulated to yield hoped-for conclusions, might result in documentation that conforms to *Uniform Guidelines* requirements for transported validity, yet fails to support an inference of validity based on a reasonable standard of informed professional judgment. In transportability work the practitioner must ensure an inference of validity is supportable under both standards. Transportability is a useful strategy for developing evidence for validity in circumstances in which situational specificity is known not to operate, or is so trivial that it cannot subvert validity. Practitioners must judge this when conducting transportability research.

Research Base

Because transportability was derived from the *Uniform Guidelines* as opposed to spawning from and being debated in research literature, relatively little exists in professional literature that is explicitly focused on methods or proper uses for transporting validity evidence. Researchers tend to ignore transportability, as it is usually conducted for legal compliance rather than answering research questions about properties of a test or test battery. In fact, Guion (1998) characterized discussion of transportability as "quaint" given the current state of the validity generalization research. He also noted that, although still part of the legal context,

> It is less certain that broader similarity is truly necessary, and very nearly certain (from research done in the 1970s) that demographic similarity is not necessary . . .

As we now discuss, there are a limited number of references to transporting validity evidence in the literature.

A recent discussion of transportability in published research was in the larger context of defining and classifying techniques to generalize validity evidence as opposed to specifying methods or applications. Hoffman and McPhail (1998) compared and contrasted test transportability, validity generalization, and synthetic validity. After discussing the *Uniform Guidelines* requirements for borrowing validity evidence, they discuss challenges inherent in applying a transportability strategy. These complexities include requiring permission to use a source study, as well as the fact that applicable source studies may not contain the job analysis data necessary to conduct an examination of job similarity. Hoffman and McPhail also noted that many modern jobs are too fluid or change too rapidly to make a criterion-related validation study feasible, and consequently no source study could exist.

There are limited examples of actual methods for establishing job similarity discussed in the literature. Hoffman (1999) and Hoffman, Holden, and Gale (2000) both provided practical examples of a Position Analysis Questionnaire (PAQ)–based method of establishing similarity between job families; however, this example is not applicable to most situations as it requires a sizable sample of jobs with PAQ data. Johnson and Jolly (2000) provided a practical example of establishing job similarity between jobs at different business units within the same company for the purpose of supporting use of a test battery. This study provides a step-by-step process that the authors used to determine if use of a test battery was appropriate at additional facilities, as well as a description of the statistical methods and professional judgment required to make this determination. Brannick (2001) and Rafilson, Allscheid, and Weiss (1994) also discussed methods for establishing job similarity. The methods in these articles are applicable in idiosyncratic situations when job analysis data are available in certain formats or data have been collected regarding a large number of jobs.

Although most of the aforementioned articles do focus on the most ambiguous aspect of transporting validation evidence—establishing job similarity—most of the authors acknowledge a lack of confidence when attempting to determine the proper extent of job similarity. The question raised is: how similar is similar enough? A portion of the body of validity generalization research described below focuses on the topic of forming job families for the purpose of generalizing test constructs within a job family.

Mobley and Ramsay (1973) discussed using cluster analysis to establish job similarity. They identified two points that are still salient today regarding differences between jobs: namely, what variables to consider when comparing jobs and what index to use as an indicator of similarity. Cluster solutions do not allow a researcher to declare confidently that jobs are substantially similar or dissimilar.

Arvey and Mossholder (1977) summarized this research and present an analysis of variance (ANOVA) procedure as an alternative method to determine the degree of similarity between jobs. They assessed the similarity of a group of jobs with three raters providing PAQ ratings for each job and compared to the cluster analytic technique. This article spawned progeny (McIntyre & Farr, 1979; Lissitz, Mendoza, Huberty, & Markos, 1979; Hanser, Mendel, & Wolins, 1979; Arvey, Maxwell, & Mossholder, 1979; Lee & Mendoza, 1981), all of which compare and contrast the relative strengths and weaknesses of using ANOVA, multivariate analysis of the variance (MANOVA), and cluster analytic techniques for establishing job families. A study by Sackett, Cornelius, and Carron (1981) provided an example in which global SME judgments regarding job family membership yielded identical results to statistical methods.

A single superior method of establishing similarities or differences between jobs did not evolve from this line of research, primarily due to the fact that different methods are appropriate, given different sample sizes (of both jobs and raters) as well as varying formats of job analytic data. In addition, many of these methods involve comparing multiple jobs for job family inclusion or exclusion, whereas when transporting validity, we often seek to compare one target job to one source job or family of jobs.

The lack of published research regarding methods and applications of borrowing validation evidence is certainly disheartening to a practitioner seeking guidance in methodology or support for a decision of establishing job similarity. Practitioners must apply the culmination of knowledge and experience from other bodies of research as well as professional judgment when engaging in such endeavors.

Review of Legal Implications

There is a modest number of cases in which transportability issues have been addressed in the courts, and among these, fewer still by which transportability was central to the case or even offered as a planned validation strategy. In addition, many of the cases were adjudicated under now expired EEOC or DOJ *Guidelines* that predate and differ from the *Uniform Guidelines*. All of these issues diminish what can be leveraged from these cases; nevertheless, a review of them yields some useful information for practitioners.

In *Albemarle Paper v. Moody* (1975), the Supreme Court considered the validity of three ability tests used to select employees for numerous skilled jobs that formed six lines of progression in a paper mill. The concurrent validity study included ten small samples (based on eight to twenty-one employees each) from "job groups" formed by combing adjacent titles in the lines of progression. The high court confirmed the notion that extending validity evidence to unstudied jobs requires completion of an adequate job analysis. Relying on language from the then-current EEOC *Guidelines,* the court stated,

> Even if the study were otherwise reliable, this odd patchwork of results would not entitle Albemarle to impose its testing program under the *Guidelines.* A test may be used in jobs other than those for which it has been professionally validated only if there are "no significant differences" between the studied and unstudied jobs. 29 CFR § 1607.4 (c)(2). The study in this case involved no analysis of the attributes of, or the particular skills needed in, the studied job groups. There is accordingly no basis for concluding that "no significant differences" exist among the lines of progression, or among distinct job groupings within the studied lines of progression. Indeed, the study's checkered results appear to compel the opposite conclusion.

Perhaps most important in Albemarle, to the issue of proper use of transportability, was the court's reliance upon then-current EEOC *Guidelines* language requiring that "no significant differences" exist between studied and unstudied jobs. Clearly the court insisted that there be evidence of job similarity. Existing lines of progression in the work setting, without further study, were inadequate evidence of job similarity for this court. With so little job information for the court to consider, it is less clear what showing of job similarity might have satisfied it. However, it is interesting to examine the court's brief language describing what was missing, namely, "The study in this case involved no analysis of the attributes of, or the particular skills needed in, the studied job groups." Apparently, at least under consideration of the EEOC *Guidelines,* the high court would allow similarity to be established through an analysis of attributes of the jobs (such as tasks or work behaviors) or of the person attributes (skills, and presumably other KSAOs) needed to perform them. Whether or not adoption of the *Uniform Guidelines* subsequent to Albemarle renders this inference transitory is unknown.

In *Dickerson v. United States Steel Corp* (1978), a district court rejected as inadequate and a "fatal flaw" the defendant's job analysis based on only "existing corporate job descriptions and apprentice training syllabi." The case involved three criterion-related validation studies conducted in two settings (South Works and Fairless) that were in support of tests for numerous craft jobs. Each study addressed multiple craft jobs that were pooled together for analysis purposes; criteria included grades in classroom apprentice training and supervisory ratings of on-the-job training after an average of one year in the apprentice program. The court found that the syllabi did not contain descriptions of the courses, but were "merely a listing of each course to be taken." The court continued, "Even if this coursework analysis were adequate . . . there is no analysis of the first year on-the-job training." Of the corporate job descriptions, the court stated, "Neither the descriptions or classifications from the JDC indicate which skills are expected to be mastered." The court concluded, "The Court finds that this information, while it may constitute a superficial description of a journeyman's work, certainly does not constitute an analysis of a first-year apprentice's job."

Having found that the job analyses were " . . . either completely deficient or unrelated to the first-year apprentice work," the court concluded, "For the Fairless crafts jobs not included in any validation 'pool,' the Court holds that the test battery has not been validated. This failure to include those crafts is conclusive against USS, since the Court has rejected the conclusory evidence of all-craft similarity."

On the issue of test fairness, the court stated,

> The absence of a differential validity study in the Fairless studies, and the use of a "borrowed" study to establish racial fairness, is treated differently under the two sets of guidelines. Under the DOJ guidelines, where a user is unable to conduct its own internal analyses for racial fairness, it may rely on the analyses of others if the validity studies are otherwise properly used under the guidelines as "borrowed" studies. However, under the EEOC instructions, § 1607.7, a more stringent set of rules for "transportability" is called

into play when a test user seeks to use another's study in lieu of its own, rather than merely as corroboration. It must then substantiate "in detail" job comparability and must show the absence of "major difference in contextual variables or sample composition which are likely to significantly affect validity." This section does not allow the party seeking to rely on a borrowed validation to benefit from any inferences of assumptions of similarity. Since the Court has only been able to find a hint of task and content similarity through inference, and the evidence on similarity of the sample reveals distinct difference between the South Works and Fairless groups, this higher standard clearly has not been met.

The court noted,

> For example, the South Works sample contains: more crafts (16 as compared with 12 and 8), proportionately more minorities, and older apprentices (mean age 25.6 compared with 22.1 in Fairless III) . . . The Court sees these differences as potentially significant, and finds that USS failed to satisfy its burden of explaining them or demonstrating their non-significance.

It continued,

> What this means, to this Court using the EEOC guidelines, is that the South Works study's evidence of racial fairness cannot be considered probative of the fairness of the tests at Fairless. It is not "transportable" to the Fairless situation, and cannot be used as primary evidence. . . . Therefore, even if the Court were to accept the South Works study as corroborative on other issues, it cannot accept it as the sole evidence of the tests' racial fairness. By rejecting this evidence, the record is now barren of evidence of the tests' racial fairness.

Dickerson illustrates very clearly the importance of job analysis in transportability; it is difficult to read the decision and not conclude the defendant's case was lost largely on this issue. However, the court's reasoning on test fairness must be seen as troubling by I/O practitioners. It seems as though pertinent sections from both the EEOC and DOJ *Guidelines* were used in combination to present an insurmountable hurdle on the issue of fairness to defendants. The fairness study conducted at South Works supported a conclusion that race membership had no impact on validity. (The court did not criticize the conclusions of the fairness study itself, nor disparage the credibility of testimony supporting it; presumably the study demonstrated fairness for the two groups of interest in the sample on which it was based, and the court accepted this evidence.) With affirmative evidence of test fairness established in the only setting in which it was feasibly researched, the court concluded that such fairness evidence was irrelevant to the other studies. The court seems to have missed the meaning of test fairness: that validity is not impacted by racial group membership. The affirmative finding was itself empirical evidence that it did apply to other settings, regardless of any racial differences in samples. By citing differences in the proportion of minorities between the two settings as a reason for rejecting applicability of fairness evidence, the court may have placed an insurmountable burden on defendants to prevail on the issue.

We find it even more troubling that the court refused to apply the fairness evidence to settings in which the proportion of minorities was *smaller.* Having accepted evidence that race was *irrelevant* to validity, the court insisted that in other settings, in which fewer minorities were employed and no such research could be conducted, race *might impact* validity, and so the court rejected its probative value. In doing so, the court rejected as irrelevant the evidence that was contrary to its premise. Given that the court acknowledged " . . . only the South Works validity analysis contained a sufficiently large minority sample to conduct the differential validity analyses," it is difficult to understand how it did not view its own decision as a "Catch-22" that was impossible to overcome.

To conclude this discussion of *Dickerson,* practitioners must hope that the test fairness conclusions in the case are anomalous and can be ignored. Given the different perspective on fairness taken in the *Uniform Guidelines,* contrary court decisions noted as follows in this section, and the developed consensus based on accumulated research in the field since the time of this decision (Society for Industrial and Organizational Psychology, 2003), it seems reasonable to do so.

In *Vanguard Justice Society v. Hughes* (1979), a district court considered multiple lines of evidence in support of a written promotional exam for police sergeant, including an eleventh-hour attempt to transport validity evidence. The transportability effort did not include complete documentation of most of the borrowed validity studies or of job analysis information linking the studied and unstudied jobs. The court noted,

> Defendants have not themselves conducted any validity study. Nor have they stated any reason why they did not do so. However, defendants' expert . . . introduced documentary evidence and testified concerning validity studies conducted in other police departments in other locales. Defendants seek to borrow or, to use the professional jargon, to "transport" such other studies to Baltimore City.

The court concluded that

> . . . any study . . . is of little support to defendants because the record fails to disclose that any such study was itself conducted in accordance with the appropriate guidelines. Further, even if the said other studies relied upon by defendants were conducted in accordance with such guidelines, they are of little aid to defendants unless their transportability is established pursuant to the guidelines.

The court further observed,

> Mr. Bemis testified (Tr. 92) that the authors of the neighboring jurisdiction study examined Test No. 10 for fairness. Guidelines § 15(B)(8). However, no evidence of test fairness, i.e., in this instance, comparison of test scores of blacks and whites versus their respective job performances, was presented other than Mr. Bemis' stamp of seeming approval upon the conclusion of the psychologists who conducted the study that Test No. 10 was fair.

The court then concluded,

> In sum, the evidence presented with regard to the neighboring jurisdiction study, both considered separately and together with all other evidence, does not constitute a showing by defendants of the job-relatedness of Test No. 10. Accordingly, that test, because of its discriminatory impact, was utilized by defendants in violation of Title VII.

In *Vanguard* we are reminded that both the borrowed validity study and the job analysis transporting it must conform to *Uniform Guideline* requirements. Throughout the decision, the court seemed to rebuke casual and incomplete statements of validity. In discussing *Uniform Guidelines'* Section 9A—No Assumption of Validity, the court noted (1) there was expert testimony unsupported by court documents, (2) the expert did not bring such documents to court, (3) the expert acknowledged that a body of research referenced by him to transported validity was not "by itself" sufficient to transport validity, and (4) the expert failed to provide results from a study that he testified would be available "shortly." The court concluded by finding that the single study best documented for transportability failed to meet *Uniform Guidelines* requirements for establishing validity. Without a thorough review of all expert reports and pleadings, it is impossible to infer many issues that may have influenced the court, but *Vanguard* appears to beg for more precision and care in the presentation of relevant validation evidence and for exclusion of evidence only marginally related to support. It seems apparent that expert testimony without explicit written support of it substantially diminished the credibility of the witness.

In *Friend v. Leidinger* (1977), the District court considered the validity of an entry-level fire fighter exam based on evidence obtained elsewhere. Defendants provided expert testimony supporting transported validity of the test. Plaintiffs did not dispute the evidence directly, but instead argued that the EEOC *Guidelines* did not permit an employer to rely upon "vicarious" validation where a validity study was feasible. The court opined that both the EEOC *Guidelines* and the more recent DOJ *Guidelines* were both relevant and "of great value" but stated that "the Court will not be bound by one set of guidelines over another, but only by what the Court deems as reasonable in this case." The court concluded,

> . . . the Court finds it credible . . . that the job of a fireman in Richmond is very similar to the job of a fireman in certain California cities. Given this, the Court concludes that the City of Richmond carried its burden of showing the Firefighters B-1 (m) test to be job-related by proof that the test had been validated as job-related according to EEOC guidelines in a validation study in California, and that proof that the job for which the test was validated

was substantially the same as the job for which the test was being used in Richmond.

Upon appeal (*Friend v. Leidinger,* 1978), the appellate court affirmed the district court's judgment. The appellate court agreed that neither it, nor the trial court, need consider only the EEOC *Guidelines,* and on the issue of transportability, it concluded,

> . . . plaintiffs have shown no difference in the duties of a fireman in the 55 areas of California, where the test was validated, from the duties of a Richmond fireman. To require local validation in every city, village and hamlet would be ludicrous.

In *Friend,* the district court approved transported validity without any criticism of unmet guidelines in either the source study or the job analysis used to demonstrate job similarity. It cannot be known whether the favorable opinion would have been reached had plaintiffs challenged the evidence of transportability. However, the eloquent appellate quote must leave practitioners interested in transportability feeling empowered.

In *Bernard v. Gulf Oil Corporation* (1986), the court considered, among other issues, the validity of entry-level tests for numerous craft jobs. Having accepted criterion-related validation evidence for two crafts, the court approved the tests for all crafts based on job analysis information showing that the measured abilities were common to all crafts jobs. On remand, the district court, in an unpublished decision, again found for the defendants on all issues.

Upon appeal (*Bernard v. Gulf Oil Corporation,* 1989), the appellate court affirmed the district court's final judgment, summarizing,

> Having found that Gulf had shown the new tests were significantly correlated with performance as a boilermaker and pipefitter, the district court considered and compared the most important abilities in those two crafts with the important abilities in all the other crafts. If the most important abilities required for the other crafts are closely related to the most important abilities of the boilermaker or pipefitter, it may be concluded that the new tests, which predict significant aspects of job performance for the boilermaker or pipefitter, also predict important abilities related to the performance of all other craft jobs as well. The district court found that the most important abilities for boilermakers or pipefitters were

closely related to the important abilities for all of the other crafts, and extrapolated from that to find that the tests were job related for all of the crafts.

The district court decisions in *Bernard* permitted an important extension of transportability research that is not explicitly sanctioned in the *Uniform Guidelines*. A showing of job similarity based on common important abilities is a meaningful departure from what were previously presumed to be the requirements. It is interesting to note that none of the versions of the *Guidelines* were referenced in the earlier district decision or in the 1989 appellate decision supporting it.

In *Pegues v. Mississippi State Employment Service* (1980), the district court considered, among many issues, the validity and proper use of the General Aptitude Test Battery (GATB) by a local office of a state employment service. Although a formal transportability argument was not presented, the court nevertheless made several findings relevant to conclusions of validity for jobs not specifically studied. Among the court's findings were the following:

> Empirical research has demonstrated that validity is not perceptibly changed by differences in location, differences in specific job duties or applicant populations. Valid tests do not become invalid when these circumstances change. Plaintiffs' allegation that validity is specific to a particular location, a particular set of tasks and to a specific applicant population, or in other words, that a valid test in one set of circumstances is not valid in circumstances not perfectly identical is not true.

> The research done by Dr. John Hunter and his colleagues shows that the validity of tests is broadly generalizable across jobs, geographical locations and applicant populations. In both the 1970 EEOC *Guidelines* and the Standards of the American Psychological Association such research has been called for.

> No differences between the job duties in the research sample and the jobs in Bolivar County were specified. According to research, even gross changes in job duties did not destroy validity. It follows that small and/or hypothesized differences have little or no effect on validity. Plaintiffs have not shown that the USES tests were invalid because the tasks of the jobs in the research setting may have been different from those in Bolivar County.

The United States Employment Service (USES) tests meet all of the applicable EEOC guidelines for test usage and validation.

Section 1607.4(c)(1) has been met. Differences in location, jobs and applicant characteristics do not alter the proper interpretation of validity evidence. Further, no credible evidence exists that differences between units, jobs and applicant populations alter test validity.

Section 1607.5(b)(1) has been met. No evidence was presented that any of the samples are atypical or unrepresentative. Differences in applicant characteristics do not moderate or change validity.

The court concluded,

> When the evidence is considered as a whole, the court has con-
> cluded that plaintiffs have not shown by a preponderance of the
> evidence that they and the members of the class represented by
> them have suffered, or are likely to suffer, discrimination on the
> basis of race or sex at the hands of defendants . . .

Upon appeal (*Pegues v. Mississippi State Employment Service*, 1983; certiorari denied), the Appellate court affirmed the District court's finding that no adverse impact had been demonstrated. The court concluded,

> Because we affirm the district court's determination that the dis-
> puted tests produced no disparate impact upon black referral can-
> didates during the years involved in plaintiffs' studies, we do not
> address . . . the challenge to expert testimony on the job-validation
> issue.

Although *Pegues* is not a transportability case per se, it never-theless addressed issues highly relevant to establishing validity for unstudied jobs. The court's findings were supportive of many re-search conclusions central to both generalizing and transporting validity. Given how broadly supportive the court's conclusions were, it may be prudent to note that the findings remained intact, but without review, on appeal.

A summary of cases showing: (1) referenced *Guidelines*, (2) controlling *Guidelines*, (3) deference given, (4) transportability is-sues concluded, and (5) final judgment is provided in Table 2.1.

Table 2.1. Case Summary.

Case	Referenced Guidelines	Controlling Guidelines	Deference Given	Transportability Issues Concluded	Final Judgment
Albemarle (1975)	EEOC DOJ	EEOC	"entitled to great deference"; "measured against the Guidelines . . ."	JA must show "no significant differences" between studied and unstudied jobs	Test not validated
Dickerson (1978)	EEOC DOJ	EEOC DOJ	"looked for guidance" to both Guidelines; "not legally binding . . ."; "will use both sets . . . as an aid"	"Superficial description" of work inadequate and a "fatal flaw"	Test not validated
Vanguard (1979)	EEOC Uniform	Uniform[a]	". . . requires consideration of the applicable EEOC guidelines"; many court citations of various levels of deference to Guidelines	Borrowed study and transportability must be established in accordance with and pursuant to Guidelines	Test not validated
Friend (1977, 1978)	EEOC DOJ	EEOC DOJ	"of great value"; "not bound by one set of guidelines over another"	Borrowed test is job related, and studied and unstudied jobs are substantially the same	Test valid
Bernard (1986, 1989)	Uniform	Uniform	Unknown[b]	Permitted transportability based on common important abilities	Test valid
Pegues (1980, 1983)	EEOC Uniform	EEOC[c]	"meets applicable EEOC guidelines"; adherence to numerous specific guidelines noted	Variety of conclusions favorable to transporting and generalizing validity	Test valid

[a] The Vanguard decision stated that the *Uniform Guidelines*, "with a few modifications and clarifications, were the same as the proposed Guidelines published before trial in these cases" and defendants "have stressed that their evidence . . . is related to those Guidelines." The court then referenced the *Uniform Guidelines* throughout its decision.

[b] No reference to *Guidelines* was found in the Appellate decision, and the published District court decision referenced only the 4/5ths rule from the *Uniform Guidelines*.

[c] The Pegues decision stated: "The EEOC Guidelines on Employee Selection Procedures in effect at the time of the alleged discrimination are controlling."

As can be seen in Table 2.1, the *Guidelines* that were "controlling" for the cases varied, as did the level of "deference" given them by the courts. Since each set of *Guidelines* differs somewhat in their requirements for transportability, and since the EEOC and DOJ *Guidelines* now are expired (unless "in effect at the time of alleged discrimination"), the specific inferences we can draw from the developed case law are diminished further. This issue is perhaps more constraining to inferences regarding transportability than to other validation strategies, because transportability approaches have developed from *Guidelines* language to professional practice, more so than for traditional strategies for validation.

One other constraint of this and other reviews of case law is the limited detail provided in the court decisions. Without a thorough review of all pleadings and expert reports before the court, it is often difficult to understand precisely what issues may have influenced the judgment of the court. Even with such a review, subtleties regarding a court's weighing and judgment of witness credibility, the clarity and competence with which evidence was presented, and other intangibles cannot be completely understood in a retrospective review. Thus, the following conclusions must be tempered with caution.

The review of these cases suggests several conclusions that are consistent with language in the *Uniform Guidelines* defining transportability. First, it is feasible to establish validity and job relatedness through a strategy of transportability. The courts in *Friend* and *Bernard* supported explicit transportability strategies, and several of the court's findings in *Pegues* are supportive of transporting and generalizing validity. Second, it is clear that the borrowed validity study must itself conform to the requirements of the *Uniform Guidelines* for establishing validity. This requirement is explicit in the *Uniform Guidelines* and is not novel to transportability strategies; the courts in *Vanguard* and *Dickerson* reinforced this point.

Third, the courts inform us that casually conducted or presented job analyses offered as evidence of job similarity are probably insufficient and certainly are not prudent. Although the *Uniform Guidelines* offer less explicit instruction for establishing job similarity than they do for establishing criterion-related validity, for example, the standards imposed by the courts seem reasonable. The Supreme Court in *Albemarle* refused to infer job similarity from existing lines of job progression without further study and, in *Dickerson,* rejected a "superficial description" of work as a basis for establishing similarity. However, the courts in *Friend* and *Bernard* accepted job analysis information showing job similarity, and in *Bernard,* clarified interpretation of explicit language in the *Uniform Guidelines* to allow that similarity be established on the basis of common abilities.

In *Pegues,* the court found credible (and held) that "even gross changes in job duties did not destroy validity. It follows that small and/or hypothesized differences have little or no effect on validity." This finding and others from *Pegues* illustrate that a court may assimilate widely held research conclusions with possibly disparate regulatory requirements (in this case, the earlier *Guidelines* from the EEOC), and support varied strategies for test validation. The court's findings regarding validity and "applicant characteristics" and "populations" stand in stark contrast to the fairness conclusions in *Dickerson.*

Taken together these decisions provide useful context with which to judge how thresholds of job similarity in transportability efforts will be assessed. Though these cases vary in their instructions, they begin to inform us of the courts' view of transportability, and with regard to job similarity, how similar is similar enough?

Review of Professional Implications

The two primary sources for professional guidance regarding test validation were revised more recently than the *Uniform Guidelines.* Both the *Standards for Educational and Psychological Testing* (American Educational Research Association, American Psychological Association, & National Council on Measurement in Education, 1999) and the *Principles for the Validation and Use of Personnel Selection Procedures* (Society for Industrial and Organizational Psychology, 2003) have been updated in the past decade, and both of these documents reflect evolution in research regarding generalizing validity evidence. Although the *Uniform Guidelines* were adopted when the tenets of situational specificity were still widely accepted, the *Standards* and the *Principles* both support the accumulation of validity evidence by gathering data from multiple studies regarding the specific test or construct being studied in situations similar to the target environment.

The *Principles* define transportability as:

A strategy for generalizing evidence of validity in which demonstration of important similarities between different work settings is used to infer that validation evidence for a selection procedure accumulated in one work setting generalizes to another work setting (p. 71).

The *Principles* denote transportability as one of three methods of generalizing validity evidence from previously conducted research, along with job component validity and synthetic validity and meta-analysis. The *Principles* provide general guidance for conducting a transportability study, such as the recommendation that care be taken when evaluating the technical merits of a source validation study as well as consideration of the comparability between the target job and the source job. "Job comparability" is described as the similarity of job "content or requirements." No preferred method for comparing and contrasting two jobs is specified in the *Principles*. The more general considerations of the job context and candidate group are listed as additional factors for establishing job comparability. Specific aspects of the source study that should be documented according to the *Principles* are possible sampling biases, aspects of the target population which may not be representative of the source study population, as well as range restriction that may have occurred during the source study.

Although the above-mentioned recommendations regarding statistical considerations (that is, range restriction) seem to refer to the process of transporting validity from a criterion-related validation study, another section in the *Principles* implies that transporting validity evidence from studies that employ other validation strategies is appropriate as well. In the section describing meta-analysis, the *Principles* state:

While transportability and synthetic validity/job component validity efforts may be based on an original study or studies that establish the validity of inferences based on scores from the selection procedures through a content-based and/or a criterion-related strategy, meta-analysis is a strategy that only can be applied in cases in which the original studies relied upon criterion-related evidence of validity. (p. 28)

This compare-and-contrast statement widens the definition of transportability from the original in the *Uniform Guidelines* to include borrowing validity evidence from a source study or group of studies that used either a criterion-related strategy or a content strategy. The effect of this evolution is to broaden the usefulness of transportability to apply to the types of assessments that typically evolve from a content strategy, such as job knowledge or work sample assessments. This is especially useful, given that content validity studies often are site- or organization-specific. Relying on a transportability strategy to support validity inferences allows organizations to spread these selection procedures across multiple sites without expending the resources for a second content validity study. However, the work steps required to transport validity from a content validation study would be similar to conducting a separate content validation study at the target location. Both studies would involve a thorough job analysis and documentation of how the tested constructs relate to the job. This endeavor would not qualify as transportability as sanctioned by the *Uniform Guidelines,* but it may be an example of how professionally accepted norms in the field continue to outgrow the aging *Uniform Guidelines.*

The *Standards* never actually use the term *transportability,* but they do refer to strategies for borrowing validity evidence from other sources. Standard 14.6 cautions against borrowing validation evidence from a single source unless the study was conducted under favorable conditions. Regarding the issue of job similarity, the *Standards* state the "current situation must closely correspond to the previous situation" (p. 159). The general nature of that statement is daunting; however, the comment following it recommends a job analysis to identify if the job requirements and underlying constructs are the same for the source job and the target job. The mention of predictor-criterion relationships and sample size implies that the reference is to borrowing validity evidence from a criterion-related validation study (as opposed to content validation); however, that is not explicitly stated. Similar to the *Principles,* the *Standards* promote gathering evidence of validity from as many sources of validation evidence as possible, as evidence gathered at different locations can bolster support for validity.

Neither the *Principles* nor the *Standards* provide much guidance for practitioners seeking to determine if a situation is appropriate for transporting validity evidence. In a situation in which a practitioner seeks to borrow validation evidence from a particular study or group of studies, it seems advantageous to set a threshold or statistical standard for the level of similarity between target and source jobs. In an isolated case of borrowing validation evidence, it may prove that professional judgment of the level of similarity is more appropriate. Although variables such as tasks, KSAOs, minimum qualifications, and requirements can be quantified and compared using quantitative methods, those variables can be affected by larger, more nebulous factors such as organizational culture, place in hierarchy, and other administrative duties. Because such factors may not be consistent between sites or organizations, careful professional judgment is required in all situations when evaluating job similarity. This indeterminacy may be why authors of the *Standards* and the *Principles* refrained from making specific procedural recommendations.

Practical Development

This section addresses some of the practical issues that may be encountered when conducting transportability studies. A sample study is used to illustrate some of the concepts. The sample study is contrived; it is based on several client situations encountered in our transportability work. The details and data have been changed or omitted both to provide anonymity to client organizations and to optimize our illustration and discussion of the data and decision issues.

The simplest situation in which a transportability approach can be applied is one involving two jobs: a source job, in which criterion-related validation evidence (and a fairness study, if feasible) has been established, and a single target job to which that evidence is to be transported. A basic approach may follow closely the pertinent *Uniform Guidelines* language (quoted in earlier sections of this chapter).

The job analysis approach for transporting validity focuses on a showing of substantial similarity in major work behaviors for the jobs under review. With only two jobs under consideration, this effort can be relatively straightforward. The process entails (1) an appropriate job analysis effort to identify the major work behaviors on a common metric for both jobs and (2) a mechanism for judging the degree of job similarity. Judging job similarity is the most ambiguous aspect of the process, and various methods for this comparison are described as follows.

Situation Scenario

The following details provide some context for this example. The client organization is a paper and wood products manufacturer with several production facilities. An ability-testing program for the skilled trade job of millwright was validated and implemented for existing paper mills several years ago. Recently, the company acquired a plywood plant from a competitor, and there was a strong desire to standardize employee selection procedures and to extend the ability test, with validation support, for use in selecting among millwright applicants at the new plant. A company HR representative familiar with skilled plant jobs worked with plant personnel to better understand any differences in the jobs due to different work processes, production facilities, or plant organizational structure. Based on a favorable cursory review, the company asked an I/O psychologist to advise them about extending the testing program and any prudent and cost-effective validation that might be conducted. The project steps and a discussion of the issues considered at each work step are discussed as follows.

Step One. Review Existing Job Information and Develop Preliminary Project Plan.

Overview. This effort should result in a basic understanding of the relevant information that will shape a successful project plan. It is at this preliminary phase where feasibility, risk, and any known or anticipated problems should be identified, including numerous general "consultative" issues. These issues include historic or ongoing enforcement activity, the equal employment posture and status of the organization, presence and severity of adverse impact, presence of and constraints from bargaining agreements, and other stakeholder issues. In the interest of space, we will focus on only those issues that are specifically pertinent to transportability.

Project Details. The following should be accomplished:

A. A practitioner should attempt to identify if basic information required for the study is available. This information includes full documentation of the source study—likely in the form of a technical report—as well as needed data not contained in the report. It is prudent to verify that subject matter experts (SMEs) will be available at the target location to provide job analysis information. Any available job information, such as job descriptions, training manuals, or other relevant documentation, should be collected and reviewed.

B. To properly explore the feasibility of the project, the following considerations must be explored:

What is the exact purpose of validation?

An organization may engage in a test validation project for multiple reasons, some more potentially contentious than others. It is necessary to understand the context under which a study will be conducted. Important contextual information includes the possible existence (or anticipation) of a legal challenge, the stance of the organization on adverse impact and other equal employment issues, and the specific problem or concern that is prompting the need for testing at the target location.

What is known about the source and target jobs?

Subject matter experts at both the source and target locations should be consulted for knowledge of possible differences in job tasks, possible variations in complexity of the jobs (perhaps due to technology or autonomy), or possible differences between positions or shifts. Other information to be collected could include demographic data and the existence of any recruiting or relevant labor pool issues. An important issue with serious consequences is the nature of the planned use of the test within an applicant flow process. If the target location plans to use the test subsequent to more (or fewer) screening hurdles than the source location, the pass rate and selection ratio could be substantially different from those observed in the current implementation.

What is known about the source study?

A full review of the source study should occur at this point. A complete understanding of the assessed test constructs and how they are combined, weighted, and used is necessary. The currency of the study is important to consider, as the transportability effort may be futile if the study is approaching obsolescence in the short or medium term. It is ideal to borrow validation evidence from a trusted source or a study author with whom communication is possible. As indicated in the *Uniform Guidelines* requirements, it is optimal if an analysis of test fairness was conducted. Knowledge of the state of the testing program as it exists for the source job is key, as any problems occurring will likely carry over to the target location. Any changes that have occurred in the source job since the study was conducted also should be considered.

C. Develop a basic project plan. Strategies for conducting the job analysis—ideally including interviews, observations, and a data collection effort—should be developed.

Outcomes. If step one is completed successfully, any knowable barriers to success will have been identified, and sound decisions about how (or whether) to proceed can be made. It is at this phase when deal breakers or insurmountable problems should be identified. Sometimes a preliminary desire to use transportability is reversed here, and the project morphs into something different or otherwise ends before it begins. Although this phase entails a relatively cursory review, much of what will be learned later can be anticipated and predicted here.

Issues and Commentary. Several practical barriers to transportability work may be identified during this early phase of inquiry. A common one relates to ownership of the source study and data, and a frequent desire to shield an existing testing program supported by the source study from expanded risk of review or litigation. Even within a single corporate environment, perceived risk can result in a study "owner" choosing to restrict use of a desired source study. Complications can arise regarding data ownership during mergers and acquisitions and when facilities participating in a testing program are sold. If particular locations participated in the validation study or conducted a transport study, the question of that location's right to use a test battery must be considered. Many test publishers face difficult questions regarding data ownership when allowing clients to borrow validation evidence from data compiled from past studies. Efforts should be made in advance of borrowing validation evidence to formally designate study and data ownership rights.

Another concern that can be difficult to judge occurs when an organization desires to leverage a relatively modest source study in support of a much larger testing program. If the resources used in the source study appear to be "upside down" when compared to those available for the target job(s), and especially if adverse impact may be an issue, it may be prudent to advise against a transportability approach; although scientific rationale for caution may not exist, practical experience with enforcement begs for caution here. Finally, preliminary information may suggest sufficient possible differences between source and target jobs to make a transportability approach a risky strategy. In general, it is useful to know at the outset whether or not the study is exploratory or whether there is reasonable confidence that job similarity will likely be established.

Situation Scenario Update. Step one resulted in a preliminary decision to proceed with a transported validity project for the plywood plant millwright job. No discovered risk issues or technical barriers to success were identified. The I/O psychologist judged the credibility of all of the information exchanged to be high, and there was good reason to believe the source and target jobs were the same in complexity and very similar in major work behaviors and tasks.

Step Two. Review Source Study.

Overview. Although this review must confirm that the study meets *Uniform Guidelines* requirements for establishing criterion-related validation evidence, we will focus on only those issues pertinent to leveraging such studies in transportability work. This effort should result in a determination of whether the source study, if substantial similarity in jobs is shown, provides adequate evidence of validity to support its transport.

Project Details. The following should be accomplished:

A. Examine the job(s) comprised by the original research sample to understand the source of validation data. For studies based on a single job title, this evaluation can be straightforward. However, if similar titles have been combined in the validation study, or job families have been developed and sampled from, this step may require much more effort.

B. Examine the job analysis approach used in the source study. In general, there is a need to connect the source and target jobs based on a common format of job analysis data. It is difficult to compare two datasets that used different metrics in data collection and will make quantitative comparisons of any kind difficult or impossible. It may be necessary to obtain the actual job analysis questionnaire from the original study (or other relevant data collection tool) to use in collecting SME data for the target job.

C. Examine the effects of the test. All of the information in the source study regarding subgroup differences in mean scores and pass rates should be reviewed and considered in the target environment. Consider the appropriateness of the existing cutting score and the likely effect in the applicant pool at the target location.

Outcomes. If step two is completed successfully, the practitioner will have a thorough understanding of the testing program itself as well as the likely consequence of its use in the target location. A plan for collecting target job analysis data in the same format as in the source study should be developed, and any normative data or pass rate information should be considered in the context of the target location.

Issues and Commentary. The source study review should provide information that directs the strategy for continuing the transportability effort. Often, job titles are combined in validation studies to obtain sufficient sample size or because they require the same aptitudes at the time of hire. When validation analyses in the source study are based on more than one job and the data are described by a job family profile, it may be difficult to determine precisely which "job" from the source study to compare to the target of transportability. In some cases, the raw data on which validity coefficients were computed in the source study will not be available, and segmenting the study sample and computing coefficients for only one job will not be feasible. Even when feasible, doing so may produce undesirable results because the job initially may have been combined with others to create enough statistical power to detect an effect. In these cases it is important to know that the description of the study sample (often a centroid or other statistical average) is weighted appropriately to reflect the actual validation data that is to be transported. If the only basis of comparison provided in the source study is a centroid calculated from unit-weighted job analysis data for jobs assigned to the family, it may not fairly represent the computed validity data and therefore is not optimal as a basis of comparison for transportability. If the jobs that make up the computed validity data cannot be determined with precision, then judgment of similarity to the target job should be qualified accordingly.

Understanding the job analysis data is the primary component of step two. In a sense, a practitioner should attempt to reproduce the method used to collect the data, as the relationship between these two datasets forms the foundation on which the validation evidence is to be generalized. The practitioner should have a thorough understanding of how cut scores were devised, as well as any weighting or compensatory scheme that contributes to a battery score. It is important to assess the applicability of the theory behind a multiple hurdle or compensatory approach and its relevance in the target location. Alternatively, there should be a plan to address these important test use issues based on other information, whether from the target setting or from other experience with the tests.

A decision must be made regarding the variables that will be considered for the purpose of establishing job similarity. The *Uniform Guidelines* state that the target job and the source job should have "substantially the same major work behaviors." Work behavior is defined as including "observable (physical) components as well as unobservable (mental) components." This definition (and the court's opinion in *Bernard*) suggests that a review of knowledge, skills, and abilities is certainly within the scope of consideration for the purpose of establishing job similarity. Substantial task overlap implies that the underlying KSAOs for the target and source jobs will be analogous, as it is unlikely that similar activities are being performed without a similar skill set supporting the behavior. A comparison of KSAOs should focus on the level of assessed KSAOs, to establish that the source and target jobs do not differ in the level of complexity of tested constructs. If the level of assessed KSAOs is different, it may result in the test battery being inappropriate for use at the target location. This issue is addressed further in the Constraints and Risks section of this chapter.

Situation Scenario Update. Step two resulted in a favorable review of the source study. A cognitive test battery measuring mechanical comprehension and reasoning skills was validated against several measures of job performance. The validity evidence documented was compelling, with significant and sizable computed validities based on a reasonable sample size. The study included useful job analysis information collected on a task-based job analysis questionnaire (JAQ) and associated data. No fairness study was conducted, but it was determined to be unfeasible in the current sample. Job analysis ratings were collected at the Work Behavior level as well as at the task level. This issue led to a preliminary decision to examine job similarity both on the basis of work behaviors as well as on that of common tasks.

Step Three. Develop Procedures, Plan Analyses, and Gather Data to Examine Job Similarity.

Overview. This effort should result in the design of a JAQ that will be used to collect SME ratings regarding the target job, along with a plan to gather data and analyze it. The plan and JAQ should address all issues critical to the analysis of job similarity. There should be a high degree of confidence before the data are collected that the obtained data will support the analyses needed to properly inform an assessment of job similarity, to judge an inference of transported validity, and to support needed documentation.

Project Details. The following should be accomplished:

A. Identify an appropriate job analysis tool and group of job experts to provide job analysis information. The job experts should understand the purpose and nature of the rating task and provide ratings based on the entry-level job. It is important that the job experts receive instructions similar to those given to the job experts in the source study, with one exception: the SMEs in the target job should be given the opportunity to add any tasks performed that are not included on the rating form. There may be tasks performed by the target job incumbents that are not included in the source study job analysis form. Ratings of these tasks should be provided as well to allow the practitioner to decide on their relevance to the process of establishing job similarity. Alternatively, there must be a mechanism to otherwise conclude that no additional important tasks were relevant to the target job but omitted from the rating form. The intent is to ensure that all important elements of the job are understood.

B. Compile the job analysis results and create a dataset to pre-pare for conducting analyses of similarity. A preliminary examina-tion of the results should prove useful to identify anomalous ratings. If there are additional tasks performed by the target job incumbents, consider the importance of these tasks to the job and whether or not they affect the level of complexity in any of the testable construct areas.

C. Based on thorough knowledge of the source study and the data requirements, similarity analyses should be planned. At this point, the practitioner should decide on a threshold of similarity that will be acceptable as an indicator of similarity.

Outcomes. If step three is completed successfully, the job analysis data regarding the target job will be collected and prepared for analysis. Decisions will be made regarding the relevance of any ad-ditional tasks performed by the target job. Analyses will be planned and decision rules for job similarity will be decided upon.

Issues and Commentary. It is important to collect the job analysis data in a format and method parallel to the source study, to pro-vide a sound basis of comparison to the source job. The identified SMEs must be capable of providing accurate information regard-ing the target job (for example, journey-level millwright incum-bents or supervisors in our client scenario). In some cases, the rating scales used in the rating form from the source study will eas-ily support a rational distinction between critical and noncritical tasks or work behaviors. In some cases, perusal of the job analysis data from the source study can provide a basis for inferring a rea-sonable threshold. Whether or not a firm decision regarding any needed thresholds is made prior to data collection, the issues should be carefully weighed and considered. In some cases, dis-tinguishing critical from unimportant tasks is so subjective that an alternative approach based on continuous data is preferable.

Situation Scenario Update. Step three resulted in a decision to use the existing JAQ to investigate job similarity. A focus group meeting with SMEs was used to explore whether or not the tasks and work behaviors identified in the previous study were current and comprehensive. This and a review of the JAQ instructions and rating scales indicated that data parallel to those existing in the original source study could support a careful examination of job similarity. Thus, the JAQ could be used without modification to gather information on the millwright job at the plywood plant, and the resulting data would provide a basis for judging similarity. Representative incumbent and supervisor SMEs for the plywood millwright job completed the JAQ. The JAQ used, with rating scales, and tasks nested under the identified work behaviors, is presented in Exhibit 2.1.

A measure of overall task and work behavior salience had been computed in the source study by multiplying the time spent and importance ratings for each work behavior and for each task. This measure of task and work behavior salience was judged to be useful and sufficient for analyses of job similarity between the target job and the source job. A rational and defensible method for distinguishing critical and noncritical tasks and work behaviors on the basis of salience indices was developed. All feasible combinations of time spent and importance ratings are shown in Table 2.2 (p. 68), along with the threshold value identified for designating tasks as critical.

The following summary question was used to document whether tasks identified in the JAQ were comprehensive, thereby providing a mechanism to ensure important job elements were not omitted.

Summary: Considering all of the tasks performed on the job, how many hours per week (in a typical forty-hour work week) have been accounted for by the tasks on this list? (Circle one.)

6   35 or more hours
5   30 to 34 hours
4   25 to 29 hours
3   20 to 24 hours
2   15 to 19 hours
1   10 to 14 hours
0   Fewer than 10 hours

Exhibit 2.1. Instructions for Rating Work Behaviors.

On the following pages is a list of work behaviors with associated tasks performed on various maintenance jobs at Client Company. Please indicate whether each task is performed by incumbents in the job you are rating by answering the first question below. Do this for each task or work behavior. The work behavior ratings are at the top of each section. Work behavior should be rated first, followed by each task below that is a component of the work behavior. Answer each of the following questions for each work behavior and associated task.

First, is the task/work behavior normally performed as part of the job?

1 = YES, task/work behavior is performed

0 = NO, task/work behavior is not performed

If the task or work behavior is not performed, mark "0" for "NO" and do not answer the second and third questions for the task.

Second, how much time is spent performing this task/work behavior? (If the time varies from week to week, indicate the average over a month or a year.) Use the following scale:

5 = *Much more time* than other job tasks/work behaviors

4 = *More time* than other job tasks/work behaviors

3 = *About the same* amount of time as other job tasks/work behaviors

2 = *Less time* than other job tasks/work behaviors

1 = *Much less time* than other job tasks/work behaviors

Third, how important is it to successful job performance to perform this task/work behavior acceptably? Use the following scale:

4 = Critical

3 = Very Important

2 = Moderately Important

1 = Somewhat Important

0 = Of No Importance

To answer these questions, refer to these scales and mark your ratings directly on the task list. After you have completed the task ratings, answer the summary question at the end of the task list.

Millwright

Work behaviors are in the shaded section of each table. Please rate the work behavior first, then rate the task set associated with each work behavior.

Performed?	Time Spent	Importance	
——	——	——	*Installs Equipment* (pumps, turbines, compressors, motors, gearboxes, rolls, valves, and so on) in accordance with accepted safety standards as well as layout plans, blueprints, or other drawings in order to generate power and maintain plant operations.
——	——	——	1. Reads blueprints, sketches, and schematic drawings
——	——	——	2. Builds scaffolding and other supports
——	——	——	3. Obtains parts, materials, and supplies
——	——	——	4. Moves materials and equipment using cherry picker, mobile cranes, fork lifts, boom trucks, electric hoists, cables, nylon slings, come-alongs, and so on
——	——	——	5. Constructs bases for machines and equipment
——	——	——	6. Assembles equipment
——	——	——	7. Aligns machines and equipment
——	——	——	8. Connects power to equipment, up to 440 volts
——	——	——	9. Connects piping to equipment
——	——	——	10. Secures machines to solid structures using bolts, welds, rivets, or other fasteners
——	——	——	*Inspects and Maintains Equipment* by watching for potential problems and taking corrective actions in order to comply with safety standards and prevent equipment failure.
——	——	——	11. Checks lubrication
——	——	——	12. Observes flow and pressure indicators

Performed?	Time Spent	Importance
____	____	____	13. Examines parts for visible flaws
____	____	____	14. Checks clearances between parts
____	____	____	15. Listens to mechanical devices in operation
____	____	____	16. Tests vibration using a vibration analyzer
____	____	____	17. Checks temperature by touch or with a temperature probe
____	____	____	18. Checks general structural conditions (painting, corrosion, and so on)
____	____	____	19. Reads gauges for strainers and filters
____	____	____	20. Checks alignment of equipment
____	____	____	21. Examines welded joints for external defects
____	____	____	22. Checks safety equipment (backup alarms, beacons, flag switches, pressure shutdown, level shutdown, temperature shutdown, and so on)
____	____	____	23. Cleans equipment
____	____	____	24. Adjusts packing
____	____	____	25. Measures parts using calipers, micrometers, rules, and other devices
____	____	____	26. Notifies appropriate personnel of problems

Repairs Equipment (gearboxes, pumps, compressors, hydraulic cylinders, rolls, valves, turbines, and so on) according to blueprints, diagrams, and technical manuals so that defective machinery can be returned to normal operation.

Performed?	Time Spent	Importance
____	____	____	27. Dismantles equipment
____	____	____	28. Replaces worn parts
____	____	____	29. Realigns gears and adjusts bearing clearance
____	____	____	30. Adjusts clutches
____	____	____	31. Adjusts brakes

Performed?	Time Spent	Importance	
____	____	____	32. Fabricates parts
____	____	____	33. Joins metal parts using a variety of welding procedures (electric arc welding, acetylene, oxyacetylene, oxyhydrogen, and so on)
____	____	____	*Trains Workers* by following specified procedures to expand the technical job knowledge of maintenance personnel.
____	____	____	34. Explains procedures
____	____	____	35. Demonstrates procedures
____	____	____	36. Observes performance
____	____	____	37. Provides feedback
____	____	____	*Maintains Records* according to specified procedures in order to document worker and maintenance activities.
____	____	____	38. Lists tools, equipment, and materials needed
____	____	____	39. Records inspection and maintenance data
____	____	____	40. Completes personnel forms (time cards, vacation request slips, floating holiday requests, and so on)
____	____	____	*Cleans Work Area* using good housekeeping rules and established procedures to ensure a safe and efficient work environment.
____	____	____	41. Sweeps floor
____	____	____	42. Removes trash and scrap
____	____	____	43. Wipes up spills
____	____	____	44. Washes equipment
____	____	____	45. Stores tools and equipment

Table 2.2. Distinguishing Critical and Noncritical Tasks and Work Behaviors.

	Amount of Time Spent				
Importance	Much More Time – 5	More Time – 4	About the Same – 3	Less Time – 2	Much Less Time – 1
Critical – 4	20	16	12	8	4
Very Important – 3	15	12	9	6	3
Moderately Important – 2	10	8	6	4	2
Somewhat Important – 1	5	4	3	2	1
Of No Importance – 0	0	0	0	0	0

Note: Tasks or work behaviors with salience indices ≥ 6 are designated critical.

Step Four. Complete Analyses of Job Similarity and Document Study Results

Overview. This effort entails examination and analysis of job similarity data, the weighing of evidence regarding an inference of transported validation evidence, and documentation of the study results.

Details. The following should be accomplished:

A. Many indices are available for comparing two arrays of task data. A practitioner must consider the nature of the dataset and make decisions regarding the best methods for examining differences. A list of job similarity indices is presented at the end of this section.

B. Weigh the evidence of the analyses. The result of quantitative comparisons between two task arrays is the starting point for a decision regarding job similarity. One must closely examine the data and pinpoint specific tasks or work behaviors for which differences exist between the source and target jobs. The most important similarities are those regarding aspects of the job that involve the testable constructs in question. Any deviations in job similarity in terms of complexity of testable abilities are especially troublesome and should be given proper deference. Their existence may indicate that an inference of transportability is not appropriate, despite the results of statistical comparisons.

C. Document the results in a technical report. After any validation effort, the study steps and results should be described in a final technical report.

Outcomes. When assessing job similarity, a practitioner should be intimate with the job analysis results. Any deviations in job tasks should be identified and understood. After carefully weighing the evidence, a decision should be made regarding the appropriateness of the use of the test or test battery at the target location. A final technical report should contain the study steps and results to comply with all relevant legal and professional guidelines.

Issues and Commentary. The decision on whether or not a target job is "substantially similar" to a source job is a multifaceted verdict. The job similarity indices presented in this section provide initial indicators of the overall correspondence between the tasks performed on two jobs. Further investigation beyond this global evaluation is necessary any time two jobs are compared. Other matters must be considered: most saliently, those issues that involve the level of the testable constructs required at the time of entry into the jobs. A practitioner must not lose sight of the purpose and nature of a testing program and its likely effects on applicants. For example, if the job similarity index indicates a strong relationship between the jobs, but differences are found in a group of tasks that involve automation of a complex function, the possible result could be that an ability test appropriate for the source job is inappropriate for the target job.

The practitioner must employ a combination of quantitative and qualitative judgment to arrive at a final decision regarding job similarity. A responsible choice to borrow validity evidence will require a thorough understanding of the target job and the source job and the nature of any differences in job requirements. Relying solely on the result of a quantitative comparison of tasks or work behaviors is inadvisable because it may be insensitive to important differences or similarities in KSAO importance and thus result in erroneous conclusions.

Situation Scenario Update. The data obtained from the JAQ are summarized in Table 2.3, along with computed task salience indices and identified critical tasks. The SMEs all responded to the summary question by marking "6," indicating that their job was adequately described by the task list.

The planned analyses entailed identification of critical work behaviors and critical tasks based on analysis of salience indices as previously described. Perusal of the data indicated some modest differences, but also that the two jobs share most critical tasks and all but one critical work behavior.

One method of quantifying the degree of job similarity involves examining the overlap of critical tasks or work behaviors. There are several overlap indices that might be used (some are listed at the end of this section). One is based on the following formula:

$$ SI = \frac{N_C}{\sqrt{N_S * N_T}} $$

where N_S and N_T are the number of critical tasks for the source and target jobs, respectively, and NC is the number of critical tasks common to both jobs. A Similarity Index greater than 0.5 indicates that the two jobs are more alike than different in critical tasks. Choosing a threshold based on this index for designating jobs as substantially similar involves judgment, but the authors generally look for values greater than 0.75.

For the JAQ data summarized earlier, the similarity index yields a value of 0.94 for critical tasks and 0.91 for critical work behaviors, indicating the jobs are substantially similar and that an inference of job similarity is, at least initially, supportable. However, further examination of the job tasks is warranted to identify the nature of any dissimilarities.

Table 2.3. Source Job and Target Job Analysis Results.

Work Behavior or Task	Source Job				Target Job			
	Average Time Spent	Average Importance	Salience	Average Critical?	Average Time Spent	Importance	Salience	Critical?
Installs Equipment	3.0	3.5	10.5	√	3.0	3.0	9	√
Task 1	3.0	4.0	12	√	3.0	4.0	12	√
Task 2	1.0	3.0	3		1.0	2.5	2.5	√
Task 3	3.0	4.0	12	√	3.0	4.0	12	√
Task 4	3.0	4.0	12	√	3.0	4.0	12	√
Task 5	1.5	4.0	6	√	2.0	3.5	7	√
Task 6	4.0	4.0	16	√	4.0	4.0	16	√
Task 7	4.0	4.0	16	√	4.0	4.0	16	√
Task 8	1.0	2.0	2		0.0	0.0	0	
Task 9	3.0	4.0	12	√	3.0	3.5	10.5	√
Task 10	4.0	4.0	16	√	4.0	4.0	16	√
Inspects or Maintains Equipment	3.0	4.0	12	√	3.0	3.5	10.5	√
Task 11	3.0	3.5	10.5	√	3.0	3.0	9	√
Task 12	3.0	4.0	12	√	3.0	3.0	9	√

Table 2.3. Source Job and Target Job Analysis Results.

Work Behavior or Task	Source Job				Target Job			
	Average Time Spent	Average Importance	Salience	Average Critical?	Average Time Spent	Importance	Salience	Critical?
Task 13	3.0	4.0	12	✓	3.0	3.0	9	✓
Task 14	3.0	4.0	12	✓	3.0	3.0	9	✓
Task 15	3.0	3.5	10.5	✓	3.0	3.5	10.5	✓
Task 16	3.0	3.5	10.5	✓	0.0	0.0	0	
Task 17	3.0	3.5	10.5	✓	3.0	3.0	9	✓
Task 18	3.0	3.0	9	✓	3.0	3.0	9	✓
Task 19	3.0	3.5	10.5	✓	3.0	3.0	9	✓
Task 20	3.0	4.0	12	✓	3.0	3.5	10.5	✓
Task 21	3.0	3.5	10.5	✓	3.0	3.5	10.5	✓
Task 22	3.0	4.0	12	✓	3.0	4.0	12	✓
Task 23	3.0	3.5	10.5	✓	3.0	3.0	9	✓
Task 24	3.0	3.0	9	✓	3.0	3.0	9	✓
Task 25	3.0	4.0	12	✓	3.0	3.5	10.5	✓
Task 26	3.0	4.0	12	✓	3.0	4.0	12	✓
Repairs Equipment	3.0	3.5	10.5	✓	3.0	3.0	9	✓
Task 27	3.0	4.0	12	✓	3.0	3.5	10.5	✓
Task 28	3.0	3.5	10.5	✓	3.0	3.5	10.5	✓

Task 29	3.0	4.0	12	✓	3.0	3.0	9	✓
Task 30	3.0	3.5	10.5	✓	3.0	3.0	9	✓
Task 31	3.0	3.5	10.5	✓	3.0	3.5	10.5	✓
Task 32	3.0	3.5	10.5	✓	3.0	3.5	10.5	✓
Task 33	3.0	4.0	12	✓	3.0	4.0	12	✓
Trains Workers	3.0	3.5	10.5	✓	1.0	3.0	3	✓
Task 34	2.5	3.5	8.75	✓	1.0	3.0	3	
Task 35	3.0	4.0	12	✓	1.5	3.0	4.5	
Task 36	2.5	3.5	8.75	✓	1.0	2.5	2.5	
Task 37	3.0	4.0	12	✓	1.0	3.0	3	
Maintains Records	3.0	4.0	12	✓	3.0	3.5	10.5	✓
Task 38	3.0	4.0	12	✓	3.0	3.0	9	✓
Task 39	3.0	4.0	12	✓	3.0	4.0	12	✓
Task 40	3.0	4.0	12	✓	3.0	3.5	10.5	✓
Cleans Work Area	3.0	3.0	9	✓	3.0	3.0	9	✓
Task 41	3.0	3.0	9	✓	3.0	3.0	9	✓
Task 42	3.0	3.0	9	✓	3.0	3.0	9	✓
Task 43	3.0	3.0	9	✓	3.0	3.0	9	✓
Task 44	3.0	2.5	7.5	✓	3.0	2.5	7.5	✓
Task 45	3.0	3.0	9	✓	3.0	2.5	7.5	✓

Task #16, "Tests vibration using a vibration analyzer," was a critical task for the source job, but was not performed at all in the target job. Further investigation revealed that this task is trained well after the time of hire and is not especially complex, so it would not affect the level of ability required for the source job.

Tasks #34 through #37, all relating to the work behavior "Trains Workers," met the criticality threshold in the source job; although each was performed in the target job, none was designated critical. The overall work behavior of "Trains Workers" also indicated that it is performed, but it is not a very important aspect of the target job. Follow-up discussion with plant personnel revealed a somewhat different approach to worker training between the source and target plants, and this in turn was reflected in the JAQ data. Since the plant personnel in both plants engage in some training, preliminary discussions of the source and target jobs did not reveal this modest difference in job structure.

The job differences in tasks comprised by the work behavior "Trains Workers" reflects the only important difference identified between the source and target jobs. Consideration of the complexity and cognitive skills required for the shared tasks comprising the other work behaviors led to a conclusion that the differences in training tasks did not undermine an inference of transportability. These considerations also led to the conclusion that a summary of job similarity based on the task-level data would meaningfully reflect the similarity of jobs for purposes of judging transportability.

This scenario was purposefully simplistic for the purpose of illustrating the process of a transportability project, although the authors did attempt to present realistic decision points and issues for consideration, many based on previous experiences. The decision to borrow validity evidence is frequently not as straightforward as it may initially seem. Our goal was to present a practical approach that could prove useful for a practitioner who is seeking to use this validation strategy.

Job Similarity Indices

A quantitative examination of job analysis ratings forms an important basis for a job similarity argument. The following are examples of some indices of job similarity that have proven useful to the authors in the past. Although these indices may allow a practitioner to compare arrays of task, work behavior, or KSAO data, the judgment of the level of similarity that is required as a threshold of establishing job similarity should be a function of both a qualitative as well as these quantitative analyses.

A. Pearson Product Moment correlation. A correlation between two arrays of job analysis data can provide an indicator of the strength of the relationship between the two jobs. The result of this analysis will provide a global evaluation of the relationship. The data should be further examined to pinpoint the nature of differences in the SME job analysis ratings.

B. Critical Task Overlap (Fleishman & Quaintance, 1984). Computing the critical task overlap between two different task lists provides an indication of the level of similarity among those tasks that are important to each job. This index does not take into consideration the overlap or lack thereof for tasks deemed as not important to the job. Also, the practitioner must identify an appropriate threshold for criticality.

$$S = \frac{n_s}{n_d + n_s}$$

where
S = Proportion of overlap of critical tasks
n_s = Number of important tasks common to both source and target jobs (tasks are the same)
n_d = Number of important tasks that are important to one job but not the other job (tasks are different)

C. Squared Euclidean Distance (Aldenderfer & Blashfield, 1984). Distance statistics are useful indications of the amount of deviation by task from the target job. This type of statistic is especially useful for examining the distance between a job and aggregate job family ratings. A useful decision rule is to assign the target into the job family if it is not farther from the centroid than the farthest job already in the job family.

$$D^2 = \Sigma \ (X - X)^2$$
where
D^2 = Squared Euclidean distance between measures
X = Task rating index

Constraints and Risks

Transportability can provide a cost-effective method for establishing validity and legal defensibility by formally leveraging validation research conducted in other settings. There are a number of challenges and limitations to the method, however, that can impact its feasibility or usefulness in any given situation.

Primary among these is the need for an adequate source study and an appropriate method for establishing job similarity. Insufficient planning often results in inadequate job analysis information to support a comparison of jobs, thereby prohibiting a transportability approach. Often, where adequate studies do exist, stakeholder interests are divided, and source study owners do not have sufficient incentive to overcome the perceived risk of sharing the source study data. Where incentives are aligned, such as in the test publishing industry, publishers may still narrowly restrict critical information that companies or consultants desire due to proprietary interests. When source studies are offered without adequate details to enable a thorough understanding of their technical features, some companies and consultants may decline to use them. Further, for a variety of reasons, some companies and consultants prefer to conduct local empirical validation research to support and inform their test use. With relatively modest attention given transportability in the *Uniform Guidelines,* and few court cases examining their use, some attorneys involved in compliance are less familiar with and therefore wary of transportability approaches. All of these pragmatic obstacles serve to limit transportability research.

Other challenges and limitations relate to job analyses needed to establish job similarity. Unfortunately, job analysis is a complex endeavor that requires professional judgment and is necessarily somewhat subjective. There is no standard job analysis method for establishing job similarity, nor is there a standard index of comparison or an agreed-upon threshold required to affirm similarity among jobs. With so many decision points requiring professional judgment, the opportunity for challenge or dispute among interested parties may be substantial.

Work behaviors and tasks as written often vary in their levels of specificity and detail. The level of both will influence job analysis data and the results of any comparison among jobs. Whether working at a general level of work behaviors or a specific level of tasks, the amount of detail included in them will influence their meaning and, consequently, JAQ data obtained based on them. In general, if less detail is provided in a behavioral description, that description becomes easier to endorse. This point is illustrated as follows, using examples in the sample study from the previous section. Each successive level shown provides less detail and as a result each becomes somewhat easier to endorse. This is true for both work behaviors and tasks.

Work Behavior #1

Level 1: Installs equipment (pumps, turbines, compressors, motors, gearboxes, rolls, valves, and so on) in accordance with accepted safety standards as well as layout plans, blueprints, or other drawings in order to generate power and maintain plant operations.

Level 2: Installs equipment in accordance with accepted safety standards as well as layout plans, blueprints, or other drawings in order to generate power and maintain plant operations.

Level 3: Installs equipment in accordance with accepted safety standards as well as layout plans, blueprints, or other drawings.

Level 4: Installs equipment in accordance with plans.

Level 5: Installs equipment.

Task #4

Level 1: Moves materials and equipment using cherry picker, mobile cranes, fork lifts, boom trucks, electric hoists, cables, nylon slings, come-alongs, and the like.

Level 2: Moves materials and equipment.

The examples just presented illustrate how the choice of taxonomic level and detail may influence job analysis data, making conclusions of similarity or dissimilarity more likely. Sound professional judgment is required throughout the job analysis process to ensure that a conclusion of job similarity and transported validity is supportable and appropriate. An incorrect affirmative inference of validity will occur when undetected differences in tasks or work behaviors diminish the importance of the target KSAOs to performance of the job. This concern is true of detected differences in tasks as well. Recalling the sample study from the previous section, there was no threat to an inference of transported validity for an ability test battery due to the differences between jobs in training tasks. The training tasks were not particularly complex, whereas most remaining shared tasks were. Hence the millwright job at the plywood plant was comparable in complexity to the source job, requiring mechanical and reasoning abilities for much of it. The jobs shared most critical tasks, and this overlap permitted an affirmative inference of transported validity supported both by the study documentation (for compliance purposes) and by sound professional judgment.

It is interesting to note, however, that confidence in a conclusion of substantial similarity and transported validity for tests of other KSAOs might have been lower. For example, if the test battery to be transported had included a test related to trainer style or interpersonal skill, the identified task differences would threaten an inference of validity. Perusal of the task list reveals no other tasks involving training or even interaction with other workers. Although the task differences between jobs were modest, they happened to influence dramatically the difference in importance of other KSAOs. It is important to remember that this example is contrived; there was no validated test of interpersonal skill in the source study, probably because it was associated with a small portion of the source job. Nevertheless, the example is useful because it illustrates that a focus on tasks and work behaviors can be insensitive to differences in KSAO importance to the respective jobs. For measures of KSAOs that are ubiquitous in job performance, there is little concern that modest or even substantial differences in tasks will result in diminished importance of a ubiquitous KSAO. Because it is ubiquitous, the KSAO will be required for many remaining shared tasks, and possibly for tasks novel to the target job. In this regard, a transportability approach that follows *Uniform Guidelines* requirements focused on similarity in work behaviors is "forgiving"; it is unlikely to result in an incorrect affirmative inference of transported validity for tests of ubiquitous KSAOs.

This reasoning is consistent with the results of meta-analysis and validity generalization research, and research examining moderators of ability test validity (Ackerman & Humphreys, 1990; Callender & Osburn, 1980; Hartigan & Wigdor, 1989; Hunter & Hunter, 1984; Schmidt & Hunter, 1998; Schmidt, Hunter, & Pearlman, 1981). This research suggests that for tests of ability, most observed variability in validity is attributable to statistical artifacts and not to situational variables that differ from one setting to another. Further, where variability in true validity exists, it is associated with differences in job complexity and not with modest or even substantial differences in tasks. Thus, it is the importance of the measured KSAO to overall job performance, and not the specific tasks performed, that is important to a proper inference of validity.

Despite complexities in job analysis, perusal of developed case law indicates that courts will accept, as an adequate defense of Title VII claims, a well-documented transportability study that includes an adequate source study and a reasonable showing of substantial job similarity. Although the *Uniform Guidelines* language focuses on transportability on the basis of job similarity in work behaviors and not in abilities, language in the *Albemarle* decision appeared to have invited the latter, and in *Bernard,* the court accepted it. In *Pegues,* the court did not rule on transportability per se, but it did demonstrate a court's willingness to embrace findings widely held in the profession that are discordant with language in the *Uniform Guidelines.* Taken together these cases suggest that practitioners should view transportability as a viable option for test validation; although an approach based on work behaviors may be less vulnerable to challenge, the courts may permit strategies that are not specifically sanctioned by *Uniform Guidelines* language. Whether the courts will move to accept validity generalization strategies and render transportability efforts obsolete cannot be known at this time.

Our advice to practitioners conducting transportability studies is to approach the endeavors with as much rigor as possible and to provide a clear chain of evidence linking the source study and target job. Risk of litigation and risks to effective selection will be minimized if an inference of transported validity is supported by both the study documentation and by sound professional judgment.

References

Ackerman, P. J., & Humphreys, L. G. (1990). Individual differences theory in industrial and organizational psychology. In M. D. Dunnette & L. M. Hough (Eds.), *Handbook of industrial and organizational psychology* (2nd ed., Vol. 1, pp. 223–282). Palo Alto, CA: Consulting Psychologists Press.

Albemarle Paper Company et al. v. Moody, 422 U.S. 405 (1975).

Aldenderfer, M. S., & Blashfield, R. K. (1984). *Cluster analysis.* Thousand Oaks, CA: Sage.

American Educational Research Association, American Psychological Association, & National Council on Measurement in Education. (1999). *Standards for educational and psychological testing.* Washington, DC: American Educational Research Association.

Arvey, R. D., Maxwell, S. E., & Mossholder, K. M. (1979). Even more ideas about methodologies for determining job differences and similarities. *Personnel Psychology, 32,* 529–538.

Arvey, R. D., & Mossholder, K. M. (1977). A proper methodology for determining similarities and differences among jobs. *Personnel Psychology, 30,* 363–374.

Bernard v. Gulf Oil Corporation, 643 F. Supp. 1494 (E.D.TX 1986).

Bernard v. Gulf Oil Corporation, 890 F.2d 735 (5th Cir. 1989).

Brannick, M. T. (2001). Implications of empirical Bayes meta-analysis for test validation. *Journal of Applied Psychology, 86,* 468–480.

Callender, J. C., & Osburn, H. G. (1980). Development and testing of a new model of validity generalization. *Journal of Applied Psychology, 65,* 543–558.

Dickerson v. U.S. Steel Corp., 472 F. Supp. 1304 (1978).

Equal Employment Opportunity Commission, Civil Service Commission, Department of Labor, & Department of Justice. (1978). *Uniform guidelines on employee selection procedures. Federal Register, 43*(166), 38290–38315.

Fleishman, E. A., & Quaintance, M. K. (1984). *Taxonomies of human performance.* Orlando: Academic Press.

Friend v. Leidinger, 446 F. Supp. 361 (E.D. VA 1977).

Friend v. Leidinger, 588 F.2d 61 (4th Cir.) (1978).

Guion, R. M. (1998). *Assessment, measurement, and prediction for personnel decisions.* Mahwah, NJ: Erlbaum.

Hanser, L. M., Mendel, R. M., & Wolins, L. (1979). Three flies in the ointment: A reply to Arvey and Mossholder. *Personnel Psychology, 32,* 511–516.

Hartigan, J. A., & Wigdor, A. K. (Eds.) (1989). *Fairness in employment testing.* Washington, DC: National Academy Press.

Hoffman, C. C. (1999). Generalizing physical ability test validity: A case study using transportability, validity generalization, and construct validation evidence. *Personnel Psychology, 52,* 1019–1041.

Hoffman, C. C., Holden, L. M., & Gale, K. (2000). So many jobs, so little "N": Applying expanded validation models to support generalization of cognitive test validity. *Personnel Psychology, 53,* 955–991.

Hoffman, C. C., & McPhail, S. M. (1998). Exploring options for supporting test use in situations precluding local validation. *Personnel Psychology, 50*, 987–1003.

Hunter, J. E., & Hunter, R. F. (1984). Validity and utility of alternative predictors of job performance. *Psychological Bulletin, 96*, 72–88.

Johnson, M., & Jolly, J. (2000). Extending test validation results from one plant location to another: Application of transportability evidence. *The Journal of Behavioral and Applied Management, 1*(1), 127.

Lee, J. A., & Mendoza, J. L. (1981). A comparison of techniques which test for job differences. *Personnel Psychology, 34*, 731–748.

Lissitz, R. W., Mendoza, J. L., Huberty, C. J., & Markos, H. V. (1979). Some further ideas on a methodology for determining job similarities/differences. *Personnel Psychology, 32*, 517–528.

McIntyre, R. M., & Farr, J. L. (1979). A comment on Arvey and Mossholder's "A proposed methodology for determining similarities and differences among jobs." *Personnel Psychology, 32*, 507–510.

Mobley, W. H., & Ramsay, R. S. (1973). Hierarchical clustering on the basis of inter-job similarity as a tool in validity generalization. *Personnel Psychology, 26*, 213–225.

Pegues et al. v. Mississippi State Employment Service, 488 F. Supp. 239 (N.D. Miss. 1980), 699 F. 2d 760 (5th Cir.) 464 U.S. 991 (1983).

Rafilson, F. M., Allscheid, S. P., and Weiss, J. G., (1994). Transportability of validity of the National Police Officer selection test for a large eastern metropolitan police department. *Psychological Reports, 75*, 707–718.

Sackett, P. R., Cornelius, E. T., & Carron, T. J. (1981). A comparison of global judgment versus task oriented approaches to job classification. *Personnel Psychology, 34*, 791–804.

Schmidt, F. L. & Hunter, J. E. (1998). The validity and utility of selection methods in personnel psychology: Practical and theoretical implications of 85 years of research findings. *Psychological Bulletin, 124*, 262–274.

Schmidt, F. L., Hunter, J. E., & Pearlman, K. (1981). Task differences as moderators of aptitude test validity in selection: A red herring. *Journal of Applied Psychology, 66*, 166–185.

Society for Industrial and Organizational Psychology. (2003). *Principles for the validation and use of personnel selection procedures* (4th ed.). Bowling Green, OH: Society for Industrial and Organizational Psychology.

Tippins, N. T., McPhail, S. M., Hoffman, C. C., & Gibson, W. M. (1999, April). Transporting validity in the real world. Continuing Education Workshop presented at the 14th Annual Conference of the Society of Industrial/Organizational Psychology, Atlanta, GA.

Vanguard Justice Society v. Hughes, 471 F. Supp 670 (D. MD 1979).

CHAPTER 3

Job Component Validity: Background, Current Research, and Applications

Calvin C. Hoffman, Boris Rashkovsky, and Erika D'Egidio

Organization of the Chapter

The goals of this chapter are to (1) provide background on the concept of job component validity, (2) provide research on the job component validity (JCV) model operationalized in the Position Analysis Questionnaire (PAQ; McCormick, Jeanneret, & Mecham, 1972), (3) describe how the JCV model was developed, (4) review research on the accuracy and efficacy of JCV, and (5) describe a variety of organizational applications of JCV. The section on organizational applications provides enough detail on how to use JCV that interested readers can replicate such research or design and conduct their own JCV studies. Because readers will vary widely in their preexisting levels of knowledge about and experience with JCV, this chapter takes several different paths to cover these concepts.

Synthetic Validity and JCV

Mossholder and Arvey (1984) stated that synthetic validity "describes the logical process of inferring test-battery validity from predetermined validities of the tests for basic work components" (p. 323). Mossholder and Arvey provided an overview of synthetic validation, contrasting two versions in the J-coefficient (Primoff, 1955) and job component validity as operationalized in the PAQ. Mossholder and Arvey also compared synthetic validation with VG, noting a major distinction between the two approaches: the former requires more detailed analysis of the job(s) in question than does the latter.

Jeanneret (1992) discussed synthetic validation, focusing on options available through the PAQ, including descriptions of both the JCV and the PAQ attributes analysis procedures. The JCV procedure provides a range of potentially useful information, including estimated validity of General Aptitude Test Battery (GATB) constructs for predicting job performance, estimated mean test scores for GATB subtests, and estimated mean scores for commercially available tests measuring the same constructs as the GATB (McCormick, DeNisi, & Shaw, 1979). Jeanneret (1992) described multiple applications of the JCV procedure and argued that JCV is a viable validation option in its own right, particularly where small sample sizes or other organizational constraints preclude other validation options.

Recently, Scherbaum (2005) reviewed and updated the published and unpublished literature on synthetic validation in its broadest sense. Readers interested in synthetic validation models—such as the J-coefficient (Primoff, 1955; 1957; 1959), Guion's (1965) approach to synthetic validity, the synthetic validity model of Hollenbeck and Whitener (1998), and even more recent work such as the Army's synthetic validity project (Peterson, Wise, Arabian, & Hoffman, 2001) and McCloy's (1994; 2001) multilevel modeling approach—should carefully review Scherbaum's (2005) article as well as Johnson (2007) in this volume. Because the focus of this discussion is confined to JCV models and applications, other synthetic validity models are not addressed in detail in this chapter.

Steel, Huffcutt, and Kammeyer-Mueller (2006) provided an extensive review of synthetic validity and how this concept overlaps with that of validity generalization. Steel et al. review both JCV and J-coefficient methodologies and describe in detail the steps involved in developing synthetic validity solutions across job domains. Steel et al. tied the development of synthetic validity in its broadest sense into conceptualizations of how work is structured and how predictions of work performance are made. That paper effectively treats JCV and other synthetic validity models as approaches wherein the researcher is attempting to estimate validity in settings in which no criterion-related data exist, but one has knowledge of the job (or jobs) in question. They also make compelling arguments that synthetic validity and validity generalization have much in common, and they suggest ways in which methodological advancements from VG can be incorporated into synthetic validity. Those interested in theoretical justifications for synthetic validity and likely future developments in the area of synthetic validity are encouraged to read the Steel et al. article. These potential developments notwithstanding, our focus in this chapter is on current and recommended applications of JCV as they now exist rather than on expected developments in JCV methodology.

Job Component Validity Defined

Job component validity, like other methodologies derived from synthetic validity, is a means of inferring the validity of a test or battery of tests without the direct measurements employed in traditional criterion-related validity strategies. Job component validity relies on two assumptions: (1) if different jobs have a common component, the attributes or skills needed to fulfill the requirements of that component are the same across jobs, and (2) the validity of a predictor of a job component is consistent across jobs requiring the component (Jeanneret, 1992). Research has provided consistent support for these two assumptions (Jeanneret, 1992; McCormick et al., 1972; Mecham, 1985).

Job component validity is assessed by analyzing the relationship between quantitative job analysis data and test data across jobs (Jeanneret, 1992). The first step in developing a JCV model is to conduct a structured job analysis to document work behaviors and required worker characteristics for the target job. The job analysis procedure should describe each job with common descriptors and a common scale, so data can be analyzed across jobs. Once profiles of descriptors from a variety of different jobs are collected using a structured job analysis tool, these profiles are matched with aggregate levels of incumbent scores on the tests used to predict performance on the same jobs (Brown & Harvey, 1996). In JCV models, the job is the unit of analysis. Two sets of data are associated with each case (that is, job): (1) job analytic data (such as ratings) and (2) criterion-related validity data (that is, test data including test means and validity coefficients for a particular job). In a JCV study, often the job analytic data and test data do not come from the same sample; rather, the job and test data are typically found in different databases and are matched according to the job titles in each database (Brown & Harvey, 1996) or by DOT codes (Rashkovsky & Hoffman, 2005).

It should be noted that there are many potential JCV models. Brown and Harvey (1996) developed a JCV approach linking the Common-Metric Questionnaire (CMQ) and the Myers-Briggs Type Indicator. Johnson, Carter, and Tippins (2001) developed a JCV model linking a proprietary job analysis questionnaire with proprietary predictors (cognitive and situational judgment) for a large telecommunications company. All that is required to develop a JCV model is (1) quantifiable job analysis data for a large number of jobs and (2) predictor information (mean test scores, validity, and the like) for the predictor(s) of interest.

JCV and the Gravitational Hypothesis

One theoretical basis for the JCV model lies in the "gravitational hypothesis" (McCormick et al., 1979). The gravitational hypothesis holds that, over the course of a person's career, the individual gravitates toward jobs compatible with his or her interests, abilities, values, and skills (McCormick et al., 1979; Wilk, Desmarais, & Sackett, 1995). In essence, the rationale for this hypothesis is based on the observation that individuals who are overqualified for a position tend to leave or be promoted to higher-level positions, and underqualified individuals tend to be terminated or voluntarily move to occupations where performance is higher and job failure is lower (Brown & Harvey, 1996). This hypothesis postulates that over large samples, the mean test scores of employees in a particular job reflect the job-required levels of the constructs measured by the tests. Thus, incumbents in a particular job would have a distribution of test scores on specific constructs that overlap with the requirements for successful job performance. To the extent that work requirements are associated with specific levels and types of individual characteristics (that is, aptitudes or personal characteristics), test score requirements can be estimated for other jobs that contain the same work requirements (Mecham, 1985).

Research by Wilk et al. (1995) and Wilk and Sackett (1996) provided empirical support for the gravitational hypothesis. Wilk and Sackett (1996) conducted a thorough test of the gravitational hypothesis in a study using more extensive data and different analytical techniques than in the earlier research. Results provided support for the gravitational hypothesis in both datasets; that is, individuals moved into jobs that were commensurate with their ability. In addition, the findings showed that cognitive ability plays a role in occupational mobility beyond its relationship with educational attainment; however, the results also suggested "cognitive ability is not the sole determinant of job complexity change" (Wilk & Sackett, 1996). Although most JCV research has been conducted with ability tests, the Wilk and Sackett (1996) study suggested similar results might be found for other characteristics (such as interest and personality factors).

The Case for Applied Use of JCV

Applied researchers working in the selection arena must grapple with disparities between established legal requirements versus developing consensus regarding sound professional practice while conducting applied validation research. The *Uniform Guidelines* (Equal Employment Opportunity Commission, Civil Service Commission, Department of Labor, & Department of Justice, 1978), although now dated due to subsequent advancements in the field, must still be accorded great deference. The *Uniform Guidelines* tell us that job analysis and validation research—whether content-oriented, criterion-related, or construct validation—are always needed prior to using a test in a new location. Although the *Uniform Guidelines* make allowance for alternative validation strategies such as test transportability, the requirements for transportability are still demanding (namely, the previous validation study must have met all requirements of the *Uniform Guidelines,* including conducting a fairness analysis).

Validity generalization (VG) research has demonstrated that for cognitive ability tests, situational differences do not moderate validity, and that differences between jobs are relatively unimportant (Pearlman, Schmidt, & Hunter, 1980; Schmidt & Hunter, 1977). If one followed the letter of recommendations regarding application of VG in applied settings, little research would seem needed where use of cognitive ability predictors is contemplated. Minimal job analysis would be required, which would probably focus on knowing enough about the job to place it into a *Dictionary of Occupational Titles* (1977) job family (see Pearlman et al., 1980).

In contrast to VG recommendations downplaying the need for job analysis and local validation research, selection-related case law demonstrates that job analysis is a necessary ingredient for successful defense of selection systems (*Griggs v. Duke Power,* 1971; *Albemarle Paper Company v. Moody,* 1975). See Thompson and Thompson (1982) for a review of court cases dealing with job analysis. Validity generalization has had an inconsistent track record in court, primarily because of its failure to incorporate detailed job analysis information (Shultz, Riggs, & Kottke, 1999). This weakness of VG does not apply to synthetic validity or JCV (Hoffman & McPhail, 1998; Scherbaum, 2005), because use of such methods is predicated on conducting a detailed job analysis.

Landy (1986) argued that the *Uniform Guidelines* were set up for "stamp collectors," and that blindly following the *Uniform Guidelines* interferes with the development of I/O psychology as a science. Landy urged researchers to continue finding new and better ways to support inferences of validity and not to allow themselves to be limited by the constraints imposed by the *Uniform Guidelines.* In a similar theme, Binning and Barrett (1989) demonstrated there are many different ways to marshal evidence regarding the validity of measures and argued that all forms of validation evidence are special cases of construct validity.

Guion (1991) noted that the need for more detailed job analysis and validation research increases in situations in which the risk of legal challenge is elevated. Regarding the amount and detail of job analysis information required to support use of a selection system, Guion (1991) stated: "The level of detail *desired* [emphasis in original] may also be determined by the likelihood of litigation. Prudent personnel researchers attend not only to the best wisdom of their profession but to the realities of the courtroom. In a specific situation, a detailed job analysis may not be necessary technically, but failure to have evidence of an 'adequate' job analysis, in the view of the trial judge, may result in an adverse decision in court" (p. 332).

Because we believe practitioners must address concerns about managing legal exposure, one of the major assumptions driving this chapter is that the amount, type, and detail of validation evidence needed varies by setting when conducting applied validation research. Applied researchers and practitioners cannot simply implement the latest, most current innovations from the scientific side of the field while citing the latest published research—they must also pay attention to practical concerns such as legal exposure. Given such concerns, how should applied researchers balance the current wisdom of the field with the demands for legal defensibility? Synthetic validity may represent a reasonable compromise (see Hoffman & McPhail, 1998; Scherbaum, 2005). A later section of this chapter illustrates the concepts of risk management in conducting validation research and outlines which applications of JCV might be viewed as more or less risky in different settings or types of organizations.

Although the *Uniform Guidelines* do not specifically discuss either synthetic validity or JCV, the *Uniform Guidelines* do make provisions for developments in the field of applied psychology. In Section 60–3.5, General Standards for Validity, part A, the *Uniform Guidelines* state: "New strategies for showing the validity of selection procedures will be evaluated as they become accepted by the psychological profession." In part C of Section 60–3.5, the *Uniform Guidelines* clarify the role of professional standards in determining validation requirements:

C. *Guidelines are consistent with professional standards.*
The provisions of these guidelines relating to validation of selection procedures are intended to be consistent with generally accepted professional standards for evaluating standardized tests and other selection procedures, such as those described in the

Standards for Educational and Psychological Tests prepared by a joint committee of the American Educational Research Association, the American Psychological Association, and the National Council on Measurement in Education (American Educational Research Association, 1974) and standard textbooks and journals in the field of personnel selection.

Although earlier versions of the *Principles for the Validation and Use of Personnel Selection Procedures* (Society for Industrial and Organizational Psychology, 2003) did not explicitly mention synthetic/job component validity, the most recent edition of the *Principles* recognizes synthetic validity and job component validity as one of several strategies researchers and practitioners can follow to support inferences of validity. The *Principles* state:

> A defining feature of synthetic validity/job component validity is the justification of the use of a selection procedure based upon the demonstrated validity of inferences from scores on the selection procedure with respect to one or more domains of work (job components). Thus, establishing synthetic validity/job component validity requires documentation of the relationship between the selection procedure and one or more specific domains of work (job components) within a single job or across different jobs. (p. 27)

PAQ JCV Model Development

The PAQ's JCV procedure (McCormick et al., 1972) was based on a series of cross-validated multiple regression models in which PAQ dimension scores were used as independent variables, and observed test validity and incumbent mean test scores for a range of jobs were used as dependent variables. The regression models are an early form of validity generalization research in that the models treated jobs as the unit of analysis and cumulated results across multiple validation studies. The JCV model differs in part from later VG efforts because the JCV model made no attempt to correct for statistical artifacts like sampling error, range restriction, or attenuation in the criterion, as is typically done in VG research. Additionally, the JCV model used multiple regression to attempt to answer the question "To what extent are the validity results obtained previously accounted for by job components?" McCormick

(1976) viewed JCV in terms of a validity generalization framework, although JCV actually preceded the development of meta-analytic VG. Because the JCV regression model used observed test validity coefficients rather than population or corrected validity coefficients as the basis for estimating operational validity, the resulting predictions of estimated validity will always be conservative when compared to the corrected values of rho reported in VG studies (Hoffman & McPhail, 1998; Scherbaum, 2005).

The JCV regression models were built using data from U.S. Employment Service validation studies (McCormick et al., 1972), so validity coefficients largely were based on using supervisory ratings and training criteria. As Nathan and Alexander (1988) demonstrated with clerical jobs, validity for a given predictor and type of job varies depending on the type of criterion being used. For example, supervisor ratings criteria and productivity criteria were about equally well predicted by cognitive ability tests, whereas training criteria produced higher validity coefficients than supervisor ratings criteria when using cognitive ability tests as predictors. Training criteria (such as job knowledge tests and hands-on performance tests) are typically more accurately predicted by cognitive ability measures than are supervisory ratings criteria of job performance. Because the PAQ JCV model was developed using validity coefficients based on supervisor ratings criteria, it is likely that estimated validity coefficients are conservative compared to what one would expect if the models were replicated using data from validation studies with training criteria alone (Hoffman, Holden, et al., 2000).

Another way to think of the PAQ JCV model is that it represents, on the one hand, the relationship between job differences captured via PAQ dimension scores, and on the other hand, differences between jobs in mean test scores or test validity. Not surprisingly, job complexity, as captured via PAQ dimension scores related to decision making and information processing requirements, is associated with higher validity of cognitive ability predictors (Gutenberg, Arvey, Osburn, & Jeanneret, 1983).

Jeanneret (1992) provided more detail on the development of the PAQ JCV model. Jeanneret (1992) stated that JCV multiple regression models predict mean test scores better (median $R = 0.69$) than they predict test validity (median $R = 0.26$). The relatively modest "validity" of the PAQ JCV procedure for estimating observed validity was noted by Sackett (1991), who found the multiple *R*'s "have not been as large as one might have hoped for" (p. 320). It is likely that the modest *R* obtained for estimating observed validity is due to the constraints of using a less than ideal metric like the correlation coefficient as a dependent variable in multiple regression (Hoffman & McPhail, 1998; Scherbaum, 2005). Because readers may be unfamiliar with recent studies of JCV, published research along with research presented at professional conferences is reviewed in the next section.

Recent JCV Research

This section provides a brief overview of recently published articles, followed by an overview of recent (unpublished) conference papers.

Hoffman and McPhail (1998)

This study compared mean JCV validity estimates across fifty-one clerical jobs with mean observed validity coefficients compiled and reported by Pearlman et al. (1980) in their VG analysis of cognitive ability tests for clerical jobs. Mean observed validity coefficients extracted from the Pearlman et al. article were used as benchmarks against which to examine the accuracy of mean JCV validity estimates. Comparisons were made by DOT job category and across all jobs examined. Correlations between mean observed validity and mean JCV estimate for five cognitive ability constructs (G, V, N, S, Q) ranged from 0.85 to 0.96 depending on job category; the correlation across all clerical jobs examined was 0.97.

Hoffman and McPhail's (1998) findings are significant because earlier research had examined the ability of the JCV model to predict observed validity coefficients at the level of the individual job; such research treated the observed validity coefficient as the benchmark against which to compare JCV validity estimates. In contrast, this study made comparisons between JCV and VG at either the DOT job category level or the entire job family level. Because there would be some amount of error associated with any given job analysis, it is likely that JCV estimates are impacted by this error. Likewise, it is well known that sampling error is a problem when

evaluating correlation coefficients at the level of the individual validation study. By averaging across JCV validity estimates and comparing those averages with average, sample-size weighted validity
coefficients from Pearlman et al. (1980), Hoffman and McPhail
(1998) were better able to account for several sources of error.

Hoffman, Holden, and Gale (2000)

A major theme of this research was application of "expanded validation models" espoused by Landy (1986) and Binning and Barrett
(1989). Landy and Binning and Barrett supported the notion of developing and reporting multiple lines of validation evidence, and
the development of such multiple and converging lines of validation evidences played a central role in this study. Although validation research in the organization in question had been performed for "larger" jobs (those with more incumbents), roughly 20
percent of the job titles studied accounted for about 80 percent of
its nonmanagement workforce. Rather than attempting to conduct
additional validation studies on progressively smaller and smaller
jobs, the authors elected to apply multiple validation strategies to
support broader test use in the organization.

Data from the PAQ were available for every job title included
in the study, as the organization had conducted a large-scale job
evaluation study prior to the onset of this project. PAQ data were
used in a number of ways, including these: (1) PAQ dimension
scores were used to derive eleven job families via cluster analysis,
(2) JCV validity estimates were used to estimate validity of cognitive ability constructs for job families, and (3) JCV predicted mean
scores were used to provide guidance regarding levels of ability
needed and to guide setting cut scores. The results of the job family analysis, examination of JCV validity estimates, and comparison
to existing empirical validity estimates provided multiple lines of
evidence to support broader test use in the organization.

Hoffman, Haase, and Babasa (2000)

JCV test score predictions were used by Hoffman, Holden, et al.
(2000) to guide initial cut score choice for test batteries implemented for eleven job families. In a follow-up study, Hoffman,

Haase, et al. (2000) examined the extent to which initial battery cut scores approximated the desired percentile for several applicant groups and found the initial cut score estimates to be quite accurate for two of three test batteries. Hoffman, Holden, et al. (2000) and Hoffman, Haase, et al. (2000) provide detailed logic for translating test score predictions for individual predictors into a cut score for a battery comprising the same individual predictors.

Morris, Hoffman, and Shultz (2002)

One of the concerns this study addressed was the degree of accuracy with which JCV estimates correspond with observed validity coefficients between commercially available aptitude tests and supervisory ratings of overall job performance across a range of jobs. The authors used archival data to compare JCV predictions for a variety of jobs with the results of a bare-bones meta-analysis (correction only for sampling error) of empirical validation results for the same jobs. Findings demonstrated that for five of the six GATB test constructs (V-Verbal Aptitude, N-Numerical Aptitude, S-Spatial Aptitude, P-Perceptual Aptitude, Q-Clerical Aptitude), average JCV estimates fell within the 95-percent confidence interval (CI) of mean observed validity as calculated using bare-bones meta-analysis.

For the five constructs falling within the 95-percent CI, three (S, P, and Q) fell toward the lower end of the CI, suggesting that these JCV estimates are likely to be conservative estimates of validity of these constructs. On the other hand, V and N estimates, although still within the 95-percent CI, were both at the upper end of the CI. The biggest concern was that the JCV estimate for G fell above the high end of the 95-percent CI, suggesting that for the limited number of validation studies included in this research, JCV estimates of G were somewhat optimistic. This study demonstrated that sampling error alone accounted for most of the variance in observed validity coefficients across studies (minimum of 76.0 percent and maximum of 95.3 percent of variance).

The small number of available studies for G was first thought to be responsible for the average JCV estimate of 0.29 falling above the 95-percent CI for observed mean validity (range of 0.19 to 0.27). However, a closer look at the structure of the GATB demonstrates that G is not a single construct but rather is a composite estimate comprising the constructs V, N, and S. The JCV model was developed based solely on USES validation studies in which the GATB was used as the predictor. It may be that since the GATB measure of G is a composite predictor or battery score, JCV estimates of G are approximating the uncorrected true validity of a battery assembled based on JCV estimates for the "other" constructs in the GATB. Hoffman, Morris, and Shultz (2003) performed this comparison.

Hoffman, Morris, and Shultz (2003)

These authors sought to extend the univariate JCV model into the multivariate domain—that is, predictions combined to estimate the validity of a battery of tests. Although the JCV procedure provides validity estimates for individual test constructs, it would be rare in practice for decisions to be made based on the results of a single test (Morris et al., 2002). More commonly, multiple predictors are combined into a test battery, either unit-weighted or optimally weighted. Hoffman et al. (2003) developed two variations on a procedure for estimating the validity of a test battery based on individual JCV predictions. Study One reviewed predictions of battery validity made using these "battery validity" estimates; Study Two provided an empirical test of battery validity estimates by comparing them with observed and corrected battery validity coefficients from an extant selection system.

The two procedures for estimating battery validity varied based on the assumed predictor intercorrelation matrix being used. One estimation procedure used population values of the intercorrelation matrix of the GATB as the basis for estimating battery validity; the second estimation procedure used an intercorrelation matrix derived from published, commercially available tests (since the GATB is not commercially available). Not surprisingly, the GATB intercorrelation matrix showed a much higher average predictor intercorrelation (0.64) than the published predictor matrix (0.37).

Results from Study One showed that the estimated validity of a test battery assembled using univariate JCV estimates would be higher than the highest validity of any predictor construct included in that battery, regardless of whether intercorrelations among GATB or published tests were used. Use of the GATB intercorrelation matrix always provided battery validity estimates that were lower than battery validity estimates based on using the matrix derived from published, commercially available tests.

In Study Two, the unit-weighted test battery described in Hoffman, Nathan, and Holden (1991) was examined for how well JCV battery validity predictions by job progression estimated the observed validity of a unit weighted test battery by job progression. The analysis provided an empirical test of the JCV battery procedure developed in Study One. Battery validity estimates for a JCV cognitive battery (G, V, N) and JCV perceptual battery (S, P, Q) resulted in estimated multiple R's of 0.34 and 0.25 (respectively) using the published test intercorrelation matrix, and multiple R's of 0.30 and 0.24 using the GATB intercorrelation matrix. These values reflected increases in validity of 15 percent and 16 percent for cognitive and perceptual batteries, respectively, when compared with the single highest JCV estimate.

JCV Research with Noncognitive Predictors

The research reviewed to this point has focused exclusively on the cognitive ability predictor domain, and it examines how well the JCV model predicts mean test scores or observed validity coefficients. The discussion that follows describes attempts to extend JCV into the domains of physical ability (Hoffman, 1999) and personality (D'Egidio, 2001; Rashkovsky & Hoffman, 2005).

PAQ and Physical Ability—Hoffman (1999)

This study used PAQ dimension scores and PAQ attributes scores to develop support for expanded use of a validated physical ability test (PAT) battery to task-dissimilar jobs with similar physical demand. Multiple lines of validation evidence were combined to support inferences of PAT validity, including participation in a consortium-based concurrent validation study (American Gas Association [AGA], 1990), published VG evidence based on the same predictor (Jackson Evaluation System, described in Blakely, Quinones, Crawford, & Jago, 1994), test transportability evidence, and demonstrated similarity of job families and physical ability attributes requirements based on PAQ dimension and attributes scores.

This study was conducted because of limitations in the test transportability protocol provided in the consortium (AGA) validation study. That transportability protocol required a 75-percent overlap of *physically demanding tasks* between jobs involved in the study and jobs to which the PAT was to be transported. Having a transportability protocol was an advantage of the consortium study, as too few validation studies make provisions for later transportability of a test battery to other jobs or organizations (for a discussion of the advantages and disadvantages of test transportability, see Hoffman & McPhail, 1998, and Gibson & Caplinger, 2007).

Existing PAQ data were used to derive job families similar to procedures described in Hoffman, Holden, et al. (2000). The PAQ data included a subset of PAQ divisional dimension scores relevant to physically demanding work, along with z-scores for four PAQ attributes (Explosive Strength, Static Strength, Dynamic Strength, and Endurance). Cluster analysis of thirteen PAQ divisional dimension scores for ninety-five jobs was used to develop job families within the organization. (The same thirteen PAQ divisional dimension scores had been used in the AGA consortium study to develop job families.) Cluster analysis results suggested the ninety-five jobs should be sorted into five job families. After job families were derived statistically, a panel of twenty-five SMEs reviewed placement of jobs in families and moved five of the ninety-five jobs between families, for an agreement of about 95 percent between statistical and rational processes. Mean physical ability attribute scores were calculated by job family and are provided in Table 3.1.

As shown in Table 3.1, jobs in the Construction family had substantial physical ability requirements as captured via PAQ physical ability attributes, with average z-scores placing them in roughly the eighty-second percentile of jobs in the PAQ Services database. The medium-high-demand Mechanical and Technical family had twenty-six jobs, with two of these jobs also present in the consortium study. Physical ability attributes scores for this family placed these jobs at about the sixty-ninth percentile of jobs in the PAQ Services database.

The Clerical and the Mapping and Planning families (forty-three and eleven job titles, respectively) had very similar physical attributes profiles, with z-scores placing them in about the thirty-fifth and thirty-second percentiles of jobs in the PAQ database.

Table 3.1. Physical Demands of Job Families and Mean (Z-Score) Attribute Requirements.

Job Family	No. of Jobs	Physical Demand	Mean PAQ Attribute Score			
			Dynamic Strength	Static Strength	Explosive Strength	Endurance
1. Construction	6	High	+0.86	+0.94	+1.00	+0.95
2. Mechanical and Technical	26	Medium	+0.43	+0.48	+0.56	+0.18
3. Clerical	43	Low	−0.31	−0.45	−0.42	−0.83
4. Mapping and Planning	11	Low	−0.46	−0.46	−0.46	−0.80
5. Warehouse	9	Medium-high	+0.72	+0.76	+0.86	+0.54

Note: Refer to Table 2, p. 1033, in Hoffman (1999) for more details and procedures for assigning jobs to job families.

None of these jobs was involved in the consortium study, and none was envisioned as requiring use of a PAT. The fifth job family (Warehouse) included nine job titles, most of which were involved in warehouse- or storeroom-related activities. The physical attributes profile for these jobs was in about the seventy-eighth percentile in the PAQ database. The study provided three lines of validity evidence (test transportability, VG, and construct validation) for the Construction and the Mechanical and Technical job families; see Table 3.2.

Taken as a whole, the study may be viewed as a construct validation effort. From a practice perspective, the original task-based transportability protocol provided in the consortium study was not as generalizable as the transportability protocol developed based on worker behaviors and required physical attributes. Given the large differences in physical ability attribute scores across the five job families, it is likely that PAQ dimension scores could be used to predict mean PAT scores for jobs across a range of physical demand with a high degree of accuracy (that is, extending the JCV model to incorporate predictions of mean PAT scores and validity).

**Table 3.2. Sources of Evidence Supporting
Inferences of PAT Validity by Job Family.**

	Sources of Validity Evidence			
Job Family	Transportability Evidence	VG Evidence	Construct Evidence	Comments
Construction	Yes	Yes	Mean strength attribute z-score +0.93 (82nd percentile)	Two jobs from heavy-demand AGA job family
Mechanical and Technical	Yes	Yes	Mean strength attribute z-score +0.49 (69th percentile)	Two jobs from medium-demand AGA job family
Clerical	No	No	Mean strength attribute z-score +0.93 (82nd percentile)	No jobs from medium-demand AGA job family
Mapping and Planning	No	No	Mean strength attribute z-score +0.93 (82nd percentile)	No jobs from medium-demand AGA job family
Warehouse	No	Yes	Mean strength attribute z-score +0.93 (82nd percentile)	No jobs from medium-demand AGA job family

Note: Adapted from Hoffman (1999), Table 4, p. 1037.

O*NET and Job Component Validity—D'Egidio (2001)

This study attempted to predict mean test scores and validity coefficients, as in the PAQ's JCV model, using the O*NET (Peterson, Mumford, Borman, Jeanneret, & Fleishman, 1999) job analysis data. The Occupational Information Network (O*NET) was developed as a result of a U.S. Department of Labor (DOL) initiative to update the *Dictionary of Occupational Titles* (DOL, 1977) and to create a comprehensive database of job information for virtually all jobs in the United States.

Jeanneret and Strong (1997) described a model linking job analysis results to assessment outcomes (aptitude test scores). On the job analysis side of their model, two types of information—PAQ item ratings and PAQ job dimension scores—were related to assessment outcomes. D'Egidio extended Jeanneret and Strong's (1997) research by examining the relationship between O*NET Skills and General Work Activities (GWAs) and commercially available measures of cognitive ability and personality.

Hypotheses were based on previous PAQ JCV research, Jeanneret and Strong's (1997) exploratory study, the characteristics of the O*NET level and importance rating scales, and the gravitational hypothesis (McCormick et al., 1979). To the extent that work requirements are associated with specific levels and types of individual characteristics (that is, aptitudes or personal characteristics), test score requirements can be estimated for other jobs having the same work requirements (Mecham, 1985).

Data for the study were drawn from: (1) job analysis data from the O*NET database and (2) test data from test manuals, test publisher databases, consultant databases, and validity studies reported in the Validity Information Exchange published in *Personnel Psychology*. The unit of analysis for all hypotheses was the occupational level.

Regression analyses were conducted for nine Employment Aptitude Series tests (Verbal Comprehension, Numerical Ability, Visual Pursuit, Visual Speed and Accuracy, Space Visualization, Numerical Reasoning, Verbal Reasoning, Word Fluency, and Symbolic Reasoning) published by Psychological Services, three Workplace Literacy Tests (Prose, Document, and Quantitative), and the seven primary scales of the Hogan Personality Inventory. Similar to the results found with the PAQ, mean test scores were more predictable than validity coefficients for test constructs (see Table 3.3). The cognitive ability measures showed more consistent predictability than the personality constructs and perceptual ability measures, which demonstrated mixed results.

The predictions of mean scores and validity coefficients for personality scales were weaker than those found for cognitive tests. If the gravitational hypothesis holds true for personality constructs, there is likely a less defined hierarchy of scores for personality constructs than for cognitive ability, because many jobs require similar levels

Table 3.3. Using O*NET Skill and GWA Level and Importance Ratings to Predict Mean Test Scores and Validity Coefficients.

	Mean Test Scores from Skill Level Ratings	Mean Test Scores from GWA Level Ratings	Validity Coefficient from Skill Importance Ratings	Validity Coefficient from GWA Importance Ratings
Cognitive Ability	Adjusted R^2	Adjusted R^2	Adjusted R^2	Adjusted R^2
Verbal Comprehension	0.50	0.48	0.00	0.00
Numerical Ability	0.58	0.61	0.22	0.16
Visual Pursuit	0.00	0.27	0.00	0.06
Visual Speed and Accuracy	0.06	0.47	0.01	0.02
Space Visualization	0.00	0.57	0.00	0.00
Numerical Reasoning	0.50	0.45	0.27	0.02
Verbal Reasoning	0.52	0.20	0.07	0.16
Word Fluency	0.00	0.00	—	—
Symbolic Reasoning	0.51	0.66	—	—
Personality (HPI)	Adjusted R^2	Adjusted R^2	Adjusted R^2	Adjusted R^2
Adjustment	0.00	0.06	0.00	0.04
Ambition	0.10	0.07	0.02	0.15
Sociability	0.09	0.20	0.03	0.11
Likeability	0.00	0.00	0.00	0.11
Prudence	0.00	0.00	0.02	0.00
Intellectance	0.03	0.11	0.16	0.00
School Success	0.42	0.58	0.00	0.14

Note: n (number of job titles) ranges from twenty-three to fifty-five.

Source: D'Egidio, 2001.

of personality constructs. For example, Barrick and Mount (1991) argued that conscientiousness is a key component for most jobs.

Regardless of these issues, some positive results were found for personality constructs, suggesting that additional data and more complex analyses may prove beneficial in the prediction of personality constructs using a job component validation model. The results provide further support for the gravitational hypothesis that underlies the concept of job component validity (Jeanneret, 1992; Wilk et al., 1995; Wilk & Sackett, 1996).

PAQ and JCV Predictions of Personality— Rashkovsky and Hoffman (2005)

Rashkovsky and Hoffman (2005) also sought to extend the job component validity model into the domain of personality predictors. They did so by examining the extent to which PAQ dimension scores and attribute scores could be used to make meaningful and significant predictions of mean Big Five personality factor scores, as measured by the Hogan Personality Inventory (HPI). The HPI was designed to measure normal personality by capitalizing on the five-factor model (FFM) of personality (Hogan & Hogan, 1995). As described previously, D'Egidio (2001) conducted an initial evaluation of job component validity models using O*NET job analysis data personality data from the HPI. This study is the first, to our knowledge, that has attempted to link the PAQ to a FFM instrument, though Mecham performed earlier analyses linking the PAQ to the Myers-Briggs Type Indicator.

Extending the JCV model to incorporate personality would enhance the utility of the JCV model that is currently used in making predictions about ability-based predictors. This study used archival data obtained from PAQ Services, Inc., and Hogan Assessment Services. Data from Hogan Assessment Services included job title or a brief job description or both, inconsistent availability of DOT or O*NET code, mean scores on each of the seven HPI scales, and validity information for HPI scales (some studies). Data from PAQ Services included DOT code, mean dimension scores, and attribute scores.

The study yielded significant multiple regression equations for predicting six of the seven HPI scale scores, with adjusted R^2 ranging between 0.127 and 0.415. The seventh regression equation (Likeability) was not significant at the 0.05 level but was close enough ($p=.059$) to show promise for future research. Additionally, and contrary to prior research using the PAQ to predict scores on cognitive ability predictors, PAQ attribute scores performed better as predictors of mean HPI scale scores than did the PAQ dimension scores for four of the seven HPI scales.

Given the retrospective nature of this study and the fact that PAQ dimension and attribute scores and HPI mean scale scores came from different sources, the findings from this study should be considered as indicative of the potential to extend the JCV model into the personality domain. Given the small sample size (number of studies) available, and the fact that not all studies provided validity information, it was not feasible to regress validity coefficients for the HPI scales on the PAQ job analysis data.

Comparing JCV Results using O*NET and PAQ Data

In preliminary work on similar JCV models, D'Egidio (2001) used O*NET data and Rashkovsky and Hoffman (2005) used PAQ data to predict HPI mean scale scores. Table 3.4 briefly summarizes findings from the two studies.

Strengths of JCV

Table 3.5 provides a brief summary of some of the strengths and weaknesses of the PAQ and the JCV. Perhaps the greatest strength of the JCV model is the amount and quality of research that has focused on the PAQ and applications of the PAQ. The PAQ has been reviewed in recent court cases (*Taylor v. James River,* 1989; *McCoy et al. v. Willamette Industries,* 2001) and was found to meet the requirements of a professional job analysis instrument in both rulings. Likewise, these two cases provide legal support (albeit limited) for use of the JCV model for estimating test validity, mean test scores, and probability of use.

The JCV approach to providing validation support is far less expensive than conducting local empirical validation studies, and the ability to aggregate multiple job titles into job families means

Table 3.4. Comparing Results from D'Egidio (2001) and Rashkovsky and Hoffman (2005): Predicting Mean HPI Scale Scores Using O*NET and PAQ Job Analysis Data.

	D'Egidio (2001)[a]		Rashkovsky & Hoffman (2005)[b]	
	Mean Test Scores from Skill Level Ratings	Mean Test Scores from GWA Level Ratings	Mean Test Scores from PAQ Dimension Scores	Mean Test Scores from PAQ Attribute Scores
Personality (HPI)	Adjusted R^2	Adjusted R^2	Adjusted R^2	Adjusted R^2
Adjustment	0.00	0.06	0.10	0.34
Ambition	0.10	0.07	0.18	0.38
Sociability	0.09	0.20	0.09	0.16
Likeability	0.00	0.00	0.00[c]	0.08
Prudence	0.00	0.00	0.08	0.03
Intellectance	0.03	0.11	0.11	–0.02
School Success	0.42	0.58	0.13	0.34

Note: n (number of jobs) ranged from twenty-three to fifty-five for D'Egidio; n was fifty-one for Rashkovsky & Hoffman.

[a]Study using O*NET job analysis information.

[b]Study using PAQ job analysis information.

[c]None were identified per criteria set

that criterion-related validation studies would be more technically feasible than where individual job titles were examined. The JCV model is applicable to small, even single incumbent jobs, making it a practical methodology for supporting test use in small N settings such as small- to medium-sized organizations, or in larger organizations that wish to transport validity results across divisions or geographically dispersed locations.

The PAQ's implementation of JCV has a number of strengths and weaknesses. The next section describes these and addresses their practical implications.

Table 3.5. Strengths and Weaknesses
of Job Component Validity.

Strengths	Weaknesses
Thorough and well-done job analysis increases legal defensibility of selection studies.	
SIOP *Principles* (2003) now list synthetic validity or job component validity as one of several strategies for cumulating validity evidence.	JCV is not explicitly acknowledged in the *Guidelines* (1978) and so may not be construed by some as an "approved" validation strategy.
Conducting JCV analyses is less expensive than performing local empirical validation studies.	PAQ and other published job analysis inventories have a substantial learning curve (extensive rater training is required; complex items and rating scales).
Once a model is developed, JCV is applicable to N=1 jobs.	At present, PAQ JCV model is the only one commercially available.
JCV validity estimates are conservative, as no statistical corrections were made prior to performing the original regression analyses.	JCV validity estimates do not correlate highly with empirical validity estimates (Jeanneret, 1992; Sackett, 1991).
JCV mean test score estimates are potentially useful in setting cutoff scores.	JCV references are sometimes obscure and hard to locate.
	Despite empirical support, criticisms of gravitational hypothesis continue to exist.
JCV model has received support in legal proceedings (*Taylor v. James River*, 1989; *McCoy v. Willamette Industries*, 2001).	Legal proceedings have not been at a high enough level to fully gauge JCV acceptability.
JCV model has the capability of being extended into physical ability domain (Hoffman, 1999) and personality domain (see D'Egidio, 2001; Rashkovsky & Hoffman, 2005).	

**Table 3.5. Strengths and Weaknesses
of Job Component Validity, Cont'd.**

Strengths	Weaknesses
JCV model has the capability of being extended into the multivariate domain (multiple predictors and multiple criteria).	JCV model is based on predicting validity coefficients likely to be observed using supervisor ratings criteria.

PAQ and JCV Weaknesses

Criticisms of the PAQ and JCV fall into at least three categories: (1) concerns about the PAQ, its items, rating procedures, and so on, (2) concerns about the efficacy of the JCV model and the assumptions underlying it (gravitational hypothesis), and (3) concerns about the legal status of JCV and synthetic validity.

Cascio (1982) noted that the PAQ has a high level of reading difficulty and suggested that persons with reading levels below college should not complete the instrument. Cascio also expressed concern that because the PAQ's items are worker behaviors rather than tasks, two jobs can be viewed as similar even though there are task differences between jobs.

As discussed in more detail in Hoffman (1999) and earlier in this chapter, the ability to compare task-dissimilar jobs can be considered an advantage of the PAQ. If one is attempting to demonstrate that two jobs have similar worker requirements, despite task differences, the worker-oriented nature of the PAQ is a distinct advantage. In fact, it is difficult if not impossible to make task-based comparisons of job similarity if two jobs have nonoverlapping tasks. Conversely, if one were attempting to establish content validity, a worker-oriented approach like the PAQ would be unavailing.

Levine and colleagues (Levine, Bennett, & Ash, 1979; Levine, Ash, & Bennett, 1980; Levine, Ash, Hall, & Sistrunk, 1983) reported on a series of studies that compared perceptions of experienced job analysts on the advantages, disadvantages, cost, and usefulness of a number of different job analysis methods. Across the three studies, the PAQ was evaluated less favorably in terms of issues like reading level and use of non-job-specific job language, and it was viewed as least favorable for supporting content validation efforts. Those working in settings in which content validation efforts are common are likely to find the PAQ less useful than task-based job analysis approaches. In two of the three studies just cited (Levine et al., 1979; Levine et al., 1980), job analysts who compared the PAQ to other job analysis strategies were in public sector settings; that is, state and local government. The study by Levine et al. (1983) incorporated job analysts from across a range of organization types (colleges and universities, state and local government, private business, and private consulting companies) and found that the PAQ was viewed positively by experienced job analysts on dimensions related to level of standardization, off-the-shelf availability, and cost. Perhaps the most important points to be learned from this series of studies are (1) no single job analysis method seems to be superior for all applications, and (2) multiple method job analyses are preferable to single method job analyses.

Harvey (1991) raised several concerns about the PAQ, with much of his criticism related to the Does Not Apply (DNA) rating available on many PAQ rating scales. Harvey noted that since many jobs have a relatively high percentage of DNA items, endorsement of the DNA rating could mask substantial rater disagreement on items rated as relevant to the job. Harvey demonstrated that it was possible to achieve interrater reliability in the 0.60 to 0.70 range using randomly generated data with varying percentages of DNA items. There are at least two responses to the DNA criticism: (1) trained and experienced PAQ analysts often produce interrater reliability coefficients in the high 0.80 range and above, and (2) having job analysts agree on whether a given worker behavior applies in a given job under analysis is in itself a form of rater agreement.

The PAQ JCV model has been criticized concerning the tenability of the gravitational hypothesis. As discussed earlier, the gravitational hypothesis criticism is based on the idea that individuals gravitate to jobs in which the worker requirements match the ability of those individuals—low-ability individuals tend to gravitate toward jobs with lower ability requirements, and higher-ability individuals gravitate towards jobs having greater ability requirements (see McCormick et al., 1979; Scherbaum, 2005; Steel et al., 2006; Wilk, Desmarais, & Sackett, 1995). The gravitational hypothesis also posits that people stay in jobs for which they are ability matched.

Although the JCV model appears to be fairly accurate in estimating mean test scores, a concern raised is that the ability to predict mean test scores does not address the validity of the gravitational hypothesis. Regarding that hypothesis, Wilk et al. (1995) conducted a large-scale longitudinal study of job movement over time and demonstrated convincingly that individuals did in fact tend to move toward jobs better fitting their measured level of ability. Steel et al. (2006) went so far as to say: "The gravitational hypothesis is based on the supported and uncontroversial notion that those who are retained in a job should be at least minimally competent (for example, Wilk et al., 1995). Any mean differences in relevant KSAOs among jobs indicate that those with insufficiently adequate levels or characteristics were either 'removed or self-selected out'" (p. 39).

Risk Management: JCV Usage Continuum

We recognize that the opinion of any number of psychologists describing or predicting the likely outcome of court cases dealing with synthetic validity or JCV is no substitute for an appellate or Supreme Court decision dealing with this validation strategy. Until such time as we have actual case decisions, the topic of JCV and the law revolves around the level of risk an organization is willing to incur.

Discussions regarding deciding whether and how to apply the JCV model to solve organizational problems would be incomplete without a discussion of risk tolerance. Put another way, the user may have faith in the research reported here and elsewhere regarding JCV findings but be unwilling or unable to risk significant legal exposure. The continuum presented in Table 3.6 describes a number of potential applications of the JCV model along with our estimates of the risk involved.

At the low end of the continuum (step one), the user chooses not to use JCV, VG, or other "non–*Uniform Guidelines*" methods. The choice here is likely dictated by the user's concerns that JCV is not an approved validation methodology in the *Uniform Guidelines,* and that JCV has not been reviewed in any legal proceeding higher than the federal district courts. Given the broad base of research support for the JCV model, this appears to be an overly conservative approach to applying JCV.

Table 3.6. JCV Risk Tolerance Continuum.

Lower risk tolerance		Moderate risk tolerance		Higher risk tolerance
←				→
1	2	3	4	5
Do not use JCV or other related strategies, as JCV is not in the *Guidelines*.	Use JCV to identify prospective predictor constructs; validate locally.	Use JCV to support test transportability efforts.	Use JCV to develop and implement test batteries; conduct later empirical validation.	Use JCV to to develop and implement test batteries with no local validation.

At step two of the continuum, JCV is applied as a method for identifying relevant predictor constructs, but measures operationalizing those constructs would be subject to local validation efforts in a concurrent or predictive criterion-related validation study before the system is used in practice. In this example, JCV findings are used to provide an additional line of evidence to document choice of predictors, but the user does not take JCV predicted validity estimates (if using the PAQ) at face value. There appears to be little risk in using JCV in this manner, especially since the PAQ provides another method of job analysis, in line with recommended practice to include multiple job analysis methods (Levine et al., 1983) when conducting validation research and consistent with the *Uniform Guidelines* lack of preference for job analysis methods.

The third step of the continuum uses JCV (and perhaps other PAQ-related evidence) to support test transportability efforts. To perform a study of this type, the user must have access to an existing empirical validation study, PAQ data for the job(s) involved in that study, and PAQ data for one or more jobs to which validity inferences are to be transported. This approach incorporates evidence from an existing validation study and ties in the concept of test transportability as described in the *Uniform Guidelines,* both of which would seem to make this strategy somewhat less risky. On the other hand, test transportability as described in the *Uniform Guidelines* seems somewhat more focused on task similarity and not on the similarity of job behaviors, PAQ dimension scores, or PAQ attribute scores. This stretching of *Uniform Guidelines* prescriptions regarding conducting validity transportability research does not seem overly risky in our view but would likely entail a greater risk than steps one or two on the continuum.

Step four of the continuum entails a slightly higher risk. In this example, JCV is used to identify relevant predictors and help guide choice of cut score, and then the completed selection system is implemented without conducting a local validation study. Validation efforts are subsequently undertaken with the goal of empirically validating the selection system implemented based on JCV evidence. This approach is ideal in a "green field" type of setting (new plant, reorganized work, and the like), and requires the user to work with client SMEs regarding planned jobs. Job analyses are completed for jobs as they are envisioned based on SME input. It is hard to argue that validation studies should be conducted before jobs even exist, and using JCV in this manner allows the organization to do a better job of staffing a new start-up or redesigned organization than many other potential approaches. The *Uniform Guidelines* do allow the use of selection procedures while validation efforts are under way, so this example may actually be less risky than as described here.

In the example at step five, JCV is used to develop and implement a selection system, and no further validation efforts are performed. Although this step of the continuum appears to be the most risky, it also represents the case in which JCV is likely to have its biggest impact for small- to medium-sized organizations, and it likely represents the direction in which synthetic validity research is taking the field (Steel et al., 2006). A common problem in small organizations is the lack of resources in dollars and staff to conduct local validation, coupled with a lack of persons who can participate as subjects in validation efforts. Since the lack of "*N*" means empirical validation is not "technically feasible" per the *Uniform Guidelines,* the user has the choice in such settings of (1) doing nothing to support test use (not recommended), (2) relying on test publisher claims or testimonials (not recommended), or (3) taking the more rigorous approach of conducting a job analysis, applying the JCV model, and using job analysis findings to support validation efforts.

Practice Recommendations

The growing body of evidence (Jeanneret, 1992; McPhail, 1995; Hoffman, Haase, et al., 2000; Hoffman, Holden, et al., 2000; Hoffman & McPhail, 1998; Morris et al., 2002; Scherbaum, 2005; Steel et al., 2006) regarding the accuracy and usefulness of the PAQ JCV model suggests that JCV is a viable option for supporting local test use in situations in which sample sizes are inadequate to make empirical validation technically feasible. Although there is considerable research regarding the development and accuracy of the JCV model, there is relatively little information available to guide practitioners wishing to apply the model in their work. Having made extensive use of JCV in our applied work, we briefly discuss a few key choice points at which professional judgment is needed when applying JCV.

Examples of JCV Implementation

Given our extensive applied experience with JCV, we felt it was important to provide readers with concrete examples that illustrate the type and range of problems that can be addressed using JCV.

Identifying Aptitude Requirements Followed by Local Validation

Hoffman (1987; 1988) conducted a criterion-related validation study of thirteen mechanically oriented jobs in a utility company. Job analysis included review of existing job descriptions, job analysis interviews with incumbents and supervisors, development of a task and KSAO survey followed by administration to job incumbents, and completion of PAQs for each of the thirteen jobs by three trained job analysts.

Results of job analysis interviews, task survey results, and PAQ attributes results were used to identify relevant aptitudes needed for successful job performance. Attributes analyses and JCV predictions identified numerical, spatial, and clerical perception as necessary for these jobs, and an experimental test battery was developed and administered to over two hundred incumbents. Multiple criteria were used in the study, including supervisory ratings of performance, a research-only self-assessment of performance, an objective measure of production quantity, and an objective measure of production quality (see Hoffman et al., 1991). Later analysis of validation results demonstrated that all the test constructs identified were relevant predictors, and JCV predicted validity estimates were conservative compared to observed validity results.

Test Transportability

Landkammer (1990) conducted a test transportability study seeking to transport validity evidence from an earlier criterion-related validation study performed at a utility company to a meter repair classification. The earlier studies (Hoffman, 1987; 1988) had used a task-based job analysis survey and the PAQ as part of the validation of a single battery of cognitive ability tests for thirteen mechanically oriented jobs. Job analysis of the meter repair classification used the same task inventory as well as the PAQ. Job similarity was assessed from a number of perspectives, including similarity of tasks performed, similarity of PAQ dimension profiles, similarity of required cognitive ability attributes, and similarity of predicted validity coefficients for cognitive ability attributes.

Based on the several lines of evidence just described, the same test battery that was developed and validated in the earlier mechanical validation study (Hoffman, 1988) was applied to the meter repair technician classification. In retrospect, the meter repair classification could have been added to the mechanical job family via cluster analysis, but a study examining a large number of jobs in the company was not performed and described until a number of years later (Hoffman, Holden, et al., 2000).

Developing Job Families

As noted elsewhere (see Hoffman & McPhail, 1998), there are a number of advantages to developing job families. Use of job families allows the researcher to combine similar jobs for research purposes, resulting in larger combined sample sizes and thus making criterion-related validation studies more feasible. Using job families also means that practitioners do not need to develop and validate selection systems for a large number of job titles and can therefore streamline both the validation process and the implementation of selection systems.

Two projects by the first author (Hoffman, 1999; Hoffman, Holden, et al., 2000) used PAQ dimension scores to develop job families. Jobs examined in both of these studies included ninety-five of the most-populated nonmanagement jobs in the organization, and both studies relied on using data from an existing job evaluation database. In Hoffman (1999), a subset of thirteen of the thirty-two PAQ divisional dimension scores was examined via cluster analysis. The thirteen dimension scores were selected based on a prior consortium study that developed job families among physically demanding jobs in the utility industry (AGA, 1990).

The Hoffman (1999) study (described earlier in the context of validation for a physical ability test) found five job families with varying levels of physical demand. Jobs that were expected to have moderate or higher physical demand were identified by the cluster analysis as fitting into one of the three job families having moderate to high physical demand. Jobs that were not expected to fit into physically demanding families were identified by the cluster analysis as fitting into one of two nondemanding job families.

Hoffman, Holden, et al. (2000) examined the same ninety-five jobs examined in the earlier physical demand study, but used all thirty-two PAQ divisional dimension scores as the basis for cluster analysis. A total of eleven job families were identified, with a number of the families having similar cognitive ability requirements but differing physical requirements. The job families developed in Hoffman, Holden, et al. (2000) were used for broader application of existing test validation research, with multiple lines of validation evidence provided, including concurrent validation, test transportability, and job component validity.

The two job family studies described here both relied on using job analysis data in cluster analyses to derive job families. Although these studies used PAQ job dimensions scores, cluster analytic procedures can be used with a variety of job analysis data. In neither of the studies just described were the results of the statistical procedure taken at face value. As a second, "reality testing" phase of research, SME panels were asked to review the statistical findings to determine whether the cluster groupings that had been made based on purely statistical criteria made practical sense. In both studies, the SMEs recommended moving a relatively small number of jobs between job families. The agreement between statistical criteria and pooled judgment of the SME panels was above 90 percent for both studies. We encourage other researchers conducting job family analyses to follow up on statistical procedures with such independent review for practical reality. For another example of developing job families using a proprietary job analysis system, see Johnson et al. (2001).

Slotting or Assigning Jobs to Job Families

An additional feature of both job family studies was that a mean dimension score profile (centroid) was calculated for each of the five physically demanding job families, and for each of the eleven more general job families. Job slotting routines were then developed that allowed comparing a "new" profile to each of the five and eleven job families. A measure of distance (D^2) was calculated for each of the sixteen job families, allowing new jobs to be slotted into one of the five physically demanding families for physical ability testing (if needed) and into one of the more general families for cognitive ability testing (if needed).

Suggestions for Using the PAQ JCV Procedure

While the JCV procedure has many and varied applications, practitioners must exercise sound professional judgment in its use. The following examples better illustrate some of the common choice-points faced by those attempting to implement JCV in applied settings.

Selecting Predictor Constructs

The authors support use of JCV as a validation option, but researchers should expect to exercise professional judgment when using JCV. Although the PAQ JCV procedure estimates validity for six GATB cognitive constructs (G, V, N, S, P, Q), estimated JCVs for G are almost invariably larger than JCV estimates for other constructs. Probability of use estimates provided by the JCV selection report, which reflect the likelihood a construct would be included in a Specific Aptitude Test Battery developed by the United States Employment Service, may not identify G as a relevant predictor. This outcome may be surprising to novice users, especially because G will invariably be listed as having the highest estimated validity. G is typically "flagged" as relevant by the JCV routine for jobs of moderate or greater complexity or those jobs having higher cognitive demands. Researchers must decide whether to rely primarily on the estimated probability of use when selecting predictor constructs, or to temper this decision with the knowledge that G is a ubiquitous predictor of training and job performance (Ree, Earles, & Teachout, 1994).

Operationalizing Predictor Constructs

The process of deciding how to operationalize predictor constructs that the researcher has chosen is another area requiring professional judgment. For example, it is useful to know that the construct N (Numerical Aptitude) was flagged by the JCV procedure as a relevant predictor. Once the practitioner has decided to incorporate a construct, however, the question becomes one of which test to use to operationally measure that construct. It cannot be overemphasized that job analysis information should be used to inform this decision. For example, numerical aptitude requirements for a job that requires use of Ohm's Law to solve for unknowns in an equation (as do many technical jobs involving electricity and electronics) may be better represented by a test of basic algebra rather than a test of basic computation. McPhail (1995) indicated that close matching of construct operationalization with job requirements tends to produce observed validity coefficients higher than JCV estimates. Job analysis plays a critical role when using JCV.

Setting Cut Scores

A third area in which professional judgment is needed in applying JCV is that of cut score choice. Sackett (1991) suggested that predicted scores from the JCV procedure might provide useful guidance in setting cut scores. Just as attempting to use multiple predictors identified by the JCV procedure complicates matters in terms of estimating validity, so too does using multiple predictors complicate cut score choice. Unless the researcher is willing to use a multiple hurdle process, some means of developing an overall cut score for the test battery is needed. Although use of predicted test score information from the JCV procedure to guide cut score choice is beyond the scope of this chapter, interested readers are referred to Hoffman, Holden, et al. (2000) for an example related to setting up initial cutoff scores using JCV test predictions, and to Hoffman, Haase, et al. (2000) for an empirical follow-up to the 2000 study.

Study Documentation

As a final note regarding professional judgment in using JCV: documenting job analysis procedures and findings is a critical part of the process. Unless the researcher's job analysis activities, findings, and choice points are properly documented, there is little chance a validation study can survive even the most cursory legal scrutiny (Thompson & Thompson, 1982). Practitioners using JCV to support local test use should pay particular attention to making concrete the linkage between tasks performed on the job(s) and the predictor constructs being measured. Documentation of tasks or behaviors that clearly reflect such a linkage, as in the Ohm's Law example just mentioned, helps establish a construct framework as well as augmenting the face validity of the tests chosen. Documentation of multiple lines of validation evidence (that is, synthetic validation or JCV, construct linkages, and content overlap) helps buttress arguments about the validity of inferences one can make regarding the selection process (Landy, 1986; Binning and Barrett, 1989; Hoffman & McPhail, 1998; Hoffman, 1999).

JCV Alone or in Combination?

Regarding sole reliance on JCV to support local test use, Hoffman and McPhail (1998) stated:

> At a minimum, the results reported here support broader use of the JCV model in developing selection systems in practice. Whether a practitioner uses JCV predictions to identify predictors and then conducts a local validation study (as in McPhail, 1995 or Holden, 1992), or simply implements tests based on those predictions is to some degree a matter of risk management; the former is probably a too-conservative use of JCV given the results reported here and elsewhere, while the latter might be seen as too risky by some. (p. 1001)

A large body of evidence supports the development of the JCV model (Mecham & McCormick, 1969; Marquardt & McCormick, 1974; McCormick, Mecham, & Jeanneret, 1977; McCormick, Mecham, & Jeanneret, 1989). A growing body of more recent research regarding the accuracy of JCV predictions (Hoffman & McPhail, 1998; Hoffman, 1999; Holden, 1992; Jeanneret, 1992; McPhail, 1995;

Hoffman, Holden, et al., 2000; Morris et al., 2002) provides practitioners with greater confidence in the JCV model as a viable validation option. Based on this body of research evidence, we believe sole use of JCV to underpin local use of cognitive ability measures is preferable to conducting local validation studies with inadequate samples and, hence, inadequate power.

This chapter has reviewed and summarized JCV from a number of different perspectives. Regardless of whether one uses the existing JCV model incorporated in the PAQ or develops a unique JCV model (Brown & Harvey, 1996; D'Egidio, 2001; Johnson et al., 2001), we believe JCV has many applications and deserves wider acceptance and use. We hope the material discussed in this chapter will help contribute to the continued development of JCV.

References

Albemarle Paper Company et al. v. Moody, 422 U.S. 405 (1975).

American Gas Association (1990). American Gas Association Physical Abilities Study. (Vols. 2, 3, 4, 5, 8a) Houston: Jeanneret and Associates.

Barrick, M. R., & Mount, M. K. (1991). The Big Five personality dimensions and job performance: A meta-analysis. *Personnel Psychology, 44*, 1–26.

Binning, J. F., & Barrett, G. V. (1989). Validity of personnel decisions: A conceptual analysis of the inferential and evidential bases. *Journal of Applied Psychology, 74*(3), 478–494.

Blakely, B. R., Quinones, M. A., Crawford, M. S., & Jago, J. A. (1994). The validity of isometric strength tests. *Personnel Psychology, 47,* 247–274.

Brown, R. D., & Harvey, R. J. (1996, April). Job-component validation using the MBTI and the Common-metric questionnaire (CMQ). Paper presented at the Annual Conference of the Society for Industrial and Organizational Psychology, San Diego.

Cascio, W. F. (1982). *Applied psychology in personnel management.* Reston, VA: Reston.

D'Egidio, E. L. (2001). *Building a job component validity model using job analysis data from the Occupational Information Network.* Unpublished doctoral dissertation, University of Houston, Texas.

Equal Employment Opportunity Commission, Civil Service Commission, Department of Labor, & Department of Justice. (1978). *Uniform guidelines on employee selection procedures. Federal Register, 43*(166), 38290–38315.

Gibson, W., & Caplinger, J. A. (2007). In S. M. McPhail (Ed.), *Alternative validation strategies: Developing new and leveraging existing validity evidence* (pp. 29–81). San Francisco: Jossey-Bass.

Griggs v. Duke Power Co., 401 U.S. 424, 426, (1971).

Guion, R. M. (1965). Synthetic validity in a small company: A demonstration. *Personnel Psychology, 18,* 49–63.

Guion, R. M. (1991). Personnel assessment, selection, and placement. In M. D. Dunnette and L. Hough (Eds.), *Handbook of industrial and organizational psychology* (2nd ed.). Palo Alto, CA: Consulting Psychologists Press.

Gutenberg, R. L., Arvey, R. D., Osburn, H. G., & Jeanneret, P. R. (1983). Moderating effects of decision-making/information processing job dimensions on test validities. *Journal of Applied Psychology, 36,* 237–247.

Harvey, R. J. (1991). Job analysis. In M. D. Dunnette & L. Hough (Eds.), *Handbook of industrial and organizational psychology* (2nd ed.). Palo Alto, CA: Consulting Psychologists Press.

Hoffman, C. C. (1987). Unpublished technical report, Southern California Gas Company, Los Angeles.

Hoffman, C. C. (1988). Unpublished technical report, Southern California Gas Company, Los Angeles.

Hoffman, C. C. (1999). Generalizing physical ability test validity: A case study using test transportability, validity generalization, and construct-related validity evidence. *Personnel Psychology, 52,* 1019–1041.

Hoffman, C. C., Haase, S., & Babasa, B. (2000). *Using JCV predicted scores in setting test battery cut scores.* Paper presented at the annual conference of the Society for Industrial and Organizational Psychology, New Orleans.

Hoffman, C. C., Holden, L. M., & Gale, E. K. (2000). So many jobs, so little "N": Applying expanded validation models to support generalization of cognitive test validity. *Personnel Psychology, 53,* 955–991.

Hoffman, C. C., & McPhail, S. M. (1998). Exploring options for supporting test use in situations precluding local validation. *Personnel Psychology, 51,* 987–1003.

Hoffman, C. C., Morris, D., & Shultz, K. (2003). *Development and test of an extension to the Job Component validity model.* Paper presented at the annual conference of the Society for Industrial and Organizational Psychology, Orlando.

Hoffman, C. C., Nathan, B. R., & Holden, L. M. (1991). A comparison of validation criteria: Objective versus subjective and self versus supervisor ratings. *Personnel Psychology, 44,* 601–619.

Hogan, R., & Hogan, J. (1995). Hogan personality inventory manual (2nd ed.). Tulsa, OK: Hogan Assessment Systems.

Holden, L. M. (1992). *Job analysis and validity study for the distribution planning office technical progression.* Unpublished technical report, Southern California Gas Company, Los Angeles.

Hollenbeck, J. R., & Whitener, E. M. (1988). Criterion-related validation for small sample contexts: An integrated approach to synthetic validity. *Journal of Applied Psychology, 73*, 536–544.

Jeanneret, P. R. (1992). Applications of job component/synthetic validity to construct validity. *Human Performance, 5*, 81–96.

Jeanneret, P. R., & Strong, M. H. (2003). Linking O*NET job analysis information to job requirement predictors: An O*NET application. *Personnel Psychology, 56*, 465–492.

Johnson, J. W. (2006). Synthetic validity: a technique of use (finally). In S. M. McPhail (Ed.), *Alternative validation strategies: Developing new and leveraging existing validity evidence* (pp. 122–158). San Francisco: Jossey-Bass.

Johnson, J. W., Carter, G. W., & Tippins, N. T. (2001). A synthetic validation approach to the development of a selection system for multiple job families. In J. W. Johnson & G. W. Carter (Chairs), *Advances in the application of synthetic validation.* Symposium conducted at the 16th Annual Conference of the Society for Industrial and Organizational Psychology, San Diego.

Landkammer, K. (1990). Unpublished technical report, Southern California Gas Company, Los Angeles.

Landy, F. J. (1986). Stamp collecting versus science: Validation as hypothesis testing. *American Psychologist, 41*(11), 1183–1192.

Levine, E. L., Ash, R. A., & Bennett, N. (1980). Exploratory comparative study of four job analysis methods. *Journal of Applied Psychology, 65*, 524–535.

Levine, E. L., Ash, R. A., Hall, H. L., & Sistrunk, F. (1983). Evaluation of job analysis methods by experienced job analysts. *Academy of Management Journal, 26*, 339–347.

Levine, E. L., Bennett, N., & Ash, R. A. (1979). Evaluation and use of four job analysis methods for personnel selection. *Public Personnel Management, 8*, 146–151.

Marquardt, L. D., & McCormick, E. J. (1974). *The job dimensions underlying the job elements of the Position Analysis Questionnaire* (PAQ Form B; Tech. Rep. No. 4). West Lafayette, IN: Purdue University, Psychological Sciences Department.

McCloy, R. A. (1994). Predicting job performance scores without performance data. In B. F. Green & A. S. Mavor (Eds.), *Modeling cost and performance for military enlistment: Report of a workshop.* Washington, DC: National Academy Press.

McCloy, R. A. (2001). Predicting job performance scores in jobs lacking criterion data. In J. Johnson and G. Carter (Cochairs), *Advances in the application of synthetic validity.* Symposium conducted at the 16th annual conference of the Society for Industrial and Organizational Psychology, San Diego, CA.

McCormick, E. J. (1976). Job and task analysis. In M. D. Dunnette (Ed.), *Handbook of industrial and organizational psychology* (pp. 651–696). Chicago: Rand McNally.

McCormick, E. J., DeNisi, A. S., & Shaw, J. B. (1979). Use of the Position Analysis Questionnaire for establishing the job component validity of tests. *Journal of Applied Psychology, 64,* 51–56.

McCormick, E. J., Jeanneret, P. R., & Mecham, R. C. (1972). A study of job characteristics and job dimensions based on the Position Analysis Questionnaire (PAQ). *Journal of Applied Psychology, 56,* 347–368.

McCormick, E. J., Mecham, R. C., & Jeanneret, P. R. (1977). *Technical manual for the Position Analysis Questionnaire (PAQ).* Logan, UT: PAQ Services. (Available through PAQ Services, Inc., 1625 North 1000 East, Logan, UT 84321.)

McCormick, E. J., Mecham, R. C., & Jeanneret, P. R. (1989). *Technical manual for the Position Analysis Questionnaire (PAQ).* Logan, UT: PAQ Services. (Available through Consulting Psychologists Press Inc., Palo Alto, CA.)

McCoy et al. v. Willamette Industries, Inc. U.S. District Court for the Southern District of Georgia, Savannah Division, Civil Action No. CV401–075 (2001).

McPhail, S. M. (1995, May). Job component validity predictions compared to empirical validities. Paper presented as part of the symposium Current Innovations in PAQ-Based Research and Practice, C. C. Hoffman (chair), at the annual conference of the Society for Industrial and Organizational Psychology, Orlando.

Mecham, R. C. (1985, August). Comparative effectiveness of situational, generalized, and job component validation methods. In P. R. Jeanneret (Chair), *Job component validity: Job requirements, estimates, and validity generalization comparisons.* Symposium conducted at the annual convention of the American Psychological Association, Los Angeles.

Mecham, R. C., & McCormick, E. J. (1969). *The use of data based on the Position Analysis Questionnaire in developing synthetically derived attribute requirements of jobs* (Tech. Rep. No. 4). West Lafayette, IN: Purdue University, Occupational Research Center.

Morris, D. C., Hoffman, C. C., & Shultz, K. S. (2002). *A comparison of job component validity estimates to meta-analytic validity estimates.* Paper presented at the annual conference of the Society for Industrial and Organizational Psychology.

Mossholder, K. W., & Arvey, R. D. (1984). Synthetic validity: A conceptual and comparative review. *Journal of Applied Psychology, 69,* 322–333.

Nathan, B. B., & Alexander, R. (1988). A comparison of criteria for test validation: A meta-analytic investigation. *Personnel Psychology, 41,* 517–535.

Pearlman, K., Schmidt, F. L., & Hunter, J. E. (1980). Validity generalization results for tests used to predict job proficiency and training success in clerical occupations. *Journal of Applied Psychology, 65,* 373–406.

Peterson, N., Mumford, M., Borman, W., Jeanneret, P., & Fleishman, E. A. (1999). *An occupational information system for the 21st century: The development of O*NET.* Washington, DC: American Psychological Association.

Peterson, N. G., Wise, L. L., Arabian, J., & Hoffman, R. G. (2001). Synthetic validation and validity generalization: When empirical validation is not possible. In J. P. Campbell and D. J. Knapp (Eds.), *Exploring the limits in personnel selection and classification* (pp. 411–451). Mahwah, NJ: Erlbaum.

Primoff, E. S. (1955). *Test selection by job analysis: The J-coefficient: What it is, how it works* (Test Technical Series, No. 20). Washington, DC: U.S. Civil Service Commission, Standards Division.

Primoff, E. S. (1957). The J-coefficient approach to jobs and tests. *Personnel Administration, 20,* 31–40.

Primoff, E. S. (1959). Empirical validation of the J-coefficient. *Personnel Psychology, 12,* 413–418.

Rashkovsky, B., & Hoffman, C. C. (2005). *Examining a potential extension of the JCV model to include personality predictors.* Paper presented at the annual meeting of the Society for Industrial and Organizational Psychology.

Ree, M. J., Earles, J. A., & Teachout, M. S. (1994). Predicting job performance: Not much more than *g. Journal of Applied Psychology, 79,* 518–524.

Sackett, P. R. (1991). Exploring strategies for clustering military occupations. In A. K. Wigdor and B. F. Green (Eds.), *Performance assessment for the workplace* (Vol. II, pp. 305–332). Washington, DC: National Academy Press.

Scherbaum, C. A. (2005). Synthetic validity: Past, present, and future. *Personnel Psychology, 58,* 481–515.

Schmidt, F. L., & Hunter, J. E. (1977). Development of a general solution to the problem of validity generalization. *Journal of Applied Psychology, 62,* 529–540.

Shultz, K. S., Riggs, M. L., & Kottke, J. L. (1999). The need for an evolving concept of validity in industrial and personnel psychology: Psychometric, legal, and emerging issues. *Current Psychology, 17,* 265–286.

Society for Industrial and Organizational Psychology. (2003). *Principles for the validation and use of personnel selection procedures* (4th ed.). Bowling Green, OH: Society for Industrial and Organizational Psychology.

Steel, P.D.G., Huffcutt, A. I., & Kammeyer-Mueller, J. (2006). From the work one knows the worker: A systematic review of the challenges, solutions, and steps to creating synthetic validity. *International Journal of Selection and Assessment, 14*(1), 16–36.

Taylor v. James River Corporation, CA 88–0818-T-C (TC) (S.D. AL, 1989).

Thompson, D. E., & Thompson, T. A. (1982). Court standards for job analysis in test validation. *Personnel Psychology, 35,* 872–873.

U.S. Department of Labor. (1977). *Dictionary of occupational titles* (4th ed.). Washington, DC: U.S. Department of Labor.

Wilk, S. L, Desmarais, L. B., & Sackett, P. R. (1995). Gravitation to jobs commensurate with ability: Longitudinal and cross-sectional tests. *Journal of Applied Psychology, 80,* 79–85.

Wilk, S. L., & Sackett, P. R. (1996). Longitudinal analysis of ability–job complexity fit and job change. *Personnel Psychology, 49,* 937–967.

CHAPTER 4

Synthetic Validity: A Technique of Use (Finally)

Jeff W. Johnson

Synthetic validation is a technique that can be used to assemble a test battery or calculate validity coefficients for jobs in which there are too few incumbents to conduct a traditional criterion-related validity study, or when necessary data are otherwise unavailable (see, for example, Guion, 1965; Hoffman & McPhail, 1998; Hollenbeck & Whitener, 1988). Synthetic validation is the process of inferring validity in a specific situation based on (1) the identification of basic components of the job, (2) a determination of test validity for predicting performance on those components, and (3) a combination or synthesis of the component validities into a whole (Cascio, 1987). The term *synthetic validation* was first introduced by Lawshe (1952) over fifty years ago, but it has had little impact on the field of personnel selection. In a review of synthetic validity research and applications, Mossholder and Arvey (1984) stressed that the synthetic validity approach holds a great deal of promise. However, they concluded their review by noting that ". . . only after additional development will synthetic validation be more properly referred to as a technique of use instead of a technique of promise" (p. 331). A more recent review (Scherbaum, 2005) concluded that, although synthetic validation still has not captured the interest of most selection experts, recent developments have made it a more prominent and well-developed technique.

Synthetic validation is based on two assumptions. First, when a job component (that is, a cluster of related work behaviors) is common across multiple jobs, the human attributes predictive of performance on that component are similar across jobs. The implication of this assumption is that a test measuring a particular attribute should be a valid predictor for any job that contains a component for which the attribute is required. Second, the validity of a test for predicting performance of a job component is similar across jobs and situations. In other words, any differences in the relationship between a test and performance on a job component across jobs is due to sampling error, unreliability, or other random factors. Synthetic validation assumptions are therefore similar to those made for validity generalization (Jeanneret, 1992), a concept that has received considerable research support (American Educational Research Association, American Psychological Association, & National Council on Measurement in Education, 1999; Schmidt, Hunter, & Pearlman, 1982; Society for Industrial and Organizational Psychology, 2003).

Guion (1965) summarized the basic steps in applying the synthetic validation paradigm. First, isolate the work behaviors (or job components) that are common to the jobs of interest. Second, validate tests for predicting performance of those work behaviors. Finally, assemble a valid test battery for a job by using those tests found valid for predicting the specific work behaviors performed in that job. For example, assume the jobs of interest are made up of components A, B, C, and D. If job one is made up of components A, B, and D, the test battery for that job would consist of the tests that have been found to be valid for predicting components A, B, and D.

Note that synthetic validity is not a "type of validity." Synthetic validation is a process by which evidence for the interpretation of a test or test battery score is inferred for a particular job based on the validities (either empirical or judgmental) of the test or tests for predicting performance on the components of which the job is composed. An essential step in this process is determining the extent to which a test predicts performance on each important job component. The validity of a test for predicting a particular job component may be determined using any of a variety of research strategies (such as content sampling, experimental design, criterion-related correlations, or expert judgment) or a combination of strategies.

In this chapter, I distinguish between job component validity and other synthetic validation methods. Job component validity (JCV) is a term coined by McCormick (1959) to describe a specific type of synthetic validation technique in which validity coefficients are predicted rather than computed or estimated. In the JCV method, a set of equations is used to predict mean test scores and validity coefficients from job component scores. McCormick and colleagues (for example, McCormick, DeNisi, & Shaw, 1979; McCormick, Jeanneret, & Mecham, 1972) used the Position Analysis Questionnaire (PAQ) job dimensions to create equations to predict General Aptitude Test Battery (GATB) mean test scores and validity coefficients using jobs as the unit of analysis. The PAQ is a worker-oriented job analysis instrument, factor analyzed to produce forty-two job dimensions. All synthetic validation techniques involve job components, but the specific term *job component validity* is usually reserved for McCormick's approach. JCV is the topic of Chapter Three (Hoffman, Rashkovsky, & D'Egidio (2007) this volume), so this chapter focuses on other approaches to synthetic validation.

The synthetic validation techniques emphasized in this chapter have their roots in the J-coefficient approach introduced by Primoff (1957; 1959). This approach uses job analysis to identify the job components that are common across multiple jobs and the predictor measures that predict performance on those job components. The J-coefficient is a mathematical index of the relationship between the test battery and job performance. There are many different J-coefficient formulas, most of which involve a vector of the relationships between the predictors and the job components and a vector defining the relationships between the job components and job performance (Hamilton & Dickinson, 1987).

The elements of the J-coefficient formula can be estimated either empirically or using SME judgments. Because empirical correlations between predictors and job components require large overall sample sizes and performance ratings, the use of SME judgments is more typical (Scherbaum, 2005). For example, the relationship between predictors and job components could be estimated by asking SMEs to rate the relevance of each predictor to each job component. Alternatively, test experts or I/O psychologists could estimate the validity coefficients between predictors and job components (see Schmidt, Hunter, Croll, & McKenzie, 1983).

There are two primary differences between JCV and the synthetic validation techniques discussed in this chapter. First, the JCV approach links tests and performance constructs indirectly by demonstrating that, across jobs, job incumbents' test scores or test validity coefficients are related to the importance of the attribute measured by the test, as determined by a standardized job analysis survey (Mossholder & Arvey, 1984). Other types of synthetic validation approaches depend on more direct linkages between tests and performance constructs. Second, the JCV approach is based on the assumption that high-ability individuals tend to gravitate toward jobs with high-ability requirements and low-ability individuals tend to gravitate toward jobs with low-ability requirements (McCormick et al., 1979)—the "gravitational hypothesis" (Wilk, Desmerais, & Sackett, 1995). Although the gravitational hypothesis has garnered some empirical support, it is also a source of some criticism (Scherbaum, 2005).

Recent Synthetic Validation Research

Since Mossholder and Arvey's (1984) review, there have been several applications of the synthetic validation approach. Although much of the research has involved the JCV method (Hoffman, Holden, & Gale, 2000; Hoffman & McPhail, 1998; Jeanneret & Strong, 2003), several studies have incorporated other types of synthetic validation methods.

Hollenbeck and Whitener (1988) extended the traditional synthetic validity paradigm by suggesting a different order of aggregation. In traditional approaches (Guion, 1965; Primoff, 1959), the relationships between tests and job components are determined first and then aggregated into an overall estimate of validity for a single job. In Hollenbeck and Whitener's approach, job component performance scores are weighted by their importance for an individual's job (determined by a job analysis) and aggregated. Thus, each employee in the validation study has an overall performance score based on the weighted sum of the job component scores, and the weights applied to each job component differ according to the employee's job. Test scores are also aggregated, such that each employee has an overall test battery score. The result is an aggregate test score and an aggregate performance score for each employee. Then the correlation between aggregated test scores and aggregated performance scores is computed across all employees. This results in one correlation between the overall test battery scores and the overall performance scores, rather than many correlations between individual predictors and individual job components that are then aggregated into an overall validity coefficient. Thus, the sample size for the validity estimate is the number of employees included in the validation study and is not limited by the smallest sample sharing test and job component data. Rather than providing validity estimates for test batteries within each of a number of different jobs in an organization, this approach provides a single estimate of validity for a test battery within the organization as a whole. Although this approach would be useful for small organizations, it has had very little impact so far (Scherbaum, 2005).

In the U.S. Army's Synthetic Validity project (Peterson, Wise, Arabian, & Hoffman, 2001), synthetic validity equations were derived for several military occupational specialties (MOS), and validity estimates using these equations were compared to estimates from traditional criterion-related validation studies conducted as part of Project A. Industrial and organizational psychologists estimated the magnitude of the relationship between each predictor (taken from the Project A test battery) and each job component, and these estimates served as the basis for developing a weighting scheme for each MOS for predicting core technical proficiency and overall performance. Results showed very little difference between the validity coefficients developed from the synthetic validation approach and the validity coefficients obtained in the traditional manner.

Peterson et al. (2001) also examined the extent to which a synthetic validity equation derived for one MOS predicted criterion performance for another MOS. There was very little discriminant validity, in that mean differences between validity coefficients derived from MOS-specific equations and equations specific to other MOS were typically very small. The test batteries were very cognitively loaded, however, and cognitive ability tends to predict performance in a wide variety of jobs (Scherbaum, 2005). Highly intercorrelated tests would also minimize the differential effects of alternative weighting schemes (Wainer, 1978).

Johnson, Carter, and Tippins (2001) applied a synthetic validation technique to a selection system development project in a large private-sector organization. In this organization, a single selection system was desired for approximately four hundred nonmanagement jobs. It was not feasible to conduct a validity study for each job. Even when jobs were grouped into job families, the population of employees in some job families was very small, making inferences based on within-family correlations suspect. The job title structure also changed rapidly, and it was necessary to use the selection system for new jobs that did not exist at the time the validation study was conducted. Faced with this situation, a synthetic validation strategy was considered the most appropriate for this project.

A job analysis questionnaire (JAQ) was developed and administered, and the data were used to identify eleven job families and twenty-seven job components. Twelve tests were developed to predict supervisor-rated performance on these job components, and a concurrent, criterion-related validation study was conducted to collect test and job component data for 1,926 incumbents. A test composite was chosen for each job component, based on a combination of psychologist judgments and empirical relationships. In other words, both expert judgments of the relationships between tests and job components and empirical correlations between test scores and performance ratings on job components were available. A test was determined to be relevant for a job component if expert judgments or correlations indicated a strong relationship. A test battery was chosen for each job family based on its important job components. Using the equation for computing the correlation between two composites (for example, Nunnally & Bernstein, 1994; see Equation One later in this chapter), a validity coefficient for predicting a composite of performance on each job family's important job components was synthesized for each job family's test battery. Because test intercorrelations, job component intercorrelations, and correlations between tests and job components could be computed across job families, an overall validity coefficient could be computed for each job family by using the equation rather than by actually computing composite scores and calculating the correlations within job families. This approach allowed the researchers to take advantage of the large overall study sample size to compute stable validity estimates, even for very small job families. A great deal more detail is provided on this study later in this chapter in the Illustrative Example section.

Because sample sizes within some job families were relatively large, Johnson, Carter, and Tippins (2001) were able to compare synthetic validity coefficients to traditional validity coefficients calculated within those job families. The synthesized validity coefficients were very similar to empirical within-family validity coefficients for many families, indicating that validity coefficients computed from test-job component correlations calculated across job families are reasonable substitutes for traditional validity coefficients calculated within large job families. The differences between validity coefficients computed using the synthetic validation approach and validity coefficients computed using the traditional method within job families are presented in Table 4.1. Among the ten job families with at least forty cases, synthetic validity coefficients were substantially different (that is, > .05) from within-family validity coefficients for only three job families. Nevertheless, the synthetic validity coefficient was within the 90-percent confidence interval (CI) in all families, so sampling error is a possible explanation for this difference.

Johnson, Carter, and Tippins (2001) also examined several ways of weighting tests and job components when computing synthetic validity coefficients. Weighting of job components in calculating validity did not provide an advantage over unit weights. On the predictor side, however, results indicated that a simple weighting strategy can yield slightly higher validities than with unit weights. A test was included in a job family battery if that test was included in the prediction equation for at least one job component relevant to the job family. It stands to reason that a test that is relevant to several job components should have greater predictive power with respect to overall performance than will a test that is relevant to only one job component. As expected, weighting each test by the number of job components to which it was relevant yielded consistently higher validities than did unit weighting of each test.

Johnson, Paullin, and Hennen (2005) applied a similar synthetic validity procedure to a large public-sector organization, for several reasons. First, the five jobs included in the study had many job components in common, allowing validity coefficients to be com-

Table 4.1. Deviations Between Synthetic Validity Coefficients and Within-Family Validity Coefficients.

Job Family	Difference Between Within-Family and Synthetic Validity Coefficient	Within-Family N	Standard Error of Within-Family r	90% CI (SE ± 1.645)
1. Secretarial and Staff Support	±.001	254	.060	±.099
2. Technical Support	±.003	274	.057	±.094
3. Customer Service and Sales	±.033	252	.060	±.099
4. Operator	.103	189	.066	±.109
5. Craft A	±.049	146	.081	±.133
6. Craft B	±.074	203	.070	±.115
7. Engineering Support	.037	134	.081	±.133
8. Warehouse, Transportation, and Other Services	.005	133	.084	±.138
9. Building Maintenance	.194	40	.133	±.219
10. Vehicle Maintenance	.002	51	.137	±.225

Note: Reproduced from Johnson, Carter, & Tippins (2001).

puted on a larger sample size. It is always beneficial to increase the sample size for computing a validity coefficient. A larger sample size decreases the standard error around the validity coefficient, providing more confidence in the results. Second, the available sample size for one of the five jobs was too small to allow meaningful validity coefficients to be computed for that job alone. The synthetic validation approach allows stable validity coefficients to be computed even for jobs with very small sample sizes. Finally, the organization expected that test batteries would be needed in the near future for a number of other jobs similar to those included in the synthetic validation study. The synthetic validation approach allows the computation of validity coefficients for jobs that were not included in the validation study, as long as they are composed of job components for which validation data are available. Faced with these issues, the synthetic validation strategy was considered the most appropriate for this project.

Johnson et al. (2005) also examined alternative predictor and criterion weighting schemes. As with the previous study (Johnson, Carter, & Tippins, 2001), validity coefficients were highest when job components were unit weighted and predictors were weighted according to the number of job components to which they were relevant. Similar to Peterson et al. (2001), applying a common set of weights to all jobs as opposed to using job-specific weights resulted in very small differences in validity.

A noteworthy aspect of the Johnson et al. (2005) study is the range of predictors included. Scherbaum (2005) observed that most synthetic validity studies have examined cognitive, perceptual, and psychomotor ability tests, and called for more research including constructs such as personality and vocational interests. Johnson et al. (2005) included tests measuring cognitive ability, perceptual speed, biographical data, and six different personality constructs (such as conscientiousness, interpersonal skill, initiative, and service orientation).

Johnson and colleagues also extended the synthetic validity paradigm to the testing of differential prediction hypotheses (Johnson, Carter, Davison, & Oliver, 2001). The hypothesis of slope or intercept differences for different subgroups of examinees is typically difficult to test because of low power (Aguinis & Stone-Romero, 1997). To increase sample size and therefore power, Johnson, Carter, Davison, and Oliver showed that the same procedures used to compute correlations between tests and job components across jobs can be used to compute correlations between job component scores and the other variables necessary for differential prediction analyses (that is, a dummy-coded subgroup variable and the cross-product of the subgroup variable and the predictor score). Equations for computing correlations between a variable and a linear composite or correlations between two linear composites are used to create the matrix of synthetic correlations between overall performance, test scores, subgroup membership, and cross-product terms. This matrix is used to conduct the moderated multiple regression analyses necessary to determine if there is differential prediction across groups. Johnson, Carter, Davison, and Oliver illustrated the procedure by showing that the sample size for one job was 149 for a traditional within-job differential prediction analysis, but was increased to 1,361 by using synthetic differential prediction analysis. This analysis increased the power to detect a significant effect from .17 to .97.

McCloy (1994, 2001) combined a synthetic validity approach with hierarchical linear modeling to create prediction equations for jobs in which criterion data are not available. McCloy created a multilevel regression equation that related (1) individual scores on job-specific hands-on performance tests to characteristics of the individuals (level-one equation) and (2) job-specific, level-one regression parameters to job characteristics determined by a job analysis (level-two equations). Job analysis data for jobs lacking criterion data are entered into the level-two equations, yielding estimated level-one parameters. These level-one parameters are then applied to the individual characteristic variables to yield predicted performance scores for each individual. McCloy (2001) provided evidence showing that the linkage methodology provides predictions of job performance for jobs without criterion data that are very similar to predictions obtained from cross-validated least-squares regression equations when criterion data are available.

Legal Implications

Although there have been some court cases involving selection procedures based on JCV, the legal defensibility of other types of synthetic validity has not yet been challenged. The *Uniform Guidelines on Employee Selection Procedures* (Equal Employment Opportunity

Commission, Civil Service Commission, Department of Labor, & Department of Justice, 1978) do not address synthetic validity directly, but Trattner (1982) argued that the operational definition of construct validity provided by the *Uniform Guidelines* is actually a description of a synthetic validity model. The *Uniform Guidelines* state:

> . . . if a study pertains to a number of jobs having common critical or important work behaviors at a comparable level of complexity, and the evidence satisfies . . . criterion-related validity evidence for those jobs, the selection procedure may be used for all the jobs to which the study pertains. (p. 38303)

Trattner (1982) interpreted this definition of construct validity as meaning that a selection instrument can be used when work behaviors are important in any occupation within a class of occupations, as long as there is criterion-related validity evidence linking the instrument to the work behaviors for incumbents in the class. Trattner concluded that the synthetic validity approaches of Primoff (1959) and Guion (1965) were consistent with this interpretation of the *Uniform Guidelines*. The approaches of Peterson et al. (2001) and Johnson (Johnson, Carter, & Tippins, 2001; Johnson et al., 2005) also appear to meet these requirements of the *Uniform Guidelines*.

It is more difficult to infer how a synthetic validity study that is based only on SME judgments would be received in light of the *Uniform Guidelines*. The *Uniform Guidelines* clearly state that criterion-related validity evidence is required, so there is no direct support in the *Uniform Guidelines* for a synthetic validity study in which linkages between tests and job components are provided by SMEs. Of course, the *Uniform Guidelines* define an acceptable content validation strategy as demonstrating that the content of a selection procedure is representative of the important aspects of performance on the job. This demonstration is precisely what is done in a synthetic validation study when SMEs link the selection procedure content to job components and the only content included for a particular job has been linked to the important job components for that job. Thus, it seems likely a synthetic validity study based on a content validity strategy would meet the requirements of the *Uniform Guidelines*.

Scherbaum (2005) identified several reasons why synthetic validity should be legally defensible. First, any synthetic validity approach requires a comprehensive job analysis. The first step of a well-constructed selection study is a thorough job analysis; a selection procedure that is not based on an appropriate job analysis will rarely pass muster with the court. Second, using a synthetic validity approach forces the personnel specialist to create a test battery that is job relevant. Tests are chosen to measure attributes that have been determined to be relevant to important components of the job. Third, Scherbaum noted that Varca and Pattison (1993) believed that concepts like synthetic validity could more easily be added to the validity frontier based on the trends of recent decisions.

There are also legal implications when using the synthetic differential prediction analysis of Johnson, Carter, Davison, and Oliver (2001). These authors recommended considering the effect size when conducting differential prediction analyses, because the large sample sizes that are possible could lead a meaningless effect to be statistically significant. If a significant slope or intercept difference increases R^2 by less than .01, that could be considered too small an effect to be meaningful. They noted that this argument may not hold up in court, where it may be more difficult to ignore a statistically significant result.

It appears that the synthetic validation approach discussed in this chapter is consistent with the *Uniform Guidelines*, but there is no case law as yet to directly support these procedures. The quality of the job analysis, the appropriateness of the procedures used, and the nature of the inferences made by the users will determine the ultimate defensibility of any synthetic validation procedure (Scherbaum, 2005).

Professional Implications

Despite the long history of the synthetic validation concept, it is not explicitly mentioned in the most recent version of the *Standards for Educational and Psychological Testing* (American Educational Research Association, American Psychological Association, & National Council on Measurement in Education, 1999). Nevertheless, the principles for validating employment tests presented in the *Standards* are consistent with a synthetic validation approach. For example, Standard 14.4 states that "all criteria used should represent important work behaviors" (p. 159), based on systematic collection of job information. The synthetic validation method dictates the identification of important work behaviors from a job analysis. The *Standards* further state that a linkage must be established between the predictor measure and the criterion construct domain. The synthetic validation method is based on linking predictors to job components, so this prerequisite is clearly met. The *Standards* advocate the use of validity generalization where appropriate and note that type of job is one of the situational facets on which prior studies included in a meta-analysis may vary. This acknowledgment appears to support the idea that predictor-job component relationships can generalize across jobs.

The *Principles for the Validation and Use of Personnel Selection Procedures* (Society for Industrial and Organizational Psychology, 2003) do explicitly mention synthetic validity as an approach to generalizing validity evidence. The *Principles* state that the validity of a selection procedure may be established for different job components, and the validity of that procedure can be established for a given job by combining across the job components that are relevant to that job. The *Principles'* inclusion of synthetic validity along with validity transportability and meta-analytic validity generalization gives synthetic validity a status as a defensible validation strategy that it had not previously achieved.

Illustrative Example

In this section, I illustrate the application of synthetic validation by describing a synthetic validation project and working through each step of the procedure. This example is taken from Johnson, Carter, and Tippins (2001), who employed a synthetic validity approach to develop a selection system for all nonmanagement jobs in a large organization. The synthetic validity approach was applied for two primary reasons. First, it was not feasible to conduct a validity study for every job to which the selection system would be applied. Even after grouping jobs into job families, the population of incumbents in some job families was still very small. Second, the organization wanted to use the selection system for new jobs that did not exist at the time of the validation study.

The synthetic validity approach we employed consisted of the following steps, each of which is described in detail in the ensuing sections:

1. Job analysis
2. Develop measures of important predictor constructs
3. Develop job performance criteria
4. Collect predictor and criterion data
5. Compute correlations between predictors and criteria
6. Choose predictors for each job component
7. Choose predictor battery for each job family
8. Calculate overall validity coefficient
9. Develop transportability procedures

Step One. Job Analysis

The purpose of the job analysis was to identify (1) job families, (2) predictor constructs, and (3) job components. We developed a JAQ consisting of 483 work behaviors and 68 worker characteristics (skills, abilities, and other characteristics). Although the JCV method bases job components on worker characteristics, our synthetic validity approach based the job components on clusters of similar work behaviors. As Trattner (1982) pointed out, the *Uniform Guidelines* specify work behaviors as the preferred element for the determination of predictor validity. In addition, less inference is required on the part of supervisors or incumbents to rate the importance of work behaviors than to rate the importance of skills, abilities, or other characteristics. Thus, job components were based on clusters of similar work behaviors, and job families were based on clusters of similar jobs, in terms of similarity in work behaviors performed.

Job families were identified by clustering together jobs with similar task requirements. This was accomplished with a hybrid Q-factor analysis and cluster analysis (see Colihan & Burger, 1995, for an overview of this methodology) of the mean task importance ratings for each job. The following job families were created:

- Secretarial and Staff Support
- Technical Support
- Customer Service and Sales

- Operator
- Technician A (higher level)
- Technician B (lower level)
- Engineering Support
- Warehouse, Transportation, and Other Services
- Building Maintenance
- Equipment Operations
- Vehicle Maintenance

Job components were identified by factor analyzing the task importance ratings. Although Cranny and Doherty (1988) warned against factor analysis of job analysis importance ratings, their arguments applied to the situation in which a single job is analyzed. When the primary source of variance in importance ratings is the job, however, factor analysis is appropriate (Johnson, 2000). Little research exists on the dimensionality of task inventories, because factor analysis of the hundreds of task statements on such inventories is difficult in both application and interpretation (Harvey, 1991). Our JAQ consisted of 483 task statements, so we used a procedure similar to that used in identifying job families to identify job components (Johnson, 2003). Specifically, task importance ratings were factor analyzed and fifty factors were extracted. Rather than attempting to interpret these fifty factors by examining the items that had their largest loading on each factor, the factor loadings were cluster analyzed using Ward's method and squared Euclidean distances. This way, loadings on every factor were considered in clustering tasks together, rather than just the factor on which the task had its largest loading. Clusters were further combined rationally if they were conceptually similar, and the tasks were performed by people in the same job families. These analyses resulted in a final set of twenty-six job components.

Job component scores were calculated by computing the mean of the importance ratings for the tasks included in each job component. Mean job component scores were calculated for each job, and the mean of these scores was calculated across jobs within each job family. We established a cutoff for considering a job component to be relevant to a job family by examining the mean job component scores in light of our understanding of the job families. In other words, we selected job components that we knew were relevant to the majority of jobs within a job family, based on the job analysis results, and determined what minimum mean job component score at the job family level was necessary to ensure that those job components remained relevant to the job family. Given the level of aggregation from task to job component and from incumbent to job family in this study, the cutoff was set relatively low to ensure that relevant job components were not excluded for any job. A grid showing the job component labels and which job components were considered relevant to each job family is provided in Table 4.2. The number of job components relevant to a family ranged from eight to sixteen.

Step Two. Develop Measures of Important Predictor Constructs

Predictors could be commercially available tests or measures developed specifically for the situation. For this study, tests were developed by experienced industrial and organizational psychologists to measure the skills and abilities determined to be important to the jobs in this organization during the job analysis. The following tests were developed for this study:

- Coding
- Checking for Accuracy
- Language Usage
- Mechanical Comprehension
- Numerical Reasoning
- Reading Comprehension
- Reasoning
- Assembling Objects (Spatial)
- Spelling
- Situational Judgment – General
- Situational Judgment – Customer Contact

Step Three. Develop Job Performance Criteria

A single performance-rating scale was created for each of the twenty-six job components identified in the job analysis. Each scale was a seven-point behavior summary scale, with written descriptions of what should be considered high, medium, and low performance on that job component. Raters had the option of rating the job

Table 4.2. Job Components Relevant to Each Job Family.

Job Component	Job Family										
	1	2	3	4	5	6	7	8	9	10	11
1. Plan, Prioritize, Organize, or Coordinate Work	X	X	X	X	X	X	X	X	X	X	X
2. Make Decisions and Solve Problems	X	X	X	X	X	X	X	X	X		X
3. Work with Others	X	X	X	X	X	X	X	X	X	X	X
4. Communication	X	X	X	X	X	X	X	X	X		X
5. Keep Job-Relevant Knowledge Current	X	X	X	X	X	X	X	X	X	X	X
6. Handle Telephone Calls	X	X	X	X	X	X	X	X	X		X
7. Customer Service	X	X	X	X	X	X	X	X	X		X
8. Clerical/Administrative Duties	X	X	X				X	X	X		
9. Computer Usage	X	X	X		X		X	X	X		
10. Drafting or Specifying Technical Devices, Parts, or Equipment							X				
11. Handle and Maintain Materials								X			
12. Inspect, Repair, or Maintain Building Equipment or Systems									X		
13. Sales-Related Activities			X								
14. Handle Service Orders or Repair Requests		X									
15. Handle Bills, Payments, Adjustments, or Credit Research			X								

	1	2	3	4	5	6	7	8	9	10	11
16. Maintain Supplies or Materials	X		X		X	X					
17. Operate Tools, Equipment, or Vehicles	X	X	X		X	X					
18. Wire and Cable Distribution, Telecommunications Equipment Installation and Maintenance					X						
19. Assist with Listings, Calling Procedures				X							
20. Install, Operate, or Maintain Complex Equipment and Computer Systems						X					
21. Operate Document Production Equipment							X				
22. Repair or Maintain Vehicles, Vehicle Equipment, or Mobile Power Units											X
23. Handle Work Stress					X	X	X	X	X	X	X
24. Demonstrate Effort and Take Initiative					X	X	X	X	X	X	X
25. Help Others					X	X	X	X	X	X	X
26. Organizational Commitment					X	X	X	X	X	X	X

component as not applicable to the job of the person they were evaluating. Great care was taken to write job component definitions and performance-level descriptions that were general enough that they would be applicable to each job family to which the job component was relevant. Thus, one rating scale could be used across multiple job families. Initial rating scales were revised based on meetings with supervisors representing each job family. A pilot study with a subset of supervisors indicated that supervisors had no difficulty using the rating scales and believed that the scales targeted to the jobs they represented were relevant and appropriate.

Step Four. Collect Predictor and Criterion Data

Tests were administered to job incumbents as a battery during work time in four- to five-hour blocks. To save testing time, tests were not administered to incumbents if the job analysis indicated that the construct was not relevant to their job family. For example, the Mechanical Comprehension test was not relevant to the Customer Service and Sales job family, so there was no need to administer that test to incumbents in that family.

Supervisors completed most performance ratings in small groups during work time. The session administrator provided a brief rater training session, focusing on how to use the rating scales and awareness of common rating errors. Supervisors who were unable to attend these sessions completed the ratings on their own and returned them by mail. These supervisors received the rater training in written form.

The final sample with both predictor and criterion data included 1,926 incumbents. Eight of the job families had sample sizes ranging from 144 to 306. The remaining three job families had sample sizes of 58, 44, and 8. It was for these smaller job families that the synthetic validation strategy was most useful.

Step Five. Compute Correlations
Between Predictors and Criteria

When calculating correlations between test scores and job component performance ratings, it would not be appropriate to simply compute a correlation without regard to job family, because of the nature of the criterion. It would not be unusual for the relationship between the predictor and the criterion to be stronger within job families than across job families, if the job family itself is expected to cause differences in predictor scores that are independent of differences in criterion scores.

For example, imagine the predictor is the Reasoning test, and the criterion is the supervisor rating of the Make Decisions and Solve Problems job component. Technician A is a relatively high-level, technical job family, and Warehouse, Transportation, and Other Services is a relatively low-level job family. We would expect differences in the mean level of reasoning ability between the incumbents in each of those job families. The supervisors would, however, probably base their ratings on how their employees compare to other people within the same job family, so the mean performance rating within each job family may be the same. Thus, differences in mean Reasoning scores would not correspond to differences in mean ratings of Make Decisions and Solve Problems. This situation is illustrated in Figure 4.1.

Figure 4.1. Example of a Situation in Which Within-Job Relationships Are Obscured by Calculating Correlations Across Jobs.

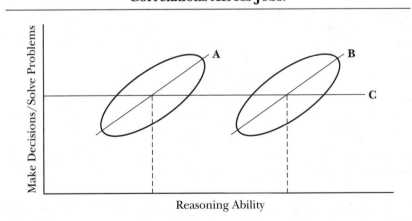

Note: A and B are within-job regression lines, and C is the across-job regression line.

There are two simple ways to deal with this situation. First, correlations can be computed within jobs and then a sample-size weighted average calculated across jobs (that is, a meta-analytic approach); second, all variables can be standardized within jobs and then correlations calculated across jobs (Sackett & Arvey, 1993). Either of these methods will yield the same correlations, but the former would allow for correction for statistical artifacts (such as range restriction), if desired. Uncorrected correlations were used in this study, so we standardized predictor and criterion scores within job families and calculated correlations across families, because this approach was simpler.

Step Six. Choose Predictors for Each Job Component

Choosing predictors for each job component involved several substeps: (1) obtaining expert judgments on the relevance of each potential predictor to each job component, (2) identifying potential predictors for each job component based on a set of rules, and (3) choosing the final set of predictors for each job component.

Expert Judgments

A primary consideration in choosing predictors was to avoid capitalizing on chance relationships in the data, so one of the criteria used to choose predictors was expert judgments of the relationships between tests and job components. Expert judgment surveys were completed by twenty-three industrial and organizational psychologists who were associated with the organizations involved in this project. The expert judgment survey asked for estimates of the extent to which each test would be relevant for predicting performance on each job component, using the following scale:

5 = Extremely relevant for predicting performance; one of the best available predictors

4 = Relevant for predicting performance; definitely a solid predictor

3 = Somewhat relevant for predicting performance; a secondary predictor at best

2 = Minimally relevant for predicting performance; contributes little to prediction

1 = Not at all relevant for predicting performance; no relationship between predictor and criterion

Each participant was provided with information about each test, which included a description of what the test measured and how it was set up, abbreviated instructions for the test-taker, and several sample items. Each participant was also provided with a definition of each performance dimension.

Potential Predictors

The first step in creating a predictor composite for each job family was to create a predictor composite for each job component. This step required identifying a set of potential predictors to include in such a composite for each job component. Relevant predictors were based on a combination of the ratings obtained from the expert judgment exercise and empirical validity.

Two sets of rules were devised for selecting potential predictors. The first set of rules was for large-N job components only. A large-N job component was defined as a job component for which both test and criterion data were available from at least four hundred valid cases. A minimum of four hundred was chosen because the standard error of the correlation is no more than .05 at $N = 400$, so correlations based on samples this large are quite stable. A test was considered relevant to a large-N job component if it met one of the following criteria: (1) mean expert relevance rating ± 3.50, (2) mean expert relevance rating ± 3.00 and correlation ± .10, or (3) mean expert relevance rating ± 2.50 and correlation ± .15. This sliding scale meant the less relevant the experts perceived a test to be, the higher the empirical validity had to be to consider including it.

For small-N job components (fewer than four hundred cases), empirical validity information was not considered, so as not to capitalize on chance. Thus, the only criterion for considering a test to be relevant to a small-N job component was that the mean expert relevance rating was at least 3.00.

Final Composites for Each Job Component

We followed three steps to choose the final predictor composite for each job component. First, we created a number of alternative unit-weighted predictor composites for each job component from the tests that were eligible for consideration. Note that some job components required different composites for different job families because some tests were not available for all families. For example, Communication is a relevant job component for all job families, but Reading and Situational Judgment – General were the only potential tests for the Communication composite that were taken by all examinees. Language Usage and Spelling were taken by examinees in Families 1, 2, 3, and 4, and Situational Judgment – Customer Contact was taken only by examinees in Families 2, 3, and 4. Thus, three separate test batteries were required. One set of test batteries was created for Families 2, 3, and 4, considering all possible tests. Another set of test batteries was created for Family 1, considering all tests but Situational Judgment – Customer Contact. A third set of test batteries was created for the remaining families, considering only Reading and Situational Judgment – General. Ten job components required more than one test battery because of this situation. Composite validities and adverse impact statistics were then calculated for each alternative composite.

Finally, the project team came to a consensus on the best composite to choose from the set of possible composites for each job component. The goal was to choose the best composite in terms of maximizing validity and minimizing adverse impact. For small-N job components, only adverse impact was considered. When the best composite was not clear, the most parsimonious composite (that is, the one with the fewest predictors) of those being considered was chosen. The tests that were included in the final composite for each job component are shown in Table 4.3.

Step Seven. Choose Predictor Battery for Each Job Family

The predictor battery for each job family was determined by simply including the tests in the composites for the job components relevant to that family. For example, if job components 1 and 2 are relevant to a particular job family, the predictor composite for that job family includes all the tests included in the composites for job components 1 and 2. Table 4.4 presents a grid showing the final predictor battery for each job family.

Table 4.3. Tests Included in Final Composites for Each Job Component.

JC	Label	CD	CK	NR	RD	RS	LU	SPE	MC	SPA	SJ	SJC
1.	Plan, Prioritize, Organize, or Coordinate Work					X					X	
2.	Make Decisions and Solve Problems[a]			X	X	X					X	X
3.	Work with Others[a]										X	X
4.	Communication[a]				X		X	X			X	X
5.	Keep Job-Relevant Knowledge Current				X							
6.	Handle Telephone Calls[a]						X				X	X
7.	Customer Service[a]										X	X
8.	Clerical/Administrative Duties[a]	X	X		X		X					
9.	Computer Usage	X	X	X	X							
10.	Drafting or Specifying Technical Devices, Parts, or Equipment								X	X		
11.	Handle and Maintain Materials									X		
12.	Inspect, Repair, or Maintain Building Equipment or Systems					X			X	X		
13.	Sales-Related Activities					X					X	X

Table 4.3. Tests Included in Final Composites for Each Job Component, Cont'd.

JC	Label	CD	CK	NR	RD	RS	LU	SPE	MC	SPA	SJ	SJC
14.	Handle Service Orders or Repair Requests	X									X	X
15.	Handle Bills, Payments, Adjustments or Credit Research	X				X					X	X
16.	Maintain Supplies or Materials	X										
17.	Operate Tools, Equipment, or Vehicles								X	X		
18.	Wire and Cable Distribution, Telecommunications Equipment Installation and Maintenance					X			X			
19.	Assist with Listings, Calling Procedures	X						X				X
20.	Install, Operate, or Maintain Complex Equipment and Computer Systems					X				X		
21.	Operate Document Production Equipment											
22.	Repair or Maintain Vehicles, Vehicle Equipment, or Mobile Power Units								X	X		
23.	Handle Work Stress[a]										X	X
24.	Demonstrate Effort and Take Initiative[a]										X	X
25.	Help Others[a]										X	X
26.	Organizational Commitment[a]										X	X

Note: CD = Coding; CK = Checking for Accuracy; NR = Numerical Reasoning; RD = Reading Comprehension; RS = Reasoning; LU = Language Usage; SPE = Spelling; MC = Mechanical Comprehension; SPA = Spatial; SJ = Situational Judgment; SJC = Situational Judgment – General; SJC = Situational Judgment – Customer Contact.

[a]All families did not have data for all tests in this composite.

Table 4.4. Test Batteries for Each Job Family.

Test	Job Family										
	1	2	3	4	5	6	7	8	9	10	11
Coding	X	X	X	X	X	X	X	X	X	X	X
Checking for Accuracy	X		X								
Numerical Reasoning	X	X	X		X	X	X	X	X		X
Reading Comprehension	X	X	X	X	X	X	X	X	X	X	X
Reasoning	X	X	X		X	X	X	X	X	X	X
Language Usage	X	X	X	X							
Spelling	X			X							
Mechanical Comprehension					X	X	X	X	X		X
Assembling Objects (Spatial)					X	X	X	X	X	X	X
Situational Judgment– General	X	X		X	X	X	X	X	X	X	X
Situational Judgment – Customer Contact	X	X	X								

Step Eight. Calculate Overall Validity Coefficient

A validity coefficient between the test battery and the overall performance composite would traditionally be calculated by computing a test composite score and a job component composite score for each person, then correlating the two scores. The synthetic validity approach allows us to base validity calculations on all available data across all job families. Of course, this means actual test and job component composites would not be computed to determine validity; rather, the test-job component correlations that are relevant to a particular job family are combined using standard formulae to yield an overall validity coefficient for that job family.

The following equation is used to calculate the correlation between the test composite and the overall performance composite (Nunnally & Bernstein, 1994):

$$r_{y_c x_c} = \frac{\overline{r_{y_i x_i}}}{\sqrt{\overline{r_{yy}}} \; \sqrt{\overline{r_{xx}}}} , \tag{1}$$

where

$$r_{y_c x_c}$$

= correlation of a unit-weighted sum of standardized test scores x_i with a unit-weighted sum of standardized job component scores y_i,

$$\overline{r_{y_i x_i}}$$

= mean correlation between all scores y_i making up one composite and all scores x_i making up the other composite,

$$\overline{r_{yy}}$$

= mean of all elements in the R_{yy} intercorrelation matrix, and

$$\overline{r_{xx}}$$

= mean of all elements in the R_{xx} intercorrelation matrix.

When the correlation between a composite and a single variable is of interest (for example, between a test battery and a single job component), the following equation is used (Nunnally & Bernstein, 1994):

$$r_{yx_c} = \frac{\overline{r_{yx_i}}}{\sqrt{\overline{r_{xx}}}} \qquad (2)$$

where

$$r_{yx_c}$$

= correlation of a unit-weighted sum of standardized scores x_i with a variable y,

$$\overline{r_{yx_i}}$$

= mean correlation between a variable y and all scores x_i making up the composite,

$$\overline{r_{xx}}$$

= mean of all elements in the R_{xx} intercorrelation matrix.

These equations can also incorporate any type of weighting of tests or job components by appropriately weighting the elements of the correlation matrices before applying Equation 1 or 2 (Nunnally & Bernstein, 1994). Ghiselli, Campbell, and Zedeck (1981) provided an equivalent equation for the correlation between a variable and a unit-weighted composite, and Trattner (1982) gave an equivalent equation for the correlation between a variable and a weighted composite.

To illustrate how to calculate an overall synthetic validity coefficient, Table 4.5 presents correlations between tests and job components that are relevant to the Operator job family. Note that the actual correlations are proprietary, so the correlations in Table 4.5 are fabricated just to illustrate the calculation. To compute

$$\overline{r_{y_i x_i}},$$

calculate the weighted mean of all correlations in the table. Note that Nunnally and Bernstein's (1994) equations do not require that correlations be transformed to Fisher's z values before computing the mean. Assuming that predictors and criteria are unit-weighted, the mean of all correlations in Table 4.5 is .119.

When computing

$$\overline{r_{yy}}$$

and

$$\overline{r_{xx}},$$

all elements of the correlation matrix must be included in the calculation, including the ones on the diagonal and the above-diagonal elements. Note that the Ghiselli et al. (1981) and Trattner (1982) equations use the mean of only the below-diagonal elements. For this example,

$$\overline{r_{yy}}$$

= .572 and

$$\overline{r_{xx}}$$

= .425. Inserting these values into Equation 1 yields an overall validity coefficient for the test battery predicting a unit-weighted composite of relevant job components of .242.

Step Nine. Develop Transportability Procedures

One of the advantages of the synthetic validity approach is that test batteries can be constructed and validity coefficients computed for jobs that were not included in the original validation study. We designed a transportability tool that identifies a test battery and computes a validity coefficient for new jobs that come online. The input to the tool is JAQ responses from those knowledgeable about

Table 4.5. Correlations Between Predictors and Job Components Relevant to Operator Job Family.

Job Component	Coding	Reading Comprehension	Language Usage	Spelling	SJ – General	SJ – Customer Contact
2. Make Decisions and Solve Problems	.13	.22	.16	.07	.21	.19
3. Work with Others	.06	.07	.08	.04	.15	.12
4. Communication	.14	.23	.19	.09	.16	.18
5. Keep Job-Relevant Knowledge Current	.11	.18	.11	.05	.09	.10
6. Handle Telephone Calls	.09	.12	.14	.08	.11	.17
7. Customer Service	.12	.08	.12	.09	.13	.24
19. Assist with Listings, Calling Procedures	.18	.18	.16	.14	.14	.22
23. Handle Work Stress	.11	.09	.06	.03	.15	.13
24. Demonstrate Effort and Take Initiative	.09	.11	.05	.02	.16	.15
25. Help Others	.06	.06	.05	.03	.18	.16
26. Organizational Commitment	.05	.04	.07	.05	.17	.16

the new job. The job component profile for the new job is first compared to the job component profiles for the existing job families. If possible, the new job is placed in the job family in which it fits best. If a new job is not adequately similar to any existing family, a new test battery can easily be developed for the new job, based on the job component profile for the job. Just as with the original job families, the new test battery is composed of the tests that were included in the predictor batteries for the job components that are important to the new job. The synthetic validity coefficient of the test battery for the new job can be computed using the existing data.

This ability to develop new scoring algorithms and provide validity evidence for new jobs even if they do not fit into current job families is a substantial advantage of the application of the synthetic validation strategy for organizations in which jobs change quickly. This approach is predicated on the assumption that the existing JAQ captures a large majority of the important tasks for the new job.

Constraints and Risks

Several requirements must be met when conducting a synthetic validation study such as the one described in the example. First, there must be a structured job analysis instrument that can be used across jobs, so that the important components of each job or job family can be identified. The sample size must be large enough that reliable job analysis data can be collected. A well-conducted job analysis is the primary requirement of any synthetic validation study, and it cannot be compromised. Incorporating O*NET into synthetic validity approaches may make an adequate job analysis more attainable in smaller organizations (Scherbaum, 2005).

Second, the job analysis instrument must include almost all of the important tasks for the job or jobs under study. If a very important component of performance for a particular job is not captured by the job analysis instrument, the resulting test battery may be deficient in that a predictor for that important job component may be excluded. Also, the estimated validity coefficient is likely to be inaccurate because overall performance would not be defined by a composite of the available job components.

The third requirement is a means of linking the predictor measure or measures to the job components. In the example we employed a criterion-related validation study, but a content- or construct-oriented strategy is also acceptable. The criterion-related strategy offers the advantage of being able to apply synthetic differential prediction analysis (Johnson, Carter, Davison, & Oliver, 2001), but doing so requires a large overall study sample size with sufficient numbers within each subgroup of interest, even though the within-job sample sizes may be small.

Finally, job component measures must be consistent across jobs. In other words, the definition of the job component and rating scale anchors must be applicable to each job to which the component is relevant. This requires considerable development effort, involving extensive review and pretesting by SMEs with knowledge of the content of the jobs studied.

Scherbaum (2005) noted that another limitation of synthetic validation is the lack of discriminant validity, in that equations developed for one job yield almost equal validity when applied to another (see Peterson et al., 2001). This result could be due to the primary use of cognitively oriented predictors in most synthetic validation studies, which do not exhibit much discriminant validity across most jobs (Schmidt & Hunter, 1998). A more recent study including many noncognitive predictors, however, also found little discriminant validity across jobs (Johnson et al., 2005).

A current constraint on the use of synthetic validity is the need to identify and validate predictors for the job components with each new synthetic validity study. There is very little accumulated research on specific predictor measures because most synthetic validity studies have included predictor measures that are not commercially available (Mossholder & Arvey, 1984; Scherbaum, 2005). Hough (2001; Hough & Ones, 2001) called for the creation of a database to be used with synthetic validation models to build prediction equations for specific situations. The idea is to conduct primary studies that report relationships between predictor constructs and job components, then use meta-analysis to cumulate the results of those studies. Such a database would allow us to use synthetic validity techniques to estimate the validity of a battery of predictors for any job that includes job components on which research is available. When such a database is large enough, practitioners will be able to buy or develop measures of predictor constructs that have been shown to predict performance on job components relevant to any job of interest and to calculate a validity coefficient for that job. The development of this type of database should be the ultimate goal of synthetic validation research.

There is risk associated with using a synthetic validation approach to support the use of a selection procedure. So far, the synthetic validation approach as discussed in this chapter has not been challenged in court. The lack of challenge may be due to the small number of synthetic validation studies that have been conducted. As discussed previously, there is reason to believe that a well-designed synthetic validation study has a good chance of successfully withstanding legal scrutiny, based on its emphasis on job analysis and linking predictors directly to criterion constructs. Nevertheless, this method has yet to be subjected to judicial review, and there is always some legal risk associated with using an approach that does not yet have case law supporting its use, despite its clear scientific and professional support.

Conclusion

The synthetic validation approach discussed in this chapter has a number of practical benefits. First, it allows for the calculation of stable validity estimates, even for jobs with small sample sizes. Second, it makes it possible to develop new test batteries for jobs that were not included in the validation study and to support use of the selection system for these jobs with solid validity evidence and explicit consideration of disparate impact in constructing the relevant batteries. Third, in some cases it is possible to test differential prediction hypotheses with adequate statistical power even in cases in which within-job sample sizes are small. Finally, the synthetic validity approach forces the researcher to use a construct-oriented approach to personnel selection, which is the best way to maximize validity (Schneider, Hough, & Dunnette, 1996). There is relatively little risk associated with the approach, stemming primarily from the unknown of employing a procedure that has not been tested explicitly in court. Given the logic associated with its development and recent research showing the success with which it can be applied, I believe the synthetic validity strategy has gone beyond a technique of promise to become a technique of use and should be considered when planning any validation study.

References

Aguinis, H., & Stone-Romero, E. F. (1997). Methodological artifacts in moderated multiple regression and their effects on statistical power. *Journal of Applied Psychology, 82,* 192–206.

American Educational Research Association, American Psychological Association, & National Council on Measurement in Education. (1999). *Standards for educational and psychological testing.* Washington, DC: American Educational Research Association.

Cascio, W. F. (1987). *Applied psychology in personnel management* (3rd ed.). Englewood Cliffs, NJ: Prentice-Hall.

Colihan, J., & Burger, G. K. (1995). Constructing job families: An analysis of quantitative techniques used for grouping jobs. *Personnel Psychology, 48,* 563–586.

Cranny, C. J., & Doherty, M. E. (1988). Importance ratings in job analysis: Note on the misinterpretation of factor analyses. *Journal of Applied Psychology, 73,* 320–322.

Equal Employment Opportunity Commission, Civil Service Commission, Department of Labor, & Department of Justice. (1978). *Uniform guidelines on employee selection procedures. Federal Register, 43*(166), 38295–38309.

Ghiselli, E. E., Campbell, J. P., & Zedeck, S. (1981). *Measurement theory for the behavioral sciences* (rev. ed.). San Francisco: Freeman.

Guion, R. M. (1965). Synthetic validity in a small company: A demonstration. *Personnel Psychology, 18,* 49–63.

Hamilton, J. W., & Dickinson, T. L. (1987). Comparison of several procedures for generating J-coefficients. *Journal of Applied Psychology, 72,* 49–54.

Harvey, R. J. (1991). Job analysis. In M. D. Dunnette & L. M. Hough (Eds.), *Handbook of industrial & organizational psychology* (2nd ed., pp. 71–163). Palo Alto, CA: Consulting Psychologists Press.

Hoffman, C. C., Holden, L. M., & Gale, K. (2000). So many jobs, so little "N": Applying expanded validation models to support generalization of cognitive test validity. *Personnel Psychology, 53,* 955–991.

Hoffman, C. C., & McPhail, S. M. (1998). Exploring options for supporting test use in situations precluding local validation. *Personnel Psychology, 51,* 987–1003.

Hoffman, C. C., Rashkovsky, B., & D'Egidio, E. (2007). Job component validity: Background, current research, and applications. In S. M. McPhail (Ed.), *Alternative validation strategies: Developing new and leveraging existing validity evidence* (pp. 82–121). San Francisco: Jossey-Bass.

Hollenbeck, J. R., & Whitener, E. M. (1988). Criterion-related validation for small sample contexts: An integrated approach to synthetic validity. *Journal of Applied Psychology, 73,* 536–544.

Hough, L. M. (2001). I/Owes its advances to personality. In B. W. Roberts & R. T. Hogan (Eds.), *Applied personality psychology: The intersection of personality and industrial/organizational psychology* (pp. 19–44). Washington, DC: American Psychological Association.

Hough, L. M., & Ones, D. S. (2001). The structure, measurement, validity, and use of personality variables in industrial, work, and organizational psychology. In N. R. Anderson, D. S. Ones, H. K. Sinangil, & C. Viswesvaran (Eds.), *Handbook of industrial, work & organizational psychology* (Vol. 1, pp. 233–277). New York: Sage.

Jeanneret, P. R. (1992). Applications of job component/synthetic validity to construct validity. *Human Performance, 5,* 81–96.

Jeanneret, P. R., & Strong, M. H. (2003). Linking O*NET job analysis information to job requirement predictors: An O*NET application. *Personnel Psychology, 56,* 465–492.

Johnson, J. W. (2000). Factor analysis of importance ratings in job analysis: Note on the misinterpretation of Cranny and Doherty (1988). *Organizational Research Methods, 3,* 267–284.

Johnson, J. W. (2003). *A procedure for conducting factor analysis with large numbers of variables.* Poster presented at the 18th Annual Conference of the Society for Industrial and Organizational Psychology, Orlando, FL.

Johnson, J. W., Carter, G. W., Davison, H. K., & Oliver, D. (2001). A synthetic validity approach to testing differential prediction hypotheses. *Journal of Applied Psychology, 86,* 774–780.

Johnson, J. W., Carter, G. W., & Tippins, N. T. (2001, April). A synthetic validation approach to the development of a selection system for multiple job families. In J. W. Johnson & G. W. Carter (Chairs), *Advances in the application of synthetic validity.* Symposium conducted at the 16th Annual Conference of the Society for Industrial and Organizational Psychology, San Diego, CA.

Johnson, J. W., Paullin, C., & Hennen, M. (2005). Validation and development of an operational version of Exam 473. In C. Paullin & J. W. Johnson (Eds.), *Development and validation of Exam 473 for the United States Postal Service* (Institute Report #496). Minneapolis: Personnel Decisions Research Institutes.

Lawshe, C. H. (1952). Employee selection. *Personnel Psychology, 6,* 31–34.

McCloy, R. A. (1994). Predicting job performance scores without performance data. In B. F. Green & A. S. Mavor (Eds.), *Modeling cost and performance for military enlistment: Report of a workshop.* Washington, DC: National Academy Press.

McCloy, R. A. (2001, April). Predicting job performance scores in jobs lacking criterion data. In J. W. Johnson & G. W. Carter (Chairs), *Advances in the application of synthetic validity.* Symposium conducted at the 16th Annual Conference of the Society for Industrial and Organizational Psychology, San Diego, CA.

McCormick, E. J. (1959). The development of processes for indirect or synthetic validity: III. Application of job analysis to indirect validity. A symposium. *Personnel Psychology, 12*, 402–413.

McCormick, E. J., DeNisi, A. S., & Shaw, J. B. (1979). Use of the Position Analysis Questionnaire for establishing the job component validity of tests. *Journal of Applied Psychology, 64*, 51–56.

McCormick, E. J., Jeanneret, P. R., & Mecham, R. C. (1972). A study of job characteristics and job dimensions based on the Position Analysis Questionnaire (PAQ). *Journal of Applied Psychology, 56*, 347–368.

Mossholder, K. W., & Arvey, R. D. (1984). Synthetic validity: A conceptual and comparative review. *Journal of Applied Psychology, 69*, 322–333.

Nunnally, J. C., & Bernstein, I. H. (1994). *Psychometric theory* (3rd ed.). New York: McGraw-Hill.

Peterson, N. J., Wise, L. L., Arabian, J., & Hoffman, G. (2001). Synthetic validation and validity generalization: When empirical validation is not possible. In J. P. Campbell & D. J. Knapp (Eds.), *Exploring the limits of personnel selection and classification* (pp. 411–451). Mahwah, NJ: Erlbaum.

Primoff, E. S. (1957). The J-coefficient approach to jobs and tests. *Personnel Administrator, 20*, 31–40.

Primoff, E. S. (1959). Empirical validation of the J-coefficient. *Personnel Psychology, 12*, 413–418.

Sackett, P. R., & Arvey, R. D. (1993). Selection in small *N* settings. In N. Schmitt & W. C. Borman (Eds.), *Personnel selection in organizations* (pp. 418–447). San Francisco: Jossey-Bass.

Scherbaum, C. A. (2005). Synthetic validity: Past, present, and future. *Personnel Psychology, 58*, 481–515.

Schmidt, F. L., & Hunter, J. E. (1998). The validity and utility of selection methods in personnel psychology: Practical and theoretical implications of 85 years of research findings. *Psychological Bulletin, 124*(2), 262–274.

Schmidt, F. L., Hunter, J. E., Croll, P. R., & McKenzie, R. C. (1983). Estimation of employment test validities by expert judgment. *Journal of Applied Psychology, 68*, 590–601.

Schmidt, F. L., Hunter, J. E., & Pearlman, K. (1982). Progress in validity generalization: Comments on Callender and Osburn and further developments. *Journal of Applied Psychology, 67*, 835–845.

Schneider, R. J., Hough, L. M., & Dunnette, M. D. (1996). Broadsided by broad traits: How to sink science in five dimensions or less. *Journal of Organizational Behavior, 17*, 639–655.

Society for Industrial and Organizational Psychology. (2003). *Principles for the validation and use of personnel selection procedures.* Bowling Green, OH: Society for Industrial and Organizational Psychology.

Trattner, M. H. (1982). Synthetic validity and its application to the Uniform Guidelines validation requirements. *Personnel Psychology, 35,* 383–397.

Varca, P. E., & Pattison, P. (1993). Evidentiary standards in employment discrimination: A view toward the future. *Personnel Psychology, 46,* 239–258.

Wainer, H. (1978). On the sensitivity of regression and regressors. *Psychological Bulletin, 85,* 267–273.

Wilk, S. L., Desmarais, L., & Sackett, P. R. (1995). Gravitation to jobs commensurate with ability: Longitudinal and cross-sectional tests. *Journal of Applied Psychology, 80,* 79–85.

CHAPTER 5

Validity Generalization as a Test Validation Approach

Michael A. McDaniel

Validity generalization is an application of meta-analysis to the correlations between an employment test and a criterion, typically job or workplace training performance. By employment test, I mean any method used to screen applicants for employment, including cognitive ability tests, personality tests, employment interviews, and reference checks. The purpose of this chapter is to review the use of validity generalization as a test validation strategy. I begin by reviewing the issues of situational specificity, differential validity, differential prediction, and racial and ethnic differences in test performance. In the 1970s, these were issues for which professional consensus had not been reached or professional consensus was later shown to be incorrect. These issues prominently influenced the *Uniform Guidelines on Employee Selection Procedures* (Equal Employment Opportunity Commission, Civil Service Commission, Department of Labor, & Department of Justice, 1978). Subsequent to adoption of the *Uniform Guidelines,* compelling research findings have altered professional consensus on these issues such that the *Uniform Guidelines* are at variance with current professional guidance, thus rendering the *Uniform Guidelines* technically flawed and in need of revision.

Situational Specificity

Dating from the 1920s, researchers observed that different studies using the same employment test showed different validity results (Schmidt & Hunter, 1998). This led to the hypothesis that there were yet-to-be-discovered characteristics of the validity setting (the situation) or the job that caused tests to be valid in one situation but less valid or not valid in another situation. This phenomenon was termed the "situational specificity" hypothesis (Schmidt & Hunter, 1998). It also appeared that the yet-to-be-discovered differences in situations and jobs that caused the varying validity results could not be identified through job analysis. Because the validity of a test appeared to vary across settings, it was argued that employers who used employment tests would need to conduct local studies to determine the validity of the tests in their settings with their jobs. By the 1970s, the situational specificity theory had come to be regarded as a well-established fact (Guion, 1975; Schmidt & Hunter, 2003), and the practice of local validation studies was common.

Beginning in 1977, Schmidt and Hunter began to develop and report data questioning the situational specificity hypothesis. They observed that sampling error was the major source of variation in validity coefficients across studies (Schmidt & Hunter, 1977). They also observed that measurement error reduces observed validity coefficients and that differences across studies in the degree of measurement error would also cause validity coefficients to vary across studies. They further observed that range restriction similarly reduced observed validity coefficients and that likewise differences across studies in the degree of range restriction result in variation in validity coefficients.

As a result and in support of this research, Schmidt and Hunter (1977) developed psychometric meta-analytic procedures (Hunter & Schmidt, 2004) for determining the extent to which the variation in validity across studies was due to sampling error and differences across studies in measurement error and range restriction. They continued to confirm in subsequent research that most of the variation across studies was due to these statistical artifacts (Pearlman, Schmidt, & Hunter, 1980; Schmidt, Gast-Rosenberg, & Hunter, 1980).

Thus, it was confirmed that the variation across studies that had been previously attributed to mysterious situational factors was largely due to these statistical artifacts, primarily simple random sampling error. This application of meta-analysis became known as *validity generalization* when applied to employment validity results. The groundbreaking work of Schmidt and Hunter (1977) and many subsequent meta-analyses of test validity data indicated that the hypothesis of situational specificity, which had been thought to be well-established, was disconfirmed. Unfortunately, the *Uniform Guidelines* had been adopted before this information regarding the situational specificity hypothesis became well known.

Differential Validity and Differential Prediction

By the 1970s, the concept of situational specificity and racial and ethnic differences in test scores also fueled the debate concerning differential validity and differential prediction (Boehm, 1972; Bray & Moses, 1972; Kirkpatrick, Ewen, Barrett, & Katzell, 1968). These hypotheses held that validity or prediction accuracy might vary by racial or ethnic subgroup. Since it appeared that some unknown situational factors caused the validity of tests to vary, it was possible that other unknown factors could cause a test to be valid for Whites but not for minorities. The common finding that Blacks, on average, scored lower than Whites on employment tests fueled the speculation that local validation studies were the best way to determine if a test was valid for all subgroups. However, by the mid-1980s it had become clear that differential validity is very rare (Schmidt, 1988; Schmidt & Hunter, 1981; Wigdor & Garner, 1982). Research on differential validity evolved into research on differential prediction, because even if a test were equally valid for all subgroups, the optimal regression lines to predict job performance might differ. Differential prediction might occur in either differing slopes or differing intercepts. However, research indicated that differing slopes occur at no higher than chance levels (Bartlett, Bobko, Mosier, & Hannan, 1978). Differing intercepts are somewhat less rare, but the error in prediction tends to favor minority groups; that is, when the prediction of job performance for minority groups and Whites is based on a common regression line, performance of the minority groups is often overpredicted when differential prediction exists (Hartigan & Wigdor, 1989; Schmidt, Pearlman & Hunter, 1980). Thus, in the 1980s, it became clear that differential validity is a rarely detected phenomenon, and differential prediction, to the extent that it does exist, does not bias employment tests against minorities. Unfortunately, the *Uniform Guidelines* were written before this research was conducted and widely recognized.

Mean Racial Differences in Employment Test Scores

It is difficult to find an example of a cognitively loaded employment test on which Black or Hispanic minorities perform as well as Whites, on average. Over time, these differences have proven intractable despite various efforts to reduce them, and the magnitude of the differences has been relatively stable. To date there appear to be few, if any, interventions that are consistently effective in reducing these mean differences (Sackett, Schmitt, & Ellingson, 2001). A comprehensive review of Black-White mean differences on general cognitive ability tests indicated that White mean scores are about one standard deviation higher (Roth, BeVier, Bobko, Switzer, & Tyler, 2001). Previous research had indicated smaller differences, but Roth et al. showed how such differences were due to restricted range in the samples. Thus, mean racial differences are smaller in college samples because college samples only include those who have obtained a high school diploma and met other selection criteria of the college. Research places the Hispanic-White mean score difference as somewhat smaller but still substantial. Minority groups have also shown lower mean scores than Whites on less cognitively loaded measures, such as employment interviews (Roth, Van Iddekinge, & Huffcutt, 2002), assessment centers (Fiedler, 2001; Goldstein, Yusko, & Braverman, 1998; Goldstein, Yusko, & Nicolopoulos, 2001), and situational judgment tests (Nguyen, McDaniel, & Whetzel, 2005). To the extent (albeit limited) that personality tests show mean racial differences, they tend to disfavor Blacks (Goldberg, Sweeney, Merenda, & Hughes, 1998; Hough, Oswald, & Ployhart, 2001). Virtually all employment tests show mean racial differences.

Although there had been some early evidence that Black scores were substantially lower than White scores on measures of general cognitive ability, the size and the intractability of that difference became more apparent after the end of the 1970s. Unfortunately, the *Uniform Guidelines* were written before the extent and persistence of racial or ethnic score differences were fully appreciated. Under the *Uniform Guidelines,* when an employer's test use results in differential hiring rates based on this very common finding of mean racial or ethnic score differences, the employer is faced with requirements to demonstrate validity and business necessity. Specifically, employers need to offer validity evidence, which may require the employer to conduct a local validation study, to prepare validity transport evidence, or to participate in a consortium validity study—all of which are activities that require substantial resources.

Addressing the Uniform Guidelines

The widespread acceptance of situational specificity in the 1970s, concerns over potential differential validity and differential prediction, and general uneasiness concerning racial and ethnic mean score differences all formed a part of the world view when the *Uniform Guidelines* were adopted. It is not surprising that the authors of the *Uniform Guidelines* incorporated a number of viewpoints into the regulations that are inconsistent with current scientific thinking. Specifically, the *Uniform Guidelines* are biased in favor of

- Conducting local validation studies
- Conducting differential validity and differential prediction studies
- Requiring detailed and costly job analysis data

In addition, when there are racial disparities in hiring as a result of mean racial differences in test performance, the *Uniform Guidelines* encourage a close examination of the validity of the test rather than viewing the racial difference in test performance as a common finding consistent with many years of cumulative data. Worse yet, they may influence employers to shun employment testing or to follow nonoptimal selection practices such as setting low cutoff scores, banding, and other methods of gerrymandering employment test results in attempts to eliminate the disparity in hiring rates. Thus, the provisions of the *Uniform Guidelines* may encourage employers to make nonoptimal selection decisions that result in productivity losses. Specifically, if an employer engages in nonoptimal implementation of their selection process in order to hire minorities at about the same rates as Whites, they may avoid inquiries by the Equal Employment Opportunity Commission (EEOC) and the Office of Federal Contract Compliance Programs (OFCCP). Ironically, an employer's failure to screen effectively on cognitive skills in its hiring decisions can exacerbate mean racial differences in job performance (McKay & McDaniel, 2006) that may also trigger enforcement agency scrutiny. Use of nonoptimal selection practices can cause serious detriment to the productivity of organizations.

It should be noted that employers may follow nonoptimal selection practices without pressure from enforcement agencies. For example, an employer might seek to hire more minority employees than would be hired using selection tests in the most optimal way because they feel a social, public relations, or business need to do so. However, the *Uniform Guidelines* increase the pressure on employers to make such selection decisions.

Shortly after the adoption of the *Uniform Guidelines,* the Executive Committee of the Society of Industrial and Organization Psychology (SIOP) sent a letter to the authoring agencies of the *Uniform Guidelines* documenting how they were inconsistent with professional guidance. The letter did not result in a revision of the *Uniform Guidelines.* Thus, although the *Uniform Guidelines* state that they are intended to be consistent with professional standards, the federal agencies that are responsible for them have not called for their revision.

Professional Guidelines and Validity Generalization

In contrast to the *Uniform Guidelines,* professional associations have updated professional standards relevant to employment testing to recognize the significant merit of validity generalization analyses. The *Standards for Educational and Psychological Testing* are professional guidelines issued jointly by the American Educational Research Association, the American Psychological Association, and the National Council on Measurement in Education (1999). The *Principles for the Validation and Use of Personnel Selection Procedures* are published by the Society for Industrial and Organizational Psychology (2003). Both the *Standards* and the *Principles* were adopted by the APA and thus have "formal professional status" (Jeanneret, 2005, p. 49). These documents are important because they summarize the best judgment of the profession concerning the state of the science regarding acceptable validation research. They are also important because the *Uniform Guidelines* state:

> The provisions of these guidelines relating to validation of selection procedures are intended to be consistent with generally accepted professional standards for evaluating standardized tests and other selection procedures, such as those described in the Standards for Educational and Psychological Tests prepared by a joint committee of the American Psychological Association, the American Educational Research Association, and the National Council on Measurement in Education . . . and standard textbooks and journals in the field of personnel selection. (Section 5C)

In addition, the *Uniform Guidelines* (Section 5A) state that "New strategies for showing the validity of selection procedures will be evaluated as they become accepted by the psychological profession." Thus, to the extent that the *Uniform Guidelines* are in conflict with professional principles and standards as well as scientific knowledge in textbooks and journals, one can argue that they should be read in concert with those more current professional sources in developing validation evidence for employment tests.

Both the *Standards* and the *Principles* endorse the use of validity generalization as a means for establishing the validity of an employment test. The *Standards* recognize that local validation studies are not preferred over validity generalization evidence. The *Principles* share this view and state:

> Meta-analysis is the basis for the technique that is often referred to as "validity generalization." In general, research has shown much of the variation in observed differences in obtained validity coefficients in different situations can be attributed to sampling error

and other statistical artifacts (Barrick & Mount, 1991; Callender & Osburn, 1980; 1981; Hartigan & Wigdor, 1989; Hunter & Hunter, 1984). These findings are particularly well established for cognitive ability tests; additional recent research results also are accruing that indicate the generalizability of predictor-criterion relationships for noncognitive constructs in employment settings. (p. 28)

The *Principles* also acknowledge that validity generalization is often a better source of validity information than a local validity study (p. 29). In summary, both the *Standards* and the *Principles* have endorsed the usefulness of validity generalization for drawing inferences about the validity of an employment test.

Validity Generalization in Court

In contrast to the effects of validity generalization on the practice and knowledge of personnel selection, the methodology has received limited attention by the courts. Landy (2003) provides an overview of validity generalization in court proceedings and the following draws in part on his overview.

Although predating validity generalization, a case concerning screening for firefighters in Richmond, Virginia, addressed the extent to which validity results are transportable across employers (*Friend et al. v. Leidinger et al.*, 1977). The court found that the firefighter job in Richmond was very similar to the firefighter job in California, where the test had been the subject of a validation study, and that the California study was sufficient validity information for the test to be considered valid in Richmond. The Court of Appeals (*Friend et al. v. City of Richmond et al.*, 1978) agreed with the decision and noted that "To require local validation in every city, village, and hamlet would be ludicrous" (p. 65) (see Gibson & Caplinger (2007) of this volume).

In a reverse discrimination case in the City of Detroit, White applicants claimed reverse discrimination because the City did not use strict rank ordering on a test to select applicants for the fire academy (*Van Aken et al. v. Young and City of Detroit et al.*, 1982). The plaintiff's expert witness used validity generalization to argue that the test should have been used in a top-down manner to achieve maximum utility. The expert argued that cognitive ability tests are valid for all jobs. The court did not accept the argument and noted that the expert knew nothing specific about the Detroit Fire Department and the academy curriculum. I note that the expert's testimony was consistent with the then (and still) current state of scientific knowledge, specifically that cognitive ability tests are valid for all jobs. Thus, it appears that in 1982 the situational specificity hypothesis still influenced some court decisions.

Validity generalization fared better in *Pegues v. Mississippi State Employment Service* (1983). The expert witness provided testimony on the validity generalization based on his analysis of the General Aptitude Test Battery (GATB) validity evidence. The judge cited research indicating that even gross changes in job duties do not destroy validity. He concluded that "Plaintiffs have not shown that the USES tests (in this case the GATB) were invalid because the tasks of the jobs in the research setting may have been different from those in Bolivar County" (p. 1136). Here the judge accepted the scientific conclusions of validity generalization research and clearly rejected situational specificity.

In *EEOC v. Atlas Paper Box Company* (1987), the expert witness used validity generalization research in support of the validity of a cognitive ability test. The trial judge concluded that the sample sizes at Atlas would have been too small to provide meaningful local validity studies. However, in 1989 the Sixth Circuit of Appeals rejected the validation generalization argument:

> The expert witness offered by the defendant, John Hunter, failed to visit and inspect the Atlas office and never studied the nature and content of the Atlas clerical and office jobs involved. The validity of the generalization theory utilized by Atlas with respect to this expert testimony under these circumstances is not appropriate. Linkage or similarity of jobs in this case must be shown by such on site investigation to justify application of such a theory. (p. 1490)

In a concurring but separate opinion, one of the judges stated:

> The first major problem with a validity generalization approach is that it is radically at odds with *Albermarle Paper Co v. Moody* . . . and *Griggs v. Duke Power* and the EEOC *Guidelines,* all of which require a showing that a test is actually predictive of performance of a specific job. (p. 1499)

The judged concluded that "As a matter of law, Hunter's validity generalization is totally unacceptable under relevant case law and professional standard" (p. 1501). Landy (2003) noted that as a Circuit Court of Appeals opinion, this opinion carries much more weight than a trial court opinion. It is binding in the Sixth Circuit Court and would be influential in other circuit courts.

Two cases have been decided with courts giving deference to validity generalization research. In *Bernard v. Gulf Oil Corp.* (1989), the Fifth Circuit upheld the district court decision, which found in favor of the defendant based in part on Drs. Hunter and Sharf's testimony that the cumulative knowledge of the validity of the Bennett Mechanical Comprehension Test supported generalizing validity for selecting craft workers at Gulf refineries. Likewise, in *Taylor v. James River Corp.* (1989), the court gave deference to Dr. Sharf's testimony and ruled the Bennett Mechanical Comprehension Test was valid based on validity generalization evidence.

In sum, some previous court decisions have taken note of what I would refer to as the situational specificity doctrine of the *Uniform Guidelines* and have been unpersuaded by more recent scientific findings. Other decisions have accepted validity generalization scientific findings. The existing and growing disjunction between the *Uniform Guidelines* and the state of the science raises the question of why the federal enforcement agencies have not undertaken to revise the *Uniform Guidelines*.

Why Haven't the Uniform Guidelines Been Revised?

In this section, I offer speculation on why the *Uniform Guidelines* have not been revised. Given that the *Uniform Guidelines* are inconsistent with scientific knowledge, they are not serving their original intention of providing "a framework for determining the proper use of tests and other selection procedures" (Section 3.1). The *Principles* and *Standards* provide guidance on test validity that is consistent with the scientific findings.

Why have the *Uniform Guidelines* not been revised to be consistent with professional standards? It appears to the author that a primary use of the *Uniform Guidelines* is to pressure employers into using suboptimal selection methods in order to hire minorities and

Whites at approximately the same rates. If employers do not hire minorities at about the same rates as Whites, the *Uniform Guidelines* are invoked by enforcement agencies and plaintiffs to require the employer to prepare substantial validity documentation.

It is noted that a revision of the *Uniform Guidelines* would likely cause uncertainty for employers. Currently, employers know what to expect. Revised rules would likely be followed by new litigation serving to clarify ambiguities. For a time, employers would have a less clear understanding of the new rules. Also, a revision of the *Uniform Guidelines* could make matters worse. A new set of *Uniform Guidelines* might continue to ignore current scientific findings and end up even more problematic than the current set. However, the current *Uniform Guidelines* are close to thirty years old and are substantially disparate from scientific findings and other professional principles and standards. In other areas of federal regulations and guidelines, such regulations and guidelines are often updated to reflect scientific knowledge and professional practice. It is well past the time for the *Uniform Guidelines* to be revised.

Validity Generalization and Suggestions for Interpreting Validity Generalization in Support of Test Validity

To use generalization as a test validation strategy, one must find or conduct a meta-analytic study that is applicable to one's needs. Locating such studies is not difficult. Validity generalization studies have been conducted for cognitive ability tests (Hunter, 1980; Hunter & Hunter, 1984; Pearlman, Schmidt, & Hunter, 1980), assessment centers (Winfred, Day, & McNelly, 2003; Gaugler, Rosenthal, Thornton, & Benson, 1987), personality tests (Barrick & Mount, 1991; Hurtz & Donovan, 2000; Salgado, 1997; Tett, Jackson, & Rothstein, 1991), college grades (Dye & Reck, 1989), psychomotor tests (Hunter & Hunter, 1984), short-term memory tests (Verive & McDaniel, 1996), biodata instruments (Carlson, Scullen, Schmidt, Rothstein, & Erwin, 1998; Gandy, Dye, & MacLane, 1994; Rothstein, Schmidt, Erwin, Owens, & Sparks, 1990), customer service tests (Frei & McDaniel, 1998), interviews (Huffcutt & Arthur, 1994; McDaniel, Whetzel, Schmidt, & Maurer, 1994), training and experience assessments (McDaniel, Schmidt, & Hunter, 1988a,

1988b), length of job experience (McDaniel, 1986; McDaniel, Schmidt, & Hunter, 1988b), integrity tests (McDaniel & Jones, 1986; Ones, Viswesvaran, & Schmidt, 1993, 1995, 2003), and job knowledge measures (Dye, Reck, & McDaniel, 1993). Analyses have also been conducted for specific jobs or classes of jobs, including clerical (Pearlman, Schmidt, & Hunter, 1980), police (Hirsh, Northrop, & Schmidt, 1986), fire fighter (Barrett, Polomsky, & McDaniel, 1999), petroleum occupations (Schmidt, Hunter, & Caplan, 1981a, 1981b), and computer programmers (Schmidt, Gast-Rosenberg, & Hunter, 1980).

Considerations in Applying Validity Generalization Results as Support for Test Validation

In this section, I review issues that should be considered when drawing validity inferences about the local use of a test from a validity generalization study. Some of the issues raised should be viewed as the responsibility of the validity generalization researcher in preparing the meta-analysis report. Other issues are better viewed as the responsibility of the employer seeking to use a validity generalization study as evidence supporting test use and interpretation in a local setting. I also refer the reader to Sackett (2003) and the "Suggestions for enhancing the contribution of meta-analysis" section of Rothstein (2003).

Are the jobs in the meta-analysis comparable to the job for which the employer seeks test validity support? There are two issues here. The first issue is whether the job content matters in drawing conclusions about the validity of the test. The second is whether there are some jobs or classes of jobs for which the test has no validity.

If the validity generalization study targets a specific job or class of jobs and the job for which one seeks test validity support is not one of those jobs, one might question the usefulness of the validity generalization study. For example, Pearlman, Schmidt, and Hunter (1980) reported a meta-analysis of tests for clerical jobs. It would not be prudent to rely on that study to support the validity of a test for petroleum engineers. However, there is little evidence that small differences in the tasks performed across jobs within the same job family (Schmidt, Hunter, & Pearlman, 1980) result in substantive differences in relationships with relevant criteria. Many meta-analyses do not report validity differences between jobs or job classes (Gaugler et al., 1987; Hurtz & Donovan, 2000; McDaniel et al., 1994; McDaniel et al., 1988a, 1988b; McDaniel, Morgeson, Finnegan, Campion, & Braverman, 2001). Here, the task would be to argue that the local job is comparable to the jobs in the meta-analysis or that the content of the job is not relevant to the validity of the test.

Some meta-analyses have categorized jobs by the job's characteristics rather than its content. For example, some studies have grouped jobs by the degree of cognitive complexity, where a cognitively complex job is one that places substantial cognitive demands on the incumbent (Hunter & Hunter, 1984; Hunter, 1980; McDaniel, 1986). Thus, the job of rocket scientist has high cognitive complexity whereas the job of poultry eviscerator has lower cognitive complexity. Tests of general cognitive ability are more valid for jobs higher in cognitive complexity, although the validity of cognitive ability tests for jobs at the lowest level of cognitive complexity is still positive. The author knows of no validity generalization studies showing that a test of cognitive ability is valid for one job but not valid for another.

When determining the relevance of a validity generalization study for a local test validation, it would be useful if meta-analysis authors specified the types of jobs contributing data to the meta-analysis. The *Principles* have argued for clear specification of the scope of the meta-analysis. An example is provided of a meta-analysis of interviews, which concludes that "a cumulative database on interviews where content, structure, and scoring are coded could support generalization to an interview meeting the same specification" (p. 30). The *Principles* encourage that the boundary conditions of the meta-analysis be specified with respect to the content, structure, and scoring of the tests. It is suggested that it would be reasonable also to describe the scope of the jobs covered in the meta-analysis.

Is the test examined in the meta-analysis comparable to the test for which one seeks test validity support? Often it is clear that the tests analyzed in the meta-analysis are similar to the test for which one seeks test validation evidence. For example, Ones, Viswesvaran, and Schmidt (1993) listed the names of tests they analyzed in their meta-analysis of integrity tests. Short of listing the names of tests in a meta-analysis, there might be clear evidence that the meta-analysis is relevant to an employer's validation needs. For example, measures of general cognitive ability are highly correlated with each other. Thus, if one seeks validation support for a measure of general cognitive ability, there are several validity generalization studies that document the validity of tests of general cognitive ability (Hunter, 1980; Hunter & Hunter, 1984; McDaniel, Schmidt, & Hunter, 1988a; Pearlman, Schmidt, & Hunter, 1980), so an employer could offer evidence that their test is a cognitive ability test—and that past validity generalization research has demonstrated that cognitive ability tests are valid for all jobs.

The answer to the question of whether a given employer's test is comparable to the tests in the validity generalization study is different when the meta-analysis addresses the validity of a method (for example, an interview, a situational judgment test, an assessment center) than when the meta-analysis addresses the validity of a construct (for example, cognitive ability, conscientiousness). In the case of a method, validity generalization has shown that following a specific procedure, such as a procedure to develop a structured interview, results in a valid measure. The *Principles* argue that inferences from a validity generalization study of a method are more complicated because the interviews may measure different constructs. Another point of view is that validity inferences are not dependent on knowing the constructs assessed; rather, the validity generalization study reflects the validity of a measure developed by following a procedure, such as a procedure for developing a job-related structured interview. From this perspective, the inference from the validity generalization of a method is not more constrained than the inferences drawn from validity generalization of a construct.

Can the reliability and range restriction corrections be defended as accurate? Hartigan and Wigdor (1989) reviewed the use of the GATB and validity generalization. Although validity generalization was accepted by this National Academy of Science Committee, they expressed some concern regarding assumed values of range restriction corrections. Hartigan and Wigdor also expressed some concerns over the assumed values of reliabilities used in corrections. I encourage meta-analytic researchers to specify the details of any assumed values of reliability and range restriction so that an employer using the study as a test validity defense can point to the reasonableness of the corrections. As noted by Sackett (2003), there is still some controversy about the appropriate use of some reliability estimates in meta-analytic corrections.

Are the criteria used in the meta-analysis appropriate for drawing validity inferences regarding a local test? For most meta-analyses, the answer to this question is straightforward because the criterion used in most meta-analyses is job performance, typically assessed through supervisor ratings. However, in some validity generalization analyses based on small numbers of studies, criteria may be grouped in combinations that might serve to hinder efforts to generalize the validity to a local test. For example, Hurtz and Donovan (2000) combined performance rating criterion data with objective sales data in their meta-analysis of personality test validity. Thus, if an employer wanted to use the Hurtz and Donovan data to support the validity of a personality test for a nonsales job, an adversary might argue that the data do not permit an inference to a nonsales job.

Is the meta-analysis sufficiently credible to use as a validity defense? Some meta-analyses are better than others. Consider, for example, an early meta-analysis of integrity tests by McDaniel and Jones (1986). The criteria were almost entirely self-report theft measures. Many would find self-report theft to be an inadequate criterion. Fortunately for those who seek validity generalization studies of integrity tests, more comprehensive studies have been conducted (Ones, Viswesvaran & Schmidt, 1993, 2003). The number of studies summarized in the meta-analysis might also limit its credibility. McDaniel, Schmidt, and Hunter (1988a) reviewed the validity of methods of evaluating training and experience. One type of training and experience (the task method) was based on only ten underlying studies. Although the meta-analytic summary provided the best available validity evidence regarding the task method at that time, an adversary might point out that the validity estimate is based on limited information. A rebuttal argument is that the ten studies provide ten times as much information as a local validation study.

Are the studies in the meta-analysis representative of all studies? Publication bias occurs when the effect sizes (correlations in the case of validity data) analyzed by the researcher are not representative of all available effect sizes. Statistical methods for evaluating potential publication bias have been developed in the medical literature (Rothstein, Sutton, & Borenstein, 2005), but instances of their application to validity data are few. Vevea, Clements, and Hedges (1993) conducted a publication bias analysis of the GATB validity data and concluded that any bias present did not meaningfully affect the conclusion about the validity of cognitive ability tests. However, emerging research results on the employment interview are more unsettling. Readers of the validity generalization studies on the employment interview will likely conclude that structured interviews are substantially more valid than unstructured interviews. Duval (2005) analyzed the data from the McDaniel et al. (1994) meta-analysis of interviews and concluded that there was evidence of publication bias in the distribution of structured interviews such that the validity of structured interviews was overestimated. Although the Duval (2005) analysis is not the final word for the validity of structured employment interviews, it does suggest that it would be prudent for meta-analyses to incorporate publication bias analyses. McDaniel, Rothstein, and Whetzel (in press) applied publication bias methods to data in the technical manuals of three employment test vendors. Evidence of publication bias was found in the analyses of two of the four test vendors. Validity data had been selectively reported by the test vendors and served to overestimate the validity of the test. This unfortunate circumstance could be used by an adversary to question the value of any meta-analysis that has incorporated the vendor's data. I suggest that the validity generalization studies that have evaluated and ruled out publication bias in their data will offer more compelling evidence of validities than those that do not.

Summary and Recommendations

In sum, validity generalization provides reasonable and scientifically defensible evidence for the validity of an employment test and finds support in professional guidelines and research literature. However, the *Uniform Guidelines* were written prior to the development and acceptance of meta-analytically based validity generalization. In addition to encouraging the revision of the *Uniform Guidelines* to be consistent with the scientific knowledge, one can argue that the they can and should be more broadly interpreted. As was noted in discussing the role of professional standards, to the extent that the *Uniform Guidelines* are in conflict with those *Principles* and *Standards,* they should be read in concert. Practitioners must exercise prudent professional judgment in interpreting both the regulatory and the scientific issues. The *Uniform Guidelines* state that they are intended to be consistent with professional guidelines and scientific knowledge. Employers can argue that because the validity inferences they draw from validity generalization studies are consistent with professional principles and scientific knowledge, the validity evidence should be judged as consistent with the underlying requirements of the *Uniform Guidelines.*

References

American Educational Research Association, American Psychological Association, & National Council on Measurement in Education (1999). *Standards for Educational and Psychological Testing.* Washington, DC: American Educational Research Association.

Barrett, G. V., Polomsky, M. D., & McDaniel, M. A. (1999). Selection tests for firefighters: A comprehensive review and meta-analysis. *Journal of Business and Psychology, 13,* 507–514.

Barrick, M. R., & Mount, M. D. (1991). The Big Five personality dimensions and job performance: A meta-analysis. *Personnel Psychology, 44,* 1–26.

Bartlett, C. J., Bobko, P., Mosier, S. B., & Hannan, R. (1978). Testing for fairness with a moderated multiple regression strategy: An alternative to differential analysis. *Personnel Psychology, 31,* 233–241.

Bernard v. Gulf Oil Corporation, 890 F.2d 735, 744 (5th Cir. 1989).

Boehm, V. R. (1972). Differential prediction: A methodological artifact? *Journal of Applied Psychology, 62,* 146–154.

Bray, D. W., & Moses, J. L. (1972). Personnel selection. *Annual Review of Psychology, 23,* 545–576.

Carlson, K. D., Scullen, S. E., Schmidt, F. L., Rothstein, H., & Erwin, F. (1999, Fall). Generalizable biographical data validity can be achieved without multi-organizational development and keying. *Personnel Psychology, 52*(3), pp. 731–755.

Duval, S. J. (2005). The "trim and fill" method. In H. Rothstein, A. J. Sutton, & M. Borenstein (Eds.), *Publication bias in meta analysis: Prevention, assessment, and adjustments* (pp. 127–144). New York: Wiley.

Dye, D. A., & Reck, M. (1989). College grade point average as a predictor of adult success. *Public Personnel Management, 18,* 235–241.

Dye, D. A., Reck, M., & McDaniel, M. A. (1993). The validity of job knowledge measures. *International Journal of Selection and Assessment, 1,* 153–157.

Equal Employment Opportunity Commission, Civil Service Commission, Department of Labor, & Department of Justice. (1978). *Uniform guidelines on employee selection procedures. Federal Register, 43*(166), 38290–39315.

Equal Employment Opportunity Commission v. Atlas Paper Box Company, 680 F. Supp. 1184 (U.S. Dist. 1987).

Fiedler, A. M. (2001). Adverse impact on Hispanic job applicants during assessment center evaluations. *Hispanic Journal of Behavioral Sciences, 23,* 102–110.

Frei, R., & McDaniel, M. A. (1998). The validity of customer service orientation measures in employee selection: A comprehensive review and meta-analysis. *Human Performance, 11,* 1–27.

Friend et al. v. City of Richmond et al., 588 F.2d 61 (4th Cir. 1978).

Friend et al. v. Leidinger et al., 446 F. Supp. 361 (U.S. Dist. 1977).

Gandy, J., Dye, D., & MacLane, C. (1994). Federal government selection: The individual achievement record. In G. Stokes, M. Mumford, & G. Owens (Eds.), *Biodata handbook: Theory, research, and use of biographical information in selection and performance prediction* (pp. 275–310). Palo Alto, CA: CPP Books.

Gaugler, B. B., Rosenthal, D. B., Thornton, G. C., & Benson, C. (1987). Meta-analysis of assessment center validity. *Journal of Applied Psychology, 72,* 493–511.

Gibson, W. M., & Caplinger, J. A. (2007). Transportation of validation results. In S. M. McPhail (Ed.), *Alternative validation strategies: Developing new and leveraging existing validity evidence* (pp. 29–81). San Francisco: Jossey-Bass.

Goldberg, L. R., Sweeney, D., Merenda, P. F., and Hughes, J. E. (1998). Demographic variables and personality: The effects of gender, age, education, and ethnic/racial status on self-descriptors of personality attributes. *Personality and Individual Differences, 24,* 393–403.

Goldstein, H. W., Yusko, K. P., & Braverman, E. P. (1998). The role of cognitive ability in the subgroup differences and incremental validity of assessment center exercises. *Personnel Psychology, 51,* 357–374.

Goldstein, H. W., Yusko, K. P., & Nicolopoulos, V. (2001). Exploring Black-White subgroup differences of managerial competencies. *Personnel Psychology, 54,* 783–807.

Guion, R. M. (1975). Recruiting, selection and job placement. In M. D. Dunnette (Ed.), *Handbook of industrial and organizational psychology* (pp. 777–828). Chicago: Rand McNally.

Hartigan, J. A., & Wigdor, A. K. (Eds.). (1989). *Fairness in employment testing: Validity generalization, minority issues, and the General Aptitude Test Battery.* Washington, DC: National Academy Press.

Hirsh, H. R., Northrop, L., & Schmidt, F. L. (1986). Validity generalization results for law enforcement occupations. *Personnel Psychology, 39,* 399–420.

Hough, L. M., Oswald, F. L., & Ployhart, R. E. (2001). Determinants, detection and amelioration of adverse impact in personnel selection procedures: Issues, evidence and lessons learned. *International Journal of Selection and Assessment, 9,* 152–194.

Huffcutt, A. I., & Arthur, W. (1994). Hunter and Hunter revisited: Interview validity for entry jobs. *Journal of Applied Psychology, 79,* 184–190.

Hunter, J. E. (1980). *Validity generalization for 12,000 jobs: An application of synthetic validity and validity generalization to the General Aptitude Test Battery (GATB).* Washington, DC: U.S. Department of Labor, Employment Service.

Hunter, J. E., & Hunter, R. F. (1984). Validity and utility of alternative predictors of job performance. *Psychological Bulletin, 96,* 72–98.

Hunter, J. E., & Schmidt, F. L. (2004). *Methods of meta-analysis: Correcting error and bias in research findings* (2nd edition). Newbury Park, CA: Sage.

Hurtz, G. M, & Donovan, J. J. (2000). Personality and job performance: The Big Five revisited. *Journal of Applied Psychology, 85,* 869–879.

Jeanneret, R. (2005). Professional and technical authorities and guidelines. In F. J. Landy (Ed.), *Employment discrimination litigation: Behavioral, quantitative, and legal perspectives* (pp. 47–100). San Francisco: Jossey-Bass.

Landy, F. J. (2003). Validity generalization: Then and now. In K. R. Murphy (Ed.), *Validity generalization: A critical review* (pp. 155–195). Mahwah, NJ: Erlbaum.

Kirkpatrick, J. J., Ewen, R. B., Barrett, R. S., & Katzell, R. A. (1968). *Testing and fair employment.* New York: New York University Press.

McDaniel, M. A. (1986). *The evaluation of a causal model of job performance: The interrelationships of general mental ability, job experience, and job performance.* Doctoral dissertation, The George Washington University.

McDaniel, M. A., & Jones, J. W. (1986). A meta-analysis of the employee attitude inventory theft scales. *Journal of Business and Psychology, 1,* 31–50.

McDaniel, M. A., Morgeson, F. P., Finnegan, E. B., Campion, M. A., & Braverman, E. P. (2001). Use of situational judgment tests to predict job performance: A clarification of the literature. *Journal of Applied Psychology, 86,* 730–740.

McDaniel, M. A., Rothstein, H., & Whetzel, D. L. (in press). Publication bias: A case study of four test vendors. *Personnel Psychology.*

McDaniel, M. A., Schmidt, F. L., & Hunter, J. E. (1988a). A meta-analysis of methods for rating training and experience in personnel selection. *Personnel Psychology, 41,* 283–314.

McDaniel, M. A., Schmidt, F. L., & Hunter, J. E. (1988b). Job experience correlates of job performance. *Journal of Applied Psychology, 73,* 327–330.

McDaniel, M. A., Whetzel, D., Schmidt, F. L., & Maurer, S. (1994). The validity of the employment interview: A comprehensive review and meta-analysis. *Journal of Applied Psychology, 79,* 599–616.

McKay, P., & McDaniel, M. A. (2006). A re-examination of Black-White mean differences in work performance: More data, more moderators. *Journal of Applied Psychology, 91,* 538–554.

Nguyen, N., McDaniel, M. A., & Whetzel, D. L. (2005, April). *Subgroup differences in situational judgment test performance: A meta-analysis.* Paper presented at the 20th Annual Conference of the Society for Industrial and Organizational Psychology, Los Angeles.

Ones, D. L., Viswesvaran, C., & Schmidt, F. L. (1993). Comprehensive meta-analysis of integrity test validities: Findings and implications for personnel selection and theories of job performance. *Journal of Applied Psychology, 78,* 679–703.

Ones, D. L., Viswesvaran, C., & Schmidt, F. L. (1995). Integrity tests: Overlooked facts, resolved issues, and remaining questions. *American Psychologist, 50,* 456–457.

Ones, D. L., Viswesvaran, C., & Schmidt, F. L. (2003). Personality and absenteeism: a meta-analysis of integrity tests. Personality and industrial, work and organizational applications. *European Journal of Personality, 17*(Suppl. 1), S19–S38.

Pearlman, K., Schmidt, F. L., & Hunter, J. E. (1980). Validity generalization results for tests used to predict job proficiency and training criteria in clerical occupations. *Journal of Applied Psychology, 65,* 373–406.

Pegues v. Mississippi State Employment Service, 488 F. Supp. 239 (N.D. Miss. 1980), aff's 699 F.2d 760 (5th Cir. 1983), cert denied, 464 U.S. 991, 78 L. Ed. 2d 679, 104 S. CT. 482 (1983).

Roth, P. L., BeVier, C. A., Bobko, P., Switzer, F. S., III, & Tyler, P. (2001). Ethnic group differences in cognitive ability in employment and educational settings: A meta-analysis. *Personnel Psychology, 54,* 297–330.

Roth, P. L., Van Iddekinge, C. H., & Huffcutt, A. I. (2002). Corrections for range restriction in structured interview ethnic group differences: The values may be larger than researchers thought. *Journal of Applied Psychology, 87,* 369–376.

Rothstein, H. R. (2003). Progress is our most important product: Contributions of validity generalization and meta-analysis to the development and communication of knowledge in I/O Psychology. 115–154. In K. R. Murphy (Ed.), *Validity generalization: A critical review*. Mahwah, NJ: Erlbaum.

Rothstein, H. R., Schmidt, F. L., Erwin, F. W., Owens, W. A., & Sparks, C. P. (1990). Biographical data in employment selection: Can validities be made generalizable? *Journal of Applied Psychology, 75*, 175–184.

Rothstein, H. R., Sutton, A. J., & Borenstein, M. (2005). *Publication bias in meta-analysis: Prevention, assessment and adjustments*. West Sussex, England: Wiley.

Sackett, P. R. (2003). The status of validity generalization research: Key issues in drawing inferences from cumulative research findings. In K. R. Murphy (Ed.), *Validity generalization: A critical review* (pp. 91–114). Mahwah, NJ: Erlbaum.

Sackett, P. R., Schmitt, N., & Ellingson, J. E. (2001). High-stakes testing in employment, credentialing, and higher education: Prospects in a post-affirmative-action world. *American Psychologist, 56*, 302–318.

Salgado, J. F. (1997). The five factor model of personality and job performance in the European community. *Journal of Applied Psychology, 82*, 30–43.

Schmidt, F. L. (1988). The problem of group differences in ability test scores in employment selection. *Journal of Vocational Behavior, 33*, 272–292.

Schmidt, F. L., Gast-Rosenberg, I. F., & Hunter, J. E. (1980). Validity generalization results for computer programmers. *Journal of Applied Psychology, 65*, 643–661.

Schmidt, F. L., & Hunter, J. E. (1977). Development of a general solution to the problem of validity generalization. *Journal of Applied Psychology, 62*, 529–540.

Schmidt, F. L., & Hunter, J. E. (1981). Employment testing: Old theories and new research. *American Psychologist, 36*, 1128–1137.

Schmidt, F. L., & Hunter, J. E. (1998). The validity and utility of selection methods in personnel psychology: Practical and theoretical implications of 85 years of research findings. *Psychological Bulletin, 124*, 262–274.

Schmidt, F. L., & Hunter, J. E. (2003). History, development, evolution and impact of validity generalization and meta-analysis methods, 1975–2001.

Schmidt, F. L., Hunter, J. E., & Caplan, J. R. (1981a). *Selection procedure validity generalization (transportability) results for three job groups in the petroleum industry*. Washington, DC: American Petroleum Institute.

Schmidt, F. L., Hunter, J. E., & Caplan, J. R. (1981b). Validity generalization results for two job groups in the petroleum industry. *Journal of Applied Psychology, 66,* 261–273.

Schmidt, F. L., Hunter, J. E., & Pearlman, K. (1980). Task difference and validity of aptitude tests in selection: A red herring. *Journal of Applied Psychology, 66,* 166–185.

Schmidt, F. L., Hunter, J. E., Pearlman, K., & Hirsh, H. R. (1985). Forty questions about validity generalization and meta-analysis (with commentary by P. R. Sackett, M. L. Tenopyr, N. Schmitt, J. Kehoe, & S. Zedeck). *Personnel Psychology, 38,* 697–798.

Schmidt, F. L., Pearlman, K., & Hunter, J. E. (1980). The validity and fairness of employment and educational tests for Hispanic Americans: A review and analysis. *Personnel Psychology, 33,* 705–724.

Society for Industrial and Organizational Psychology. (2003). *Principles for the validation and use of personnel selection procedures* (4th ed.). Bowling Green, OH: Society for Industrial and Organizational Psychology.

Taylor v. James River Corp., 1989 WL 165953 (S.D. Ala. 1989).

Tett, R. P., Jackson, D. N., & Rothstein, M. (1991). Personality measures as predictors of job performance: A meta-analytic review. *Personnel Psychology, 44,* 703–742.

Van Aken et al. v. Young and City of Detroit et al., 541 Supp. 448 (U.S. Dist. 1982).

Verive, J. M., & McDaniel, M. A. (1996). Short-term memory tests in personnel selection: Low adverse impact and high validity. *Intelligence, 23,* 15–32.

Vevea, J. L., Clements, N. C., & Hedges, L. V. (1993). Assessing the effects of selection bias on validity data for the General Aptitude Test Battery. *Journal of Applied Psychology, 78,* 981–987.

Wigdor, A. K., & Garner, W. R. (Eds.). (1982). *Ability testing: Use, consequences, and controversies.* Washington, DC: National Academy Press.

Winfred Jr., A., Day, E. A., & McNelly, T. L. (2003). A meta-analysis of the criterion-related validity of assessment center dimensions. *Personnel Psychology, 56,* 125–154.

CHAPTER 6

Generalizing Personality-Based Validity Evidence

Joyce Hogan, Scott Davies,
and Robert Hogan

Prior to 1977, criterion-related validity research involved testing the hypothesis that a particular predictor variable (such as a cognitive ability measure) covaried reliably with a particular criterion variable (such as performance in training). Researchers then repeated this test using different samples, predictors, and criterion measures. Not surprisingly, results from these studies often differed between locations with similar jobs, and this variability made firm generalizations difficult. More important, this variability challenged the scientific integrity of the entire enterprise of personnel selection.

Researchers often explained the differences in study results in terms of situational specificity: the view that the validity of a measure is specific to the contexts and jobs under study (Gatewood & Feild, 1994; Ghiselli, 1966; Ghiselli & Brown, 1955). These differences required conducting separate validation studies for each organization, job, or group of employees. Using a large database, Schmidt and Hunter (1977) presented evidence showing that the variability in validity coefficients in single-location studies is due to statistical and procedural factors (Guion, 1998, p. 368)—idiosyncratic factors that can be ignored or statistically corrected.

Schmidt and Hunter introduced meta-analysis to psychometric research (as discussed earlier in this book, meta-analysis is a methodology for aggregating correlation coefficients from independent studies testing the same hypothesis). They argued that differences in a test's validity across studies reflect statistical artifacts (such as sampling deficiency) and measurement problems (such as predictor or criterion unreliability, range restriction) and not unique jobs or situations. Subsequent research suggests that the correlations between performance measures and cognitive ability tests (Schmidt & Hunter, 1977), biographical data inventories (Schmidt & Rothstein, 1994), personality inventories (Barrick & Mount, 1991; Barrick, Mount, & Gupta, 2003; Hogan & Holland, 2003; Hough, 1992; Judge, Bono, Ilies, & Gerhardt, 2002; Salgado, 1997, 1998; Tett, Jackson, & Rothstein, 1991), assessment center exercises (Arthur, Day, McNelly, & Edens, 2003; Gaugler, Rosenthal, Thornton, & Bentson, 1987), and situational judgment tests (McDaniel, Morgeson, Finnegan, Campion, & Braverman, 2001) generalize across studies.

Validity generalization (VG) evidence, when available, may be used in place of local validation studies to support the use of a selection procedure (Gatewood & Feild, 1994; Society for Industrial and Organizational Psychology, 2003). As indicated by the *Principles for the Validation and Use of Personnel Selection Procedures* (Society for Industrial and Organizational Psychology, 2003):

> At times, sufficient accumulated validity evidence is available for a selection procedure to justify its use in a new situation without conducting a local validation research study. In these instances, use of the selection procedure may be based on demonstration of the generalized validity inferences from that selection procedure, coupled with a compelling argument for its applicability to the current situation. Although neither mutually exclusive nor exhaustive, several strategies for generalizing validity evidence have been delineated: (a) transportability, (b) synthetic validity/job component validity, and (c) meta-analytic validity generalization. (p. 27)

This chapter illustrates the use of personality measures in VG research. We describe a conceptual model that links personality variables to workplace behavior. We illustrate strategies for using validity evidence from previous studies to apply to new jobs. We use research from managerial jobs as examples of the VG strategy. We then discuss the limitations of these methods and considerations for VG analyses.

Personality Measurement

Most important personality characteristics can be described in terms of five broad dimensions. The five-factor model (FFM) (cf. De Raad & Perugini, 2002; Digman, 1990; Goldberg, 1992; John, 1990, p. 72; McCrae & Costa, 1987; Wiggins, 1996), which is based on fifty years of factor analytic research on the structure of observer ratings (Norman, 1963; Thurstone, 1934; Tupes & Christal, 1961), suggests that we think about and describe people (Goldberg, 1990) in terms of the following themes:

I. *Surgency/Extraversion*—the degree to which a person seems outgoing and talkative
II. *Agreeableness*—the degree to which a person seems pleasant and rewarding to deal with
III. *Conscientiousness*—the degree to which a person complies with rules, norms, and standards
IV. *Emotional Stability*—the degree to which a person appears calm and self-accepting
V. *Intellect/Openness to Experience*—the degree to which a person seems creative and open-minded

The FFM is the basis for several personality inventories constructed over the last twenty years, such as the NEO-PI (Costa & McCrae, 1985), the Hogan Personality Inventory (Hogan, 1986; Hogan & Hogan, 1995; Hogan, Hogan, & Busch, 1984), and the Personal Characteristics Inventory (PCI) (Mount & Barrick, 2001). The FFM provides a useful taxonomy for classifying individual differences in social behavior. In addition, evidence suggests that all existing multidimensional personality inventories can be reconfigured in terms of these five dimensions (De Raad & Perugini, 2002; Wiggins & Pincus, 1992). Consequently, the FFM is useful for classifying personality predictors for VG research (De Raad & Perugini, 2002; Hogan & Holland, 2003).

The FFM is based on observers' descriptions of others, and those descriptions reflect reputation (Hogan, 1983; Hogan & Shelton, 1998). Reputations are based on social consensus regarding consistencies in another person's behavior, as seen in the person's interactions at work and elsewhere; reputations are ubiquitous and enduring facts of social life. Peoples' social behavior consists, at least in part, of efforts to establish, defend, or enhance their reputations (cf. Goffman, 1958). Reputations are public, they tell us about observable tendencies in the others' behaviors, they can be measured reliably, and they can be used to forecast future behavior (cf. Emler, 1990; Ozer & Benet-Martinez, 2006). A person's reputation is an invaluable source of information about work-related strengths and shortcomings, and it also influences the direction of a career.

Personality assessment samples self-presentational behavior—that is, how a person portrays him or herself to others across situations. Assessment instruments allow us to aggregate these behavioral samples, assign them numbers or scores according to certain agreed-upon rules, and then use these scores to make predictions about a person's future behavior. The research described in this chapter used the Hogan Personality Inventory (HPI) (Hogan & Hogan, 1995) to provide data for generalizing validity evidence. The HPI was the first measure of normal personality developed explicitly to assess the FFM in everyday life. The HPI was developed using samples of working adults, and its measurement goal is to predict real-world outcomes—including job performance.

The HPI is a 206-item true-false inventory that contains seven primary scales that are aligned with the FFM. The HPI splits the FFM dimension of Extraversion into Ambition and Sociability (Hogan & Hogan, 1995, p. 11) and Intellect-Openness to Experience into Inquisitive, which reflects creativity, and Learning Approach, which reflects achievement orientation. The internal consistency and test-retest reliability of the scales are as follows: Adjustment (0.89/0.86), Ambition (0.86/0.83), Sociability (0.83/0.79), Interpersonal Sensitivity (0.71/0.80), Prudence (0.78/0.74), Inquisitive (0.78/0.83), and Learning Approach (0.75/0.86). Hogan and Holland (2003) summarize considerable validity evidence for predicting occupational criteria.

Why Personality Matters at Work: A Domain Model of Job Performance

To understand why the validity of personality measures generalizes across contexts, we first need to organize social behavior in terms of its underlying motivational themes. There are two such themes:

(1) most people want to be liked and accepted by others ("getting along"), and (2) most people want power, status, and success ("getting ahead"). Next, we need a framework for classifying performance. We approach this using competencies; we believe every competency model that has been proposed can be classified in terms of four domains, which we call Intrapersonal, Interpersonal, Technical, and Leadership (cf. Bartram, 2005; Hogan & Warrenfeltz, 2003). The structure of our performance domain model with 40 competencies appears in Table 6.1. Previous atheoretical reviews of predictor-performance relationships are useful for estimating the consequences of using a particular class of measures for selection decisions. In principle, however, theory-driven data aggregation should lead to results that are more generalizable. The domain model provides a systematic account of the links between personality and occupational performance.

Metaconcepts and Job Performance Models

We now review this conceptual model in somewhat more detail. Socioanalytic theory (Hogan, 1983, 1996) proposes two generalizations about human nature: (1) people always live (work) in groups, and (2) groups are always structured in terms of status hierarchies. These generalizations suggest two conclusions. First, people need acceptance and approval and want to avoid rejection. These needs translate into behavior designed to "get along" with other members of the group. Supervisors and peers evaluate individuals who are skilled at "getting along" as team players, who are rewarding people with whom to deal. Second, people need status and control of resources, and they try to avoid losing them. At work, these needs translate into behavior designed to "get ahead" or achieve status vis-à-vis other members of the group. Supervisors and peers evaluate individuals who are skilled at "getting ahead" as having initiative and getting results.

Getting along and getting ahead are traditional themes in personality psychology and are often called *agency and communion* (cf. Adler, 1939; Bakan, 1966; Rank, 1945; Wiggins & Trapnell, 1996). Empirical research also shows that these constructs are related to performance outcomes (Barrick, Stewart, & Piotrowski, 2002). Additionally, anthropologists (for example, Redfield, 1960, p. 345) note that societies depend on their members "getting a living and

**Table 6.1. Domain Model of Job Performance,
Example Competencies, and Personality Measures.**

Metaconcept	Domain	Example Competency	FFM Measurement
Getting Ahead	Leadership	Achievement Building Teams Business Acumen Decision Making Delegation Employee Development Initiative Leadership Managing Performance Resource Management	Surgency/Extraversion
	Technical	Analysis Creating Knowledge Decision Making Political Awareness Presentation Skills Problem Solving Safety Technical Skill Training Performance Written Communication	Openness to Experience
Getting Along	Interpersonal	Building Relationships Communication Consultative Skills Cooperating Influence Interpersonal Skill Organizational Citizenship Service Orientation Teamwork Trustworthiness	Agreeableness Surgency/Extraversion
	Intrapersonal	Dependability Detail Orientation Flexibility Following Procedures Integrity Planning Respect Risk Taking Stress Tolerance Work Attitude	Conscientiousness Emotional Stability

living together." "Getting a living" concerns being successful at life tasks, and "living together" concerns maintaining group solidarity—esprit de corps. There are solid conceptual and empirical reasons for organizing the structure of job performance around these metaconcepts of getting along and getting ahead.

Other models of job performance also reflect these themes. Campbell, McHenry, and Wise (1990) proposed that performance in entry-level jobs in the U.S. Army could be evaluated in terms of five dimensions: core proficiency, general soldier proficiency, effort and leadership, personal discipline, and physical fitness and military bearing. Campbell, McCloy, Oppler, and Sager (1993) expanded this taxonomy to include eight factors: job-specific task proficiency, non-job-specific task proficiency, written and oral communication task proficiency, demonstrating effort, maintaining personal discipline, facilitating peer and team performance, supervision and leadership, and management and administration. In Campbell's models, "getting along" is represented by personal discipline and facilitating peer and team performance, whereas "getting ahead" is represented by the proficiency and leadership dimensions.

Borman and Motowidlo (1993) distinguished between task performance and contextual performance—which is non-task performance that is important in all jobs. Task performance seems to correspond to getting ahead and contextual performance corresponds to getting along with others. Borman and Motowidlo then construct a five-dimensional model of contextual performance. Their non-task criterion space overlaps considerably with that described by Campbell, Gasser, and Oswald (1996), and Rotundo and Sackett (2002). In addition, Motowidlo, Borman, and Schmit (1997) described performance in terms of episodes and evaluated it in terms of the perspective of the observer—that is, they organized occupational episodes around the agendas and roles that people use to get along and get ahead.

Hunt (1996) proposed a nine-dimensional model of entry-level job performance based on factor analyses of performance ratings. His model highlighted technical proficiency, but also emphasized contextual performance, organizational citizenship, and pro- versus antisocial behavior, all of which concern getting along at work. Tett, Guterman, Bleier, and Murphy (2000) described a taxonomy that synthesized twelve models of managerial performance. They identified fifty-three performance dimensions, the content of which suggested the well-known factors of structure and consideration (Bass, 1990; Fiedler, 1967; Fleishman, 1953). Managers who provide structure enable groups to get ahead; managers who are considerate facilitate the ability of groups to get along.

Finally, Bartram (2005) analyzed the structure of the universe of competencies, defined as "sets of behaviors that are instrumental to the delivery of desired results" (Bartram, Robertson, & Callinan, 2002, p. 7). He began with two metaconcepts that corresponded to "getting along" and "getting ahead." He expanded the metaconcepts to include eight broad competency factors—"the Great Eight." Competencies that promote getting along included Supporting and Cooperating, Interacting and Presenting, Organizing and Executing, and Adapting and Coping; competencies that promote getting ahead included Leading and Deciding, Analyzing and Interpreting, Creating and Conceptualizing, and Enterprising and Performing. Bartram's competencies overlap with the generalized work activities that Jeanneret, Borman, Kubisiak, and Hanson (1999) proposed as a comprehensive taxonomy of work behaviors required in the U.S. economy.

Job Performance Domains, Their Competencies, and Their Measurement

McClelland and his colleagues (for example, Boyatzis, 1982) introduced the concept of *competency,* which they defined as performance capabilities that distinguish effective from ineffective personnel. McClelland defined competencies empirically in terms of the requirements of particular jobs in particular contexts. This rigorous approach is rare in a field characterized by ad hoc competency models.

As noted previously, we believe that every existing competency model can be organized in terms of a "domain model" first proposed by Warrenfeltz (1995). The model contains four domains: (1) intrapersonal skills; (2) interpersonal skills; (3) technical skills; and (4) leadership skills. Hogan and Warrenfeltz (2003) argued that these four domains form a natural, overlapping developmental sequence, with the later skills depending on the appropriate development of the earlier skills. These domains also form a hierarchy of trainability, in which the earlier skills are harder to train and the later skills are easier to train.

Intrapersonal Skills

Intrapersonal skills develop early in childhood and then have important consequences for career development in adulthood. Two components underlie the domain of intrapersonal skills. The first is core self-esteem (Erez & Judge, 2001; Judge & Bono, 2001), emotional security, or resiliency. People with core self-esteem are self-confident, even-tempered, and positive; they are not easily frustrated, and they bounce back quickly from reversals and disappointments. Persons who lack core self-esteem are self-critical, moody, unhappy, easily frustrated, and need frequent reassurance. Core self-esteem is easily assessed using any well-validated personality measure of emotional stability from the FFM. More important, measures of core self-esteem predict a wide variety of career outcomes, including job satisfaction and performance evaluations (Judge & Bono, 2001).

The second component of intrapersonal skills concerns self-control. Self-controlled people follow rules and respect authority; they are conforming, socially appropriate, and easy to supervise. Persons with low self-control ignore rules and procedures; they are rebellious, refractory, and hard to supervise. Self-control is easily assessed using well-validated personality measures of FFM emotional stability and conscientiousness (Hogan & Hogan, 1989); self-control predicts a wide variety of career outcomes, including supervisors' ratings of satisfactoriness (Hogan & Holland, 2003).

Intrapersonal skills form the foundation on which careers develop. Persons with good intrapersonal skills project integrity; integrity is perhaps the most important characteristic in employability. It is prerequisite for getting along with others because persons who act with integrity gain reputations for being responsible, dependable, and trustworthy.

Interpersonal Skills

Interpersonal skills concern building and sustaining relationships. People with good interpersonal skills seem socially adept, approachable, and rewarding to deal with. Hogan and Warrenfeltz (2003) describe interpersonal skills in terms of three components.

The first is a disposition to put oneself in the place of another person, to anticipate how that person sees the world and what he or she expects during an interaction. The second component involves getting it right when one seeks to anticipate. The third component involves incorporating the information about the other person's expectations into one's subsequent behavior.

Interpersonal skill concerns building and maintaining relationships with a variety of people who might differ from oneself in terms of demographic and psychological characteristics. Interpersonal skill is easily measured using well-validated personality measures of FFM extraversion and agreeableness (Bartram, 2005). Good measures of interpersonal skill predict a wide range of occupational outcomes, including supervisory performance (cf. Hogan & Hogan, 2001; Riggio, 1989). These skills are prerequisite for getting along with others because they are the foundation for establishing and sustaining relationships.

Technical Skills

The domain of technical skills is included in every comprehensive model of performance; it differs from the preceding two domains in several ways. Technical skills can be taught, and they are the least dependent on being able to deal with other people. Technical skills involve comparing, copying, compiling, computing, analyzing, coordinating, innovating, synthesizing, and so on (Peterson, Mumford, Borman, Jeanneret, & Fleishman, 1999). These skills can be assessed using work simulations, assessment center exercises, and content-valid tests; the best predictors of individual differences in technical skills are measures of cognitive ability (Hunter & Hunter, 1984; Ree & Earles, 1992).

Interest in training and acquiring new technical knowledge is also part of this domain. The tendency to value education can be assessed using well-validated measures of the FFM dimension of openness to experience. These measures predict technical outcomes such as supervisor ratings of judgment, market savvy, training progress, and job knowledge (Hogan & Holland, 2003). Technical skills are prerequisite for getting ahead because persons who seem knowledgeable and competent are a resource for the performance of their group.

Leadership Skills

Leadership skills are relevant for performance in virtually any job. Leadership skills, which concern building and maintaining effective teams, can be understood in terms of five components—which depend on intrapersonal, interpersonal, and technical skills.

The first component is recruiting talented people to a team. The second component involves retaining that talent once it is recruited. The third component of leadership skills concerns motivating a team; other things being equal, a motivated team will outperform a talented but less motivated group. Recruiting, retaining, and motivating team members all depend on building positive relationships with each team member, a capability that builds on the interpersonal skills described above. The fourth component concerns developing and promoting a vision for the team. The vision legitimizes the team enterprise. Technical competence is needed to develop the vision, and interpersonal skills are needed to sell it. The final component of leadership skill concerns being persistent and hard to discourage. Persistence probably depends on core self-esteem and conscientiousness, although there is little research on the topic.

Leadership skill can be assessed using any number of well-validated procedures, although the most effective assessment uses a combination of methods. Historically, assessment centers have been used extensively. Recent meta-analyses indicate that measures of cognitive ability (Judge, Colbert, & Ilies, 2004) and personality substantially predict both leadership emergence and effectiveness (Judge, Bono, Ilies, & Gerhardt, 2002). Leadership skills are prerequisite for getting ahead because leadership by definition involves the pursuit of status.

Summary

We use the domain model to organize the content of performance and its measurement in VG research. The metaconcepts (getting along and getting ahead) and four competency domains are inclusive and exhaustive; they also resemble Hough and colleagues' notion of taxons (Hough & Ones, 2001; Hough & Schneider, 1996). Both approaches are flexible and inclusive, and in VG research, flexibility and inclusiveness are essential because every organization views its jobs as unique.

Converging Validity Generalization Evidence

The *Standards for Educational and Psychological Testing* (American Educational Research Association, American Psychological Association, & National Council on Measurement in Education, 1999) and the *Principles* use the term VG to refer to meta-analysis, transportability of validity, and synthetic or job component validity. These three techniques are used to evaluate the validity of selection procedures in particular cases. Although best practice dictates using multiple sources of validity evidence to evaluate a test (Binning & Barrett, 1989; Messick, 1995), we know little about using multiple VG models for this purpose. Projects by Hoffman, McPhail, and their colleagues (for example, Hoffman, Holden, & Gale, 2000; Hoffman & McPhail, 1998) and Johnson, Carter, and their colleagues (for example, Johnson, Carter, Davison, & Oliver, 2001), which used cognitive measures for VG across several job families in a single organization, are notable exceptions. Combining validity information from various sources requires technical expertise and professional judgment (Hoffman et al., 2000; Landy, 1986), but doing so should yield more defensible selection procedures than using a single strategy as endorsed by the *Uniform Guidelines on Employee Selection Procedures* (Equal Employment Opportunity Commission, Civil Service Commission, Department of Labor, & Department of Justice, 1978).

We generalize validity evidence from the HPI using the domain model (Table 6.1) and the Hogan Archive, which contains over two hundred validity studies spanning twenty-five years. Meta-analysis and synthetic or job component validity research depend on using archival validity data that can be aggregated. VG research is appropriate when resources preclude local validation, when an organization needs to hire immediately for newly created jobs, or when many jobs contain only a single incumbent. The research proceeds through five steps:

1. Analyze the personality-based job requirements for the marker job, and use the results to guide the subsequent study.

2. Aggregate meta-analytic validity evidence for the marker job from the published literature and the Hogan Archive.
3. Conduct transportability of validity research using criterion-related validity data from the "original study" in the Hogan Archive to the "new location" as required by the *Uniform Guidelines*.
4. Conduct synthetic validity or job component validity research using competency ratings, examples of which are illustrated in Table 6.1. Using the Hogan Archive, meta-analyze correlations between personality predictors and competency ratings, then use the results to define and evaluate a test battery.
5. Examine the validity evidence from the three VG sources, compose a battery for the new job, and simulate the consequences of various cutoff scores using archival data.

In the following sections, we go through these steps using managerial jobs as an example of how to conduct personality-based VG studies.

Step One. Analyze Personality-Based Requirements for the Marker Job

The *Uniform Guidelines* emphasize that all validity studies should be based on a job analysis or review. The *Uniform Guidelines* require documenting (1) the required work behaviors or outcomes, (2) the criticality of the work behaviors or outcomes, and, if applicable, (3) the evidence and rationale for grouping two or more jobs. Tippins and McPhail (2002) described these requirements in detail. Generalizing validity requires information about the job for which validity evidence is available and the job to which one wants to generalize. The goal is to evaluate the similarity of the two jobs. We use standardized job analysis methods to determine similarity; this allows us to estimate the defensibility and the possible error associated with a VG analysis. We use a mixed-method, multiple-step job analysis as follows:

1. Review existing information about the marker job.
2. Code the important dimensions from the job descriptions.
3. Match the job to existing databases, including the O*NET (Peterson et al., 1999) descriptions and DOL job family typology.

4. Ask subject matter experts (SMEs) to complete a worker-oriented, personality-based job analysis, the Job Evaluation Tool (JET) (Hogan Assessment Systems, 2000).
5. Conduct job observations, interviews, and critical incident focus groups with incumbents.

Typically, organizations have position descriptions for the marker job that contain useful information. We also use O*NET codes to determine the similarity of jobs, and the JET is rationally linked to O*NET classifications. D'Egidio (2001) also provided empirical links between the HPI and O*NET ratings.

Most people assume that job analysis is a well-defined methodology. Cornelius (1988, p. 48) concluded that it is not; based on decades of research, he suggested that the best way to identify "necessary job traits" is to review "mental, social, and physical" traits using the Position Analysis Questionnaire (PAQ) (McCormick, Jeanneret, & Mecham, 1972). Dunnette and Borman (1979) and Guion (1998) referred to the PAQ as a milestone in worker-oriented job analysis, and the PAQ is good way to understand the cognitive requirements of a job. But the PAQ provides little information about a job's noncognitive demands. Other than in Raymark, Schmit, and Guion's (1997) Personality-Related Position Requirements Form, the noncognitive domain is not emphasized in any well-established, standardized job analysis method. We developed the Performance Improvement Characteristics (PIC) checklist to identify personality-based job requirements; it is part of the JET.

We use the JET to determine the critical requirements of a job in terms of (1) the personal capabilities that would improve performance and (2) the critical competencies required for effective performance. The JET contains five sections covering various taxonomies of job performance; sample items from the JET are included in Exhibit 6.1. We use the PIC and the Competency Evaluation Tool (CET) sections of the JET for personality-based VG research. They are used to evaluate the competencies and personality requirements of the domain model (Table 6.1).

Quantitative Job Analysis

The PIC checklist identifies (1) the personal characteristics (see measurement constructs in Table 6.1) needed for a job, and (2) the degree to which performance on the job is enhanced by them

(Hogan & Rybicki, 1998). SMEs rate jobs on scales ranging from 0 (*Does Not Improve Performance*) to 3 (*Substantially Improves Performance*). Harvey (1991) recommends expressing job analysis methods and selection constructs in common terms; thus the forty-eight PIC items form seven scales that align with the seven HPI scales (see Table 6.2). Internal consistency reliability estimates for the PIC scales range between 0.76 (Adjustment) and 0.87 (Interpersonal Sensitivity); the average is 0.83. Test-retest reliability, estimated over a one-month interval, ranges between 0.60 (Learning Approach) and 0.84 (Inquisitive), with reliabilities of 0.80, 0.73, 0.69, 0.69, and 0.64 for the Ambition, Sociability, Interpersonal Sensitivity, Prudence, and Adjustment scales, respectively.

We obtain PIC scale scores by (1) summing the item ratings on each of the seven scales, (2) averaging the scores for each scale across raters, and (3) converting the average scale scores to percentiles using a national database. The raw scores for each scale and their standard errors of measurement are used to compare PIC profiles across different jobs. Previous research indicates that the PIC checklist differentiates among jobs, and scores on PIC scales correlate with the HPI scales that predict job performance (Foster & Anderson, 2006; Rybicki, 1997; Tett, Holland, Hogan, & Burnett, 2002). The results of these studies support the validity of the PIC results for job analyses across different jobs and organizations (Harvey & Wilson, 2000).

SMEs use the CET portion of the JET to rate the criticality of forty competencies for successful job performance (see Exhibit 6.1). SMEs evaluate the importance of each competency for the target job using a five-point scale, where 0 is defined as *Not associated with job performance* and 4 is defined as *Critical to job performance*. The forty CET competencies map onto the four performance domains presented in Table 6.1, as well as onto other competency and performance models described previously in this chapter.

Internal consistency reliability estimates for domain scores, using ratings across 951 archived jobs for the forty CET items, are 0.76 for Intrapersonal, 0.72 for Interpersonal, 0.77 for Technical, and 0.89 for Leadership; the average is 0.78. Average SME interrater reliability within a job was estimated using intraclass correlations (Shrout & Fleiss, 1979). Across thirty-five jobs, average interrater reliability is 0.44 for a single rater, and 0.82 for a set of seven raters (Hogan Assessment Systems, 2006).

Exhibit 6.1. Sample Items from the Job Evaluation Tool.

JET Section

Performance Improvement Characteristics (PIC)

The forty-eight-item PIC job analysis identifies (1) the personal characteristics needed to execute successfully the requirements of a job and (2) the degree to which possession of these personal characteristics improves job performance.

Sample Item

Would job performance IMPROVE if a _____[a] . . . ?

> Is steady under pressure
>
> Has clear career goals
>
> Seems to enjoy social interaction
>
> Is kind and considerate

Derailment Characteristics (DC)

The twenty-two-item DC job analysis identifies (1) personal characteristics that can inhibit performance in a specified job, and (2) the degree to which these personal characteristics degrade job performance.

Sample Item

Would job performance DECLINE if a _____[a] . . . ?

> Becomes irritable when frustrated
>
> Resents criticism and takes it personally
>
> Avoids taking any risks
>
> Is typically silent and uncommunicative

Motives and Interests (MI)

The forty-item MI job analysis assesses the environment in which an employee works and the values that help define workgroup climate.

Sample Item

The _____[a] work group(s) in our organization . . .

> Do things to improve the appearance of offices and facilities
>
> Enjoy meeting new people
>
> Show sympathy for those with personal problems
>
> Set clear financial goals for the work group

Exhibit 6.1. Sample Items from the Job Evaluation Tool, Cont'd.

Competency Evaluation Tool (CET)

The CET allows SMEs to indicate the criticality of performance competencies to successful job performance.

Sample Item

> Stress Tolerance—Handles pressure without getting upset, moody, or anxious
>
> Teamwork—Works well in groups and is a good team player
>
> Decision Making—Evaluates issues and uses sound reasoning to make decisions
>
> Initiative—Takes action before being told what to do

Cognitive Job Analysis

The thirty-item cognitive job analysis measure allows SMEs to assess the strategic reasoning, tactical reasoning, and operations for reasoning components of job performance.

Sample Items

Please rate the importance of each reasoning statement for performance on the job.

> Anticipate opportunities that will affect planning and direction
>
> Follow problems back to their cause
>
> Interpret information in text, numeric, or graphic media accurately

[a]Blanks represent where job titles should be inserted.

Job Analysis Results for a Marker Managerial Job: Case Study

A multinational telecommunications company wanted to improve its selection procedures for entry-level management jobs because the jobs are the starting point for management succession. The organization thought its current selection system could be enhanced by using valid personality assessments. The organization provided a description of a job corresponding to the 11–1021.00 "General and Operations Managers" O*NET code. The O*NET description is

> Plan, direct, or coordinate the operations of companies or public and private sector organizations. Duties and responsibilities include

Table 6.2. Performance Improvement Characteristics and Hogan Personality Inventory Scale Definitions.

Scale Name	Definition Sample PIC Item
Rating Instruction	The degree performance improves if an incumbent . . .
Adjustment	Is calm, self-accepting, and even-tempered
	Is steady under pressure
Ambition	Is socially self-confident and competitive
	Takes initiative—solves problems on own
Sociability	Seems to need and/or enjoy interacting with others
	Seems to enjoy social interaction
Interpersonal Sensitivity	Is seen as perceptive, tactful, and socially sensitive
	Is warm and friendly
Prudence	Seems conscientious, conforming, and dependable
	Is self-controlled and conscientious
Inquisitive	Seems creative and interested in intellectual matters
	Is imaginative and open-minded
Learning Approach	Seems to value learning or training for its own sake
	Keeps up on advances in the profession

formulating policies, managing daily operations, and planning the use of materials and human resources, but are too diverse and general in nature to be classified in any one functional area of management or administration, such as personnel, purchasing, or administrative services. Includes owners and managers who head small business establishments whose duties are primarily managerial.

SMEs ($N = 225$) described the job using the PIC and CET sections of the JET. SMEs had an average of 6.3 years experience supervising the job they rated and 3.2 years experience as incumbents in these jobs. SMEs rated a representative sample of management-level jobs. The PIC results defined the personal characteristics associated with effective job performance. As seen in Figure 6.1, these included leadership (Ambition), resilience (Adjustment), conscientiousness (Prudence), and staying up to date (Learning Approach). Enjoying social interaction (Sociability) was less important for the

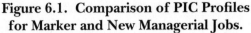

Figure 6.1. Comparison of PIC Profiles for Marker and New Managerial Jobs.

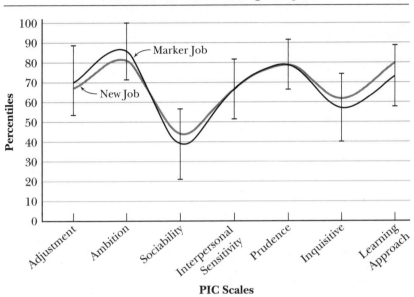

job. Note that this profile combines the elements of getting along and getting ahead, which are important for success as a manager.

SMEs also evaluated job competencies using the CET. Thirteen competencies had mean ratings greater than 3, which is interpreted as *Important to job performance.* Descriptive statistics for these ratings appear in Table 6.3. Average interrater reliability across the forty CET competencies was 0.89. They suggest that effective managers must act with integrity, make timely and well-reasoned decisions, be technically skilled, and provide vision—themes that appear in the job descriptions for management-level employees and are consistent with implicit leadership theory (Lord, DeVader, & Alliger, 1986).

Step Two. Analyze Meta-Analytic Evidence from Validity Studies for the Marker Job

The *Principles* recognize meta-analysis as a method "that can be used to determine the degree to which predictor-criterion relationships are specific to the situations in which the validity data

Table 6.3. Descriptive Statistics for CET Dimensions Rated as Important to Job Performance for Target Job.

Competency	Mean SME Rating	Standard Deviation	Performance Domain
Integrity	3.69	0.50	Intrapersonal
Decision Making	3.50	0.52	Technical
Business Acumen	3.38	0.51	Leadership
Resource Management	3.38	0.57	Leadership
Flexibility	3.28	0.55	Intrapersonal
Stress Tolerance	3.28	0.60	Intrapersonal
Achievement	3.20	0.58	Leadership
Teamwork	3.19	0.61	Interpersonal
Communication	3.17	0.69	Interpersonal
Initiative	3.17	0.57	Leadership
Leadership	3.15	0.54	Leadership
Planning	3.14	0.66	Intrapersonal
Employee Development	3.13	0.61	Leadership

Note: $N = 225$. Ratings made on a five-point scale, ranging from 0 (*Not associated with job performance*), to 4 (*Critical to job performance*). A rating of 3 is anchored with *Important to job performance*.

have been gathered or are generalizable to other situations, as well as to determine the sources of cross-situation variability" (Aguinis & Pierce, 1998, p. 28). Pearson (1904; as cited in Rosenthal & Di-Matteo, 2001) reported meta-analytic results evaluating the efficacy of vaccinations over one hundred years ago. However, the method was not used to evaluate selection test validity until the late 1970s, and it was not the first method to be used (cf. Lawshe, 1952). Of the three VG methods, meta-analysis provides the most generalizable results, but it relies exclusively on criterion-related validity studies. Transportability and synthetic or job component validity research is less generalizable, but can use either content or criterion-related research as source data.

Meta-analysis averages findings from multiple studies of the same relationship to provide a best estimate of ρ (that is, the population correlation) by controlling for error due to sampling, measurement range restriction, and moderators (Smith & Glass, 1977). In addition, there are standardized criteria for deciding what studies to include, what variables to code, effect size comparisons, and moderator identification. Ideally, a meta-analysis includes all relevant studies; however, this is often impossible because studies with insignificant results are less likely to be published. Rosenthal (1979) notes that such omissions are problematic for meta-analytic research based on few studies, small sample sizes, and an atheoretical base.

According to the *Principles,* "reliance on meta-analysis results is more straightforward when they are organized around a construct or set of constructs" (p. 30). Schmidt and Hunter (1977) used a construct orientation in their well-known meta-analysis of cognitive ability measures. Hogan and Holland (2003) did the same using the domain model in Table 6.1 as the basis for a meta-analysis of the validity of personality predictors (see Table 6.1). A construct-driven approach has two advantages. First, theory drives professional judgment, which is unavoidable when compiling data from multiple studies. Second, a theory-driven approach provides a framework for interpreting the results. The remainder of this section describes a meta-analysis of personality measures and managerial jobs.

Meta-Analysis of Personality Measures for a Managerial Job: Case Study

We proceeded in two phases. First, we identified a set of studies whose predictors and criteria are relevant for the job family. Several meta-analyses have focused on managerial jobs. Barrick and Mount (1991) found that FFM factors Conscientiousness ($\rho = 0.22$) and Extraversion ($\rho = 0.18$) predicted all managerial performance criteria (that is, job proficiency, training proficiency, and personnel data). Barrick and Mount (1993) reported once again that Conscientiousness ($r = 0.25$) and Extraversion ($r = 0.14$) were significantly related to job performance. More recently, Hurtz and Donovan (2000) found that Conscientiousness ($\rho = 0.17$), Extraversion ($\rho = 0.12$), and Emotional Stability ($\rho = 0.12$) reliably predict managerial performance. Focusing on leadership, Judge, Bono, Ilies, and Gerhardt (2002) found that Emotional Stability ($\rho = 0.24$), Extraversion ($\rho = 0.31$), Openness to Experience ($\rho = 0.24$), and

Conscientiousness ($\rho = 0.28$) predict performance. The most generalizable measure across samples and criteria was Extraversion (which includes Ambition). Finally, Larson, Rottinghaus, and Borgen (2002) and Barrick, Mount, and Gupta (2003) examined the relationship between the FFM and Holland's RIASEC occupational types. Extraversion ($\rho = 0.41$) predicted interest in persuading and leading others to reach organizational or economic goals. Together, these analyses suggest that Emotional Stability, Extraversion, Conscientiousness, and Openness to Experience predict performance in the managerial-level job family.

Second, we searched the Hogan Archive for studies that include supervisor as well as entry-level, middle, and executive management jobs (Foster & Hogan, 2005) and identified thirty-five such studies. Each study reported correlations between the HPI scales and job performance criteria. We aggregated the correlations for each scale across studies, using meta-analysis (Hunter & Schmidt, 1990) to estimate the true relationship between the predictor variables and job performance.

All studies used zero-order product-moment correlations. We corrected for sampling error, unreliability in the measures, and range restriction. We estimated the reliability of the personality measures using within-study coefficient alpha [$M = 0.78$; range = 0.71 (Prudence) to 0.84 (Adjustment)], rather than using the values reported in the HPI manual. Following Barrick and Mount (1991) and Tett et al. (1991), we used the 0.508 reliability coefficient proposed by Rothstein (1990) to estimate the reliability of supervisory ratings of job performance. We also computed a range restriction index for HPI scales. Following Hunter and Schmidt (1990), we divided each HPI scale's within-study standard deviation by the standard deviation reported in the test manual. This yields an index of range restriction for each HPI scale for each study. When a within-study standard deviation was unavailable, we used mean replacement within job family to estimate range restriction correction factors for each scale.

We averaged correlations within studies so that each sample contributed only one estimate per scale. Note that this procedure uses negative and positive correlations rather than absolute values for averaging correlations, which differs from the analyses reported by Tett et al. (1991, p. 712). We did not correct correlations to estimate validity at the construct level. Although some (for example, Mount & Barrick, 1995; Ones, Viswesvaran & Schmidt, 1993) have argued this artifact can be corrected, we believe it is premature to estimate the validity of the perfect construct when there is no agreement about the definition of the perfect construct.

Table 6.4 contains the correlations for managerial performance. Consistent with previous research, HPI Adjustment and Ambition (FFM Emotional Stability and Extraversion [in part]) are the best predictors of performance. Again consistent with earlier results, Prudence and Interpersonal Sensitivity (FFM Conscientiousness and Agreeableness) predict overall performance, but less well. Finally, Sociability, Inquisitiveness, and Learning Approach (FFM Extraversion [in part] and Openness) had positive but small correlations with job performance, suggesting that they might be important in some specific cases.

Every meta-analytic study reviewed here (that is, Barrick & Mount, 1991; 1993; Barrick et al., 2003; Foster & Hogan, 2005; Hurtz & Donovan, 2000; Judge et al., 2002; Larson et al., 2002) supports the use of personality measures for selection into management jobs.

Table 6.4. Meta-Analytic Correlations between HPI Scales and Overall Performance for the Managerial Job Family.

HPI Scale	N	K	r_{obs}	ρ_v	ρ
Adjustment	3,751	35	0.15	0.20	0.22
Ambition	3,751	35	0.21	0.29	0.31
Sociability	3,751	35	0.05	0.07	0.08
Interpersonal Sensitivity	3,751	35	0.09	0.13	0.15
Prudence	3,751	35	0.08	0.11	0.13
Inquisitive	3,751	35	0.05	0.07	0.08
Learning Approach	3,074	31	0.07	0.10	0.12

Note: N = number of participants across K studies; K = number of studies; r_{obs} = mean observed validity; ρ_v = operational validity (corrected for range restriction and criterion reliability only); ρ = true validity at scale level (corrected for range restriction and predictor-criterion reliability).

However, each study provides a slightly different estimate of the predictor-criterion relationships because they use different measures. Our meta-analysis (Foster & Hogan, 2005) used a single measure of the FFM (the HPI) and is consistent with the results from earlier published studies; consequently, we conclude that the HPI Adjustment ($\rho = 0.22$), Ambition ($\rho = 0.31$), Interpersonal Sensitivity ($r = 0.15$), Prudence ($r = 0.13$), and Learning Approach ($\rho = 0.12$) scales are the best predictors of managerial job performance. We used Nunnally's (1978) equation (cf. Johnson, Carter, and Tippins, 2001) to estimate the relationship between these scales and overall performance:

$$ r_{y_c x_c} = \frac{\overline{r_{y_i x_i}}}{\sqrt{\overline{r_{yy}}} \; \sqrt{\overline{r_{xx}}}} $$

Based on this estimate, the overall validity of the test battery is $r = 0.33$.

Step Three. Research Transportability of Validity from Personality Predictors

The next step in the VG process is to transport validity evidence from one job to another, similar job. The primary reference for the transportability of validity is the *Uniform Guidelines*. Hoffman, McPhail and colleagues (Hoffman & McPhail, 1998; Tippins, McPhail, Hoffman, & Gibson, 1999) discuss the technical requirements for test transportability in situations that preclude local validation and use the *Uniform Guidelines* as a reference. Johnson and Jolly (2000) provide an empirical demonstration of the method and note the lack of guidance for its appropriate use.

The *Principles* consider transportability of validity as one of three VG strategies for justifying a selection procedure. Transportability involves using a selection procedure in a new situation based on evidence established in another situation. This process assumes that the original validation study was technically sound and that the jobs are "closely related" (*Bernard v. Gulf Oil Corp.*,

1989). Situations in which transportability might apply include choosing a selection procedure for the same job across multiple locations and different companies or for different jobs with similar requirements. It might also be useful for different job titles within a single job family (see Gibson & Caplinger, 2007, this volume).

The *Uniform Guidelines,* the *Standards,* and the *Principles* all recognize transportability of selection procedures (cf. Tippins, 2003). Although employment discrimination experts distinguish between these three documents, we focus on their common themes. For example, all three require that the original research be technically adequate. The *Uniform Guidelines* emphasize the need for evidence regarding fairness as well as validity and job similarity as criteria for transportability. Personality-based selection procedures typically yield no adverse impact, which meets requirements set by the *Uniform Guidelines* and precedents in many courts (Lindemann & Grossman, 1996). However, fairness is generally considered a social rather than a psychometric issue (*Principles,* 2003, p. 31).

The *Standards* emphasize the need for good cumulative research (such as meta-analysis) and discourage relying on single local validation studies unless they are "exceptionally sound." Interestingly, the original design for transportability of a selection procedure relies on a single validation study. The *Principles* emphasize the importance of job similarity in the original and the new job. Evidence of similarity comes from job requirements, job context, and job applicants. For personality-based selection systems, demonstrating job similarity has been a problem because few job analysis methods were available. Notable exceptions are Raymark et al. (1997) and the JET methodology.

Job similarity is the key to transporting test validity. The success of the strategy rests on (1) establishing validity in a marker job and then (2) demonstrating that the marker job is comparable to the job to which the validity evidence is to be transported. We estimate similarity using converging evidence and professional judgment.

Transportability of Validity for a Managerial Job: Case Study

We conduct transportability of validity research in two steps. First, we analyze the "new location" target managerial job in qualitative and quantitative terms. Second, we identify an "original location" marker managerial job for which there is a validation study. In the present case, we identified the job in the Hogan Archive based on identical O*NET codes, similar PIC profiles (see Figure 6.1), overlapping competencies from the CET, and similar applicant pools. The O*NET typology provided a standard external metric for rating job similarity.

We evaluate the similarity of the new job to the job in the Hogan archive using PIC profiles and CET importance ratings. We determine the similarity of PIC profiles by calculating the standard error of measurement (SE_{msmt}) for each of the seven PIC scales based on the coefficient alpha for each using the following formula:

$$SE_{msmt} = s_t \sqrt{1 - r_{xx'}}$$

where s_t is the standard deviation of the PIC scale and $r_{xx'}$ is the reliability of the scale.

We construct a 95-percent confidence interval for each scale by adding and subtracting 1.96 SE_{msmt} to and from each raw score scale mean. We compare each PIC scale mean for the target job with the confidence interval for the same scale for the marker job. The jobs are sufficiently similar for transportability of validity if the seven scale means for the target job fall within the 95-percent confidence intervals. Figure 6.1 presents PIC profiles with each scale mean, defined as a percentile calculated from the raw score mean divided by total possible raw score for the scale; we calculate the confidence interval for each scale in the same way.

Overlap analyses of CET ratings provide further evidence of job similarity. In this example, twelve of the thirteen competencies rated as important for the target job were also rated as important for the marker job. We also computed Tilton's (1937) overlap statistic:

$$N_s / N_s + N_d$$

where N_s (that is, n = 41) is the number of competencies evaluated in the same way for both the target and marker jobs (that is, either both important or both not important), and N_d (that is, n = 15) is the number evaluated differently. This overlap statistic was 0.73.

Moreover, the correlation between ratings for the two jobs on the twenty important competencies was 0.96. Finally, mean differences across jobs for competencies rated as important averaged 0.21, and ranged from 0.05 to 0.3 on the 0 to 4 scale; this indicates substantial agreement among the SMEs regarding the similarity of the two jobs.

We judged similarity of applicant pools across the target and marker jobs using the demographics of the SME samples in the job analysis, the incumbent samples in the criterion studies, and the subsequent applicant pool for the positions. Specifically, the samples for each job were primarily white (64 percent and 74 percent) and male (69 percent and 71 percent). We also compare mean HPI scale scores for the two incumbent samples; mean differences between the two groups for each scale were within one standard error of measure.

Based on this converging evidence on job similarity, the similarity of the potential applicant pools, and the existence of an adverse impact study, we determined that Study #324 from the Hogan Archive was appropriate for transporting validation evidence. Table 6.5 presents correlations between the HPI scales and the important competencies for Study #324. The average corrected correlations between the HPI and the twelve competencies for this managerial sample are as follows: Adjustment (0.34); Ambition (0.20), Interpersonal Sensitivity (0.14), and Prudence (0.16). The similarity of the jobs indicates that the test battery can be transported and used for selection into the new job. Applying the equation for the correlation of a linear composite (Nunnally, 1978), the validity of the test battery for predicting overall job performance is 0.33.

Step Four. Research Synthetic Validity or Job Component Validity for Personality Measures

The most specific validity generalizability evidence comes from synthetic validity or job component validity research. Mossholder and Arvey (1984) noted that meta-analysis relies on global evaluations of job similarity, whereas synthetic validity requires a detailed examination of the work. The strategy is criterion driven and the selection procedure resembles using canonical correlations—that is,

Table 6.5. Correlations Between the HPI Scales and Competencies for Study #324.

Competency	ADJ	AMB	SOC	INT	PRU	INQ	LEA
Resource							
Management	0.30 (0.22)**	0.16 (0.11)	−0.22 (−0.16)**	0.05 (0.03)	0.20 (0.14)*	−0.02 (−0.02)	0.07 (0.05)
Initiative	0.34 (0.24)**	0.36 (0.25)**	−0.08 (−0.06)	0.22 (0.16)**	0.18 (0.12)*	0.09 (0.06)	0.22 (0.16)**
Stress Tolerance	0.47 (0.34)**	0.23 (0.16)**	−0.16 (−0.12)*	0.26 (0.19)**	0.28 (0.20)**	0.01 (0.01)	0.14 (0.10)
Communication	0.36 (0.25)**	0.19 (0.13)*	−0.13 (−0.09)	0.17 (0.12)*	0.11 (0.08)	−0.09 (−0.07)	0.05 (0.04)
Flexibility	0.26 (0.18)**	0.10 (0.07)	−0.19 (−0.14)*	0.08 (0.06)	0.16 (0.11)	−0.07 (−0.05)	0.03 (0.02)
Integrity	0.34 (0.24)**	0.07 (0.05)	−0.21 (−0.15)**	0.21 (0.15)**	0.17 (0.12)*	−0.02 (−0.01)	−0.06 (−0.05)
Teamwork	0.33 (0.23)**	0.20 (0.15)*	−0.21 (−0.15)*	0.14 (0.10)	0.20 (0.14)*	−0.03 (−0.02)	0.09 (0.06)
Achievement	0.36 (0.25)**	0.23 (0.16)**	−0.11 (−0.08)	0.07 (0.05)	0.13 (0.10)	0.02 (0.01)	0.13 (0.09)
Planning	0.30 (0.22)**	0.05 (0.03)	−0.20 (−0.14)*	0.12 (0.08)	0.12 (0.08)	−0.15 (−0.11)	−0.05 (−0.03)
Business Acumen	0.30 (0.21)**	0.13 (0.09)	−0.15 (−0.11)	0.09 (0.06)	0.03 (0.02)	−0.01 (−0.01)	−0.05 (−0.03)
Employee							
Development	0.39 (0.28)**	0.36 (0.26)**	−0.10 (−0.07)	0.16 (0.11)	0.16 (0.12)*	0.07 (0.05)	0.18 (0.13)*
Leadership	0.35 (0.25)**	0.30 (0.21)**	−0.12 (−0.08)	0.13 (0.09)	0.22 (0.16)**	0.10 (0.07)	0.15 (0.11)
Average	0.34 (0.24)	0.20 (0.14)	−0.16 (−0.11)	0.14 (0.10)	0.16 (0.12)	−0.01 (−0.01)	0.08 (0.05)

Note: Correlations are corrected for criterion unreliability. Uncorrected correlations appear in parentheses. $N = 290$; *p < .05, one-tailed. **p < .01, one-tailed. ADJ = Adjustment; AMB = Ambition; SOC = Sociability; INT = Interpersonal Sensitivity; PRU = Prudence; INQ = Inquisitive; LEA = Learning Approach.

finding the best set of predictors to maximize the best representation of the criterion space. The three VG methods fill the gaps inherent in each.

The *Uniform Guidelines* are vague about technical requirements and documentation for synthetic or job component validity, but the *Principles* explicitly include this strategy. Lawshe (1952) introduced synthetic validity over fifty years ago; however, it was largely ignored because people believed that test validity was specific to situations. The interpretive review and demonstration by Mossholder and Arvey (1984) is a rare exception. Mossholder and Arvey defined synthetic validity as "the logical process of inferring test-battery validity from predetermined validities of the tests for basic work components" (p. 323). If we know the key components of a job, we can review studies predicting those components. The valid predictors of the key job components can then be "synthesized" into a test battery for the new job (Balma, 1959; Lawshe, 1952). Primoff (1959), Guion (1965), and McCormick, DeNisi, and Shaw (1979) also examined synthetic validity. Hoffman, Holden, and Gale (2000), Jeanneret and Strong (2003), Johnson, Carter, Davison, and Oliver (2001), and McCloy (1994, 2001) have published synthetic validity research, and Scherbaum (2005) reviewed the field. Brannick and Levine (2002) point out that synthetic validity approaches allow us to build up validity evidence from small samples with common job components.

Synthetic validation involves: (1) identifying the important components of a job, (2) reviewing prior research on the prediction of each component, and (3) aggregating correlations across multiple studies for each component of the job to form a test battery (Scherbaum, 2005). Mossholder and Arvey (1984) summarized these requirements as follows: "When test battery validity is inferred from evidence showing that tests measure broad characteristics necessary for job performance, the process resembles a construct validation strategy. When scores are correlated with component performance measures, the process involves criterion-related validation. The nature of the tests used in the process (e.g., work sample vs. aptitude) may determine in part the appropriate validational strategy" (p. 323).

One version of synthetic validation, the focus of Chapter Three, is job component validity (JCV) (McCormick, DeNisi, &

Shaw, 1979). JCV has been used primarily to study the cognitive demands of jobs by correlating job dimensions using PAQ data (Jeanneret, 1992; Hoffman, Rashkovsky, & D'Egidio, 2007, this volume). Jeanneret described JCV as falling "within the rubric of construct validity" and reviewed evidence from studies using cognitive ability tests. Hoffman and McPhail (1998) examined the accuracy of JCV for predicting the observed validity of cognitive tests in clerical jobs. Few similar analyses are available for personality predictors, although Mecham (1985) and D'Egidio (2001) provide notable exceptions.

Synthetic or Job Component Validity for a Managerial Job: Case Study

As pointed out by Guion (1965), Hoffman and McPhail (1998), McCormick (1959), and Mossholder and Arvey (1984), the first step in synthetic validation is a job analysis to determine the important components of the job. Our example is the managerial position analyzed earlier, and we use the CET results from the job analysis for the synthetic part of the study. Descriptive statistics for the thirteen job dimensions the SMEs rated as important or critical for the target job are presented in Table 6.3.

Next we identify validity evidence for the important job components. Foster and Hogan (2005) have mapped each of the criteria from over two hundred validity studies in the Hogan Archive onto the CET dimensions. We then conducted a meta-analysis for each scale by competency relationship, using all of the studies that included each competency. These meta-analyses provide stable estimates of the relationships between the seven HPI scales and the thirteen critical competencies as rated by SMEs. This information is presented in Table 6.6. The correlations, averaged for the seven HPI scales across the thirteen competencies, show that Adjustment (0.15), Ambition (0.21), Interpersonal Sensitivity (0.10), and Prudence (0.11) are stable predictors of the important competencies of the manager job.

Finally, we combine the validities across predictors and job components into a single coefficient representing the link between the predictor battery and total job performance. There are several methods for doing this; these are reviewed by Scherbaum (2005).

Table 6.6. Meta-Analysis Results for Synthetic or Job Component Validities from Hogan Archives.

Competency / HPI Scale	N	K	r_{obs}	ρ_v	ρ
Integrity					
Adjustment	3660	36	0.11	0.16	0.17
Ambition	3660	36	0.02	0.02	0.02
Sociability	3660	36	−0.03	−0.04	−0.05
Interpersonal Sensitivity	3660	36	0.08	0.11	0.13
Prudence	3660	36	0.15	0.21	0.24
Inquisitive	3660	36	−0.02	−0.03	−0.03
Learning Approach	3520	34	0.02	0.03	0.03
Decision Making					
Adjustment	1105	8	0.08	0.12	0.12
Ambition	1105	8	0.13	0.19	0.20
Sociability	1105	8	0.07	0.10	0.11
Interpersonal Sensitivity	1105	8	0.04	0.05	0.06
Prudence	1105	8	0.00	−0.01	−0.01
Inquisitive	1105	8	0.13	0.18	0.20
Learning Approach	1105	8	0.09	0.13	0.15
Business Acumen					
Adjustment	89	1	0.31	0.43	0.46
Ambition	89	1	0.34	0.48	0.51
Sociability	89	1	0.06	0.09	0.10
Interpersonal Sensitivity	89	1	0.18	0.25	0.30
Prudence	89	1	0.11	0.15	0.17
Inquisitive	89	1	0.15	0.22	0.25
Learning Approach	—	—	—	—	—
Resource Management					
Adjustment	381	3	−0.11	−0.15	−0.16
Ambition	381	3	0.21	0.30	0.32
Sociability	381	3	0.22	0.30	0.33
Interpersonal Sensitivity	381	3	0.00	0.00	0.00
Prudence	381	3	−0.04	−0.05	−0.06

Table 6.6. Meta-Analysis Results for Synthetic or Job Component Validities from Hogan Archives, Cont'd.

Competency / HPI Scale	N	K	r_{obs}	ρ_v	ρ
Inquisitive	381	3	0.16	0.22	0.25
Learning Approach	381	3	−0.02	−0.03	−0.03
Flexibility					
Adjustment	3126	22	0.11	0.16	0.17
Ambition	3126	22	0.14	0.20	0.21
Sociability	3126	22	0.06	0.08	0.09
Interpersonal Sensitivity	3126	22	0.06	0.09	0.10
Prudence	3126	22	0.04	0.05	0.06
Inquisitive	3126	22	0.05	0.07	0.08
Learning Approach	3026	20	0.06	0.08	0.09
Stress Tolerance					
Adjustment	5676	52	0.20	0.28	0.30
Ambition	5676	52	0.06	0.09	0.10
Sociability	5676	52	−0.03	−0.04	−0.04
Interpersonal Sensitivity	5676	52	0.10	0.14	0.16
Prudence	5676	52	0.12	0.17	0.19
Inquisitive	5676	52	0.00	0.00	0.00
Learning Approach	5536	50	0.03	0.05	0.05
Achievement					
Adjustment	4496	48	0.06	0.08	0.09
Ambition	4496	48	0.13	0.19	0.20
Sociability	4496	48	0.00	0.00	0.00
Interpersonal Sensitivity	4496	48	0.02	0.02	0.03
Prudence	4496	48	0.04	0.06	0.07
Inquisitive	4496	48	0.01	0.02	0.02
Learning Approach	4496	48	0.02	0.03	0.04
Teamwork					
Adjustment	4417	36	0.13	0.18	0.19
Ambition	4417	36	0.03	0.05	0.05
Sociability	4417	36	−0.02	−0.03	−0.04

Table 6.6. Meta-Analysis Results for Synthetic or Job Component Validities from Hogan Archives, Cont'd.

Competency / HPI Scale	N	K	r_{obs}	ρ_v	ρ
Interpersonal Sensitivity	4417	36	0.08	0.11	0.13
Prudence	4417	36	0.12	0.18	0.20
Inquisitive	4417	36	−0.02	−0.03	−0.03
Learning Approach	3804	31	0.03	0.05	0.05
Communication					
Adjustment	5225	51	0.07	0.10	0.11
Ambition	5225	51	0.08	0.12	0.13
Sociability	5225	51	0.02	0.03	0.03
Interpersonal Sensitivity	5225	51	0.06	0.09	0.10
Prudence	5225	51	0.04	0.06	0.07
Inquisitive	5225	51	0.02	0.03	0.04
Learning Approach	4971	48	0.04	0.05	0.05
Initiative					
Adjustment	3947	26	0.11	0.16	0.17
Ambition	3947	26	0.21	0.29	0.32
Sociability	3947	26	0.06	0.09	0.09
Interpersonal Sensitivity	3947	26	0.05	0.07	0.08
Prudence	3947	26	0.08	0.12	0.13
Inquisitive	3947	26	0.09	0.13	0.14
Learning Approach	3557	22	0.09	0.12	0.13
Leadership					
Adjustment	3205	24	0.10	0.14	0.15
Ambition	3205	24	0.19	0.27	0.29
Sociability	3205	24	0.08	0.11	0.12
Interpersonal Sensitivity	3205	24	0.02	0.03	0.04
Prudence	3205	24	0.05	0.07	0.08
Inquisitive	3205	24	0.06	0.09	0.10
Learning Approach	3205	24	0.04	0.06	0.07
Planning					
Adjustment	2166	22	0.07	0.10	0.11

**Table 6.6. Meta-Analysis Results for Synthetic or
Job Component Validities from Hogan Archives, Cont'd.**

Competency / HPI Scale	N	K	r_{obs}	ρ_v	ρ
Ambition	2166	22	0.09	0.13	0.14
Sociability	2166	22	0.01	0.01	0.01
Interpersonal Sensitivity	2166	22	0.04	0.05	0.06
Prudence	2166	22	0.09	0.13	0.14
Inquisitive	2166	22	−0.01	−0.01	−0.01
Learning Approach	1893	19	0.03	0.03	0.04
Employee Development					
Adjustment	1414	10	0.04	0.06	0.06
Ambition	1414	10	0.19	0.27	0.29
Sociability	1414	10	0.10	0.14	0.16
Interpersonal Sensitivity	1414	10	0.08	0.11	0.14
Prudence	1414	10	0.06	0.08	0.09
Inquisitive	1414	10	0.06	0.08	0.10
Learning Approach	1364	9	0.02	0.03	0.03

Note: N = number of participants across K studies; K = number of studies; r_{obs} = mean observed validity; ρ_v = operational validity (corrected for range restriction and criterion reliability only); ρ = true validity at scale level (corrected for range restriction and predictor-criterion reliability).

Peterson, Wise, Arabian, and Hoffman (2001) specifically discussed various weighting options for predictor batteries. Although these authors find little difference in the outcomes of the various methods, there are differences in data requirements (such as the need for PAQ data). The data in the target study (that is, CET) dictated that we use the unit weighting procedure recommended by Johnson, Carter, and Tippins (2001). Using the equation provided by Nunnally (1978), we calculate that the overall synthetic correlation between a composite of the predictors (that is, Adjustment, Ambition, Interpersonal Sensitivity, and Prudence) and a composite of the important components for the marker job is 0.23. This evidence supports the use of the HPI Adjustment, Ambition, Interpersonal Sensitivity, and Prudence scales to predict performance in the target job.

Step Five. Examine Validity Evidence and Simulate Outcomes from the Selection Procedure

The final step involves merging the evidence from each VG method into a single profile for the target job. This step is critical, but, with the possible exception of Hoffman et al.'s (2000) work, the process is poorly described in the literature. The results from the three VG strategies for the managerial job used in this chapter, summarized by predictor and validity source, are presented in Table 6.7. The meta-analysis results support the use of five HPI scales for manager selection: Ambition, Adjustment, Prudence, Interpersonal Sensitivity, and Learning Approach. The transportability of validity evidence supports all but one of these five scales (the unsupported scale is Learning Approach). Evidence from the synthetic validity study justifies using the Adjustment and Ambition scales. On balance, however, the data in Table 6.7 support using the Ambition, Adjustment, Prudence, Interpersonal Sensitivity, and Learning Approach scales as a test battery. This conclusion, consistent with the overall corrected validity estimates (Nunnally, 1978) for the test battery, provides good coverage for prediction of the important competencies and results in no adverse impact. The mean of these corrected validity estimates is $r = 0.30$. From the multiple methods and meta-analysis of study results used to calculate this correlation, it is the best estimate of the overall validity of the HPI scales for predicting target job performance.

Setting cutoff scores for a selection system depends on three criteria: (1) the validity of each scale, (2) the client's desired pass rate based on business necessity, and (3) the results of an adverse impact study using the HPI normative data set ($N = 161,000$). The results in Table 6.7 suggest that the Adjustment and Ambition scales are the best predictors of managerial performance. This conclusion supports higher cutoff scores on these scales. The combined validity evidence for the remaining three scales suggests similar, but lower, cutoff scores for them. Based on our experience using these scales with similar applicant pools and the desired pass rate, we propose initial cutoff scores. We then conduct a simulation, using the

Table 6.7. Combined Validity Generalization Results for the Managerial Job.

	Adjustment	Ambition	Interpersonal Sensitivity	Prudence	Learning Approach	Total Validity for Predictor Battery
Meta-analysis	0.22	0.31	0.15	0.13	0.12	0.33
Transportability	0.34	0.20	0.14	0.16	0.08	0.33
Synthetic	0.15	0.21	0.10	0.11	0.06	0.23
Total Validity by Predictor	0.24	0.24	0.13	0.13	0.09	**0.30**

Note: Validity coefficients are summarized in the text. Marginal column entries for predictors across methods are the means of the three methods. Marginal row entries for methods across predictors are the means for the synthesized personality test batteries using Nunnally (1978).

HPI normative sample, to evaluate the effects of the cutoff scores on a potential applicant pool, adjusting the cutoff scores to yield the desired pass rate. At this point, we calculate adverse impact analyses with these cut scores. If adverse impact for any group is detected, based on the *Uniform Guidelines* four-fifths rule, we modify the cutoff scores until it is minimized. Once the data become available, we compare our pass rate estimates with those from the actual applicant pool. These profiles have yet to result in adverse impact with an actual applicant pool.

Discussion

In this chapter, we described how three VG approaches may be used to evaluate the validity of personality measures within a competency domain framework. The purpose of the exercise was not to determine which of these methods works best, but to illustrate how they complement each other. We believe that these three validity estimates provide the best solution for generalizing the validity of a personality-based selection procedure to a new job. This solution simply extends the unitarian view of validity (Binning & Barrett, 1989; Landy, 1986; Messick, 1995) to selection VG. We now comment briefly on each approach, and then consider outstanding future issues.

Conditions for Meta-Analysis, Transportability, and Synthetic or Job Component Validity

The availability of data usually dictates the most appropriate VG method. We agree with Hoffman and McPhail (1998) that VG should not rely entirely on meta-analysis, and we say this for two reasons. First, meta-analysis does not require job analysis—which is critical for real-world test selection. Second, meta-analysis results may fail to detect less powerful but nonetheless important predictors of job performance, as seen in this chapter. Nevertheless, many researchers (for example, Schmidt & Hunter, 1977; Peterson et al., 2001) believe that meta-analytic evidence is sufficient for VG as long as the predictor-criterion relationships are consistent across all components of job performance (that is, no moderators identified).

Hoffman and McPhail (1998) note that transportability of validity is only practical in cases in which "the test publisher has shown the forethought and taken the necessary steps to build-in this option while conducting their original validation research" (p. 988). The necessary steps to which they refer include archiving standardized job analysis information and empirical validation research on the original, marker, jobs. These two steps are essential for estimating the transportability of validity, but few test publishers maintain the requisite archives.

Synthetic or job component validation research requires data similar to the transportability of validity approach (that is, standardized job analysis and archived validity coefficients), as well as validity data archived as job component criteria (Peterson et al., 2001). These requirements are both the strength of and the challenge for the synthetic validity method. If data are available to conduct a synthetic validation study, the approach is useful for virtually any job. We developed the CET job analysis tool to facilitate synthetic validity studies and the results from the CET are stored in a searchable database. Furthermore, each synthetic or job component validity study uses meta-analytic estimates of job component validities from which a personality predictor battery can be compiled. Bartram (2005) illustrates this procedure using the Inventory of Management Competencies (SHL Group, 1993) and a database of twenty-nine validation studies based on the Occupational Personality Questionnaire family.

Regardless of the validity generalization method, we found good validity for personality measures. This finding is consistent with current meta-analytic research (for example, Hogan & Holland, 2003; Judge et al., 2002), and challenges the view (cf. Murphy & Dzieweczynski, 2005) that personality measures lack practical validity. The results of the three validity generalization studies reported here are similar in magnitude to results using other types of assessments (Hoffman et al., 2000).

Legal Basis for Validity Generalization Approaches

Unlike VG for cognitive ability tests, we found no existing case law on VG for personality-based test batteries. This may be because personality measures used for selection usually do not result in adverse impact or because personality-based VG is a new activity. Nonetheless, challenges will inevitably emerge. As soon as selection procedures include both cognitive and personality measures, adverse impact is almost guaranteed, and the adequacy of VG methods will be scrutinized. Interestingly, Guion (1965) proposed using this kind of test battery over forty years ago.

Despite the regulatory and research support for VG studies, some employers will want to augment them with local validation. This has at least two benefits. First, organizations can use their own data to support the validity of their selection procedures, thereby minimizing questions about the appropriateness of generalized research. The legal defensibility of a local validation study is appealing to employers. Second, local validation can provide evidence of utility that otherwise would not be available through VG methods. Brannick (2001) provides a Bayesian approach for combining a local validation study with existing validity generalization evidence.

Future Research Needs for Personality-Based VG

Future personality-based VG studies could benefit from the example of JCV research using the PAQ and cognitive measures. This tradition illustrates the importance of a standardized job analysis database and an archive of validity studies across jobs, construct measures, and criteria. The next generation of VG should also expand the measurement domains covered by test batteries to map more comprehensively the domain of job performance. Our work with personality measures expands the measurement domain and extends the coverage to other important competencies.

Theory-based models are essential for future progress. Once the FFM was recognized as an organizing framework, the use of personality measures for personnel selection progressed substantially. It is perhaps less well recognized that the FFM concerns acceptance (getting along) and status (getting ahead). This framework provides structure and organization to a variety of instruments that are relevant for personnel selection. These domains structure the class of predictors in a VG selection battery. As taxonomies such as the FFM, verbal and quantitative cognitive abilities, and Holland's six vocational interest factors become better defined and measurement improves, so will our VG capability.

The performance domain model in Table 6.1 is a practical guide for linking criterion and construct measures. The domain model needs to be expanded to include missing measures whose validity can be tested. Minimally, these include motivational and ability measures whose relations with the competency criteria can be estimated across each domain. Bartram's (2005, p. 1187) mapping of hypothesized measures and competency domains is a good starting point for developing a matrix of relations. In addition, the criterion competency list and its organization across the four performance domains needs additional technical and conceptual work.

For VG applications, we envision developing a matrix that provides a single system of empirically validated relations for predictors and their associated competencies. Such a system should operate at the level of job families; that is, we need to specify test batteries for the twenty-two DOL job families using meta-analysis. Once a new job is classified by job family, the test battery can be refined using competencies identified across the domain model. For each job competency, meta-analyzed predictor-criterion validity estimates should be calculated to obviate the need for expert judgment of relations. The initial work with this approach seems promising, although with an increasingly fine-grained analysis, piecemeal synthetic validity could become a daunting task (Steel, Huffcutt, & Kammeyer-Mueller, 2006, p. 31). Nevertheless, increasing the database for VG will advance our ability to deliver high-quality, comprehensive selection systems economically.

References

Adler, A. (1939). *Social interest.* New York: Putnam.

Aguinis, H., & Pierce, C. A. (1998). Testing moderator variable hypotheses meta-analytically. *Journal of Management, 24,* 577–592.

American Educational Research Association, American Psychological Association, & National Council on Measurement in Education. (1999). *Standards for educational and psychological testing.* Washington, DC: American Educational Research Association.

Arthur, W., Jr., Day, E. A., McNelly, T. L., & Edens, P. S. (2003). A meta-analysis of the criterion-related validity of assessment center dimensions. *Personnel Psychology, 56,* 125–154.

Bakan, D. (1966). *The duality of human existence: Isolation and communion in Western man.* Boston: Beacon.

Balma, M. J. (1959). The development of processes for indirect or synthetic validity. *Personnel Psychology, 12,* 395–396.

Barrick, M. R., & Mount, M. K. (1991). The Big-Five personality dimensions and job performance: A meta-analysis. *Personnel Psychology, 44,* 1–26.

Barrick, M. R., & Mount, M. K. (1993). Autonomy as a moderator of the relationship between the Big Five personality dimensions and job performance. *Journal of Applied Psychology, 78,* 111–118.

Barrick, M. R., Mount, M. K., & Gupta, R. (2003). Meta-analysis of the relationship between the Five-Factor Model of personality and Holland's occupational types. *Personnel Psychology, 56,* 45–74.

Barrick, M. R., Stewart, G. L., & Piotrowski, M. (2002). Personality and job performance: Test of the mediating effects of motivation among sales representatives. *Journal of Applied Psychology, 87,* 43–51.

Bartram, D. (2005). The great eight competencies: A criterion-centric approach to validation. *Journal of Applied Psychology, 90,* 1185–1203.

Bartram, D., Robertson, I. T., & Callinan, M. (2002). Introduction: A framework for examining organizational effectiveness. In I. T. Robertson, M. Callinan, & D. Bartram (Eds.), *Organizational effectiveness: The role of psychology* (pp. 1–10). Chichester, UK: Wiley.

Bass, B. M. (1990). *Bass & Sogdill's handbook of leadership: Theory, research, and managerial applications.* New York: Free Press.

Bernard v. Gulf Oil Co., 619 F.2d 495, 470 (5th Cir. 1980), aff d, 452 U.S. 89 (1981).

Binning, J. F., & Barrett, G. V. (1989). Validity of personnel decisions: A conceptual analysis of the inferential and evidential bases. *Journal of Applied Psychology, 74*(3), 478–494.

Borman, W. C., & Motowidlo, S. J. (1993). Expanding the criterion domain to include elements of contextual performance. In N. Schmitt, W. C. Borman, & Associates (Eds.), *Personnel selection in organizations* (pp. 71–98). San Francisco: Jossey-Bass.

Boyatzis, R. E. (1982). *The competent manager: A model for effective performance.* New York: Wiley.

Brannick, M. T. (2001). Implications of empirical Bayes meta-analysis for test validation. *Journal of Applied Psychology, 86,* 468–480.

Brannick, M. T., & Levine, E. L. (2002). Doing a job analysis study. In M. T. Brannick & E. L. Levine (Eds.), *Job analysis: Methods, research, and applications for human resource management in the new millennium* (Ch. 9, pp. 265–294). Thousand Oaks, CA: Sage.

Campbell, J. P., Gasser, M. B., & Oswald, F. L. (1996). The substantive nature of job performance variability. In K. R. Murphy (Ed.), *Individual differences and behavior in organizations* (pp. 258–299). San Francisco: Jossey-Bass.

Campbell, J. P., McCloy, R. A., Oppler, S. H., & Sager, C. E. (1993). A theory of performance. In N. Schmitt, W. C. Borman, & Associates (Eds.), *Personnel selection in organizations* (pp. 35–70). San Francisco: Jossey-Bass.

Campbell, J. P., McHenry, J. J., & Wise, L. L. (1990). Modeling job performance in a population of jobs. *Personnel Psychology, 43,* 313–333.

Cornelius, E. T. (1988). Practical findings from job analysis research. In S. Gael (Ed.), *The job analysis handbook for business, industry, and government.* New York: Wiley.

Costa, P. T., Jr., & McCrae, R. R. (1985). *The NEO Personality Inventory manual.* Odessa, FL: Psychological Assessment Resources.

D'Egidio, E. L. (2001). Building a job component validity model using job analysis data from the Occupational Information Network. Unpublished doctoral dissertation. University of Houston, Houston.

De Raad, B., & Perugini, M. (Eds.). (2002). *Big Five assessment.* Seattle, WA: Hogrefe & Huber.

Digman, J. M. (1990). Personality structure: Emergence of the five-factor model. *Annual Review of Psychology, 41,* 417–440.

Dunnette, M. D., & Borman, W. S. (1979). Personnel selection and classification systems. *Annual Review of Psychology, 30,* 477–525.

Emler, N. P. (1990). A social psychology of reputation. *European Review of Social Psychology, 1,* 173–193.

Equal Employment Opportunity Commission, Civil Service Commission, Department of Labor, & Department of Justice. (1978). *Uniform guidelines on employee selection procedures. Federal Register, 43*(166), 38290–38315.

Erez, A., & Judge, T. (2001). Relationship of core self-evaluations to goal setting, motivation, and performance. *Journal of Applied Psychology, 86,* 1270–1279.

Fiedler, F. E. (1967). *A theory of leadership effectiveness.* New York: McGraw-Hill.

Fleishman, E. A. (1953). The measurement of leadership attitudes in industry. *Journal of Applied Psychology, 37,* 153–158.

Foster, J. F., & Anderson, M. (2006, May). The validity of structured job analysis instruments. In J. Foster (Chair), Standardized job analysis tools: State of the science. Symposium conducted at the 21st Annual Conference of the Society for Industrial and Organizational Psychology, Dallas, TX.

Foster, J. F., & Hogan, J. (2005). *Validity of the Hogan Personality Inventory for job family profiles.* Technical Report. Tulsa, OK: Hogan Assessment Systems.

Gatewood, R. D., & Feild, H. S. (1994). *Human resource selection* (3rd ed.). Orlando, FL: Dryden Press.

Gaugler, B. B., Rosenthal, D. B., Thornton, G. C., & Bentson, C. (1987). Meta-analysis of assessment center validity. *Journal of Applied Psychology, 72,* 493–511.

Ghiselli, E. E. (1966). *The validity of occupational aptitude tests.* New York: Wiley.

Ghiselli, E. E., & Brown, C. H. (1955). *Personnel and industrial psychology* (2nd ed.). New York: McGraw-Hill.

Gibson, W. M., & Caplinger, J. A. (2007). Transportation of validation risks. In S. M. McPhail (Ed.), *Alternative validation strategies: Developing new and leveraging existing validity evidence* (pp. 29–81.) San Francisco: Jossey-Bass.

Goffman, E. (1958). *The presentation of self in everyday life.* New York: Doubleday.

Goldberg, L. R. (1990). An alternative "description of personality": The Big-Five factor structure. *Journal of Personality and Social Psychology, 59,* 1216–1229.

Goldberg, L. R. (1992). The development of markers for the Big-Five factor structure. *Psychological Assessment, 4,* 26–42.

Guion, R. M. (1965). Synthetic validity in a small company: A demonstration. *Personnel Psychology, 18,* 49–63.

Guion, R. M. (1998). *Assessment, measurement, and prediction for personnel decisions.* Mahwah, NJ: Erlbaum.

Harvey, R. J. (1991). Job analysis. In M. D. Dunnette & L. M. Hough (Eds.), *Handbook of industrial and organizational psychology* (Vol. 2, 2nd ed., pp. 71–163). Palo Alto, CA: Consulting Psychologists Press.

Harvey, R. J., & Wilson, M. A. (2000). Yes Virginia, there is an objective reality in job analysis. *Journal of Organizational Behavior, 21,* 829–854.

Hoffman, C. C., Holden, L. M, & Gale, E. (2000). So many jobs, so little "N": Applying expanded validation models to support generalization of cognitive ability. *Personnel Psychology, 53,* 955–991.

Hoffman, C. C., & McPhail, S. M. (1998). Exploring options for supporting test use in situations precluding local validation. *Personnel Psychology, 51,* 987–1003.

Hoffman, C. C., Rashkovsky, B., & D'Egidio, E. (2007). Job component validity: Background, current research, and applications. In S. M. McPhail (Ed.), *Alternative validation strategies: Developing new and leveraging existing validity evidence* (pp. 82–121). San Francisco: Jossey-Bass.

Hogan, J., & Hogan, R. (1989). How to measure employee reliability. *Journal of Applied Psychology, 74,* 273–279.

Hogan, J., & Holland, B. (2003). Using theory to evaluate personality and job-performance relations: A socioanalytic perspective. *Journal of Applied Psychology, 88,* 100–112.

Hogan, J., & Rybicki, S. (1998). *Performance improvement characteristics manual.* Tulsa, OK: Hogan Assessment Systems.

Hogan, R. (1983). A socioanalytic theory of personality. In M. M. Page (Ed.), *1982 Nebraska symposium on motivation* (pp. 55–89). Lincoln: University of Nebraska Press.

Hogan, R. (1986). *Manual for the Hogan Personality Inventory.* Minneapolis: National Computer Systems.

Hogan, R. (1996). A socioanalytic perspective on the five-factor model. In J. S. Wiggins (Ed.), *The five-factor model of personality* (pp. 163–179). New York: Guilford Press.

Hogan, R., & Hogan, J. (1995). *Hogan Personality Inventory manual* (2nd ed.). Tulsa, OK: Hogan Assessment Systems.

Hogan, R., & Hogan, J. (2001). Leadership and sociopolitical intelligence. In R. Riggio (Ed.), *Multiple intelligences and leadership* (pp. 65–89). San Francisco: Jossey-Bass.

Hogan, R., Hogan, J., & Busch, C. (1984). How to measure service orientation. *Journal of Applied Psychology, 69,* 157–163.

Hogan, R., & Shelton, D. (1998). A socioanalytic perspective on job performance. *Human Performance, 11,* 129–144.

Hogan, R., & Warrenfeltz, W. (2003). Educating the modern manager. *Academy of Management Learning and Education, 2,* 74–84.

Hogan Assessment Systems. (2000). *Job Evaluation Tool manual.* Tulsa, OK: Hogan Assessment Systems.

Hogan Assessment Systems. (2006). *Competency Evaluation Tool manual.* Tulsa, OK: Hogan Assessment Systems.

Hough, L. M. (1992). The "Big-Five" personality variables—construct confusion: Description versus prediction. *Human Performance, 5,* 139–156.

Hough, L. M., & Ones, D. S. (2001) The structure, measurement, validity, and use of personality variables in industrial, work, and organizational psychology. In N. R. Anderson, D. S. Ones, H. K. Sinangil, & C. Viswesvaran (Eds.), *Handbook of work psychology* (pp. 233–277). London and New York: Sage.

Hough, L. M., & Schneider, R. J. (1996). Personality traits, taxonomies, and applications in organizations. In K. R. Murphy (Ed.), *Individual differences and behavior in organizations* (pp. 31–88). San Francisco: Jossey-Bass.

Hunt, S. T. (1996). Generic work behavior: An investigation into the dimensions of entry-level, hourly job performance. *Personnel Psychology,* 49, 51–83.

Hunter, J. E., & Hunter, R. F. (1984). Validity and utility of alternative predictors of job performance. *Psychological Bulletin, 96,* 72–98.

Hunter, J. E., & Schmidt, F. L. (1990). *Methods of meta-analysis: Correcting error and bias in research findings.* Newbury Park, CA: Sage.

Hurtz, G. M., & Donovan, J. J. (2000). Personality and job performance: The big five revisited. *Journal of Applied Psychology, 85,* 869–879.

Jeanneret, P. R. (1992). Applications of job component/synthetic validity to construct validity. *Human Performance, 5,* 81–96.

Jeanneret, P. R., Borman, W. C., Kubisiak, U. C., & Hanson, M. A. (1999). Generalized work activities. In N. G. Peterson, M. D. Mumford, W. C. Borman, P. R. Jeanneret, & E. A. Fleishman (Eds.), *An occupational information system for the 21st century: The development of the O*NET* (pp. 105–125). Washington, DC: American Psychological Association.

Jeanneret, P. R., & Strong, M. H. (2003). Linking O*Net job analysis information to job requirement predictors: An O*Net application. *Personnel Psychology, 56,* 465–492.

John, O. P. (1990). The "Big-Five" factor taxonomy: Dimensions of personality in the natural language and in questionnaires. In L. A. Pervin (Ed.), *Handbook of personality theory and research* (pp. 66–100). New York: Guilford.

Johnson, J. W., Carter, G. W., Davison, H. K., & Oliver, D. H. (2001). A synthetic validity approach to testing differential prediction hypotheses. *Journal of Applied Psychology, 86,* 774–780.

Johnson, J. W., Carter, G. W., & Tippins, N. T. (2001, April). A synthetic validation approach to the development of a selection system for multiple job families. In J. Johnson & G. Carter (Chairs), *Advances in the application of synthetic validity.* Symposium conducted at the 16th Annual Conference of the Society for Industrial and Organizational Psychology, San Diego, CA.

Johnson, M. A., & Jolly, J. P. (2000). Extending test validation results from one plant location to another: Application of transportability evidence. *The Journal of Behavioral and Applied Management, 1*(1), 127–136.

Judge, T. A., & Bono, J. E. (2001). Relationship of core self-evaluations traits—self-esteem, generalized self-efficacy, locus of control, and emotional stability—with job satisfaction and job performance: A meta-analysis. *Journal of Applied Psychology, 86,* 80–92.

Judge, T. A., Bono, J. E., Ilies, R., & Gerhardt, M. W. (2002). Personality and leadership: A qualitative and quantitative review. *Journal of Applied Psychology, 87,* 765–780.

Judge, T. A., Colbert, A. E., & Ilies, R. (2004). Intelligence and leadership: A quantitative review and test of theoretical propositions. *Journal of Applied Psychology, 89,* 542–552.

Landy, F. J. (1986). Stamp collecting versus science: Validation as hypothesis testing. *American Psychologist, 41*(11), 1183–1192.

Larson, L. M., Rottinghaus, P. J., & Borgen, F. H. (2002). Meta-analyses of big six interests and big five personality factors. *Journal of Vocational Behavior,* 61, 217–239.

Lawshe, C. H. (1952). What can industrial psychology do for small business? (A symposium) 2. Employee selection. *Personnel Psychology, 5,* 31–34.

Lindemann, B., & Grossman, P. (1996). Employment discrimination law (3rd ed.). Washington, DC: American Bar Association.

Lord, R. G., DeVader, C. L., & Alliger, G. (1986). A meta-analysis of the relation between personality traits and leader perceptions. *Journal of Applied Psychology, 71,* 402–410.

McCloy, R. A. (1994). Predicting job performance scores without performance data. In B. F. Green & A. S. Mavor (Eds.), *Modeling cost and performance for military enlistment: Report of a workshop.* Washington, DC: National Academy Press.

McCloy, R. A. (2001, April). *Predicting job performance scores in jobs lacking criterion data.* In J. Johnson, & G. Carter (Chairs), Advances in the application of synthetic validity. Symposium conducted at the 16th Annual Conference of the Society for Industrial and Organizational Psychology, San Diego, CA.

McCormick, E. J. (1959). The development of processes for indirect or synthetic validity: III. Application of job analysis to indirect validity. A symposium. *Personnel Psychology, 12,* 402–413.

McCormick, E. J., DeNisi, A. S., & Shaw, J. B. (1979). Use of the Position Analysis Questionnaire for establishing the job component validity of tests. *Journal of Applied Psychology, 64,* 51–56.

McCormick, E. J., Jeanneret, P. R., & Mecham, R. C. (1972). A study of job characteristics and job dimensions based on the Position Analysis Questionnaire (PAQ). *Journal of Applied Psychology, 56,* 347–368.

McCrae, R. R., & Costa, P. T., Jr. (1987). Validity of the five-factor model of personality across instruments and observers. *Journal of Personality and Social Psychology, 52,* 81–90.

McDaniel, M. A., Morgeson, F. P., Finnegan, E. B., Campion, M. A., & Braverman, E. P. (2001). Use of situational judgment tests to predict job performance: A clarification of the literature. *Journal of Applied Psychology, 86,* 730–740.

Messick, S. (1995). Validity of psychological assessment: Validation of inferences from persons' responses and performances as scientific inquiry into score meaning. *American Psychologist, 50,* 741–749.

Mossholder, K. W., & Arvey, R. D. (1984). Synthetic validity: A conceptual and comparative review. *Journal of Applied Psychology, 69,* 322–333.

Motowidlo, S. J., Borman, W. C., & Schmit, M. J. (1997). A theory of individual differences in task and contextual performance. *Human Performance, 10,* 71–83.

Mount, M. K., & Barrick, M. R. (1995). The Big-Five personality dimensions: Implications for research and practice in human resource management. *Research in Personnel and Human Resource Management, 13,* 153–200.

Mount, M. K., & Barrick, M. R. (2001). *Personal Characteristics Inventory manual.* Libertyville, IL: Wonderlic.

Murphy, K. R., & Dzieweczynski, J. L. (2005). Why don't measures of broad dimensions of personality perform better as predictors of job performance? *Human Performance, 18,* 343–357.

Norman, W. T. (1963). Toward an adequate taxonomy of personality attributes: Replicated factor structure in peer nomination personality ratings. *Journal of Abnormal and Social Psychology, 66,* 574–583.

Nunnally, J. C. (1978). *Psychometric theory* (2nd ed.). New York: McGraw-Hill.

Ones, D. S., Viswesvaran, C., & Schmidt, F. L. (1993). Comprehensive meta-analysis of integrity test validation: Findings and implications for personnel selection and theories of job performance. *Journal of Applied Psychology, 78,* 679–703.

Ozer, D. J., & Benet-Martinez, V. (2006). Personality and the prediction of consequential outcomes. *Annual Review of Psychology, 57,* 8.1–8.21.

Peterson, N. G., Mumford, M. D., Borman, W. C., Jeanneret, P. R., & Fleishman, E. A. (1999). *An occupational information system for the 21st century: The development of the O*NET.* Washington, DC: American Psychological Association.

Peterson, N. G., Wise, L. L., Arabian, J., & Hoffman, R. G. (2001). Synthetic validation and validity generalization: When empirical validation is not possible. In J. P. Campbell & D. J. Knapp (Eds.), *Exploring the limits in personnel selection and classification* (pp. 411–451). Mahwah, NJ: Erlbaum.

Primoff, E. S. (1959). Empirical validation of the J-coefficient. *Personnel Psychology, 12,* 413–418.

Rank, O. (1945). *Will therapy and truth and reality.* New York: Knopf.

Raymark, P. H., Schmit, M. J., & Guion, R. M. (1997). Identifying potentially useful personality constructs for employee selection. *Personnel Psychology, 50,* 723–736.

Redfield, R. (1960). How society operates. In H. L. Shapiro (Ed.), *Man, culture, and society* (pp. 345–368). New York: Oxford University Press.

Ree, M. J., & Earles, J. A. (1992). Predicting training success: Not much more than g. *Personnel Psychology, 44,* 321–332.

Riggio, R. E. (1989). *Social skills inventory manual.* Palo Alto, CA: Consulting Psychologists Press.

Rosenthal, R. (1979). The file drawer problem and tolerance for null results. *Psychological Bulletin, 86,* 638–641.

Rosenthal, R., & DiMatteo, M. R. (2001). Meta analysis: Recent developments in quantitative methods for literature reviews. *Annual Review of Psychology, 52,* 59–82.

Rothstein, H. R. (1990). Interrater reliability of job performance ratings: Growth to asymptote level with increasing opportunity to observe. *Journal of Applied Psychology, 75,* 322–327.

Rotundo, M., & Sackett, P. R. (2002). The relative importance of task, citizenship, and counterproductive performance to global ratings of job performance: A policy capturing approach. *Journal of Applied Psychology, 87,* 66–80.

Rybicki, S. (1997). *Validity of personality measures for entry-level jobs.* Tulsa, OK: Hogan Assessment Systems.

Salgado, J. F. (1997). The five factor model of personality and job performance in the European community. *Journal of Applied Psychology, 82,* 30–43.

Salgado, J. F. (1998). Big Five personality dimensions and job performance in Army and civil occupations: A European perspective. *Human Performance, 11,* 271–288.

Scherbaum, C. A. (2005). Synthetic validity: Past, present, and future. *Personnel Psychology, 58,* 481–515.

Schmidt, F. L., & Hunter, J. E. (1977). Development of a general solution to the problem of validity generalization. *Journal of Applied Psychology, 62,* 529–540.

Schmidt, F. L., & Rothstein, H. R. (1994). Applications of validity generalization methods of meta-analysis to biographical data scores in employees' selection. In G. S. Stokes, M. D. Mumford, & W. A. Owens (Eds.), *The biodata handbook: Theory, research, and applications* (pp. 237–260). Palo Alto, CA: Consulting Psychologists Press.

SHL Group. (1993). *Inventory of Management Competencies: Manual and user's guide.* Thames Ditton, United Kingdom: SHL Group.

Shrout, P. E., & Fleiss, J. L. (1979). Intraclass correlations: Uses in assessing reliability. *Psychological Bulletin, 86,* 420–428.

Smith, M. L., & Glass, G. V. (1977). Meta-analysis of psychotherapy outcome studies. *American Psychologist, 32,* 752–760.

Society for Industrial and Organizational Psychology. (2003). *Principles for the validation and use of personnel selection procedures* (4th ed.). Bowling Green, OH: Society for Industrial and Organizational Psychology.

Steel, P.D.G., Huffcutt, A. I., & Kammeyer-Mueller, J. (2006). From the work one knows the worker: A systematic review of the challenges, solutions, and steps to creating synthetic validity. *International Journal of Selection and Assessment, 14*(1), 16–36.

Tett, R. P., Guterman, H. A., Bleier, A., & Murphy, P. J. (2000). Development and content validation of a "hyperdimensional" taxonomy of managerial competence. *Human Performance, 13,* 205–251.

Tett, R. P., Holland, B., Hogan, J., & Burnett, D. (2002, April). *Validity of trait-based job analysis using moderator correlations.* Paper presented at the 17th Annual Conference of the Society for Industrial and Organizational Psychology, Toronto, Ontario, Canada.

Tett, R. P., Jackson, D. N., & Rothstein, M. (1991). Personality measures as predictors of job performance: A meta-analytic review. *Personnel Psychology, 44,* 703–742.

Thurstone, L. L. (1934). The vectors of mind. *Psychological Review, 41,* 1–32.

Tilton, J. W. (1937). The measurement of overlapping. *Journal of Educational Psychology, 28,* 656–662.

Tippins, N. T. (2003, October). *Transporting the validity of assessments.* Presentation at the annual meeting of International Assessment Congress, Atlanta, GA.

Tippins, N. T., & McPhail, S. M. (2002, February). *New developments in transporting validity.* Presentation at PTC-MW education workshop, Washington, DC.

Tippins, N. T., McPhail, S. M., Hoffman, C., & Gibson, W. (1999, April). *Transporting validity in the real world.* Continuing Education Workshop presented at the 14th Annual Conference of the Society of Industrial and Organizational Psychology, Atlanta, GA.

Tupes, E. C., & Christal, R. E. (1961). *Recurrent personality factors based on trait ratings* (Tech. Rep. No. ASD-TR-61–97). Lackland Air Force Base, TX: Aeronautical Systems Division, Personnel Laboratory.

Warrenfeltz, R. B. (1995, May). *An executive-level validation of the Borman and Brush taxonomy.* Paper presented at the 10th Annual Conference of the Society for Industrial and Organizational Psychology, Orlando, FL.

Wiggins, J. S. (1996). *The five-factor model of personality.* New York: Guilford.

Wiggins, J. S., & Pincus, A. L. (1992). Personality structure and assessment. *Annual Review of Psychology, 43,* 473–504.

Wiggins, J. S., & Trapnell, P. D. (1996). A dyadic-interactional perspective on the five-factor model. In J. S. Wiggins (Ed.), *The five-factor model of personality* (pp. 88–162). New York: Guilford.

PART 2

Developing New Evidence for Validity

CHAPTER 7

Consortium Studies

Nancy T. Tippins and William H. Macey

There are a variety of practical and economic interests that determine the choice of strategy for developing evidence regarding the validity of inferences drawn from test scores. In an ideal world, the practicing psychologist would choose the strategy that provides the most definitive evidence of the validity of a selection procedure for its intended use. The problem is that practical considerations may preclude such a strategy, due to sample size considerations or reasonable business logistics. One solution to this problem is to join forces with others who have common interests—here meaning common jobs and common performance criteria. These common interests are pooled in the form of a group, or consortium, to conduct validation research, the results of which are used to support the inference of validity across the common jobs, settings, and business environments.

The consortium study provides an opportunity to use traditional validation procedures with a wider base of employees (in a content-oriented or concurrent criterion-oriented study) or applicants (in a predictive criterion-oriented study). A validation study conducted in a consortium need not require exactly identical positions, although "common interests" almost always involve similar positions across organizations. Theoretically, at least, different positions containing similar components (such as knowledge, skills, abilities, or personal characteristics, or similar job dimensions, like communications requirements) might also be the foundation for a consortium-based synthetic validation study.

For the purposes of this discussion, we are defining a consortium study as one in which independent organizations with no obligations to the other participating organizations, other than those defined specifically by the study, cooperate in test development and validity research. Thus, we are excluding studies involving organizations that are part of a larger organization and ultimately report to the same individual. For example, we are not including studies of tests for jobs in plants that are relatively autonomous but are part of the same corporate structure and report to a common manufacturing executive. Similarly, we are not including military studies, despite the relative autonomy of some units.

By their nature, many certification tests developed to credential an individual in a particular role, skill, industry, or profession are almost always developed in some form of a consortium study. Either the organizations band together to create the certification tests, or an umbrella organization creates the certification tests for the member companies. However, not all certification tests are developed via a consortium study. Exceptions include certification tests developed by a single organization to assess the competency of its employees or certification tests developed by a single organization that produces equipment or software to certify the knowledge and skills of users of their products.

Although content-oriented validation studies are possible, consortium studies frequently take some form of a criterion-related validity study, probably because content-oriented studies do not have the large sample size requirements that criterion-oriented studies have and usually can be conducted fairly easily by one organization. Despite the relatively small sample sizes necessary for content validation, one might well consider the advantages of a consortium for a content-oriented validation study when the number of linkages required is very large and beyond the tolerance limits of most subject matter experts (SMEs).

Because small samples contributed by each organization participating in a consortium prevent analysis by organization or lack the power to detect validity, consortium studies often aggregate data across participating organizations and analyze all of the data as a whole. Occasionally, consortium studies analyze the data in aggregate and also within each participating organization. In other words, a validation study is conducted by each organization, then those studies are combined meta-analytically to provide additional evidence of validity. The advantages of both analytic approaches include having multiple studies supporting the use of a test for its intended purpose and producing information to assist an organization in setting an appropriate cutoff score. The primary disadvantage to conducting the local validation study is the sample size required to make the local study feasible with sufficient power and the associated costs. Few examples of this approach exist, probably because the multiple local validation studies fail to reduce the costs, and the validity generalization analyses add additional expense.

The following section provides examples of consortia that we are considering in this chapter.

Sponsorship

Although the results of many consortium studies are not reported in the literature, a number of consortia have existed in the last thirty years for the purposes of test development and validation. These examples are probably most easily differentiated in terms of their sponsors, implicitly highlighting the motivations and resources of the participants.

Trade Associations

Trade associations—such as the Edison Electric Institute (EEI), the American Gas Association (AGA), the American Petroleum Institute (API), and LIMRA, an association for insurance companies— were created to serve the needs of member companies. Such organizations have developed and validated employee assessment tools that are then made available to member companies.

EEI regularly conducts cooperative studies for the benefit of its member companies, all of which are electric utilities. The studies have resulted in validated tests for a number of jobs ranging from clerical positions to technical positions. In EEI's consortium-based criterion-oriented validity studies, member companies fund the cost of research and depend on participating companies to provide participants, typically employees, to take experimental test batteries and supervisors to assist with criterion measures. EEI sells the tests to any member company, regardless of participation in the validation research, after a transportability process is applied. All companies using tests are bound to abide by EEI's test administration policies to protect the security of the tests.

Less broadly than EEI, the AGA has sponsored validation of tests (such as measures of physical abilities) for general application across member companies. Again, using a transportability process, the AGA assists member organizations in acquiring appropriate equipment and makes the supporting validation reports available to them.

The API focused on hourly positions, primarily in oil refineries, and sponsored extensive meta-analytic studies of selection tests. The studies were managed by industrial and organizational psychologists and HR professionals from member companies. The research was made available to all member companies regardless of their initial participation and, in many cases, served as the primary evidence for validity of the inferences made from the test battery.

Similarly, LIMRA also conducts cooperative studies for its member companies. The validation studies of instruments for the selection of personnel such as sales representatives, managers, and call center employees are criterion-oriented. LIMRA funds the research and sells tests to participating organizations, but like EEI, LIMRA depends on member companies for study participants. Tests are sold to member companies after a transportability study, with the expectation that they will abide by the test administration rules set forth.

Independent Companies

Shortly after the divestiture of ATT's operating telephone companies, some of the newly formed companies—the Regional Bell Operating Companies (RBOCs)—and other independent telephone companies formed a consortium to redo the selection procedures for entry-level professional and supervisory positions. The RBOC Consortium, led by the internal I/O psychologists and HR professionals in each organization, identified a vendor to assist them in the development and criterion-oriented validation of a cognitive ability test, a situational judgment inventory, and a structured interview. The participants in this consortium shared responsibility for research costs, project leadership, requirements for research participants, and ownership of the selection materials. In addition, these companies committed to standards of test security and to sharing of information on test security breaches and subsequent applicant performance on the tests. The primary advantage to the participating companies was the reduction of consultant costs and employee participation requirements.

Vendor-Organized Consortium Studies

Over the years, several consulting firms and test publishers have organized consortia to develop and validate tests for particular groups of jobs or to extend application to additional jobs. In one case, a consulting firm organized more than twenty companies to validate tests for clerical positions. All companies were asked to administer an experimental battery to incumbents in the target positions and collect criterion data. Data collection occurred at more or less the same time and resulted in one validation report.

In a more recent example, a consulting firm organized a series of consortia to validate tests for clerical, sales, and customer service positions. Rather than try to force all participating companies to meet the same time line, the consulting firm conducted independent studies for each participating company, using experimental batteries and criteria. Each participating company received a report based on its data alone and will receive a report based on the aggregated data from all participating companies. The advantages to participating companies in these consortia are greatly reduced consulting fees, a local validation report including information about appropriate cutoff scores, a validation report based on aggregated data, and reduced fees for future test purchases.

Advantages of a Consortium Study

Organizations participate in consortium studies to develop and validate employee selection procedures for many reasons. In some cases, a validation effort would not be possible without a consortium effort. In other situations, the cost savings, in terms of both time and money, are substantial.

Feasibility

A consortium study provides a means for an organization to conduct validation research in situations in which a single-organization, local validation study is not feasible. Even large organizations may lack sufficient numbers of incumbents in particular job titles or families for validation research. Participation in a consortium study with other organizations may allow an organization to develop a specialized test battery to meet its particular needs, rather than being constrained to select from test publishers' offerings.

Sample Size

The sample sizes required in a criterion-related validity study, when expected effect sizes are small, can be quite large. Cohen, Cohen, West, and Aiken (2003) note that the power to detect a correlation coefficient of 0.20 based on a sample of one hundred people, using a two-tailed test with alpha set at 0.05, is only 0.52. To reach certainty (that is, power of 0.99), five hundred subjects would be required. Many tests that have high utility in large applicant pools have correlations with the criteria of less than 0.20. In these cases, the sample requirements for adequate power grow larger still.

Despite the sample size requirements for statistical analysis, virtually all organizations are sensitive to the removal of large numbers of employees from their jobs for research purposes. Lost employee time costs organizations money and reduces productivity. Consequently, many organizations are attracted to a consortium study because it allows a group of organizations to spread both the costs of validation research and the burden of collecting data from employees and their supervisors (or applicants and their supervisors after hire) across the participating organizations. For example, if a validation study requires a sample of two hundred participants, each participating company in a consortium of four may need to produce only fifty employees, all other things being equal.

Another related advantage of the consortium study is the ability of organizations to pool their resources for adequate sample sizes within protected classes and to conduct fairness analyses (that is, assessment of bias) that would otherwise not be technically feasible. If a consortium is composed of ten companies, each with ten women employed in the job for which tests are being developed and validated, no one company could conduct an analysis of bias; however, as a group, the sample of one hundred women across the ten companies may be sufficient to compare the regression lines of men and women.

Consulting Fees

Often, the cost of professional assistance in the development and validation process is simply beyond the means of a single organization. Spread across multiple participants, those costs may be more manageable. In some cases, the cost of conducting test research is too high relative to the benefit for positions with low hiring volumes. Even if the test is a highly valid predictor of the relevant criterion, the cost of test development and validation may result in low utility when the number of positions filled in a year is quite small. As the costs go down, the cost-benefit ratio becomes more favorable. In the case of a vendor-sponsored consortium, the costs of the consortium research effort may be underwritten in part or whole by the sponsor. The motivation for the consulting firm or test publisher to sponsor such a study is the likelihood of ongoing test sales and the allure of strong evidence of validity from numerous organizations.

Other Costs

In addition to the costs associated with contributing large numbers of employees for validation research and paying fees to external consultants, other costs are associated with validation studies and operational test use. These costs range from the costs of printing research materials (job analysis questionnaires, experimental test forms, performance assessment forms) and operational materials (test booklets, answer sheets, scoring templates) to the time of the internal consultant and his or her staff used to manage the project. Consortium studies offer opportunities for economies of scale that may reduce costs on a proportionate basis while simultaneously increasing both the amount and quality of the research data obtained.

Legal Acceptability

Another advantage of a consortium study is the direct endorsement of cooperative studies by the *Uniform Guidelines for Employee Selection Procedures* (Equal Employment Opportunity Commission, Civil Service Commission, Department of Labor, & Department of Justice, 1978). The *Uniform Guidelines* (Sec. 8.A) specifically encourages employers to cooperate in the "research, development, search for lawful alternatives, and validity studies".

> Section 8: Cooperative Studies.
> A. Encouragement of cooperative studies.
> The agencies issuing these guidelines encourage employers, labor organizations, and employment agencies to cooperate in research, development, search for lawful alternatives, and validity studies in order to achieve procedures which are consistent with these guidelines.

It is interesting to note that the *Uniform Guidelines* encourage labor organizations to participate in cooperative validation studies, but we are unaware of any study sponsored for this purpose by a labor organization.

Significantly, the *Uniform Guidelines* (Sec. 8.B) note that evidence of validity specific to each user is not required unless there are differences across organizations that would be likely to affect the validity of the resulting test.

> Section 8.B. Standards for use of cooperative studies.
> If validity evidence from a cooperative study satisfies the requirements of section 14 of this part, evidence of validity specific to each user will not be required unless there are variables in the user's situation which are likely to affect validity significantly.

However, the *Uniform Guidelines* (Sec. 15.F) are clear that evidence from a cooperative study must meet the standards for the evidence of validity set forth in other sections.

> Section 15.F Evidence of validity from cooperative studies.
> Where a selection procedure has been validated through a cooperative study, evidence that the study satisfies the requirements of sections 7, 8 and 15E should be provided (essential).

Professional Acceptability

The *Principles for the Validation and Use of Personnel Selection Procedures* (Society for Industrial and Organizational Psychology, 2003) acknowledge that a validation effort may be based on a consortium study and recognize the value of multiple sources of validity.

> The design of this effort [the validation study] may take many forms such as single local studies, consortium studies, meta-analyses, transportability studies, or synthetic validity/job component studies. More than one source of evidence or validation strategy may be valuable in any one validation effort. (p. 8)

It is useful to note that a consortium study might encompass meta-analyses, transportability studies, or synthetic validity or job component studies; that is, the consortium model is distinct from the methods applied to establish the validity of inferences to be made with a test.

Although the details of conducting consortium studies have not been thoroughly addressed in the I/O psychology literature, several published studies (for example, Motowidlo, Dunnette, & Carter, 1990; Hoffman, 1999) note that the data were collected as part of consortium efforts. Motowidlo et al. conducted a criterion-related validity study with a number of organizations; Hoffman used a job component validity approach to generalize validation evidence obtained as part of a consortium project.

Opportunities to Learn

Although psychometrics is an important part of the I/O psychology curriculum, many I/O psychologists continue to learn about test development, validation, and administration from their colleagues, and consortia provide an important vehicle for continued learning. Many decisions are made over the course of a testing project, and the collegial discussion that surrounds those decisions is often highly enlightening, particularly when the topic is new or emerging, such as unproctored Internet testing. In addition, such studies may go beyond simply educating participants and move into innovative research that explores new ways for collecting and analyzing job analysis data, developing measurement tools, and creating new analytic models.

Disadvantages

Despite the substantial cost savings, many companies eschew consortium studies, for a number of reasons.

Establishment of Job Similarity

Sometimes the practical concerns about the similarity of jobs across company boundaries prevent a consortium from forming. Participants must ask the question, "How similar is similar enough?" Is a customer service job in one telephone company the same as the customer service job in another telephone company? Is a customer service job for a bank the same as a customer service job for a computer manufacturer? There are few guidelines to direct the user; one approach is to assume that the *Uniform Guidelines* comments on the similarity of jobs for transportability studies also apply to consortium studies.

> Section 14.E(1): Evidence from criterion-related validity studies.
> a. Job information. A description of the important job behavior(s) of the user's job and the basis on which the behaviors were determined to be important should be provided (essential). A full description of the basis for determining that these important work behaviors are the same as those of the job in the original study (or studies) should be provided (essential).

Liability for Legal and Administrative Challenges

A central concern for many organizations is fear of having one employer's legal problems spill over to the other consortium participants. If one of the participating companies in a consortium has its selection procedures challenged legally and loses the challenge based on a finding that the test is not valid or is biased against a protected class, a host of questions arise: What is the status of the test in the other participating companies in the consortium? What steps should those participating companies take? (Replace the tests? Begin a new validation study?) What are the obligations of the other participating organizations to support the challenged organization? Should the other participating organizations share the legal fees? Should those organizations provide data or resources to support the challenged organization? Many consortia agree that data will be collectively analyzed and individual reports will not be created. Whether a court would mandate that the consortium decompose the aggregated data is not clear.

Administrative challenges from labor unions may also present difficult situations for a consortium study. Assume a consortium of companies is formed to validate a selection procedure for a job that is represented by the same labor union across all the participating companies. If one company loses an arbitration procedure, what precedent is set for the other members of the consortium, and what are their obligations and options?

There is little precedence to guide the I/O psychologist in answering these questions. No case law answers these important questions. A search of legal databases provided no legal cases involving a consortium study in which the nature of the study participants had an impact on the legal question posed.

Test Security

A related concern is the enforcement of security procedures to protect all of the participants' investment in test development and validation. Most consortia make an attempt to agree on the obligations of users of the jointly owned or used selection materials; however, the degree to which these obligations are enforceable is usually in question. Moreover, members of a consortium may be unaware of security problems in another organization and may suffer the consequences associated with lax test security even when their own test administration practices are vigorously enforced.

Another type of security problem occurs when companies participating in a consortium operate in the same geographical area and hire from the same pool of applicants. An applicant can literally take the same test several times in one day. If competing organizations use different cutoff scores, an applicant can "shop" for the least restrictive employer.

Cost of Coordination

Other issues that may deter participation in a consortium study include the additional costs of coordinating the research effort across multiple organizations. A major disadvantage to such studies is often the amount of coordination and cooperation required across organizations that may have different goals, time lines, and priorities. Such coordination can cost additional money and time. When an external consultant is used to conduct the research, the costs of contacts, contracts, and billing arrangements are passed on to the participants in some consortia.

Allocation of Costs

Another issue related to costs of a consortium project is the manner in which costs are allocated to participating organizations. Different models are often found. Some consortia attempt to allocate costs based on the number of employees, assuming that the number of current employees presages future hiring needs and test use. These consortia also tend to establish participant requirements based on the current employees in the job or jobs of interest, in an attempt to share the burden equally. Other consortia divide the costs and sample requirements proportionately. Still other consortia permit more complex arrangements, such as discounting fees based on the number of research participants contributed.

Speed of Progress

When a consortium is set up so that all participating organizations must collect their share of the data before analyses can begin, the consortium research moves only as fast as the slowest company. Many industrial and organizational psychologists find it difficult to keep employees and management of one company interested in a validation effort over a long period of time. Management may lose interest in the project; other more pressing problems may arise; budget dollars may disappear or be allocated to other projects; or the advocate for the testing research may leave. The problems of sustaining enthusiasm are exacerbated when the reasons for delay are not specific to the organization but arise from problems in another organization.

Differences of Opinion

Many consortium projects are managed by industrial and organizational psychologists who are internal consultants in the participating companies. Often, those individuals have ideas about the appropriate conduct of the validity study based on their own experiences, and sometimes their views conflict with those of others. Occasionally, a difficult question will arise from the data analysis, and several points of view about the best approach to resolve it will surface. The professionals representing the consortium participants must resolve the question. For example, psychologists representing the participating organizations may disagree on the value of a pilot test of the experimental tests and criterion measures. Or, a psychologist in one organization may operationally define a power test as one in which 90 percent of the test takers finish 90 percent of the items, whereas another may set a lower standard, 80 percent of test takers finishing 80 percent of the items. Matters may be further complicated when HR professionals, rather than industrial and organizational psychologists, represent their firms and make decisions regarding the development and validation process.

There are myriad ways for disagreeing on the proper conduct of the research. Organizations often fail to anticipate potential disagreements about implementation and the effects that deviations from the consortium's practice may have on all members. Consider a consortium of companies whose hourly employees are represented by the same labor union. This consortium develops and validates tests of cognitive and noncognitive abilities for these represented positions. Both tests are valid predictors of job performance, but the validity of the noncognitive test, though significant, is weaker. With typical selection ratios, the noncognitive test moderates adverse impact somewhat. If one member decides not to implement the noncognitive test because of concerns about the low, albeit significant, validity and the company's ability to develop personality characteristics, where does that leave the other members?

Loss of Competitive Advantage

Sophisticated organizations recognize that their selection processes can be a competitive advantage, allowing them to identify more capable candidates for hire. When a consortium of organizations that hire from the same geographical applicant pools is assembled, the opportunity to assemble a better-qualified workforce is diminished.

Loss of Management Control

Consulting organizations that sponsor consortium efforts have a vested interest in the completion of the research. As such, issues regarding continued sponsorship rest with the consulting firm, not the participating companies. Thus, early adopters of the effort may find themselves waiting for other organizations to join. Later adopters may find that early commitments have dissipated. Time lines can slip beyond the control of the participating organizations. In the worst-case scenario, the firm sponsoring the research may, for very good business reasons, discontinue its sponsorship. The liability of the consulting firm to the participating organizations may be limited contractually. In other forms of sponsorship, there is an implied good-faith agreement among the consortium members to "get along," and at least some form of influence exists among the member organizations. This agreement is not true within the consultant-organized consortium. In fact, the consortium members may not even know of their fellow consortium participants!

From the perspective of the consulting firm, the issues are also daunting, and those issues may account for the relative infrequency with which such efforts are attempted. Agreements dissolve, raising costs for ongoing administration. Participating organizations fail to live up to standards for data collection, raising the risk profile for all consortium members. Economic returns from test sales or licensing fees may not materialize. When business issues trump individual client needs and preferences, strain on client relationships may follow.

Definition of Variables That Affect Validity

Despite the *Uniform Guidelines,* it is not clear to what extent consortium participants have obligations to identify variables that might affect validity. It is not uncommon to find that members of a protected class are concentrated in one company and not another, due to geography, demographics, or even corporate culture. If women in a particular job are concentrated in one company, and gender differences are found, are the differences due to gender or to cultural differences associated with that one organization?

Potential Lack of Data for Establishing Operational Parameters

For consortia in which data are not analyzed by organization, each company may not have sufficient data to guide its efforts in setting a cutoff score or establishing expectancy tables for use of test results. This lack of data may be particularly problematic when a specific company's employees or applicants deviate from the mean of the distribution of abilities being assessed by the tests.

Different Standards of Performance

For many reasons (such as culture, applicant pools), organizations may have different standards for performance, which can create special problems in criterion scores. For example, assume two companies join together to validate selection tests for a job. One company has very high standards; the other, much lower standards. An employee in the "low performance" company who is rated highest on the experimental performance measure may in fact perform at the level of the average employee in the "high performance" company even though their scores are identical. Standardization of scores within company or covariance analyses may not completely solve the problem if the company means are different because of actual performance differences rather than artifacts of data collection or organizational culture.

Theoretical Development

The theoretical basis for the use of a consortium study rests on the assumption that the jobs for which tests are being developed have sufficiently similar characteristics across organizations to warrant the aggregation of data in a cooperative study, despite the cultural influences of each organization. The main theoretical advantages of the consortium study lie primarily in increased sample sizes and, hence, the more powerful statistical assessment.

Research Base

The literature on consortium studies is sparse, and what there is typically mentions the consortium effort only in passing. Virtually none of the research explores issues specific to consortium studies.

Review of Legal Implications

A review of the legal literature produced no legal cases in which consortium work was challenged because the data were collected and the results were reported in aggregate. Despite the lack of litigation, consortium studies should give the practitioner pause and raise a number of questions, such as the following:

1. What is the consortium's obligation to each organization in the consortium?
2. What is the obligation of each organization to the other organizations in the consortium?
3. What rights to the individual organization data do other members of the consortium have?
4. To what extent could a legal problem in one organization create legal issues in another?

The answers to such questions depend on the type of consortium formed. When an industry organization exists and manages the consortia for the benefit of members, the industry organization (for example, EEI, AGA, API, LIMRA) may take responsibility for the defense of a test in a legal or administrative challenge. However, a consortium in which several companies have banded together for the purposes of test development and validation may specify that each organization is responsible for its own legal defense. In the case of a trade association or a consultant who has organized a consortium study, the responsibility for defending the test is dependent on the agreement the consulting firm has with its clients or the trade association has with its members. Often, consultants are eager to defend their work.

If the consortium has decided to aggregate data across organizations and has created no means of tracing the data back to its source, the organization that has been challenged may have no other option but to provide all the aggregated data. In fact, one of the main reasons for joining a consortium is the reduction of sample size for each participating company. The data from a single organization may be insufficient to establish the validity of the inference to be made from the test.

Best practices suggest that successful consortia define the obligations of the individual to the group and the group to the individual at the start of the research, before any legal challenges have occurred.

Review of Professional Implications

Perhaps the greatest implication of consortium studies for I/O practitioners is the demand placed on their management skills. I/O practitioners need not only basic management skills but also the ability to find compromise solutions when organizations disagree on approach.

A related implication of consortium studies accrues from the close interaction with other professionals throughout the project. I/O practitioners often report learning a great deal from others about various approaches to test development and validation, project management, and test implementation. But doing so requires that they develop and exercise collegial and flexible professional relationships. Such interdependent styles are not necessarily part of graduate curricula and may be more difficult to adopt than one might think at first blush. Additionally, consortia may raise substantive and complex ethical issues such as conflicts of interest between obligations to and agreements with other professionals and the demand and interests of one's employer.

Practical Development

Although there are many approaches to forming a consortium for the purpose of testing research, we have listed the major steps in the process as follows. Sometimes the group or organization initiating the consortium undertakes these steps; other times, representatives of the participating organizations must take them.

1. Identify the jobs or job families for which selection procedures will be developed.
2. Identify and recruit possible consortium members.
3. Establish the criteria for evaluating the similarity of the target positions (or components, if a job component approach is taken).
4. Develop a research plan, including
   Steps in the job analysis, test development, and validation
   Sample size requirements for each phase of the research

      Planned analyses

      Unit(s) of analysis

      Time line

5. Develop an implementation plan that includes

      Communications among members and with participants

      Mechanisms for obtaining informed consent of participants, including communications and interface with supervisors and bargaining units

      Data collection processes

      Format of data submission

      Mileposts for reviews

6. Confirm participants in the consortium and obtain clear commitments, including contractual agreements if necessary.

7. Establish the rights and responsibilities of the consortium members concerning such topics as

      Contributions to the sample

      Adherence to data collection protocols, timing, and instructions

      Adherence to time schedules

      Resolution of disagreements

      Opportunities for review of results

      Confidentiality of data

      Test security

      Publication of research results

      Notification to participants of security breaches or legal and administrative challenges

      Responsibilities for defense of resulting tests

Constraints and Risks

As already noted, the disadvantages reflect the problems consortia often present: difficulties of staying on schedule, disagreements or differences of opinion among participants regarding the study activities or implementation procedures, lack of management control, and lack of organization-specific data. Whether an organization pursues the consortium approach to test development depends on the feasibility of a local validation study, the availability of other validation options, its own resources, and the willingness and desire of organizations with similar positions to cooperate.

Despite the problems of consortia, the primary advantages of a consortium study remain: (1) those related to cost savings due to the distribution of expenses associated with collecting data and paying for study design and analysis, (2) those related to improving the technical feasibility (and therefore quality) of the research effort, (3) those related to the enhanced defensibility of procedures when such evidence exists for transportability across relatively homogenous business environments, and (4) the endorsement and encouragement of the *Uniform Guidelines*. In some cases, joining a consortium is a matter of choice and an acceptance of the advantages along with the disadvantages of cooperative works, but in many cases the consortium study presents the best option available for establishing validity.

References

Cohen, J., Cohen, P., West, S. G., & Aiken, L. S. (2003). *Applied multiple regression/correlation analysis for the behavioral sciences*. Mahwah, NJ: Erlbaum.

Equal Employment Opportunity Commission, Civil Service Commission, Department of Labor, & Department of Justice. (1978). *Uniform guidelines on employee selection procedures. Federal Register, 43*(166), 38290–38315.

Hoffman, C. C. (1999). Generalizing physical ability test validity: A case study using test transportability, validity generalization, and construct-related validation evidence. *Personnel Psychology, 52,* 1019–1041.

Motowidlo, S. J., Dunnette, M. D., & Carter, G. W. (1990). An alternative selection procedure: The low-fidelity simulation. *Journal of Applied Psychology, 75,* 640–647.

Society for Industrial and Organizational Psychology. (2003). *Principles for the validation and use of personnel selection procedures* (4th ed.). Bowling Green, OH: Society for Industrial and Organizational Psychology.

CHAPTER 8

Application of Content Validation Methods to Broader Constructs

Damian J. Stelly and
Harold W. Goldstein

The *Uniform Guidelines on Employee Selection Procedures* (Equal Employment Opportunity Commission, Civil Service Commission, Department of Labor, & Department of Justice, 1978) appear to specifically exclude the use of a content validation strategy for supporting ability constructs such as judgment or conscientiousness. The *Uniform Guidelines* offer some guidance concerning the application of content-based validation methods for tests of knowledge, skills, abilities, and other characteristics (KSAOs), but much of the language used suggests restricting the use of such methods to testing approaches for which a clear link to observable work behaviors can be demonstrated (for example, work samples or simulations). However, a more recent understanding of content validation in the field of psychology appears to endorse the use of such an approach with broader constructs.

In this chapter we explore the question of using content validation methodologies to substantiate inferences drawn from measures of broader constructs and consider how this approach could be properly implemented. We review the pertinent literature regarding this question as well as consider the question from the viewpoint of legal standards and current professional practices of the field. Based on this review, we conclude by outlining some practical implications and associated cautions regarding how content validity methodologies can be leveraged to support the use of measures of broader constructs in selection contexts.

Theoretical Development

Conceptualizing validity into different types (for example, criterion-related, content, and construct) has caused a great deal of confusion for the field of personnel selection (McPhail, 2007, this volume). The focus of this chapter (examining the use of content validity methodologies for evaluating broader constructs) hints at another validation model—construct—that could prove to be even more problematic. In addition, although the field has progressed to embrace a unitary framework for validity—a concept that subsumes content validity as part of the evidence that is required for construct validity—notions of content validity as an independent type of validity have remained, causing Guion and Gibson (1988) to comment that content validity has proved itself to be "as durable as other superstitions" (p. 350). The concept of content validity may have such resiliency, in part, because of continued references to it in legal guidelines and testing standards—such as earlier versions of the *Standards for Educational and Psychological Testing* (American Educational Research Association, American Psychological Association, & National Council on Measurement in Education, 1999) and the *Principles for the Validation and Use of Personnel Selection Procedures* (Society for Industrial and Organizational Psychology, 2003). Alone among these, the *Uniform Guidelines* has remained static and has not progressed along with the professional thinking of the field. Thus, despite convincing arguments to the contrary (such as Dunnette & Borman, 1979; Guion, 1977, 1980; Messick, 1989; Tenopyr, 1977), the term *content validity* is still commonly referred to in personnel selection, the notion of it as a type of validity has persisted, and various techniques and procedures associated with it are commonly used.

Simply put, content validity has been defined as the degree to which a test measures the content domain it purports to measure (Sireci, 1998). Typically in personnel selection, KSAOs that are critical to the performance domain are identified, usually through job analysis procedures, and measures of the identified KSAOs are developed subsequently. Content validity involves the extent to which it is judged that the content of the test that is developed (such as the test items and tasks) is representative of the targeted content domain (Guion, 1978; Messick, 1989). These content validity judgments are typically made by subject matter experts (SMEs), who may be job analysts, trainers, or the target job's incumbents and supervisors.

Interestingly, this content validation approach in personnel selection has become viewed by many as a viable alternative method of collecting validation information when compared to other strategies that are seen as less feasible. For example, some (such as Goldstein, Zedeck, & Schneider, 1993) have noted that implementing a criterion-related validation strategy may be difficult if the situation involves small sample sizes or if there are difficulties obtaining accurate performance data (for example, supervisors who are unwilling or unable to evaluate current employees for a concurrent criterion-related validity study). Furthermore, using what has been thought of as a pure construct validation approach may be seen by organizations as requiring too much effort, time, and other resources, especially when designing initial measures of new constructs (such as emotional intelligence). As noted by Messick (1988), construct validation approaches appear complicated and vague, which makes organizations reluctant to use them. For these reasons and others, it has been noted that content validation approaches have been increasingly used in personnel selection (Goldstein, Zedeck, & Schneider, 1993).

A critical point that we want to make clear in this chapter is that although a content validation approach may be considered to be more *feasible* in certain situations than other strategies for collecting evidence of validity, it should not necessarily be viewed as *easier* to conduct. What needs to be understood is that rigor is required even (perhaps, especially) when using content-based methodologies. Based on our experiences in the field with personnel selection, this view is often not shared by those who employ content validation strategies to develop evidence for the validity of their tests. Many appear to feel that content validity is established by merely designing a test in an appropriate manner (for example, conducting a job analysis that is used to design test stimuli) and necessary steps are sometimes skipped, such as collecting judgment data from experts (for example, SME judgments regarding the content validity of test items are not collected).

Given these observations regarding the lack of rigor often found when it comes to content validity, it may be especially troublesome to consider the premise of this chapter, which is whether content validation can be used with broader constructs. Early discussions in the field of personnel selection regarding appropriate circumstances for using a content validation strategy focused on tests, such as work samples, in which the behaviors required by the test were a close approximation of the observable behaviors of the job. A common example often provided was that content validation was appropriate for assessing the validity of a typing test for measuring typing ability, because SMEs could accurately make judgments about concepts as straightforward as psychomotor tasks. In addition, these discussions stressed that content validation methods were not necessarily suitable for tests that measured unobservable broad constructs, such as aspects of intelligence and personality. If we factor in that the *Uniform Guidelines* echoed this sentiment (as will be discussed later in this chapter) and appeared specifically to restrict the use of content validation for broad psychological constructs such as judgment and conscientiousness, it is clear that great caution is needed in discussing the concept of using content validation methodologies with respect to broader constructs.

The Role of Content in Construct Validation

Current theoretical thinking in the field clearly indicates that content-oriented methods are part of the larger process of construct validation. Although original conceptualizations (such as Ghiselli, 1964) viewed validity as being constituted of three main types (criterion-related, content, and construct), the modern unitary conceptualization of validity rejects this notion. The unitary approach forgoes the idea of types of validity, instead equating the notion of validity with construct validity (Messick, 1989); that is, all validation is viewed as focused on constructs, and the various types of validity previously identified are subsumed under the general notion of construct validity (Sireci, 1995). This unitary conceptualization views content validity as providing evidence regarding the construct validity of a test (Anastasi, 1988; Messick, 1988, 1989). Under this approach, "content validity is an important component of construct validity because it provides evidence about the degree to which the elements of the assessment instrument are relevant to and representative of the targeted construct" (Haynes, Richard, & Kubany, 1995, p. 241). In other words, content validity is a strategy that contributes evidence to evaluate construct validity, which implies that content validity techniques can be employed to collect information about the validity of a test for measuring a construct. Thus, the short answer to the premise of this chapter is that current thinking in the science supports the general notion that content validity evidence can be used for constructs. However, the issue of *broad* constructs could be questionable, depending on how clearly the construct domain can be specified—a topic we will address later in this chapter.

Construct validity, which is equated with validity in general by the unitary view, is the collection of evidence for the interpretation of test scores (Messick, 1995). Content validity procedures (or what many now refer to as content-oriented procedures, to avoid terms that hint at different types of validity) are critical *parts* of the construct validation process. In contributing to construct validity, content validation methods are thought of as focusing on content relevance and representativeness (Messick, 1995; Haynes, Richard, & Kubany, 1995; Sireci, 1998). Content relevance is the extent to which the tasks of the test or assessment are relevant to the target construct domain; that is, relevance refers to whether the test items reflect the construct domain to be measured. Content representativeness focuses on the degree to which the test items cover the important parts of the construct domain. Thus, representativeness refers to the extent to which the test items are proportional to the facets of the construct domain. The content relevance and representativeness, which are commonly assessed using expert judgments (such as SME ratings), reflect the content aspect of construct validity.

By default, this view of validity provides support for the concept of content validating measures of construct domains. In some ways, the real question may be whether there is actually a clear difference between content and construct domains. As originally conceptualized, content validity focused on what was thought to be content rather than construct domains. Guion (1987) notes that a content domain is first specified and content validity indicates the extent to which the content of the test (such as the test items) is a proper sample of that domain. However, in discussing this issue, Guion goes on to make the point that there may be no clear difference between what is labeled a content domain and what is labeled a construct domain and that distinguishing between them is a judgment call at best. Messick (1988) made similar statements, noting that "typically content-related inferences are inseparable from construct-related inferences" (p. 38).

In further discussing the topic, Guion (1987) stated that what is "called a construct differs from that called a content domain mainly in the degree of abstraction, and it is time we recognized that the line where we draw the distinction is arbitrary" (p. 209). He went on to note that thinking of content validation as sampling from a narrow domain, such as the tasks and knowledge required by a job, was not necessary and that theorizing about the content domain could aim at broader cognitive and personality-based abilities (which many might consider constructs). Similarly, Sireci (1995) noted that "divergent definitions of content validity stem from long-standing ambiguity regarding what is a 'construct' and what is a 'content' domain" (p. 20). He went on to say that "distinctions between construct and content domains have typically been made on the basis of tangibility; constructs are described as unobservable and undefinable, and content domains are characterized as observable and definable" (p. 20). In summary, the level of abstraction or tangibility appears to be the main difference, and, as noted by Guion, it is a judgment as to whether an attribute is characterized as content or construct. Given this overlap, it is reasonable to conclude that content-oriented procedures can be used to provide information about construct as well as content domains, which may not be clearly differentiated in any case.

However, although content validation methods may be applicable to both content and construct domains, and content-oriented evidence may be an important aspect of establishing construct validity (that is, validity in general as conceptualized by the unitary approach), it must be understood that many would not consider content evidence to be sufficient for establishing the validity of a test; to them, content validity evidence is seen as necessary, but not sufficient, for validity. Messick (1988) notes that:

> In practice, content-related evidence usually takes the form of consensual informed judgments about the representative coverage of content in a test and about its relevance to a particular behavioral domain of interest. But this is evidence about the content of the test instrument and not evidence to support inferences from individual's test scores, which are not even addressed in typical considerations of content. Thus, in a fundamental sense, content-related evidence does not qualify as validity evidence at all, although such content considerations clearly do and should influence the nature of score inferences supported by other evidence. (p. 38)

Guion (1987) made a similar argument, stating that construct validity goes beyond content-oriented approaches to developing tests because it focuses on the inferences that can be drawn from resulting scores on the test. Messick (1989) goes on to present six distinguishable aspects of validity, with the content approach being one of them that focuses on gathering information about content relevance and representativeness. In this scheme, content-oriented evidence is important but only one aspect of the validation process. Given this line of thinking, and despite what the *Uniform Guidelines* and professional practice state about using content validation methods in specific situations (for example, with observable work behaviors as opposed to abstract constructs; with work sample and simulation styled tests), one needs to consider if content-oriented methods alone should be relied on for establishing validity of a test, regardless of whether one is focusing on a content domain or a broader construct domain.

Factors Impacting Appropriateness of a Content Validity Approach to Constructs

In reviewing the literature, a number of factors emerge that impact whether content strategies are viable for establishing validity. We will examine a few of these factors and discuss their implications for the purpose of deciding whether to use a content validity strategy on broader constructs. One key issue is that of domain specification, in that the domain being sampled must be clearly defined and understood. As noted by Guion (1987), "the development of a content domain definition may be thorough and careful or approximate and crude" but "meticulously defined domains, carefully sampled, may ordinarily be expected to measure the attribute well" (p. 208). Numerous articles focusing on what procedures should be followed for content validation (such as Crocker, 1997; Guion, 1987; Haynes, Richard, & Kubany, 1995), as well as the *Principles* and *Standards,* list domain specification as the first critical step.

This principle regarding domain specification is directly applicable to content validating a construct. Haynes, Richard, and Kubany (1995) stress the need to "define the domain and facets of the construct carefully." They note that "a construct that is poorly defined, undifferentiated, and imprecisely partitioned will limit the content validity of the assessment instrument" (p. 245). However, one should realize that this is difficult to do because a construct is thought to be more abstract and less tangible than content. With a construct, even *more* attention must be placed on carefully defining the domain and its facets. It is important to remember that "many constructs have similar labels but dissimilar domains and facets" (Haynes, Richard, & Kubany, 1995, p. 241). This diversity makes it critical to delve deeply into the domain of a construct and accurately capture it.

One must attempt to delineate clearly the boundaries of the construct (that is, where one construct ends and another begins) and what constitutes the various facets of the construct and what does not. Often a construct can be vague, which makes it more difficult to define. As discussed by Lawshe (1975), domains range from the directly observable to the highly abstract, and the higher the level of abstraction, the greater the inferential leap that SMEs need to make in assessing content relevance. Thus, the more the domain is a construct in nature as opposed to job-specific content in nature, the greater the leap that typically needs to be made. Furthermore, the broader the construct gets, the less specific and more abstract it gets, which in turn requires even greater inferential leaps to be made. Thus, the broader and more abstract a construct, the more difficult it will be to define, and the greater the effort needed to do so.

In terms of defining the domain in personnel selection, the main process used is typically job analysis. Job analysis should provide detailed information regarding the content domain in terms of the critical tasks of the job and the knowledge, skills, and abilities required to complete these tasks successfully. As the focus of the job analysis shifts toward the construct domain, careful attention must be paid to clearly defining the constructs and their various facets. Job analysis with respect to constructs should gather information on how these constructs are manifested on the job. Collecting statements that illustrate the behaviors that reflect the constructs will prove extremely useful in terms of carefully defining the domain. The need to carefully define the constructs reflects our earlier point about the rigor needed to conduct a content validation study. Doing so is often not easy, but if one intends to expand the use of content methodologies to capture broader constructs, it may prove even more difficult—thereby increasing the need for rigor.

The key point for domain definition is level of specificity. The domain definition and specification process must gather information on the target construct and, most important, how it operationalizes for the target job. The construct should not necessarily be examined in general terms; rather, efforts must be exerted to demonstrate how it emerges on the job and what behaviors reflect its presence in that context. As noted previously, many constructs have similar names at a general level but can play out much differently in terms of the job. Haynes, Richard, and Kubany (1995) note that "an assessment instrument may have satisfactory content validity for one definition of a construct but not for others" (p. 241). For instance, consider the common example from job analysis, in which it was pointed out that the skills that a manager has are similar to the skills used by a homemaker (such as time management, people skills, motivational capabilities) (Arvey & Begalla, 1975). They are similar skills, but they are needed at different levels and operationalized in different contexts. This information is critical in domain specification. In another example, a typical construct used in the workplace is creativity, but how that is manifested in jobs ranging from marketing product manager to research and development designer to customer sales representative can be extremely different in terms of the nature of the construct (such as which aspect of it is dominant) and the level of the construct required (for example, the amount needed, the degree of complexity and sophistication).

Another important issue is that in content validation all elements of a testing procedure must be considered (Goldstein, Zedeck, & Schneider, 1993; Haynes, Richard, & Kubany, 1995); that is, along with the developed test stimuli, all other aspects of a test are subject to content validation. These aspects include the test instructions, the format of the questions, and the response mode. All elements of a test are subject to content validation, including both the target content or construct tapped and the method(s) used to do so. Thus, the domain to be mapped includes not just "what" is to be assessed but also "how" it is to be measured.

In validating a content domain, this issue is commonly discussed. One frequently encountered example is that when using a multiple-choice written test to capture job knowledge, part of what is measured, in addition to the target content (that is, job knowledge), is how to respond to multiple-choice questions (for example, how to compare various possible responses, how to choose the best possible responses, how to read and write) (Goldstein, Zedeck, & Goldstein, 2002; Hakel, 1998). Consideration of these issues is important to avoid or limit content contamination arising because the test measures things unrelated to the content domain that one is trying to capture. This concern is, in part, why others have stressed the positive aspects of test fidelity to the job, thus reducing the extent to which the test format measures things unrelated to the target content (Goldsten, Zedeck, & Schneider, 1993). This issue remains a critical concern when applying content methodologies to constructs. Messick (1995) described similar concerns as a major threat to construct validity as part of construct-irrelevant variance. He noted that construct irrelevant variance could arise from aspects of the test task that are extraneous to the target construct. He provided as an example "the intrusion of undue reading comprehension requirements in a test of subject matter knowledge" (p. 742). Therefore, aspects of the test such as the instructions, the stimuli mode, and the response mode should all be considered when content validation judgments are made with regard to the target construct domain.

Another key issue in the process of using content methodologies is identification of qualified SMEs to provide content validity judgments. Typically, job incumbents or supervisors who are familiar with the content domain in question are asked to make judgments about the extent to which the content of the test items captures this target domain. In addition to job incumbents and supervisors, others may also play an SME role, such as job analysts who are familiar with the content domain and the target job. The main issue to consider in identifying SMEs for the content validity process is to ask who, in fact, has the expertise required to make the needed judgments.

When shifting to content-validating a construct, the SMEs may still be persons such as job incumbents or supervisors; however, depending on how abstract the target construct is, one may need to identify other types of SMEs. For example, Lawshe (1975) notes that the more observable the content, the greater the chance that incumbents, supervisors, or others that know the job can make sound judgments when it comes to content validity. However, Lawshe states that as the content becomes more abstract and a greater inferential leap is required, "job incumbents and supervisors normally do not have the insights to make the required judgments" (p. 566). He mentions that this is the point at which there is a need to shift from a content strategy to a construct validation approach (note that this thinking was prior to a shift to a more unitary view of validity). Given this observation by Lawshe, it seems reasonable to think that as we discuss using content validation methods with regard to constructs (a practice he cautioned against, indicating instead a need to shift to what was at the time considered a pure construct validation approach involving collection of convergent and divergent evidence), it may be that job incumbents and supervisors do not have the expertise required to be considered SMEs for making content validity judgments. In these situations, it may be that there is a need to involve persons more familiar with the targeted constructs, such as professionals from an applicable field (for example, a kinesiologist when evaluating the content validity of a test of strength or flexibility). At the very least, we must consider using a mix of SMEs representing individuals familiar with the job and others familiar with the construct. A joint effort between these groups may produce the expertise needed to make accurate judgments regarding the validity of a test designed to measure a broader construct.

Summary

The question of using content validation methodologies to generate evidence of validity for a broad construct is complex, with no clearly right or wrong answer. In many ways the literature alludes to the idea that it can be done, especially in light of the modern unitary conceptualization of validity. In that view, content validation methods are part of construct validation; moreover, the literature includes reference to the idea that it is rather arbitrary to distinguish what is a content domain versus what is a construct domain. However, a key point is that rigor is required in making the greater inferential leap to the more abstract construct; that is, the judgments required are more difficult and abstract, and issues that must be considered include (1) how clearly the domain can be defined, (2) what aspects of the test may contribute irrelevant variance to the domain, and (3) what types of SMEs are best suited to make accurate judgments about the target domain.

Research Base

Overview

When we examine the literature, it appears that little or no research has been conducted directly on the question of whether content validation methodologies can be applied to broader constructs. In fact, little research has been conducted on the topic of content validation methods in general. Although a review of the literature does identify hundreds of reported studies on the validation of various testing instruments, and many of these include content methods as an approach used, there has been little research on the methodology of content validation itself. Goldstein, Zedeck, and Schneider (1993) came to a similar conclusion when reviewing the literature for their chapter on the job analysis-content validation process. Within their chapter, they raised many critical questions regarding content validity that needed to be addressed, such as investigations into what makes for an effective SME and what factors impact the reliability of content validity judgment data. Although these questions and others have been largely neglected in practice, there has been some pertinent research conducted, the findings of which are discussed in this section. We will focus on research that has been conducted on content validation of a content domain as none specifically has been conducted on construct domains (although, as noted earlier, application of the label *content* or *construct* is somewhat arbitrary). We will return later to the issue of how the research that has been conducted applies to the idea of using content-oriented methods for broader constructs.

Methods of Collecting Test Content Data

Sireci (1995) describes two main approaches to collecting content validity data: subjective and empirical methods. He states that:

> Subjective methods refer to studies where subject matter experts (SMEs) are used to evaluate test items and rate them according to their relevance and representativeness to the content domain tested. Empirical methods refer to those procedures that analyze the data obtained from administering the test (test and item score data). (p. 27)

Subjective Methods. It is subjective methods, which rely on collecting judgment data from SMEs, that are more commonly thought of and focused on when it comes to content validation as used in the field of personnel selection. There are a wide variety of subjective methods that all involve collecting data from SMEs on the extent to which the content of the test reflects the target domain. Many of these methods focus on summarizing the subjective ratings of SMEs quantitatively, often into an index of some kind. SME ratings usually focus on evaluating the test content (such as the items of the test) regarding the extent to which it reflects the desired domain. One of the better-known subjective methods in personnel selection is Lawshe's (1975) Content Validity Index (CVI), which is computed based on the ratio of judgments from an SME panel that indicate items on a test are essential for tapping a given domain. Other researchers have developed similar approaches, such as the Item-Objective Congruence Index created by Hambleton (1980) and another validity index designed by Aiken (1980).

Sireci (1998) noted that one of the limitations of this type of approach is that respondents are usually restricted to rating the links between the test content (such as test items) and the target domain, based on the options provided by the test developer. That is, SMEs are asked to link test items to specific domains and will do so even if the item would be more reflective of a domain that is not presented. In other words, these approaches can restrict the domains considered when judging the content validity of the test. In addition, Sireci noted that these types of subjective approaches are open to typical rating errors such as leniency (that is, providing high ratings on all linkages between test items and target domains) and social desirability (such as trying to answer in a manner that the test designer wants). To address these concerns, methods must be designed to capture content validation judgments that do not bias the SMEs by providing information about how they are expected to respond.

Sireci and others have conducted research to design approaches to content validation that overcome these limitations. For example, Tucker (1961) used factor analysis to examine SME content validity ratings. He found two interpretable factors related to test content. One factor was interpreted as representing a general level of approval for the content validity of the sample items, and the second factor was interpreted as showing two schools of thought among the SMEs as to what types of items were most relevant. Sireci and Geisinger (1992) proposed the use of multidimensional scaling (MDS) and cluster analysis. This approach was built on the idea that test items that reflected similar content areas would be perceived by SMEs as more similar and therefore grouped together. They had SMEs make paired comparisons of items, and MDS was used to cluster items along content dimensions. They did not provide the SMEs with specific categories that they had to use. Based on the results of this study and follow-up research, Sireci (1995) concluded that "MDS and cluster analysis of SME item similarity ratings provided both convergent and discriminant evidence of the underlying content structure of the test" (p. 28).

Melnick and Henk (1997) conducted a study that compared two methods of content validation. One procedure was a forced choice method that provided the SMEs with content categories, which arguably could bias their responses. The second method was based on Wiley's (1967) latent partition analysis. This procedure had the SMEs read all test items and sort them into as many "meaningful and mutually exclusive" categories as they deemed appropriate.

A summary of these judgments was used as a measure of content validity. This second approach did not provide a priori domain categories to the SMEs, thus removing that potential source of bias. The authors concluded that both methods yielded a degree of content validity evidence, but that the latent review provided finer distinctions among the items and thus may provide more accurate information.

Empirical Methods. As noted previously, research has also been conducted on empirical approaches to content validity. Empirical approaches escape the potential bias of SME ratings by instead focusing on investigating test *respondent* data (as opposed to data obtained from SMEs). Such techniques also involve MDS, cluster analysis, and factor analysis, but they are used to examine the structure and dimensions of the content measured by the test (such as Oltman, Stricker, & Barrows, 1990). Recent work by Ding and Hershberger (2002) explored how structural equation modeling could be used to assess item-content structures. Based on their results, further research using such techniques is warranted. However, in general, the major drawback of most empirical methods of exploring content validity is that they do not provide information about relevance of items to a particular domain (Sireci & Geisinger, 1995).

The Quality of Content Validity Judgments

Limited research has been conducted on the quality of SME-based content relevance judgments. One area that has been examined in a few studies involves investigation of the reliability of the SME ratings. In particular, it is recommended that the level of interrater agreement among SMEs' ratings of relevance and representativeness of the test items be calculated (Grant & Davis, 1997; Rubio, Berg-Weger, Tebb, Lee, & Rauch, 2003; Waltz, Strickland, & Lenz, 1991). Levels of interrater agreement deemed acceptable in this literature range from 0.70 to 0.80. Interrater agreement substantially lower than these levels should concern the test developer in terms of the implications for the validity of the test device. More in-depth questions regarding factors that impact the reliability of SME content validity judgments have not been fully explored.

Penfield and Miller (2004) recently examined improving the quality of content ratings by using asymmetric confidence intervals. They noted that typically the mean SME rating is used in content validation studies and doing so can be problematic for a number of reasons (for example, lack of stability in the sample mean rating, lack of knowledge of how close the sample mean rating is to the actual unknown population mean). Penfield and Miller suggested that one approach for addressing these concerns is to construct a confidence interval, but they noted that content validation data are less than ideal for this purpose because of small SME sample sizes and the truncated nature of the rating scales typically found in such studies. They went on to suggest using an asymmetric score confidence interval that would overcome many of these problems, and they provided a demonstration of this technique. Such approaches that address the unique nature of content validity data (such as small sample sizes) warrant further thought and research.

Another avenue for investigating the quality of the content validity ratings is to examine how well content validity data correspond to other types of validity data. In reviewing the literature, we identified only two studies, one of which was unpublished, that examined the relationship between content validity ratings and other validity indicators. Ostroff and Schmitt (1987) investigated the correspondence between content validity ratings and concurrent criterion-related validity data for an in-basket exercise. They used Lawshe's content validity ratio (CVR) to capture the content validity data and supervisory ratings of performance to capture the criterion-related validity performance data. Their analyses generally showed nonsignificant correlations between the two types of validity data, thus providing no support for the relationship between these two validity indicators.

Carrier, Dalessio, and Brown (1990) also investigated the relationship between content validity and criterion-related validity. The study demonstrated only limited support for hypotheses regarding relationships between these validity indicators. Relationships between Lawshe's CVR and criterion-related validity coefficients yielded only moderate, yet significant, correlations for one of three interviews included in the study. Further thinking and research are needed to investigate the relationships between various indicators

of validity; however, the initial results, based on correlations between criterion-related validity coefficients and content validity ratings, are less than promising.

Research Implications for Content Validity with Broader Constructs

The research findings presented demonstrate that although some
research has been conducted on content validation methods, we
have really only just begun to examine the multitude of unan-
swered questions that need to be addressed. What can be seen is
that a number of researchers are investigating how to conduct content validity in a rigorous scientific manner that can overcome potential biases and flaws of the current process. In terms of applying
content-oriented methods to broad constructs, a key point to understand is that the rigor required is likely to be even more important. For example, with SMEs making judgments regarding
broader constructs, there is additional room for and possibility of
error. The inferential leaps that need to be made with broader constructs are even greater, and it may be much harder to evaluate
items with regard to a more abstract construct domain than it is
for a more concrete content domain. As noted by Lawshe (1975):

> The higher the level of abstraction, the greater is the "inferential
> leap" required to demonstrate validity by other than a criterion-
> related approach. For example, it is one thing to say, "This job per-
> formance domain involves the addition of whole numbers; Test A
> measures the ability to add whole numbers; therefore, Test A is
> content valid for identifying candidates who have this proficiency."
> It is quite another thing to say, "This job performance domain in-
> volves the use of deductive reasoning; Test B purports to measure
> deductive reasoning; therefore, Test B is valid for identifying those
> who are capable of functioning in this job performance domain."
> (p. 565)

The types of research just summarized, which aim to make the
content validation process more reliable and accurate, are needed
even more when trying to apply content validation methods to
broader constructs. Since the leaps that we are asking SMEs to
make are greater with broader constructs, it is essential that they
be of the highest possible quality. Accordingly, continued research
on these and other factors that impact the quality of the content

validation process is critical to development of a rigorous and scientific process in which we can have confidence.

Review of Legal Implications

Since 1978, the *Uniform Guidelines* have functioned essentially as a basic legal compliance manual for the implementation of employee selection procedures. With regard to the topic of this chapter, however, they are somewhat enigmatic. In this section, we review the *Uniform Guidelines'* instruction in relation to the application of content validation methods to broader constructs. We conclude by discussing relevant federal court cases.

The Uniform Guidelines

The *Uniform Guidelines* were intended to be consistent with professional standards (see Section 5C), yet the *Uniform Guidelines* have remained unchanged for nearly thirty years. In contrast, professional standards (that is, the *Principles* and the *Standards*) have been updated frequently to reflect our evolving understanding of the concept of validation and various sources of validity evidence. Despite the fact that the consistency goal cannot be met as long as the *Uniform Guidelines* remain a static document (with the situation worsening with the passage of time), practitioners cannot lose sight of the fact that where differences exist between the *Uniform Guidelines* and professional standards, the *Uniform Guidelines* will be given precedence by enforcement agencies (Equal Employment Opportunity Commission, Civil Service Commission, Department of Labor, & Department of Justice, 1978). Thus, despite the lack of updating, the *Uniform Guidelines'* position on content validation should be studied carefully by practitioners.

It is difficult to reach a firm conclusion concerning research contexts in which a content validation approach would be considered appropriate based on the *Uniform Guidelines*. In fact, the *Uniform Guidelines'* requirements concerning content validation have been described by one prominent industrial psychologist as "confused and confusing" (Guion, 1998, p. 183). Although we would not claim to offer the only interpretation of specific statements we cite from the *Uniform Guidelines,* we will attempt to summarize and interpret key provisions relating to the topic of content validation for broader constructs.

Some of the potential for confusion may arise from the fact that the *Uniform Guidelines* actually seem to be referring to multiple applications of content validation, yet these distinctions are not clearly delineated in the text. Perhaps the clearest indication of the different approaches discussed in the *Uniform Guidelines* is the following statement describing information to be documented in content validity research: "The evidence demonstrating that the selection procedure is a representative work sample, a representative sample of work behavior(s), or a representative sample of knowledge, skill, or ability as used as a part of a work behavior and necessary for that behavior should be provided (essential)" [15C(5)]. Thus, content validity evidence may be sought for applications such as (1) a work sample, (2) a sample of work behavior(s), or (3) a representative sample of a knowledge, skill, or ability used in work behaviors. Of these applications, the first two are more traditional applications of content methods, whereas the third application, to KSAOs, is most related to the topic of this chapter.

The *Uniform Guidelines* first address the appropriateness of content validation for KSAOs rather than work samples or direct samples of work behaviors in section 14C(1), in which they state:

> Selection procedures which purport to measure knowledges, skills, or abilities may in certain circumstances be justified by content validity, although they may not be representative samples [of the content of the job], if the knowledge, skill, or ability measured by the selection procedure can be operationally defined as provided in paragraph 14C(4) of this section, and if that knowledge, skill, or ability is a necessary prerequisite to successful job performance.

This statement makes three important points with respect to content validation for KSAOs: (1) selection procedures measuring KSAOs can be justified by content validity only in certain circumstances, (2) KSAOs measured by the selection procedure must be operationally defined as explained in 14C(4), and (3) KSAOs must be a necessary prerequisite to successful job performance (which is also a requirement applying to any application of content validation). By noting that the application of content validation research to KSAOs may be justified only in certain circumstances, the *Uniform Guidelines* appear to be subjecting this application of content validation to close scrutiny, making the issue of operational definition particularly salient. The meaning of the term "operational definition" in this context is described in Section 14C(4):

> In the case of a selection procedure measuring a knowledge, the knowledge being measured should be operationally defined as that body of learned information which is used in and is a necessary prerequisite for observable aspects of work behavior of the job. In the case of skills or abilities, the skill or ability being measured should be operationally defined in terms of observable aspects of work behavior of the job. For any selection procedure measuring a knowledge, skill, or ability the user should show that (a) the selection procedure measures and is a representative sample of that knowledge, skill, or ability; and (b) that knowledge, skill, or ability is used in and is a necessary prerequisite to performance of critical or important work behavior(s). In addition, to be content valid, a selection procedure measuring a skill or ability should either closely approximate an observable work behavior, or its product should closely approximate an observable work product.

Here the *Uniform Guidelines* distinguish between the measurement of knowledge and the measurement of skills and abilities. With respect to knowledge, it is necessary to show that the knowledge being measured is that body of learned information that is used in and is a necessary prerequisite for observable aspects of work behavior. Although knowledge tested must be linked to observable aspects of work behavior, there is no requirement that a test must in any way simulate aspects of work behavior. In contrast, skills and abilities must be operationally defined in terms of observable aspects of work behavior, and either the measure used should closely approximate an observable work behavior, or its product should closely approximate an observable work product. In either case, the selection procedure should be a representative sample of a KSAO, and the KSAO must be a necessary prerequisite to performance of critical or important work behaviors. It is noteworthy that the *Uniform Guidelines* define the term *work behavior* as follows:

An activity performed to achieve the objectives of the job. Work behaviors involve observable (physical) components and unobservable (mental) components. A work behavior consists of the performance of one or more tasks. Knowledge, skills, and abilities are not behaviors, although they may be applied in work behaviors. [Section 16Y]

Note that the excerpt from Section 14C(4) cited earlier specifies "observable" aspects of work behavior when setting forth the requirements for content validity applications involving KSAOs. Similarly, the *Uniform Guidelines* specifically warn that it is inappropriate for selection procedures justified on the basis of content validity to rely on inferences about unobservable components of work behaviors:

A selection procedure based upon inferences about mental processes cannot be supported solely or primarily on the basis of content validity. Thus, a content strategy is not appropriate for demonstrating the validity of selection procedures which purport to measure traits or constructs such as intelligence, aptitude, personality, commonsense, judgment, leadership, and spatial ability. [14C(1)]

Although not clarified in the *Uniform Guidelines,* it must be noted that an important distinction exists between tests that purport to measure traits or constructs related to mental processes (such as judgment, leadership) and tests that purport to measure similarly named KSAOs. In our view, KSAO labels that happen also to be associated with existing measures of mental processes should not automatically disallow content validation methodologies; rather, a decision concerning the appropriateness of content-based evidence under the *Uniform Guidelines* should depend on whether there is an appropriate link to work behavior with respect to a measure of a knowledge area, or an operationalization based on work behavior for a measure of a skill or ability. Corroboration of this view is offered later in our discussion of relevant court cases.

The *Uniform Guidelines* provide specific guidance regarding the documentation of job analysis evidence in content validation studies. Section 15C(3) states:

A description of the method used to analyze the job should be provided (essential). The work behavior(s), the associated tasks, and if the behavior results in a work product, the work products should be completely described (essential). Measures of criticality and/or importance of the work behavior(s) and the method of determining these measures should be provided (essential). Where the job analysis also identified knowledges, skills, abilities, and other characteristics used in work behavior(s), an operational definition for each knowledge in terms of a body of learned information and for each skill and ability in terms of observable behaviors and outcomes, and the relationship between each knowledge, skill, and ability and each work behavior, as well as the method used to determine this relationship, should be provided (essential).

This section indicates that a thorough job analysis is required, including a description of all methods used, and a complete documentation of work behaviors and work products along with how their criticality or importance were measured. With regard to KSAOs, Section 15C(3) reiterates requirements already outlined in Section 14C(4) regarding operational definitions for KSAOs and linkage of KSAOs and work behaviors, but adds the requirement of documenting of the methods used to determine these linkages. It is worth pointing out that no particular methods of linkage are described as preferred. Sections 15C(4) and 15C(5) also emphasize documentation regarding requirements stated previously in section 14C(4) with respect to showing a link between the selection procedure and a KSAO, and between a KSAO and work behavior:

Where the selection procedure purports to measure a knowledge, skill, or ability, evidence that the selection procedure measures and is a representative sample of the knowledge, skill, or ability should be provided (essential). [15C(4)]

The evidence demonstrating that the selection procedure is a representative work sample, a representative sample of work behavior(s), or a representative sample of knowledge, skill, or ability as used as a part of a work behavior and necessary for that behavior should be provided (essential). The user should identify the work behavior(s) which each item or part of the selection procedure is intended to sample or measure (essential). [15C(5)]

A recurring theme in the *Uniform Guidelines* with respect to applications of content validation methods involving KSAOs is the requirement that a selection procedure be a representative sample of a KSAO. Although the *Uniform Guidelines* do not prescribe a specific method for demonstrating representativeness, such as a strict statistical approach to representative sampling, something beyond simple relatedness seems implied. In the context of content validation, the requirement of a representative sample may be taken to imply that evidence should be provided that the operationalization of the KSAO in terms of observable work behavior is such that it is reasonable to draw some conclusion about individuals' possession of a KSAO based on their performance on the selection procedure. In other words, a test developer should ask the question "Is it rational to draw a conclusion about a given KSAO based on an individual's performance on this selection procedure?" Of course, this question is more difficult to answer in the case of broader constructs. Nevertheless, the question must still involve consideration not only of the basic link, or relatedness, between the selection procedure and the KSAO, but also the degree to which the selection procedures assess the critical components of the KSAO. Showing a basic link between a selection procedure and a KSAO is a more straightforward process than evaluating the adequacy of the link—the real crux of the representativeness argument. A decision concerning adequacy is likely a question of professional judgment, but it should be made in consideration of the information and data gathered through the job analysis and test development processes.

A final consideration is the standard required by the *Uniform Guidelines* concerning the KSAO–work behavior linkage in a content validity study. Specifically, the *Uniform Guidelines* require evidence that the knowledge, skill, or ability is used in and is a necessary prerequisite to performance of critical or important work behavior(s). Thus, it is necessary to provide evidence both that a KSAO is related to a critical or important work behavior and that the behavior cannot be performed effectively without the KSAO. This requirement is particularly salient in situations in which an assessed KSAO is fairly broad and its relationship to work behavior is more distal compared to KSAOs that are more job-specific in their construction.

Further elucidation of the *Uniform Guidelines'* requirements is provided in *Adoption of Questions and Answers to Clarify and Provide a Common Interpretation of the Uniform Guidelines on Employee Selection Procedures* (Equal Employment Opportunity Commission, Office of Personnel Management, Department of Justice, Department of Labor, & Department of the Treasury, 1979). This document offers answers to a number of questions concerning the interpretation of the *Uniform Guidelines,* including several questions related to the current topic of content validation for broader constructs. In response to question 73 ("Must a selection procedure supported by content validity be an actual 'on the job' sample of work behaviors?"), the answer provided is "No . . . the guidelines also permit justification on the basis of content validity of selection procedures measuring knowledges, skills, or abilities which are not necessarily samples of work behaviors if: (1) The knowledge, skill, or ability being measured is operationally defined in accord with Section 14C(4); and (2) that knowledge, skill, or ability is a prerequisite for critical or important work behaviors" (p. 12006). However, question 75, "Can a measure of a trait or construct be validated on the basis of content validity?" (p. 12007) is also followed by a straightforward "No. Traits or constructs are by definition underlying characteristics which are intangible and are not directly observable . . . [and therefore, are] not appropriate for the sampling approach of content validity" (p. 12007). However, the answer goes on to state the following as a clarification:

> Some selection procedures, while labeled as construct measures, may actually be samples of observable work behaviors. Whatever the label, if the operational definitions are in fact based upon observable work behaviors, a selection procedure measuring those behaviors may be appropriately supported by a content validity strategy. (p. 12007)

Although it is clear from this answer that content validation strategies should not target psychological traits or constructs, the term *construct* is typically used by psychologists in a broader sense than the way it is defined in the *Uniform Guidelines.* A more inclusive definition of the term is provided by Guion (1998) when he notes ". . . a construct is an idea or concept constructed or invoked to explain relationships between observations" (p. 43). Guion also notes that although the notion of a construct is sometimes considered "mysterious" and "grand to the point of grandiose," "a construct need be little more than an idea about how people differ in some important way" (p. 292). These descriptions of the term *construct* would certainly include KSAOs as normally defined in a job analysis and discussed in the *Uniform Guidelines*. Notwithstanding the obvious semantic issues, we believe (in part due to case law described later) that the key message in the *Uniform Guidelines* is one of operationalization, or how the KSAO is actually measured in the selection procedure. Although traditional measures of traits would not be appropriate for content validation, properly operationalized measures with trait-like labels may be suited to such an approach.

Also relevant to the current discussion are questions 77 ("Is a task analysis necessary to support a selection procedure based on content validity?"), 78 ("What is required to show the content validity of a paper-and-pencil test that is intended to approximate work behaviors?"), and 79 ("What is required to show the content validity of a test of job knowledge?") (p. 12007). The response provided for question 77 clarifies that every task need not be identified, but that a complete understanding of important work behavior must be achieved:

> A description of all tasks is not required by the *Uniform Guidelines*. However, the job analysis should describe all important work behaviors and their relative importance and their level of difficulty. (p. 12007)

This response is important for the current discussion in that it clarifies that a link between a KSAO and on the job behavior may be established at different levels of abstraction with respect to work behavior. Questions 78 and 79 relate to the more specific topic of what types of selection procedures may be justified based on content validation methodologies. With respect to paper-and-pencil tests (question 78) the answer provided is: "Where a test is intended to replicate a work behavior, content validity is established by a demonstration of the similarities between the test and the job with respect to behaviors, products, and the surrounding environmental conditions" (p. 12007). For job knowledge tests (question 79), the requirement explained is

There must be a defined, well recognized body of information, and knowledge of the information must be prerequisite to performance of the required work behaviors. The work behavior(s) to which each knowledge is related should be identified on an item by item basis. The test should fairly sample the information that is actually used by the employee on the job, so that the level of difficulty of the test items should correspond to the level of difficulty of the knowledge as used in the work behavior. (See Section 14C[1] and [4]. (p. 12007)

We now summarize the key requirements in the *Uniform Guidelines* relating specifically to the application of content-oriented methodologies for KSAOs:

- Selection procedures measuring KSAOs can be justified by content validation methods only in certain circumstances and may be subject to closer scrutiny than more traditional applications. Thus, careful consideration of the *Uniform Guidelines'* requirements is prudent.
- For application of content validation methods to KSAOs (constructs), a thorough job analysis is required, including a description of methods used and documentation of the criticality or importance of work behaviors, which should be completely described.
- The KSAO(s) being assessed by the selection procedure must be operationally defined.
- The KSAO(s) assessed must be related to a critical or important work behavior that cannot be performed effectively without the KSAO.
- A selection procedure assessing a KSAO should be a representative sample of the knowledge, skill, or ability.
- An assessed knowledge should be operationally defined as the body of learned information used in an observable aspect of work behavior.
- When sampling skills or abilities, selection procedures should reflect *observable* aspects of work behaviors. It is inappropriate for selection procedures justified on the basis of content validity to rely on inferences about unobservable components of work behaviors. Thus, either selection procedures measuring a skill or ability should closely approximate an observable work

behavior, or the product should closely approximate an observable work product.

As a final caveat, we note that this section of the chapter has focused on specific aspects of the *Uniform Guidelines* directly relevant to the current topic. However, practitioners should be aware of the other, more general requirements in the *Uniform Guidelines* relating to test development and content validity, which also must be considered when applying a content validation methodology.

We now present a discussion of relevant court cases. This discussion is intended to provide a brief history of past court decisions related to the chapter topic. However, we wish to note that our review should not be considered an exhaustive analysis of every legal finding of potential relevance—nor should it be interpreted as legal advice. Practitioners should consult with an attorney in situations warranting an in-depth analysis of case law.

Relevant Court Cases

In past court cases, plaintiffs sometimes have complained that an organization relied on content validation evidence for tests that measure constructs, which imply inferences about mental processes—a practice inconsistent with the *Uniform Guidelines*. The first case to thoroughly explore the limits of content validation, and which served as a precedent for several future cases, was *Guardians Association of the New York City Police Department, Inc. v. Civil Service Commission of the City of New York* (1980). The test in question consisted of multiple-choice items measuring abilities such as the ability to recall facts, ability to fill out forms, applying general principles to specific fact situations, and human relations skills. Items could be answered based entirely on the information provided on the test itself. This test was one component of the process for selecting entry-level police officers.

Although the case was complex and involved a number of issues, it specifically addressed the topic of content validation for broader constructs. In an earlier finding at the district court level, an attempt to validate a test based on its content was ruled inappropriate; the stated reasons for the decision were that the test measured constructs rather than abilities, and that job analysis evidence was not sufficiently precise to meet the *Uniform Guidelines'* requirements for content validation. However, in *Guardians* (1980) the Second Circuit Court of Appeals vacated these parts of the district court decision in a rather expansive analysis. The court's decision was based, in part, on a consideration of the force of the *Uniform Guidelines'* legal findings relating to violations of Title VII of the Civil Rights Act of 1964. Specifically, the Second Circuit noted that although the *Uniform Guidelines* had been relied upon by the Supreme Court in several leading cases, the Supreme Court had not ruled that every deviation from the *Uniform Guidelines* automatically results in a violation of Title VII. Thus, the Second Circuit concluded that although the *Uniform Guidelines* "should always be considered" they "should not be regarded as conclusive unless reason and statutory interpretation support their conclusions" (p. 12). In rendering its decision in this case, the Second Circuit found that:

> In specifying how the selection of validation techniques is to be made, the Guidelines adopt too rigid an approach, one that is inconsistent with Title VII's endorsement of professionally developed tests. Taken literally, the Guidelines would mean that any test for a job that included a training period is almost inevitably doomed: if the attributes the test attempts to measure are too general, they are likely to be regarded as construct, in which event validation is usually too difficult to be successful; if the attributes are fairly specific, they are likely to be appropriate for content validation, but this too will prove unsuccessful because specific attributes will usually be learned in a training program or on the job. (p. 14)

The court also observed:

> The origin of this dilemma is not any inherent defect in testing, but rather the Guidelines' definition of "content." This definition makes too sharp a distinction between "content" and "construct," while at the same time blurring the distinction between the two components of "content": knowledge and ability. The knowledge covered by the concept of "content" generally means factual information. The abilities refer to a person's capacity to carry out a particular function, once the necessary information is supplied. Unless the ability requires virtually no thinking, the "ability" aspect of "content" is not closely related to the "knowledge" aspect of "content"; instead it bears a closer relationship to a "construct." (p. 14)

In addition to pointing out problems in the *Uniform Guidelines'* terminology, the court cited relevant research addressing this point. Specifically, the court noted that Tenopyr (1977) regarded content tests as merely a measurement of a certain type of construct, and that content may be defined with respect to any ability evidenced by observable behavior (Ebel, 1977). Hence, the court concluded that "abilities and constructs are not entirely distinct" (p. 14) and that "the crucial question under Title VII is job relatedness— whether or not the abilities being tested for are those that can be determined by direct, verifiable observation to be required or desirable for the job" (p. 14). In no uncertain terms, the court states "[i]f the job involves primarily abilities that are somewhat abstract, content validation should not be rejected simply because these abilities could be categorized as constructs" (p. 15), and "as long as the abilities that the test attempts to measure are no more abstract than necessary, that is, as long as they are the most observable abilities of significance to the particular job in question, content validation should be available" (p. 15). These conclusions are made with the caveat that "the degree to which content validation must be demonstrated should increase as the abilities tested for become more abstract" (p. 15). (The court did not elaborate on this point.)

Although the test in *Guardians* was found to be an appropriate target for content validation, the Court did note that the appropriateness "would have been considerably clearer . . . if each [job analysis] panel had explained which tasks required which abilities" (p. 17). In noting that the *Uniform Guidelines* may be "unnecessarily stringent regarding the identification of this relationship of ability to task as 'essential,' . . . such identification does go far toward eliminating the ambiguities that are otherwise inherent in generalized descriptions of abilities" (p. 17). Additionally, the court noted the importance of "highly qualified assistance" in constructing items to assess abilities that present a challenge given both their abstract nature and the need to avoid rewarding prior knowledge. To this point, the court referenced the fact that the City had attempted to measure human relations skill by actually including in the test a list of "do's and don'ts" concerning human relations in order to avoid (per the *Uniform Guidelines*) testing for knowledge that could be learned on the job. However, supplying this information rendered (unintentionally) this component of the test as merely an assessment of candidates' ability to apply written standards to situations rather than human relations skill.

Section 14C[1] of the *Uniform Guidelines* states generally that a selection procedure can be supported by content validation to the extent that it is a representative sample of the job, but in discussing selection procedures purporting to measure KSAOs, the requirement seems to shift to whether the selection procedure is representative of the KSAO (and whether the KSAO is a necessary prerequisite to successful performance). In *Guardians,* however, the court's discussion of the representativeness requirement focused more on the unrealistic aspects of the *Uniform Guidelines'* requirements rather than the specific distinctions concerning the representativeness standard. The court noted that the *Uniform Guidelines* require that a test be representative of the content of the job, and that the testing procedure must be similar to the procedures required by the job itself. The Second Circuit Court referred to the *Uniform Guidelines'* actual language relating to these requirements as "somewhat inscrutable" (p. 19), noting that the dual aspects of the representativeness requirement would "foreclose any possibility of constructing a valid test" (p. 19). In this case the United States had argued that all of the KSAOs required by the job must be tested in proper proportion. However, the court noted that such a standard is "not even theoretically possible, since some of the required capacities cannot be tested for in any valid manner" and that "[e]ven if they could be, the task of identifying every capacity and determining its appropriate proportion is a practical impossibility" (p. 19). The court also noted the impossibility of testing procedures being truly representative of those procedures used on the job, given that tests "by their nature, are a controlled, simplified version of the job activities" and that "[a]n elaborate effort to simulate the actual work setting would be beyond the resources of most employers, and perhaps beyond the capacities of even the most professional test-makers" (pp. 19–20). The court concluded that "it is reasonable to insist that the test measure important aspects of the job, at least those for which appropriate measurement is feasible, but not that it measure all aspects, regardless of significance, in their exact proportions" (p. 20). (This finding has been cited in other subsequent cases, such as *Police Officers for Equal Rights v. City of Columbus, Ohio,* 1990.) Nevertheless, the court indicated that the appropriateness of the representativeness requirement is in preventing "the use of some minor aspect of the job as the basis for the selection procedure or the needless elimination of some significant part of the job's requirements from the selection process entirely" (p. 20). Additionally, the court noted that a focus on representativeness is further appropriate to prevent "distorting effects that go beyond inherent distortions present in any measurement instrument" including "pointlessly high reading level of test materials, and overly complex instructions" (p. 20).

In *Association of Mexican-American Educators v. State of California* (1996), plaintiffs contended that the test in question measured general mental aptitude rather than specific skills, and thus content validation was inappropriate. In rejecting this claim, the court wrote:

> As the *Guidelines* explain, a content validity strategy is only inappropriate where a selection device purports to measure a hypothetical construct or trait, such as leadership or spatial ability. The CBEST [the test in question in this case] is not such a selection device; it does not purport to measure a candidate's general mental aptitude, intelligence, or any other construct. Rather, it is designed to measure specific, well-defined skills in reading, mathematics, and writing. (p. 16)

Although the court recognized the potential appropriateness of content validity evidence as a method of justifying the use of tests of academic skills in employee selection, it cannot be discounted that in order for a defendant to prevail in such a case, the burden of providing adequate content validity evidence (based on the *Uniform Guidelines* and applicable professional standards) must still be met, and that standard for demonstrating content validation may increase as abilities tested for become more abstract (*Guardians*, 1980). In *Association of Mexican-American Educators v. State of California,* the test in question was used for the purpose of teacher certification—a job for which a link between academic KSAOs and work behavior would appear fairly obvious. For jobs for which such a link requires greater amounts of inference, practitioners may find it more difficult to justify such tests based on content validation evidence alone. Nevertheless, this case highlights the possibility that, in some cases, tests of academic skills will be found by the courts to be appropriate based on content validation research.

In *Gillespie v. State of Wisconsin* (1985), plaintiffs argued that KSAOs such as decision making and priority setting (used to assess candidates for the position of Personnel Specialist I or Personnel Manager I) were essentially constructs, which are inappropriate for content validation. Here the court opined that plaintiffs had failed to acknowledge the defendant's operational definitions for the KSAOs. Instead, they had resorted to lay definitions of these terms and asserted that skills in decision making and priority setting were merely "rephrasings" of constructs or traits such as common sense and judgment (traits given as examples as inappropriate for content validation in the *Uniform Guidelines*). The court concluded that such tactics were insufficient to prove that the KSAOs were too abstract to be measured with a content validated test. Moreover, the court held that the test "measured concrete characteristics in a form that simulated actual work behavior" (p. 8). The test in question in this case was an essay test that involved activities such as planning a recruiting trip and writing a job description.

Cuesta v. State of New York Office of Court Administration (1987) involved the validation of court officer examinations. In this case, plaintiffs contended that the skills and abilities tested (for example, applying information, understanding written information, memory) were too abstract to allow for content validation, and that construct validation would have been more appropriate. The court cited *Guardians* (1980) in rendering its opinion that the possibility of content validation should not be dismissed simply because the abilities in question could be categorized as constructs.

Progressive Officers Club, Inc. v. Metropolitan Dade County (1990) involved the use of an assessment center rather than paper-and-pencil tests. Similar to the cases cited previously, the plaintiffs contended that content validation was inappropriate because the assessment center attempted to measure "constructs" requiring inferences concerning mental processes or traits. The defendants argued that although some assessment center dimensions were labeled similarly to constructs, the labels functioned merely as descriptions of work behavior. The court noted that this viewpoint is consistent with Thornton & Byham's (1982) observation that although some dimension labels may resemble traits, they do not constitute personality constructs if they are operationally defined in terms of work behaviors. Additionally, the court cited *Adoption of Questions and Answers to Clarify and Provide a Common Interpretation of the Uniform Guidelines on Employee Selection Procedures* (Equal Employment Opportunity Commission, Office of Personnel Management, Department of Justice, Department of Labor, & Department of the Treasury, 1979) in which the answer for question 75 states that although some selection procedures are named similarly to constructs, they may nevertheless be samples of work behavior and may be supported by content validity evidence. The court found that the test developers in the case "were careful to ensure that when the actual test materials were created, only observable work behaviors were tested" (p. 15) and that "[t]he skill dimension labels are used primarily as a convenient way to organize the various tasks which were the actual targets of measurement in the assessment center exercises" (p. 16). It is also noteworthy that the court pointed out that assessor guides were designed in an attempt to ensure that assessors make their ratings on the basis of specific behaviors identified in the job analysis, thereby facilitating conformance with the *Uniform Guidelines*. The court also cited *Gillespie* (1985), holding that merely accusing a test of seeking to measure constructs based on KSAO labels is insufficient as proof that a test was an inappropriate target for content validation research.

The following is a summary of key points that may be taken from the findings in the previously cited court cases:

- The *Uniform Guidelines'* definition of *content* is somewhat problematic, and too sharp a distinction is made between the terms *content* and *construct*.
- When jobs involve abstract abilities, content validation should not be rejected simply because these abilities could be categorized as constructs if the abilities that the test attempts to measure are no more abstract than necessary (that is, they are the most observable abilities of significance to the particular job in question).
- The degree to which content validation must be demonstrated may increase as the abilities tested for become more abstract. Although the court in *Guardians* (1980) did not state explicitly how this statement should be interpreted, it is would appear

that rigorous research methods with careful attention to proper operationalization are important.

- Although the representativeness requirement stated in the *Uniform Guidelines* may not be entirely clear, a selection process should nevertheless measure the important aspects of the job—at least those for which appropriate measurement is feasible. It also is important to avoid (1) the use of minor aspects of the job as the basis for the selection, (2) the needless elimination of significant job requirements from the selection process entirely, and (3) measurement distortions beyond the inherent distortions present in any measurement instrument (for example, overly high reading level, complex instructions).

- Tests of academic skills may be appropriate for content validation research when such skills can be linked to work behaviors.

- Providing clear evidence concerning which tasks require which abilities can clarify the appropriateness of content validation evidence and help to eliminate inherent ambiguities in descriptions of abilities.

- The assistance of highly qualified test development professionals may be needed when constructing items to assess abilities that present a challenge given both their abstract nature and the need to avoid rewarding prior knowledge.

- A stronger case for the use of content validation methodologies involving more abstract KSAOs can be made when test developers are very careful to ensure that only observable work behaviors are tested.

- Test development procedures such as testing and assessor guides should be designed, such that ratings or scores can be made on the basis of work behaviors identified in the job analysis.

Review of Professional Standards

Beyond the legal implications of the *Uniform Guidelines* and applicable case law, it also is important to consider the current professional standards provided in the *Principles for the Validation and Use of Personnel Selection Procedures* (Society for Industrial and Organizational Psychology, 2003) and the *Standards for Educational and Psychological Testing* (American Educational Research Association,

American Psychological Association, & National Council on Measurement in Education, 1999). Unlike the *Uniform Guidelines,* however, professional standards have been periodically updated to reflect current thinking in the field of psychology. We have limited our discussion to the implications of the current versions of professional standards.

The Principles

With regard to appropriate applications of content validation methodologies, there are inconsistencies between the *Uniform Guidelines* and the professional standards consulted perhaps most frequently by industrial psychologists—namely, the *Principles.* At a general level the *Principles* state: "[t]he content-based validation study specifically demonstrates that the content of the selection procedure represents an adequate sample of the important work behaviors, activities, and/or worker KSAOs defined by the analysis of work" (p. 22). Similar to the *Uniform Guidelines,* the *Principles* emphasize thoroughness in information gathered in a job analysis, stating that: "[t]he characterization of the work domain should be based on accurate and thorough information about the work including analysis of work behaviors and activities, responsibilities of the job incumbent, and/or the KSAOs prerequisite to effective performance on the job" (p. 22). Although focusing on thoroughness in the job analysis, these statements indicate a broader acceptance of different job analysis methods than in the *Uniform Guidelines,* specifically suggesting the potential appropriateness of a job analysis that focuses solely on worker KSAOs (knowledge, skills, abilities, and other characteristics) rather than specific tasks or work behaviors. The *Principles* include several statements regarding the definition of the content domain:

> The domain need not include everything that is done on the job. The researcher should indicate what important work behaviors, activities, and worker KSAOs are included in the domain, describe how the content of the work domain is linked to the selection procedure, and explain why certain parts of the domain were or were not included in the selection process. (p. 22)

These statements appear to impose a less restrictive standard regarding the definition of the content domain, leaving out strict requirements from the *Uniform Guidelines* (that is, "the work behavior(s), associated tasks, and if the behavior results in a work product, the work products should be completely described" 15C[3]).

According to the *Principles,* "[e]vidence for validity based on content typically consists of a demonstration of a strong linkage between the content of the selection procedure and important work behaviors, activities, worker requirements, or outcomes on the job" (p. 21). When sampling the work domain using a selection procedure, test developers should provide evidence that the procedure samples "important work behaviors, activities, and/or worker KSAOs necessary for performance on the job, in job training, or on specified aspects of either" (p. 21). In addition to these statements, the *Principles* reiterate the breadth of applicability of content validation methods, stating that "[t]he content-based selection procedures discussed here are those designed as representative samples of the most important work behaviors, activities, and/or worker KSAOs drawn from the work domain and defined by the analysis of work" (p. 21).

Although the *Uniform Guidelines* and the *Principles* both require explanation of the link between the selection procedure and the job, the *Uniform Guidelines* focus more specifically on establishing a direct link between work behavior and a selection procedure measuring skills or abilities (see 14C[4]). In contrast, demonstration of a link between the selection procedure and KSAO is sufficient under the *Principles,* as indicated by the use of "and/or" in the preceding statements. An exception to the direct link requirement in the *Uniform Guidelines* is when a selection procedure targets knowledge—in this case, an indirect link to work behavior is deemed sufficient if knowledge is operationally defined in terms of a body of learned information and a description of the relationship between knowledge and work behavior is provided (see 15C[3]). An illustration of the differences between the *Principles* and the *Uniform Guidelines* is contained in Figure 8.1.

Additional guidance concerning sampling within the content domain is offered in the *Principles*: (1) "[t]he development or

Figure 8.1. Linkages Implied under the
Uniform Guidelines **and** *Principles.*

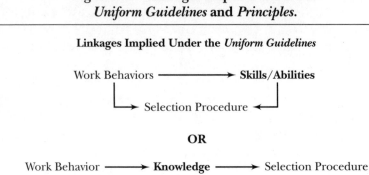

Linkages Implied Under the *Uniform Guidelines*

Work Behaviors ⟶ **Skills/Abilities**

⟶ Selection Procedure ⟵

OR

Work Behavior ⟶ **Knowledge** ⟶ Selection Procedure

Linkages Implied Under the *Principles*

Work Behavior and/or KSAO ⟶ Selection Procedure

choice of a selection procedure usually is restricted to important or frequent behaviors and activities or to prerequisite KSAOs" (p. 23), (2) "[t]he process of constructing or choosing the selection procedure requires sampling the work content domain" (p. 24), and (3) "[n]ot every element of the work domain needs to be assessed." (p. 24). It is clear, however, that there is no general expectation of random sampling, given that the *Principles* state that "[r]andom sampling of the content of the work domain is usually not feasible or appropriate" (p. 24). The *Principles* cite research suggesting that "the sufficiency of overlap between a selection procedure and work domain is a matter of professional judgment based on evidence collected in the validation effort (Goldstein et al., 1993)" (p. 25), thereby recognizing the role of professional judgment in making this determination. Thus, a judgment must be made based on the job analysis results. In making this judgment the researcher should consider whether there is "adequate coverage of work behaviors and activities and/or worker requirements from this restricted domain to provide sufficient evidence to support the validity of the inference" (p. 23). It is important to note, however, that the *Principles* state that an explanation should be provided when work behaviors, activities, and KSAOs included in the content domain are not subsequently included in the selection process. In general, the *Principles'* guidance regarding representative sampling (that is, "adequate coverage . . . to support the validity of the inference") appears to be consistent with court decisions that have rejected more extreme interpretations of the general language in the *Uniform Guidelines* (see *Guardians Association of the New York City Police Department, Inc. v. Civil Service Commission of the City of New York*, 1980). The adequacy of content validation evidence is summarized in the *Principles* as follows: "Evidence for validity based on content rests on demonstrating that the selection procedure adequately samples and is linked to the important work behaviors, activities, and/or worker KSAOs defined by the analysis of work" (p. 25).

Although less restrictive than the *Uniform Guidelines* regarding a direct link between selection instruments and specific work behaviors, the *Principles* nevertheless offer several cautions concerning the fidelity of selection instruments to the job. For example, they state that "[t]he fidelity of the selection procedure content to important work behaviors forms the basis for the inference" (pp. 23–24) and "[t]he more a selection procedure has fidelity to exact job components, the more likely it is that the content-based evidence will be demonstrated" (p. 24). Further, the *Principles* note that "[w]hen feasible, a content-based selection procedure should remove or minimize content that is irrelevant to the domain sampled" (p. 21). In contrast to the less restrictive statements in the *Principles,* these statements regarding fidelity appear to be more consistent with the *Uniform Guidelines* and relevant case law.

The *Principles* do acknowledge practical limitations concerning fidelity, noting that "[v]irtually any content-based procedure includes some elements that are not part of the work domain (e.g., standardization of the selection procedure or use of response formats that are not part of the job content, such as multiple choice formats or written responses when the job does not require writing)" (p. 21). It is noteworthy that, similar to the *Uniform Guidelines,* the *Principles* define the content of selection procedures as including "the questions, tasks, themes, format, wording, and meaning of items, response formats, and guidelines regarding the administration and scoring of the selection procedure" (p. 21). Additionally, the *Principles* recognize the need to rely on lower-fidelity selection instruments, particularly in situations in which changes in the job are likely to be frequent. The job of word processor is offered as an example (p. 24); that is, in some circumstances it would be appropriate to define content as "demonstrates proficiency with word processing principles and techniques" (lower fidelity) rather than "demonstrates proficiency with a particular word processing program" (high fidelity). Particularly relevant to the current chapter is the *Principles'* concluding comment concerning fidelity, which contains the cautionary note that more general measures "may be subject to more scrutiny because the correspondence between the measure and the work content is less detailed" (p. 24). To the extent that measures of broader constructs will often have less detailed correspondence with work content, this caution emphasizes the increased difficulty of content validation research involving broader constructs and is reminiscent of the court's statement in *Guardians* (1980) that the degree to which content validation must be demonstrated may increase as the abilities tested for become more abstract.

The Standards

The *Standards* consider validity to be a unitary concept and describe different sources of evidence that contribute to an understanding of the inferences that can be made on the basis of a selection procedure (p. 11). Although avoiding the term *content validation,* the *Standards* recognize that "[i]mportant validity evidence can be obtained from an analysis of the relationship between a test's content and the construct it is intended to measure" (p. 11). As in the *Principles, test content* is defined broadly as referring to factors such as "the themes, wording, and format of the items, tasks, or questions on a test, as well as the guidelines for procedures regarding administration and scoring" (p. 11). According to the *Standards,* evidence for validity based on test content "can include logical or empirical analyses of the adequacy with which the test content represents the content domain and of the relevance of the content domain to the proposed interpretation of test scores" and "can also come from expert judgments of the relationship between parts of the test and the construct" (p. 11). The *Standards* note that it is often the case that test developers rely on a detailed specification of content, often including a classification of content areas and types of items.

With regard to specific standards for demonstrating validity evidence based on test content, Standard 14.8 states:

> Evidence of validity based on test content requires a thorough and explicit definition of the content domain of interest. For selection, classification, and promotion, the characterization of the domain should be based on job analysis. (p. 160)

Thus, the job analysis requirement in Standard 14.8 is consistent with similar advocacy in the *Uniform Guidelines* and the *Principles.* The discussion of this standard states that "[i]n general, the job content domain should be described in terms of job tasks or worker knowledge, skills, abilities, and other personal characteristics that are clearly operationally defined so that they can be linked to test content" (p. 160). Similar to the *Principles,* this statement seems to support job analysis methods focusing on either job tasks or KSAOs, but the requirement of a clear operational definition would appear to involve some link to work behavior.

Like the *Uniform Guidelines* and the *Principles,* the *Standards* emphasize the importance of fidelity when sampling from the work domain. Standard 14.9 states "[w]hen evidence of validity based on test content is a primary source of validity evidence in support of the use of a test in selection or promotion, a close link between test content and job content should be demonstrated." This standard is further explained as follows:

> For example, if the test content samples job tasks with considerable fidelity (actual job samples, such as machine operation) or, in the judgment of experts, correctly simulates job task content (such as certain assessment center exercises), or samples specific job knowledge required for successful job performance (such as information necessary to exhibit certain skills), then content-related evidence can be offered as the principal form of evidence of validity. If the link between the test content and the job content is not clear and direct, other lines of validity evidence take on greater importance. (p. 160)

Similar to the *Principles,* Standard 14.10 emphasizes the importance of documentation when defining the content domain, stating:

When evidence of validity based on test content is presented, the rationale for defining and describing a specific job content domain in a particular way (e.g., in terms of tasks to be performed or knowledge, skills, abilities, or other personal characteristics) should be stated clearly. (p. 160)

and additionally, that

[e]vidence should include a description of the major job characteristics that a test is meant to sample, including the relative frequency, importance, or criticality of the elements. (p. 160)

Practical Development

The preceding review of the literature and legal issues documents the complex history of the concept of content validity in the field of personnel selection. We have noted that although the *Uniform Guidelines* state that content validation is inappropriate for tests of traits or constructs, KSAOs (measures of which are subject to content-based methods in the *Uniform Guidelines*) are often labeled similarly to constructs. The *Uniform Guidelines* offer operationalization as a way of dealing with abstract KSAOs. Moreover, *Adoption of Questions and Answers to Clarify and Provide a Common Interpretation of the Uniform Guidelines on Employee Selection Procedures* (Equal Employment Opportunity Commission et al., 1979) clearly states that content-based methods can go beyond work samples, and the courts have interpreted the *Uniform Guidelines* more broadly vis-à-vis content validation. Finally, professional touchstones (that is, the *Principles* and *the Standards*) rely on the more modern unitary conceptualization of validity that views content methods as providing part of the evidence required for construct validity; thus, their authors appear more open to the idea of content validation for broader constructs. Taking into consideration the range of issues addressed in this chapter, we now discuss practical recommendations for using a content validation approach for tests of broader constructs. These practical suggestions draw on many of the issues discussed previously, as well as articles that have focused on critical steps to follow in the content validation process (see Crocker, 1997; Goldstein, Zedeck, & Schneider, 1993; Haynes, Richard, & Kubany, 1995; Sireci, 1998).

The recommendations in this section should not be viewed as legal advice, especially given the divergence of the *Uniform Guidelines* and various court decisions. However, because of the greater potential for legal pitfalls, the critical question to be explored from a practical standpoint is how the content validation methodology should be applied, if used for tests of broader constructs. In this vein, we would argue that the major consideration is that validity evidence needs to be collected in a rigorous manner that yields high-quality data in which we can be confident in terms of the findings that emerge. When using content validation methods when broader constructs are the targets of assessment, a methodologically sound research approach must be designed to address a variety of concerns and questions, such as the following:

- Has the construct been adequately defined in terms of how it is used on the job?
- Do SMEs understand the construct well enough to make the judgments they are being asked to make?
- Have factors that contribute construct irrelevant variance been controlled for in the design of the test?

Designing a rigorous process means that questions like these and other related issues have been considered and addressed in how the content validation data were obtained. We now discuss a number of these issues and questions in order to provide practical guidance for the use of content-oriented methods with broader constructs.

Thorough Job Analysis

The criticality of job analysis to content validation methods has been stressed throughout the literature. Especially in light of content validity being viewed as a key step in test development (Tenopyr, 1977), it makes sense that job analysis, viewed as the foundation of test development, plays a central role in content validation procedures. Goldstein, Zedeck, and Schneider (1993) outline the necessary job analysis process in great detail and present many critical steps to be completed (for example, task identification; KSAO identification; task-KSAO linkage analysis). In applying content validity to broad constructs, consideration must be given to the high level of specificity that is required in defining and capturing the construct and how it operationalizes on the job. As noted previously, a construct label can have many different definitions and aspects to it (Haynes, Richard, & Kubany, 1995), which means that the job analysis process must be used to pinpoint the specific definition of the construct that is relevant to the given job and to delineate the key aspects of the construct, as well as its boundaries, for the target job.

In our experience reviewing and auditing content validation research, we have encountered job analysis approaches of varying detail and thoroughness. In the current context, the approach should involve identifying critical tasks and work behaviors, important KSAOs prerequisite to job performance, and the link between KSAOs and specific work behaviors. To the extent that candidates will be ranked on a selection procedure, it is also prudent to collect information regarding SME judgments concerning the linearity of the bivariate relationships between KSAOs and performance identified in the job analysis (that is, would increasingly higher levels of a KSAO tend to lead to better performance or would the relationship between the variables become asymptotic beyond some threshold level?).

When drafting construct statements and delineating the domain, one should take into consideration the level of specificity described by Goldstein, Zedeck, and Schneider (1993) when writing task and KSAO statements. Although constructs, in particular, must sometimes be defined broadly (such as "interpersonal skill"), broad labels and KSAO definitions will not serve to bolster the case for validity based on content. When feasible, a construct definition should be written to capture specifically the way the construct manifests on the job.

It should be remembered that the difference between what is a content domain and what is a construct domain is somewhat arbitrary (Guion, 1987), but that a construct domain typically is more abstract in nature. The fact that a construct is more abstract may make it more difficult to get a handle on it during job analysis. In part, it may depend a great deal not on the methodology employed in the job analysis but on the capabilities and qualifications of the

SMEs involved. To facilitate SME consideration, the construct should be defined such that it can easily be understood by the participating SMEs.

In addition, we feel that some caution is warranted concerning one of the more common practices in the field of industrial psychology in terms of job analysis (if it is to be used with content validating broader constructs)—namely, competency modeling. In many organizations, the development of selection programs for professional and management employees is based on organizational competency models in which a set of critical competencies are identified as applicable to virtually all departments, divisions, and positions in the organization. Although some complexities may be captured in the competency model (for example, defining competencies somewhat differently based on organizational level, such as professional versus managerial), the intent usually is that it be generally and broadly applicable across the organization. The development of competency models is often accomplished by using SME meetings and interviews or surveying SMEs to identify critical competencies to be included in the model. In our experience, however, selection processes based on broad competency models are often not developed using rigorous research methods. At the most basic project step—the job analysis—often minimal effort is taken to conduct a thorough job analysis to identify critical work behaviors or to link specific work behaviors to the items included in the selection instrument. In these cases, competency-based selection processes will be difficult to justify based on content evidence.

Operationalization

During the development of a selection instrument to sample a broader construct, it is important for the test developer to provide clear evidence of the link between the selection test and required work behavior. Otherwise it may be difficult to refute arguments that the test is merely serving as an assessment of mental processes. In the case of broader constructs, demonstrating the test-behavior linkage may sometimes be more difficult, given the potential for a mismatch between the level of specificity at which task statements are composed and the level of specificity at which measurements of more abstract KSAOs are operationalized in a selection instrument.

There are several ways for a practitioner to proceed in demonstrating that a selection procedure is properly operationalized as required by the *Uniform Guidelines*. One approach would involve providing an explanation of how the selection instrument relates to job tasks or duties, in addition to showing that the KSAOs assessed are related to work behavior. The identification of specific tasks or categories of tasks from the job analysis that involve behaviors in common with those elicited by the selection procedure can provide evidence of operationalization in accordance with the *Uniform Guidelines*. This approach can be more difficult when tasks are defined at a different level of abstraction compared to the behaviors elicited by the selection instrument, resulting essentially in a mismatch in behavioral specificity. When providing an explanation of the relationship between the selection procedure and actual work behavior in this situation, it may be necessary to describe specific *aspects* or *components* of tasks related to the selection instrument.

Although a clear and compelling explanation of the relationship between the selection instrument and work behavior can provide evidence of appropriate operationalization, another approach would be to collect SME ratings of such linkages. This more formal rating process might be considered if job tasks are defined at a very different level of abstraction compared to types of behaviors elicited by the selection instrument, or when the number of work behaviors is manageable, as is the case when the number of job tasks is minimal or when categories of related job tasks can be rated.

A third approach would be to have SMEs link test items to KSAOs that have been defined in the job analysis based on clear linkages to work behavior (such as arithmetic skill to compute by hand in the four basic functions for numbers and decimals up to three digits). In the case of more broadly defined KSAOs (as is typical for an organizational competency model), a test-to-work-behavior linkage can be made implicit in the KSAO-to-work-behavior linkage by asking SMEs to link test items to more broadly defined KSAOs, but with KSAO definitions qualified and further defined by a listing of the actual work behaviors linked to the KSAO in the job analysis. Thus, although a competency may have a general definition that fits a variety of jobs, the definition for a given job is further defined by the list of work behaviors for which it is required. In this manner SMEs would rate the relevance of the items as appropriate samples of the KSAO in consideration of the critical work behaviors for which the KSAO is necessary. For example, different test items would be rated as appropriate measures of the KSAO "reading ability" depending on whether the KSAO is linked to a subset of a lawyer's job tasks as opposed to a retail sales associate's job tasks. That is, the general KSAO "reading ability" has different implications depending on the types of job tasks to which it is linked—a lawyer will need reading ability to prepare court cases, whereas a sales associate may need reading ability to stock groceries or learn to operate a cash register. In this example, the job tasks define the specific type and level of reading ability actually required, and there will be job-based differences in the level of appropriateness of reading ability test items within the universe of items tapping the more general construct of reading ability.

Regardless of the method chosen, a test developer should provide a clear explanation of the link between the test instrument and work behavior and the rationale for choosing a particular testing approach as an operationalization of the work behavior. Although some might argue that direct SME ratings linking specific items to work behavior may provide the most objective evidence of the relationship, this approach is not always practical, given considerations such as test security or large numbers of test items and job tasks. In such cases, one or more of the following conditions, in addition to the practitioner's own explanation or ratings of the link between the test items and work behavior, can bolster the case for appropriate operationalization in accord with the *Uniform Guidelines*:

- SMEs provided input during the test development process regarding the sampling of KSAOs and associated work behaviors.
- Scoring procedures were developed based on SME input.
- Items were developed based on critical incidents (provided directly by SMEs or derived from job analysis interviews or observations).

When the goal is linking selection procedure content to specific work behaviors from the job analysis, a number of data collection methods may be considered. Some test developers rely on SME consensus; others collect more detailed individual ratings using a variety of types of rating scales. Moreover, it is possible to rely on a number of potential criteria for evaluating expert agreement concerning job-relatedness. Clearly, the *Uniform Guidelines* do not express a preference for a particular method for demonstrating proper operationalization. Determination of the most appropriate methods should be made on a case-by-case basis. Methods that involve a quantitative summary of ratings may sometimes hold up to greater scrutiny, given the level of detail that can be summarized in a validation report. Of course, this is true only to the extent that the methodology used to collect ratings is sound (for example, instructions are clear, rating forms are administered using a credible and unbiased data collection protocol).

The following are examples of rating procedures that could be used subsequent to the job analysis to provide evidence that selection test content is linked to work behavior.

Example One

Using the following rating scale, please rate how important it is for a candidate to be able to answer each item correctly in order to perform each work behavior successfully.

Importance of Items for Performance of
KSAO-Linked Work Behaviors

3 – Critical to successful performance. Otherwise the work behavior could not be performed at a minimally acceptable level.

2 – Important to successful performance. Otherwise it would be difficult to perform the work behavior effectively.

1 – Minor Importance to successful performance but may be useful for performing some small part of the work behavior. A candidate who answers incorrectly could still perform the work behavior effectively.

0 – Not Important to successful performance of the work behavior.

Test Items	Work Behaviors Linked to KSAO One (from Job Analysis)								
	1	2	3	4	5	6	7	8	9
Item 1									
Item 2									
Item 3									
Item 4									
Item 5									
Item 6									
Item 7									
Item 8									

Example Two

Note: For this example, KSAOs must be defined specifically in terms of work behavior or displayed for respondents along with linked work behaviors from the job analysis.

Using the following rating scale, please rate how important it is for a candidate to be able to answer each item correctly in order to demonstrate each KSAO successfully.

Importance of Items for Demonstration of Required KSAOs

3 – Critical to the demonstration of the KSAO. Otherwise the candidate could not possess the KSAO at a minimally acceptable level.

2 – Important to the demonstration of the KSAO. Otherwise it is unlikely that the candidate could possess the KSAO at a minimally acceptable level.

1 – Minor Importance to the demonstration of the KSAO. A candidate who answers incorrectly could still demonstrate the KSAO at a minimally acceptable level.

0 – Not Important to the demonstration of the KSAO.

Test Items	KSAOs								
	1	2	3	4	5	6	7	8	9
Item 1									
Item 2									
Item 3									
Item 4									
Item 5									
Item 6									
Item 7									
Item 8									

These rating scales are only examples; other types of scales may be similarly appropriate. Under some circumstances (such as job knowledge tests) it may be useful to collect ratings concerning factors such as whether candidates should be capable of answering items correctly prior to any on-the-job training or the degree to which memorization of the information presented on the test is required on the job. In cases for which a test requires open-ended responses (such as structured interviews), ratings also may be collected for potential types of responses determined during the test development process.

Relevance of Scoring Key for Open-Ended Questions

For each potential response to an item (or for behavioral anchors in the case of an interview), SMEs might be asked the following:

1. Is this response relevant to this question? **Yes or No.**
If Yes,
2. Rate the level of performance associated with such a response in relation to the job in question.

Level of performance associated with response:

1 = Unacceptable
2 = Less Than Acceptable
3 = Acceptable
4 = More Than Acceptable
5 = Outstanding
U = Unsure

Identification and Use of SMEs

SMEs obviously play a central role in content validation methods: their judgments provide the critical validation data. In content validation involving a broader construct, the question becomes, what characteristics are required of an SME who can accurately make such ratings? As noted by Sireci (1998), "as in any study involving the use of expert judges, the qualifications of the experts is critically important" (p. 315). Typically in personnel selection, the focus is on SMEs who are familiar with the target job, such as job incumbents and supervisors. However, when focusing on constructs, it would seem critical to also have SMEs who are familiar with the construct. In addition, because there are often various facets of a construct domain, SMEs should be included that are representative of these different facets in terms of expertise (Sireci, 1998).

As suggested previously, perhaps the best solution is to use a diverse sample of SMEs, some of whom understand the job and some of whom understand the construct (Gael, 1988). Together, they may be able to provide a good understanding of how the construct manifests on the job, leading to more accurate ratings about the importance of the construct for the target position. An alternative approach to consider is the use of multiple panels that have different perspectives, to determine if they see the content relationships at approximately the same levels. If they do, we can then have more confidence in the ratings. If they do not, it is important to understand why and to investigate whether there are problems regarding the measure's validity.

In addition to choosing SMEs based on expertise, the SMEs should also be representative in terms of other critical variables that may impact the way in which the construct is manifested on the job and the relationship it might have to various test items. For example, demographic variables such as geographic location, race, and gender are commonly considered when choosing an SME panel. It is also important to choose enough SMEs from whom to gather data. Often it is difficult to identify a large number of SMEs with sufficient expertise who are willing or able to participate, but it is critical to have enough SMEs that you can trust the data provided. Obtaining this participation may be a challenge, given that organizations often place constraints on the availability of their best people.

Although it is important that enough SMEs participate, such that the SME group is representative of variables affecting how constructs are manifested on the job, it should be noted that sample size alone does not guarantee the trustworthiness of the data. For example, small groups of highly motivated SMEs may provide better data than larger groups of reluctant (or resentful) participants. In general, fewer SMEs may be necessary when there are limited variables to be represented (such as smaller organizations, job homogeneity), and when highly knowledgeable and motivated SMEs are available. Another consideration that focuses specifically on improving the trustworthiness of SME judgments is to convene SME panels with which test developers (and meeting facilitators) have no relationship. Considering the problem that SMEs may want to please the test developers and thus provide positive links between the test items and the target domain, it may serve to have SME panels composed of persons who may feel less need to be supportive of the investigator.

Given all of these considerations, it is not possible to recommend one best approach to choosing SMEs. What is important is that the rationale for the approach taken is clearly documented, including taking into consideration issues such as representativeness of SMEs, qualifications and capabilities of the SMEs with regard to the types of judgments they are making, motivations of the SMEs, and sample sizes.

Analyzing the Quality of SME Ratings

Given the difficulty of the task of making inferential leaps about abstract constructs, it is especially critical to analyze the data collected to ensure that the validation evidence is of sufficiently high quality. One such analysis is the assessment of the interrater agreement among the ratings of SMEs. Agreement among raters seems to be at least the minimum level of quality that must be demonstrated, as conclusions concerning validity are predicated on appropriate interpretation of the rating data.

Should SMEs from multiple sources be used (as described in the previous section with regard to job experts and construct experts), it will be important to explore potential differences in their perceptions concerning the job relatedness of test items. When quantitative data are collected it may be appropriate to analyze them for the group as a whole and also for various subgroups. A problem with the ratings from one of the subgroups may indicate deficiency or contamination in the measure. However, there is a limit to the number of subgroup differences that should be examined. Analyzing results for every potential subgroup in a sample of SMEs may produce some differences that are merely due to chance. Thus, it is recommended that test developers focus on comparing groups for whom perspectives would be expected to differ, given earlier job analysis research or other information (such as location-specific differences in job requirements).

Determining the KSAOs or Job Representativeness of Measures

The representativeness of test content may be an issue with respect to both the adequacy of a subset of test items as a measure of a targeted KSAO and the adequacy of a test as a sample of the job domain. Strictly speaking, the *Uniform Guidelines* focus more clearly on the former with respect to tests of KSAOs, but the latter may also be of some concern, given our review of court cases (see *Guardians*, 1980). With regard to the representativeness of KSAOs, a selection instrument that targets a KSAO should reflect both the definition of the KSAO and a sample of behaviors that can be mapped directly to those work behaviors linked to the KSAO in the job analysis. There is no single accepted method for determining the representativeness of content. Such a determination may often be a matter of professional judgment. However, it would be appropriate to examine the types of evidence described earlier concerning operationalization of the construct in terms of work behavior. Representativeness may be demonstrated to the extent that qualitative or quantitative information is provided to show that test items serve as a reasonable sample of a KSAO (and do not ignore its critical components). In making a determination of representativeness, it would be important to consider factors such as whether (1) the selection procedure addresses the breadth of the KSAO, (2) the selection procedure measures a critical aspect of the KSAO, or, perhaps, (3) the selection procedure measures aspects of the KSAO that are unlikely to differ from unmeasured aspects.

Regarding a test's representativeness of the job content domain, a test developer should provide an explanation if a test assesses a limited range of KSAOs from the job content domain. For example, limited coverage may be justified if it can be demonstrated that what is being measured is so critical that proficiency in other areas cannot compensate for a weakness in this area. In such cases, a compensatory approach that involves the measurement of the full range of KSAOs may be inappropriate at an initial stage in the selection process. Alternatively, it may be shown that some KSAOs were not assessed because of their low relative importance based on the job analysis or because such assessments were deemed impractical based on general testability or organizational context (such as the extent to which bargaining units may constrain some test modalities). Nevertheless, decisions not to assess certain KSAOs should be made carefully in consideration of these issues. It may also be appropriate to consider the potential impact of such decisions, such as the potential effect on adverse impact if KSAOs are excluded from the selection process.

Use of Statistical Procedures for Assessing Content Validity

Because the degree to which validation evidence must be demonstrated might increase as the abilities tested become more abstract, it may be useful to consider statistical analysis methods for assessing content validity in these cases. Statistical analyses of job analysis data (ratings, linkages) and item ratings and linkages may provide helpful evidence for defending the job-relatedness of selection instruments based on broader constructs. Although not as commonly used as more informal analysis methods (for example, calculating rating scale means and comparing results to a predetermined threshold level), a number of agreement indices are available, such as the Content Validity Index (CVI) (Lawshe, 1975), $r_{WG(J)}$ (James, Demaree, & Wolf, 1993) and $r^*_{WG(J)}$ (Lindell & Brandt, 1999). However, for such techniques to provide meaningful information it is critically important that the research is sound, including properly designed questionnaires, interpretable rating scales, and standardized procedures for gathering data. The use of overly complex or confusing research instruments should be avoided.

Clear and Unbiased Rating Process

Because of the increased difficulty of providing validation evidence based on test content when assessing broader constructs, it is arguably more important to use formal procedures for accumulating content validity evidence (such as the collection of formal quantitative ratings from SMEs) and to follow standardized data collection procedures meticulously.

Prior to data collection, SMEs should be trained on how to complete the procedures. Clear instructions and time spent familiarizing the SMEs with the process and the ratings scales are important in terms of getting high-quality information from their ratings. Effective training techniques include (1) conducting calibration sessions in which the SMEs independently make ratings on related testing materials and (2) subsequently evaluating interrater agreement and discussing differences in order to come to consensus.

Another key issue is the choice or design of the ratings scales. There are many types of scales that can provide useful information. Thus, the key issue to be considered is not the specific scale chosen, but merely whether the scale can capture information about the relevance and representativeness of the test items with regard to the target construct domain. This consideration is important because these are two of the essential pieces of data that content-oriented strategies are supposed to contribute to construct validity within the unitary framework. Central to choosing or designing rating scales is ensuring that raters can use the procedure effectively to give accurate judgments in a manner that reduces typical rater biases. One approach is to use techniques such as paired comparisons, multidimensional scaling, and cluster analysis to gather and evaluate data. The benefit of these techniques is that they avoid "leading" raters by providing construct categories; rather, they allow the raters to decide which constructs the items measure while making it less likely that raters will respond in a socially desirable manner (that is, saying what raters think the investigator wants them to say).

If one uses a technique that provides the categories to the raters, one rigorous process check would be to provide both the constructs that are supposed to be measured as well as other constructs that were not targeted. In this way, one can see if ratings converge with the desired constructs and diverge from the constructs that were not supposed to be measured. Another approach is to leverage some of the techniques used in performance appraisal rating scales to reduce bias and error. Perhaps designing behaviorally anchored rating scales (BARS) or using other formats that reduce error such as forced distribution could be useful in this regard.

Assessing the Whole Test Instrument

It can be argued that an assessment measure focusing on broader constructs has greater potential for assessing extraneous factors not related to the job requirements. When evaluating the content relevance to the construct domain, one should consider examining the entire instrument—including the stimulus mode, response mode, nature of the instructions, and all other required types of activities. Frequently, tests involve the unintended measurement of constructs other than those targeted (for example, reading comprehension, knowledge of multiple-choice formats or other formats such as matching, categorizing, and the like), and it is important to try to minimize this construct-irrelevant variance. SMEs should be asked to consider the entire device and all of the activities that are required, not just the target constructs that were intended. Tests with higher fidelity may limit the amount of irrelevant construct variance, but tests of broader constructs can be difficult to gauge. Although high fidelity is not expected of all procedures justified based on test content, construct contamination may become problematic to the extent that performance on the test is overly affected by candidates' standing on constructs other than those of interest. When designing the test, it is important to consider carefully the rationale associated with decisions concerning the chosen test format, including the extent to which the chosen method would be expected to result in less contamination (or why the feasibility or expense associated with an alternative method was prohibitive). Such issues should be given a great deal of thought and consideration.

Test Development Expertise

In consideration of the court cases discussed earlier, the expertise of those persons involved in test construction may take on greater importance in circumstances in which more abstract KSAOs are to be assessed. The lack of such expertise may lead to lower-quality job analysis information as well as problems concerning the construction and quality of items to measure the intended KSAOs. In general, it is important that organizations consider the potential impact of using nonexperts to facilitate test construction efforts. The use of substandard test development and validation procedures may greatly increase the vulnerability of a test to legal challenges based on inadequate evidence for validity.

Types of Tests and Testing Approaches

It is difficult to categorize specific types of tests or testing approaches as uniformly appropriate or inappropriate for application of content validation methods. Clearly, tests representing straightforward attempts to measure mental constructs—such as traditional cognitive ability tests, tests of specific mental abilities (such as spatial reasoning), and personality tests—would be indefensible based on the *Uniform Guidelines*. However, an important focus of this chapter has been on pointing out that it is the operationalization of constructs, rather than their labels, that determines whether content validation methods are appropriate. It was noted earlier that tests of constructs that are given names similar to mental constructs (for example, judgment, conscientiousness, drive, initiative) would likely be acceptable, provided that the selection procedures are operationalized based on work behavior and the validation process is consistent with the *Uniform Guidelines*.

When making a decision concerning the application of such methods, it is always necessary to consider the context. Consider as an example a hypothetical aptitude test to be used to select candidates for programmer trainees from a population of inexperienced persons. It is common to discuss aptitude tests as inappropriate targets for content validation research. In this example, however, new hires would be required to successfully complete six months of training in a new computer programming language to become entry-level programmers. In this case, it is possible that a generic programming aptitude test—one requiring candidates to learn and apply a simple programming language—may be an appropriate target for content validation research. Factors affecting this determination might be whether the test is timed, whether reference material (that is, programming rules) is available during the entire test, and the degree to which applying the rules of the programming language on the test is similar to applying the rules of the programming language used on the job.

Achievement tests or other tests of academic knowledge should be used cautiously, because the test stimuli can sometimes be far removed from the actual job context. Moreover, although the skills measured by these tests may sometimes be a prerequisite for successful job performance, these variables will often appear to have a more distal relation to performance compared to more job-specific KSAOs. Nevertheless, such tests may sometimes be justified based on content, to the degree that the knowledge being assessed is knowledge that (1) is necessary to perform critical work behaviors, (2) is not taught on the job, and (3) requires a substantial amount of time to acquire (such as basic literacy).

Constraints and Risks

Although content validation for broader constructs certainly presents some additional challenges in accumulating adequate validity evidence, many of the potential legal vulnerabilities discussed here apply to any application of content validation methods. In many cases, however, challenges of the validity of a test may simply be easier to mount when a testing process involves the measurement of more abstract characteristics. When a testing program is based on broader constructs, it is prudent to place particular emphasis on a thorough job analysis to define the content domain. Job analysis methods that are more vulnerable include those that do not lead to the identification of job-specific and critical tasks or duties and those that do not specify which work behaviors are linked to critical KSAOs. The vulnerability of content validation efforts is also increased by limited consideration of factors such as which subject matter experts should be sampled to provide adequate representativeness, what locations must be sampled, what type of quantitative data should be collected, what rating scales should be considered, and how SMEs should be trained to use the rating scales.

In some test development applications, work behaviors are formally linked to KSAOs, which are in turn formally linked to test items (work behavior – KSAO – item); however, the selection procedure itself is not *directly* linked to specific work behavior(s). Although this approach may be completely appropriate from a professional standpoint, our interpretation of the *Uniform Guidelines* is that there may be some vulnerability associated with anything less than an explicit linkage to work behaviors identified in the job analysis. Moreover, the transparency of any such linkage is obviously reduced when selection procedures are measures of broader KSAOs rather than work samples. Thus, using techniques discussed in the practical applications section can help to provide the evidence needed regarding this linkage.

One issue that is particularly relevant with respect to establishing a link between the selection procedure and work behavior is the potential for conceptual mismatch between the level of specificity with which task statements are composed in the job analysis and the level of specificity with which measurements of more abstract KSAOs are operationalized in a selection instrument. Thus, the selection procedure may be operationalized such that it assesses specific *aspects* or *components* of tasks or duties defined in the job analysis rather than functioning as a direct simulation or work sample. Although this is certainly a reasonable test development strategy, given that work samples are not required by the *Uniform Guidelines,* the relationship between a selection procedure and specific aspects or components of tasks may not be readily apparent without clear documentation and may put the organization at some degree of risk.

For content validation efforts directed at KSAOs, the *Uniform Guidelines* require that a selection procedure targeting a particular KSAO should be a representative sample of the KSAO. Thus, a selection procedure measuring a KSAO is vulnerable to challenge if evidence of the representativeness of the selection procedure is not provided by the test developer. Past court cases, although not consistent with our reading of the *Uniform Guidelines'* instruction concerning content validation efforts involving measures of KSAOs, do indicate that the coverage of the entire selection procedure with respect to the job domain may also become an issue in litigation. This is likely the case because the *Uniform Guidelines'* guidance concerning this type or representativeness in relation to more traditional applications of content validity (such as work samples) has been interpreted by some as broadly applicable across all applications of content validation research. For these reasons, evidence should be provided that a selection procedure is representative of the job domain. These dual representativeness requirements present an added burden for practitioners using content validation methods to support tests of broader constructs. However, we should note an exception to the recommendation of job domain representativeness: when a particular characteristic is so critical that proficiency in other areas cannot compensate for a weakness in this area. In such cases, a compensatory approach that involves the measurement of the full range of relevant KSAOs might be argued to be inappropriate at an initial stage in the selection process. However, evidence that a KSAO truly represents a minimum requirement should be clearly documented by the researcher.

The representativeness of a selection procedure may be assailable even when positive evidence is provided for the link between the selection procedures and the job domain or particular KSAOs. Specifically, it is also important to consider whether the selection process is assessing extraneous factors that have not been demonstrated to be job related. Given their broader nature, selection procedures targeting KSAOs may have a greater potential for assessing extraneous factors (such as reading ability) compared to work samples. Although such contamination is clearly possible for any test, including work samples, the increased difficulty of linking selection procedures based on broader constructs to actual work behaviors (and the consequent difficulty of defending them against challenges based on arguments that the procedures are assessing factors that are not job related) makes it important that test developers pay close attention to this potential problem and try to anticipate sources of measurement contamination prior to developing final versions of their tests.

Representativeness is also a potential issue when job analysis research to define critical KSAOs is limited in its breadth. An example might be a situation in which an existing job analysis questionnaire designed around a vendor's assessment product is used to confirm the relevance of predetermined competencies rather than to analyze the full range of possible competencies. In this case, attorneys and their experts may more easily point to obvious yet unexplained KSAO omissions. Another example leading to vulnerability is a situation in which critical KSAOs identified in the job analysis are simply ignored after the fact (and excluded from the selection process) without any rationale or explanation.

When knowledge is assessed, it should be operationally defined as the body of learned information used in an observable aspect of work behavior, and specific linkages to work behaviors should be carefully documented. In the absence of specific evidence that the knowledge areas assessed by a selection instrument are clearly representative of the knowledge required for work behaviors, content validation arguments are clearly vulnerable in consideration of the *Uniform Guidelines*. Documentation of the importance of the knowledge assessed is particularly important for broader areas such as academic knowledge (such as a police officer's knowledge of basic grammar) compared to more job-specific knowledge requirements (such as a police officer's knowledge of traffic laws). Broader knowledge areas are often more distal antecedents of job performance, and often they are not documented in the job analysis to an extent that allows for the straightforward construction (or choice) of a fully defensible test of the broader knowledge area. For example, if a possible outcome of a job analysis and test validation project is a test of broader knowledge, the job analysis must include information concerning the specific aspects of the broader knowledge area that apply to the job of interest. For a construct such as reading ability, a goal of the job analysis might be to collect samples of material read on the job from which reading requirements (for example, the typical grammatical knowledge required, typical sentence length, and reading level) may be better understood and properly sampled in a test instrument.

When tests of broader constructs are developed, there must also be a careful focus on the development of scoring procedures. A stronger case for content validation involving more abstract KSAOs can be made when test developers are careful to ensure that *only* observable behaviors are considered in the scoring process. To the extent that the scoring process appears to require the consideration of unobservable factors, an argument for content validity may be vulnerable. This point implies that materials such as testing and assessor guides should be carefully designed, so that ratings are made on the basis of specific behaviors that SMEs have identified as relevant for the successful performance of critical tasks or duties required on the job.

Because of the potential pitfalls, test development expertise may become particularly important in circumstances in which more abstract KSAOs must be assessed. A lack of such expertise may lead to lower-quality job analysis information as well as an array of potential problems concerning the quality of items as measures of the intended KSAOs. Moreover, the vulnerabilities inherent in any test development effort may be exacerbated by the use of unqualified test developers and substandard test development procedures.

In conclusion, with regard to the risks associated with using a content validation approach with respect to broader constructs, the *Uniform Guidelines,* as well as the court cases discussed previously, suggest a number of areas in which content validation efforts may be vulnerable to challenge (or at least challenging to defend). On the other hand, the professional standards (that is, the *Principles* and the *Standards*) appear more accepting of such an approach. This divergence creates a situation that requires judgment on the part of the professionals involved in test design and implementation. Such professionals must weigh the issues discussed here, as well as the impact of the test in terms of validity and adverse impact, to determine the comfort level and risk associated with using a content validation approach with broader constructs.

The recommendations provided here are intended to provide useful guidance concerning content validation for broader constructs. However, it will always be a matter of professional judgment as to the specific strategies warranted in any particular context. We have outlined the issues that need to be considered in implementing rigorous, methodologically sound, and defensible job analysis and test development approaches involving broader constructs. Clearly, an increased focus on the quality of information gathered and the defensibility of evidence will reduce potential vulnerabilities and increase the likelihood that the effort will result in a high-quality test. However, it must be noted that although greater rigor should be a goal, different situations will call for varying degrees of focus on specific topics, such as choice of rating scales, measures of rater agreement, amount of data collected, and detail of SME sampling plans. From a practical standpoint, consideration of key factors—such as an organization's past history of litigation, the number of candidates to be tested, whether a testing approach being considered is associated in the literature with adverse impact, and specific organizational constraints—will be helpful in making decisions concerning specific methods to pursue for content validation and perhaps, at a more basic level, in deciding whether content validation should be attempted.

References

Note: Page numbers provided in text for court case citations are based on Westlaw.

Aiken, L. R. (1980). Content validity and reliability of single items or questionnaires. *Educational and Psychological Measurement, 40,* 955–959.

American Educational Research Association, American Psychological Association, & National Council on Measurement in Education. (1999). *Standards for educational and psychological testing.* Washington, DC: American Educational Research Association.

Anastasi, A. (1988). *Psychological testing* (6th ed.). New York: Macmillan.

Arvey, R. D., & Begalla, M. E. (1975). Analyzing the homemaker job using the Position Analysis Questionnaire (PAQ). *Journal of Applied Psychology, 60,* 513–517.

Association of Mexican-American Educators v. State of California (1996), 937 F. Supp. 1397.

Carrier, M. R., Dalessio, A. T., & Brown, S. H. (1990). Correspondence between estimates of content and criterion-related validity values. *Personnel Psychology, 43,* 85–100.

Civil Rights Act of 1964. (July 2, 1964) Pub. L. No. 88-352, 78 Stat. 241.

Crocker, L. (1997). Assessing content representativeness of performance assessment exercises. *Applied Measurement in Education, 10*(1), 83–95.

Cuesta v. State of New York Office of Court Administration (1987), 657 F. Supp. 1084.

Ding, C. S., & Hershberger, S. L. (2002). Assessing content validity and content equivalence using structural equation modeling. *Structural Equation Modeling, 9*(2), 283–297.

Dunnette, M. D., & Borman, W. S. (1979). Personnel selection and classification systems. In M. Rosenzweig & L. Porter (Eds.), *Annual Review of Psychology, 30,* 477–526.

Ebel, R. L. (1977). Comments on some problems of employment testing. *Personnel Psychology, 30,* 55–63.

Equal Employment Opportunity Commission, Civil Service Commission, Department of Labor, & Department of Justice. (1978). *Uniform guidelines on employee selection procedures. Federal Register, 43*(166), 38290–38315.

Equal Employment Opportunity Commission, Office of Personnel Management, Department of Justice, Department of Labor, & Department of the Treasury (1979). *Adoption of Questions and Answers to Clarify and Provide a Common Interpretation of the Uniform Guidelines on Employee Selection Procedures. Federal Register, 44*, 11996–12009.

Gael, S. (Ed.) (1988). *The job analysis handbook for business, industry, and government.* New York: Wiley.

Ghiselli, E. E. (1964). *Theory of psychological measurement.* New York: McGraw-Hill Book Company.

Gillespie v. State of Wisconsin (1985), 771 F. 2d 1035 (7th Cir. 1985).

Goldstein, H. W., Zedeck, S., & Goldstein, I. L. (2002). G: Is this your final answer? *Human Performance, 15*, 123–142.

Goldstein, I. L., Zedeck, S., & Schneider, B. (1993). An exploration of the job analysis-content validity process. In N. Schmitt & W. Borman (Eds.), *Personnel selection in organizations* (pp. 3–34). San Francisco: Jossey-Bass.

Grant, J. S., & Davis, L. L. (1997). Selection and use of content experts for instrument development. *Research in Nursing & Health, 20*, 269–274.

Guardians Association of the New York City Police Department, Inc. v. Civil Service Commission of the City of New York (1980), 630 F. 2d 79 (2nd Cir. 1980).

Guion, R. M. (1977). Content validity—The source of my discontent. *Applied Psychological Measurement, 1*, 1–10.

Guion, R. M. (1978). Content validity in moderation. *Personnel Psychology, 31*, 205–213.

Guion, R. M. (1980). On trinitarian doctrines of validity. *Professional Psychology, 11*(3), 385–398.

Guion, R. M. (1987). Changing views for personnel selection research. *Personnel Psychology, 40*, 199–213.

Guion, R. M. (1998). *Assessment, Measurement, and Prediction for Personnel Decisions.* Mahwah, New Jersey: Lawrence Erlbaum Associates.

Guion, R. M., & Gibson, W. M. (1988). Personnel selection and placement. *Annual Review of Psychology, 39*, 349–374.

Hakel, M. D. (1998). *Beyond multiple-choice: Evaluating alternatives to traditional testing for selection.* New Jersey: Erlbaum.

Hambleton, R. K. (1980). Test score validity and standard setting methods. In R. A. Berk (Ed.), *Criterion-referenced measurement: The state of the art.* Baltimore: Johns Hopkins University Press.

Haynes, S. N., Richard, D.C.S., & Kubany, E. S. (1995). Content validity in psychological assessment: A functional approach to concepts and methods. *Psychological Assessment, 7*(3), 238–247.

James, L. R., Demaree, R. G., & Wolf, G. (1993). r_{WG}: An assessment of within-group interrater agreement. *Journal of Applied Psychology, 69,* 85–98.

Lawshe, C. H. (1975). A quantitative approach to content validity. *Personnel Psychology, 28,* 563–575.

Lindell, M. K., & Brandt, C. J. (1999). Assessing interrater agreement on the job relevance of a test: A comparison of the CVI, T, $r_{WG(J)}$, and $r^*_{WG(J)}$ indexes. *Journal of Applied Psychology, 84*(4), 640–647.

McPhail, S. M. (2007). Development of validation evidence. In S. M. McPhail (Ed.), *Alternative validation strategies: Developing new and leveraging existing validity evidence.* San Francisco: Jossey-Bass.

Melnick, S. A., & Henk, W. A. (1997, February). *Content validation: A comparison of methodologies.* Paper presented at annual meeting of the Eastern Educational Research Association, Hilton Head, SC.

Messick, S. (1988). The once and future issues of validity: Assessing the meaning and consequences of measurement. In H. Wainer & H. I. Braun (Eds.), *Test validity* (pp. 33–46). Hillsdale, NJ: Erlbaum.

Messick, S. (1989). Validity. In R. L. Linn (Ed.), *Educational measurement* (3rd ed., pp. 13–104). New York: American Council on Education and Macmillan.

Messick, S. (1995). Validity of psychological assessment: Validation of inferences from persons' responses and performances as scientific inquiry into score meaning. *American Psychologist, 50,* 741–749.

Oltman, P. K., Stricker, L. J., & Barrows, T. S. (1990). Analyzing test structure by multidimensional scaling. *Journal of Applied Psychology, 75,* 21–27.

Ostroff, C., & Schmitt, N. (1987, April). *The relationship between content and criterion-related validity indices: An empirical investigation.* Paper presented at the 2nd Annual Meeting of the Society for Industrial and Organizational Psychology, Atlanta, GA.

Penfield, R. D., & Miller, J. M. (2004). Improving content validation studies using an asymmetric confidence interval for the mean of expert ratings. *Applied Measurement in Education, 17*(4), 359–370.

Progressive Officers Club, Inc. v. Metropolitan Dade County (1990), 1990 WL 270786 (S.D. Fla.).

Rubio, D. M., Berg-Weger, M., Tebb, S. S., Lee, E. S., & Rauch, S. (2003). Objectifying content validity: Conducting a content validity study in social work research. *Social Work Research, 27*(2), 94–104.

Sireci, S. G. (1995, April). The central role of content representation in test validity. Paper presented at the Annual Meeting of the National Council on Measurement in Education, San Francisco.

Sireci, S. G. (1998). Gathering and analyzing content validity data. *Educational Assessment, 5*(4), 299–321.

Sireci, S. G., & Geisinger, K. F. (1992). Analyzing test content using cluster analysis and multidimensional scaling. *Applied Psychological Measurement, 16,* 17–31.

Sireci, S. G., & Geisinger, K. F. (1995). Using subject matter experts to assess content representation: An MDS analysis. *Applied Psychological Measurement, 19,* 241–255.

Society for Industrial and Organizational Psychology. (2003). *Principles for the validation and use of personnel selection procedures* (4th ed.). Bowling Green, OH: Society for Industrial and Organizational Psychology.

Tenopyr, M. L. (1977). Content-construct confusion. *Personnel Psychology, 30,* 47–54.

Thornton, G. C., & Byham, W. C. (1982). *Assessment centers and managerial performance.* New York: Academic Press.

Tucker, L. R. (1961). Factor analysis of relevance judgments: An approach to content validity. In A. Anastasi (Ed.), *Testing problems in perspective: Twenty-fifth anniversary volume of topical readings from the invitational conference on testing problems* (pp. 577–586). Washington, DC: American Council on Education.

Waltz, C. F., Strickland, O., & Lenz, E. (1991). *Measurement in nursing research* (2nd ed.). Philadelphia: Davis.

Wiley, D. E. (1967). Latent partition analysis. *Psychometrika, 32*(2), 183–193.

CHAPTER 9

Practical Construct Validation for Personnel Selection

Timothy E. Landon and
Richard D. Arvey

Construct validation is a strategy that is seldom used as in personnel selection and is typically avoided as a legal defense. The *Uniform Guidelines on Employee Selection Procedures* (Equal Employment Opportunity Commission, Civil Service Commission, Department of Labor, & Department of Justice, 1978) assert that construct validation is complex and poorly developed, lacking a substantial literature that applies its use to personnel selection. It is described as an "extensive and arduous effort involving a series of research studies" [14D(1)]. The *Uniform Guidelines* also state that if a predictor is a measure of a construct, it cannot be validated on the basis of content validity, and any construct validation must include evidence from a criterion-related study unless there exist results of one done elsewhere that meets the standards for transportability.

In court, plaintiffs often take the strategy of labeling a variable as a construct, for if it is, it would follow that a defense would need to involve construct validation (Landy, 1986). In turn, employers try to avoid having their predictor measures labeled as construct-based. Searches for court cases in federal appeals and district courts and in state courts revealed only a small number of cases in which construct validation was used as a defense, though successfully in each case.

The newest Division 14 *Principles for the Validation and Use of Personnel Selection Procedures* (Society for Industrial and Organizational Psychology, 2003) do not even use the term *construct validation*. The *Principles* assert that validation is a unitary concept and describe evidence for validation based on (1) relationships between predictor scores and other variables, (2) test content, (3) the internal structure of a test, and (4) response or scoring processes. They refer to content relevance, criterion-relatedness, and construct meaning, all subsumed within an overarching concept of validity. We applaud the move away from the use of the trinitarian labels of criterion, content, and construct validation (Guion, 1980). Yet it may take some time before the unitarian concept of validation changes how lawyers and courts view lines of attack and defense of selection methods.

There is a stigma surrounding construct validation that unnecessarily constrains validation strategies for personnel selection. Most studies focus on criterion and content validation. At best, this limitation places blinders on us that prevent development of evidence to test hypotheses that could add to the network of inferences that our predictor measures are job-related. At worst, the focus on criterion validation leads to "dust-bowl empiricism" and the use of predictor measures that correlate with criterion measures but cannot be logically explained or justified.

Our purpose in this chapter is to explore some ways in which personnel selection practitioners can expand the range of research strategies and methods that will strengthen the evidence that predictor measures are job-related. Some of these approaches may fit the old label of construct validation, but viewed broadly, all validation is construct validation (Landy, 1986). Evidence justifying the use of a selection procedure may come from many sources. Our aim is to discuss some approaches that may hold practical value for selection practitioners, that have evidentiary value, and that are feasible, interpretable, and finite.

Part of the difficulty in discussions of validation research in general is that there is a distinction between (1) construct validation for the purpose of advancing the theory of construct domains and (2) construct validation for the purpose of linking a predictor measure to a performance domain (Guion, 1980). Advancing theory was the original purpose for construct validation, as discussed in the classic writings by Cronbach and Meehl (1955) and Campbell and Fiske (1959). In this view, the central purpose is to develop evidence about the extent to which an operational measure truly reflects the construct that is thought to underlie it. In this view, there is little immediate interest in a measure's association with a criterion or in its application to work settings, except to the extent that such relationships contributed to an understanding of the latent variable being measured. The audience to interpret validation in this context was typically other research psychologists. The evidence and inferences may be complex, with an expectation that there will be incremental advances in construct understanding through iterative studies that place the construct within a larger nomological network.(A nomological network, as introduced in Chapter One, is an interlocking system of statistical or deterministic relationships among observable variables and theoretical constructs [Cronbach & Meehl, 1955]. "Learning more about a theoretical construct is a matter of elaborating the nomological network in which it occurs, or of increasing the definiteness of the components" [p. 290].) One approach to doing this involves multitrait-multimethod (MTMM) comparisons among measures of related constructs.

On the other hand, when construct validation is applied to personnel selection, the main purpose is to develop evidence about the predictor measure's association with a criterion (most typically and specifically an indicator of performance) and its value as a predictor of that performance. In this view, the focus is on the relationships between the predictor measure and other theoretical and observable variables, particularly with job performance variables (Arvey, 1992). The evidence and inferences must be explainable to nonpsychologists involved with organizational decisions and legal defense. The generalizability of the predictor-criterion relationship is a concern— across organizations, settings, jobs, subjects, and time. In this view, there is no single dominant approach to evidence gathering; rather, there are multiple inferential paths linking a predictor measure to a performance domain. In this view, construct validation has become a process of building and confirming a model that includes predictor and performance constructs and measures.

Binning and Barrett (1989) provided a clear explanation of the multiple inferences involved with predictor and performance variables in a personnel selection context. Figure 9.1 is an adaptation of a model from their work. In Figure 9.1, inference 1 is that a performance domain represents the job behaviors identified by the organization as valuable or essential to attaining the organization's goals. Job analysis provides the basis for this inference, and all other inferences are based on the proper development of the performance domain. A performance domain is a construct representing a behavioral domain, just as psychological constructs represent behavioral domains. However, performance domains are influenced by the values and judgments of key decision makers as to how job performance contributes to the accomplishment of organizational goals (Binning & Barrett, 1989). Thus, performance domains are not simply discovered but are determined by the organization (Binning & Barrett). A performance domain can be constructed on several levels, to reflect the full set of behaviors or outcomes for a given job, a subset of behaviors or outcomes, or the behaviors or outcomes for a group of jobs combined together.

Inference 4 is the key inference for personnel selection (indicated by the heavy arrow). It is the inference that the predictor

Figure 9.1. Evidentiary Inferences.

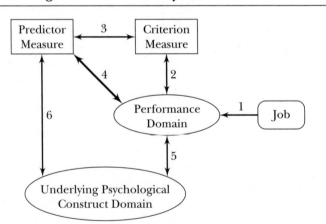

Source: Adapted from Figure 3 in Binning and Barrett (1989).

measure is related to the performance domain. All other inferences serve to support this inference 4. This inference can be demonstrated directly, using rational evidence that the predictor measure is a representative and relevant sample of the performance domain; that is, content-related validation (Binning & Barrett, 1989). Inference 4 may also be demonstrated through paths combining inferences 2 and 3 and inferences 5 and 6.

Inference 3 is that the predictor measure relates to the criterion measure. This is the inference supported by criterion-related validation research, typically based on the correlation of predictor values and criterion values. This inference is generally the main focus of attention for personnel selection.

Inference 2 is that the criterion measure is an adequate sample from the performance domain (Binning & Barrett, 1989) and is not contaminated, deficient, or biased. Evidence for this may show that the criterion measure is a representative sample of the performance domain or that the reliability and dimensionality of criterion scores supports their link to the performance domain. Criterion-related validation requires the combination of both inferences 2 and 3 to support the central inference 4. However, inference 2 has often been neglected (or given only lip service) in criterion-related validation (Binning & Barrett, 1989; Schmitt & Landy, 1993).

Inference 5 is that the predictor construct domain overlaps with the performance domain (Binning & Barrett, 1989). This inference must be justified theoretically and rationally based on accumulated knowledge about both constructs.

Inference 6 is that the predictor measure is an adequate sample of the predictor construct domain (Binning & Barrett, 1989). The typical interest for research psychologists involves empirical data and judgments about relationships that are both convergent and discriminant (Cronbach & Meehl, 1955; Campbell & Fiske, 1959). In the "advancing theory" view, inference 2 has been labeled construct validity. However, in the context of personnel selection, what has traditionally been labeled as construct validity is tied to the combination of both inference 5 and inference 6, in justifying the central inference 4.

Binning and Barrett (1989) also discuss how evidence for these inferences may be bolstered by looking at the nomological network among related variables, such as other predictor constructs or measures, alternative measures of both the predictor and criterion, or constructs and measures of behaviors outside the performance domain.

In sum, validation in personnel selection should be viewed as a process of building and testing hypotheses about relationships among predictor and performance constructs and measures (Landy, 1986). Although Figure 9.1 shows the key inferences of interest for personnel specialists, there may be a great many approaches to gathering evidence to support those inferences. As Landy points out, "the number of validity analyses available is limited only by the creativity and experience of the analyst" (p. 1186).

Some Illustrative Examples of Practical Approaches to Construct Validation

In the discussion that follows, we describe some examples of approaches to gathering evidence that involve predictor and performance constructs and their measures, and the relationships among them. We have organized these into approaches that (1) focus on development of construct-based measures, (2) build and test structural and measurement models, (3) generalize evidence from other studies, (4) incorporate predictor and performance constructs and measures into a nomological network, and (5) use experimental methods to test hypotheses about constructs and measures.

Rationalizing the Development of Predictor Measures and Performance Measures

Many approaches to construct validation involve the use of judgments as part of a rational process of developing predictor measures that are linked to performance.

Content and Construct Validation in Constructing Measures

As noted earlier, evidence for content validation can be used directly to support inference 4 in Figure 9.1, through rational judgments that the predictor measure is a representative and appropriate sample of the performance domain. Schmitt (1989) states that content validity is "just good test construction practice and is essential if our measure is to be valid in any broader or 'real' sense" (p. 340). However, it may not be clear as to whether one should present evidence to support inference 4 directly (content validation) or should present evidence to develop inferences 5 and 6 (classically defined construct validation). The problem lies in the lack of clarity about whether something is or is not a construct. The *Uniform Guidelines* lists examples of constructs (such as intelligence, aptitude, personality, common sense, judgment, leadership, and spatial ability), but they provide no guidance as to the definition of a construct. Selection tests may require candidates to demonstrate job skills through work *samples* in realistic and standardized situations, or selection tests may assess *signs* or indicators of predispositions to behave in certain ways (Wernimont & Campbell, 1968). In litigation, it is not always easy to distinguish *samples* of behavior (involving content-based item development) from *signs* of behavior (involving construct-based item development). This distinction may be a key issue in equal employment litigation, since the *Uniform Guidelines* state that a content strategy is not appropriate for predictors based on constructs, and they mandate that construct validation include a criterion-related study. It is not simply a matter of whether a demonstration of performance is observable or not (Landy, 1986). Performance on a work sample test may be observable, but various abilities (constructs or signs) may underlie that performance. It may be "easier to illuminate the typing ability or memory or strength continuum than the reasoning continuum, but all are constructs nonetheless" (Landy, 1986, p. 1189).

One illustration of construct-based item development is found in Mumford, Costanza, Connelly, and Johnson's (1996) discussion of the development of background data scales. They describe a carefully structured process that begins by identifying constructs that might contribute to performance for a particular job (such as foreign service officer). The underlying constructs are identified using both job analysis information and theory from prior research literature. This information constitutes evidence for inferences 1 and 5 in Figure 9.1.

In the Mumford et al. (1996) study, once constructs were identified, potential items for background data scales were developed by a demographically balanced panel of doctoral candidates in I/O psychology. The students completed extensive training regarding the constructs, item generation processes, and criteria. Panel members discussed and reached consensus on operational definitions for each construct and the implications of the constructs for the life histories of the target population to which the background scales would be applied. They then created items expected to elicit behavior reflecting the construct and reflecting situations to which the population of interest would likely have had exposure. Panel members also specified differences in individuals' behaviors in response to a situation, constructing a set of response behaviors reflecting differing degrees of expression of the construct.

Panel members were expected to make explicit hypotheses about how a construct would lead to the expression of behavior and to prepare multiple items reflecting a range of opportunities for manifestation of the construct. In all, these items provided multiple markers of underlying constructs, generalized across situations. All items and responses were carefully reviewed for construct relevance, social desirability, perceived bias in opportunities for exposure to the situation, faking potential, invasion of privacy, and the extent to which individuals' behavior was controllable in the situation (Mumford et al., 1996). The process used to create the items provides substantial evidence for inference 6 in Figure 9.1: that the items generated reflect the underlying constructs of interest. Exhibit 9.1 lists some examples of background data constructs and items produced using this structured approach.

A second illustration is found in Kantrowitz's (2005) study to define and create items for assessing general "soft skills" performance. She conducted semistructured interviews of subject matter experts (SMEs) to elicit a definition of soft skills performance and to build a list of behavior exemplars and critical incidents for soft skills performance. SMEs were also asked to rate the representativeness of soft skills performance for a set of behavior descriptors based on prior literature relating to soft skills performance. The result from these ratings was a master list of 107 exemplars in ten categories. This procedure provided evidence for inference 1 in Figure 9.1, in justifying a soft skills performance domain applicable to a broad range of occupations.

In the next stage of Kantrowitz's (2005) research, she asked a second set of fifty-two SMEs to perform a Q-sort exercise, which

Exhibit 9.1. Examples of Background Data Constructs and Items.

Planning

1. When an unexpected problem came up, how much has it disrupted your schedule?
2. How often has making lists been part of your regular routine?
3. How comfortable have you been when working on a number of different problems at the same time?

Achievement motivation

1. In college, how much did you enjoy self-study courses or lab work?
2. How often have you chosen classes, assignments, or projects simply to learn something new?
3. How often have your achievements been due to effort rather than ability?

Social perception

1. How often have you correctly anticipated conflict between two friends?
2. How likely have you been to change the way you present an idea when talking to different people?
3. How often have others asked you to represent the group?

Tolerance for ambiguity

1. To what extent have you put off projects when you were unclear about their objectives?
2. How important has it been for you to have friends who were similar to you?
3. How impatient have you been with problems that take a long time to solve?

Object beliefs

1. How likely have you been to do favors for people who could not return them?
2. How often have you viewed dealing with people as a game?
3. How important has it been for you to make friends with people who had good connections?

Source: Mumford, Costanza, Connelly, and Johnson (1996).

provided the basis for both cluster analysis and multidimensional scaling. These analyses yielded seven clusters of soft skills performance: communications/persuasion skills, performance management skills, self-management skills, interpersonal skills, leadership/organization skills, political/cultural skills, and counterproductive behavior (negatively signed). Then a ratings instrument was written containing 107 behavioral items in seven scales, to be completed both as a self-rating and by supervisors. The ratings provided considerable evidence for inference 2 from Figure 9.1—that the criterion measure developed is a good representation of the domain of soft skills performance.

Critical incident analyses may be especially helpful to the processes of item and test development. Critical incidents have been used in several studies as part of creating and justifying predictor constructs and measures (Ackerman & Kanfer, 1993; Kantrowitz, 2005) as well as performance constructs and measures (Campbell, Dunnette, Arvey, & Hellervik, 1973). A related methodology might be to use SMEs to create a set of job-relevant situations of varying difficulty and importance to the organization and to conduct expert analyses about the nature of involvement of constructs across the range of situations.

Rational Validation

Schmidt, Hunter, Croll, and McKenzie (1983) demonstrated that psychologists with considerable expertise in personnel selection can provide rational estimates of the empirical validities that closely match the results from empirical studies, but with less variability than is often found in criterion-related studies, due to sample size limitations. A later study (Hirsh, Schmidt, & Hunter, 1986) showed that estimates made by psychologists with high levels of expertise were more accurate with less variability than estimates made by recent doctoral graduates. One argument for these results is that the expert psychologists' rational judgments are rooted in a deep understanding of theory about predictor constructs and their relations with various performance domains, coupled with a general awareness of prior empirical studies and meta-analyses. Rational judgments from a panel of expert psychologists could provide evidence of inference 4 directly, to supplement available criterion-related studies or to replace them in situations in which criterion-related studies are not feasible.

Rational judgments from expert psychologists may also be useful in assessing inference 5, that is, in identifying predictor constructs appropriate to performance domains. A panel of such experts may bolster judgments from others, such as a panel of SMEs on performance or the judgment of the principal researchers.

Taken further, there may be rational judgments to be made about extreme groups—about characteristics or behavior of employee groups formed according to high or low levels of a predictor or performance construct. Whether one focuses on the high-level or low-level group may depend on the relationship between individual performance and organizational performance for a particular job. For instance, Jacobs (1981) discussed *guardian* jobs in which poor individual performance can lead to large organizational liabilities. This category may include jobs such as police officers, medical professionals, air-traffic controllers, or school bus drivers, or jobs in which employees represent the organization to key external constituents and can impact the organization's reputation. For *guardian* jobs, one may focus attention on those with low levels of a construct and make theory-based rational judgments about the potential impact on organizational performance. For *star* jobs (Jacobs), the highest performers can bring exponential benefits to their organization. This category may include jobs such as professional athletes, top executives, some sales professionals, medical and academic researchers, or jobs involving the production of knowledge or innovation. For *star* jobs, one may want to focus attention on rational judgments about constructs theoretically associated with the highest levels of individual performance.

Along these same lines, perhaps even "thought experiments" might prove useful in construct validation—what if an incumbent had *none* of the construct? What if an incumbent's construct level was suddenly constrained due to illness or accident?

Multivariate Methods for Linking Performance and Predictor Domains

Personnel researchers may use evidence from multivariate analyses such as factor analysis, cluster analysis, or multidimensional scaling to justify inference 5 in Figure 9.1, linking the predictor construct and performance construct domains. Essentially, these methods using statistical information about items and how they correlate with each other in justifying that a scale or factor is measuring some theoretical entity.

Borman, Rosse, and Abrahams (1980) conducted a validation study of personality constructs used in selecting Navy recruiters. In this study, the results of a job analysis and factor analysis of performance measures provided evidence that selling skills, human relation skills, and organizing skills were important to performance. Performance measures were created to assess these three constructs. Sets of personality and interest items were administered to Navy recruiters, and those items that correlated most strongly with the measures of performance on the three constructs were retained. Then factor analysis of the retained items was conducted to confirm the three-construct structure. Finally, the researchers wrote new items thought to represent each of the three constructs. This process demonstrated the researchers' understanding of the constructs and provided strong evidence for inferences 5 and 6 in Figure 9.1.

Research from Project A, a large-scale project to improve selection and placement for the U.S. Army, used exploratory and confirmatory factor analysis for a variety of measures of performance, including job knowledge and work sample tests, performance ratings, training tests, and archival performance data (Campbell, McHenry, & Wise, 1990). The results provided evidence for a conceptual model of soldier effectiveness that included general categories of determination (perseverance, conscientiousness, initiative, discipline), teamwork (cooperation, morale, goal orientation, leadership), and allegiance (following orders and regulations, respect for authority, military bearing). This development of the performance domain provided groundwork for inference 5 in developing predictor constructs.

Developing and Confirming Measurement and Structural Models

Arvey (1992) suggested that a developing perspective of construct validation for personnel selection views it as a process of specifying and confirming a range of relationships among predictor constructs and their measures, with variables representing important components of performance. Under this framework, construct validation entails building and confirming a model including predictor, performance, and related variables. From this perspective, the researcher is not just focused on confirming the test but is also interested in confirming the model, relating constructs to measures of both the predictor and performance. The determination and testing of the paths between unobservable constructs and their measures involves the *measurement model,* whereas the *structural model* refers to the components associating the predictor and performance constructs.

One example of this approach to construct validation may be seen in the work by Arvey, Landon, Nutting, and Maxwell (1992) to develop physical ability tests for selecting police officers. The researchers demonstrated a construct approach to validation, using evidence from a variety of sources.

1. Multiple approaches to job analysis supported the inference that physical activities are an important feature of police officer performance.
2. Based on the literature on physical abilities, the researchers hypothesized that two underlying physical constructs—strength and endurance—would account for variance in police officer performance and in their performance on physical tests. A model was specified in which the latent constructs of strength and endurance operated as prime determinants of both test scores and ratings. The model, shown in Figure 9.2, also included a ratings factor expected to produce common variance among all ratings measures.
3. Physical tests were administered to a random sample of incumbent police officers: an obstacle course run, a dummy drag test, a one-mile run, a climb of a five-foot fence, and a dummy wrestle simulation in which a 120-pound dummy is lifted, rotated, and carried. Supervisor ratings were gathered for the same incumbent officers regarding their effectiveness in performing job-relevant physical tasks. Archival data on the same officers was available from an annual fitness evaluation, including maximum oxygen capacity (VO_2) from a treadmill exercise, the number of bench dips in one minute, standing and running heart rate, and body-fat percentage.
4. The researchers tested the fit of the incumbent officers' test and ratings data to the model shown in Figure 9.2. The results supported the model, with the latent constructs of strength and endurance influencing both predictor scores and performance

ratings as expected. A portion of the model that included the physical tests was also confirmed, using data from an independent sample of actual applicants for police officer positions.

5. Subsequent analyses examined the relationships of the strength and endurance factor scores with the exogenous variables from the annual fitness evaluation, an overall performance rating, and an archival file rating, providing additional evidence for the interpretation and support of the strength and endurance constructs. Additional analyses examined sex and age differences and potential bias across test events and performance ratings (Arvey et al., 1992).

Figure 9.2. Hypothesized Model of Two Latent Variables— Strength and Endurance—with Test and Performance Ratings.

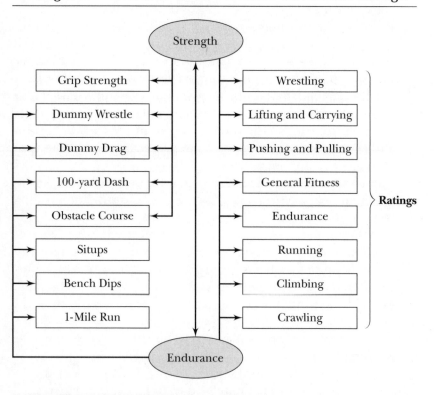

Source: Arvey, Landon, Nutting, and Maxwell (1992).

In all, this study provided a network of evidence supporting the validity of the physical ability tests. It included rational evidence in support of inferences 1, 2, 5, and 6 in Figure 9.1, as well as empirical evidence in support of inferences 2, 3, 5, and 6 through the confirmation of the structural and measurement model. It also provided evidence supporting the constructs with respect to their associations with available exogenous measures. The study included data that would constitute traditional evidence for criterion and content validation, but the totality of evidence is stronger and less vulnerable to legal challenge than would be the data from just the criterion or content evidence alone.

Another example of a model building and confirmation approach is found in Vance, Coovert, MacCallum, and Hedge (1989). The authors specified a set of constructs hypothesized to be predictive of performance by Air Force recruits. These constructs were (1) recruit capacity, measured through cognitive tests, (2) self-reported support of supervisor, and (3) recruit experience. The predictors were expected to relate to criterion constructs such as the amount of time spent on and the score on a work sample test of job performance; ratings of task performance by supervisor, peers, and self; and grades during training. The authors used a variety of methods to test and modify the model, demonstrating that cognitive ability explained significant variance in performance during training, in the work-sample performance test, and in performance ratings. Although their data included evidence of criterion validity, the advantage of their approach was that their evidence demonstrated a richer understanding of the network of variables influencing performance, including direct and mediating effects. Their model is presented in Figure 9.3.

Generalizing Validation Evidence from Other Studies

Accumulated validity evidence from other studies, external and internal, may be available to help justify the use of predictor measures for a local job or setting. There are at least three approaches to generalization of validity in the personnel selection literature (all of which are discussed in greater detail in other chapters of this volume):

Figure 9.3. A General Model of Task Performance.

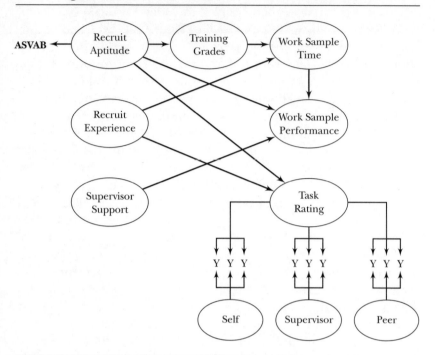

From Vance, Coovert, MacCallum, and Hedge (1989).

- *Transportability*—generalizing inferences from a study conducted on a similar job
- *Validity generalization*—generalizing inferences from many studies using meta-analysis procedures to account for variance in results due to sampling error and other artifacts
- *Synthetic validity* (or *job component validity*)—generalizing inferences across jobs that have similar subsets of performance domains (that is, job components) in common

As noted in our discussion of Binning & Barrett's (1989) model, depending on one's objective, a performance domain may be constructed for the whole job, for a family of related jobs, or for a subset of related behaviors within a job. This level of analysis of the performance domain is part of what distinguishes these three approaches to generalization of validity.

Transportability

This approach entails importing evidence from a criterion-related study conducted for another job. If job analysis demonstrates the similarity of the job studied to the local target job, an inference may be generalized about the predictor-criterion relationship for the target job (Sackett & Arvey, 1993). The *Uniform Guidelines* allow one to do so as long as the external study meets technical standards, there is evidence of test fairness, job analysis shows that the incumbents "perform substantially the same major work behaviors" in both jobs, and there are similar applicant pools of applicants for both jobs [7B(2)].

Transportability may not be a viable option if there are no prior studies for similar jobs or if other organizations are unwilling to allow access to studies. However, it may be practical if test publishers have supplied job analysis data for the jobs used in their original validations, in anticipation of organizations conducting a transportability analysis (Hoffman & McPhail, 1998).

Validity Generalization

A great deal has been written about this approach, and there is an ever-increasing number of meta-analyses performed on constructs relevant for personnel selection. In contrast to transportability, validity generalization entails generalizing from multiple studies. Validity generalization research has demonstrated that the largest proportion of variance among validity coefficients or effect sizes from multiple studies is due to statistical artifacts—the largest artifact usually being sampling error (Schmidt, Hunter, & Pearlman, 1982). Showing the similarity among jobs studied is not a major concern in generalizing results across studies; it may be sufficient to demonstrate that the job belongs the same broad group or job family (Pearlman, Schmidt, & Hunter, 1980).

Synthetic Validity

In synthetic validity strategies and approaches, evidence is generalized across jobs, but the basis for generalization is not the similarity of the entire set of job behaviors, but the fact that the jobs contain similar subsets of the performance domain. These performance domain subsets are referred to as *job components* (Sackett & Arvey, 1993). The process is to break jobs down into their components, identify predictors useful to each component, generalize validity evidence from other studies for each component, and then combine the component validities to create an estimate of overall validity for a set of tests (Schmitt & Landy, 1993).

Synthetic validity was originally conceived as a means for generalizing results from one study, or a small number of studies, for each component. However, the evidence to generalize for a given component may also come from meta-analysis of predictors. This is common in the job component validity (JCV) approach built into the reports given from the Position Analysis Questionnaire (PAQ) (McCormick, Jeanneret, & Mecham, 1972; McCormick, DeNisi, & Shaw, 1979).

An extension of synthetic validation and JCV might be useful for validating a broad selection strategy for an organization. For example, an organization may wish to use measures of general intelligence and conscientiousness as a basis for selection for all professional, technical, or managerial jobs (Behling, 1998). To support such a strategy, evidence could be gathered from job analyses to demonstrate that those jobs shared common components of problem solving and work autonomy. The organization could then generalize the findings from other studies or meta-analyses that have demonstrated strong criterion validities for those two constructs. A similar approach may be useful in the future for validation of predictors such as practical intelligence (Sternberg, 1997), emotional intelligence (Salovey & Grewal, 2005), social intelligence (Schneider, Kanfer, & Ackerman, 1996), or strategic intelligence (Streufert, Pogash, & Piasecki, 1988) that may be predictive of performance across a wide array of job families.

Examples of Studies Generalizing Validity Evidence

Hoffman (1999) used a test transportability procedure coupled with validity generalization evidence to justify the use of physical ability tests for jobs in a large utility company. A prior criterion validation of a physical abilities test battery had been conducted with a consortium of utility companies. From this prior study, four "marker" jobs were compared for similarity to the jobs in the target organization. The organization used cluster analysis to form job families for ninety-five nonmanagerial jobs with at least five incumbents—representing more than 80 percent of the firm's workforce. These jobs had a wide range of physical demands, from low to high. The input for the clustering consisted of scores on thirteen of thirty-one PAQ dimensions. The clustering analysis resulted in five job families. These job families were examined by twenty-five SMEs for the purpose of rationally reviewing the reasonableness of the statistically derived groupings. The consensus of the SMEs supported the groupings, though a few jobs were reassigned to different families (Hoffman, 1999).

Four attribute scores from the PAQ—explosive strength, static strength, dynamic strength, and stamina—determined the physical demands of each job family. The results provided evidence for transporting the prior criterion validities, in justifying the use of physical ability tests for two job families in the target organization. The study also incorporated validity generalization evidence from one published study dealing with physical abilities (Blakely, Quinones, Crawford, & Jago, 1994), as well as construct validation evidence from other studies addressing strength and endurance constructs.

Hoffman, Holden, and Gale (2000) generalized validation evidence for cognitive test use across an array of jobs, in a situation in which criterion-related validation was not technically feasible. The study combined judgmental and empirical evidence, including validity generalization research and test transportability. The organization had conducted thirteen prior internal criterion validity studies of cognitive ability measures for a variety of jobs and job groups, typically using two to four criteria for each study. Job families were formed through cluster analysis using thirty-two PAQ dimension scores. After a rational review by forty SMEs, the result was a set of eleven job families. Jobs within the same family were assumed to contain similar worker behaviors. If one or more jobs in a job family had prior criterion-related studies that had been conducted internally, then that evidence could potentially be transported to justify using the same predictor measure for the other jobs in the family (Hoffman et al., 2000). The researchers also examined JCV predictions (synthetic validity results) and sets of required attributes from PAQ reports. If they were also similar among jobs in the family, the converging construct information served to bolster the transportability inference. If the JCV and required attributes from the PAQ were not similar across the job family, the case for transportability was weakened (Hoffman et al., 2000).

The *Uniform Guidelines* speak solely to generalization of criterion-related validities. However, the logic of transportability and synthetic validity might also be applied to nonempirical evidence. For instance, rationally developed background data scales, developed for a particular performance domain, might be justified for use in another job or setting if job analysis demonstrates the similarity of the overall performance domain (transportability). Or, if jobs share some of the same component constructs but not others, rationally developed scales from several other sources could be combined through a synthetic validation process.

Incorporating Related Constructs and Measures into a Nomological Network

Construct validity has long been associated primarily with MTMM analyses (Campbell & Fiske, 1959) as a way of confirming the meaning of a construct through convergent and discriminant associations. In personnel selection, this approach may be useful in triangulating predictor constructs, performance constructs, or both, through their correlations with theoretically similar and related-but-dissimilar constructs in a nomological network. Such analyses usually provide evidence for inferences 2 or 6 in Figure 9.1—the inference that a measure truly reflects the construct intended.

Shore, Thornton, and Shore (1990) examined how final dimension ratings in assessment centers related to a range of cognitive, personality, and background data measures. They began by rationally classifying eleven assessment center dimensions into two categories: interpersonal-style dimensions (orientation toward people), and performance-style dimensions (orientation toward the task itself). Data were gathered on a large sample of participants in a corporate assessment center designed to identify management potential. After participants had completed all exercises of the three-day center, a panel of three assessors and two psychologists gave the final dimension ratings. All participants also took a battery of cognitive ability tests and a personality inventory. Their patterns of convergent and discriminant correlations generally support the authors' hypotheses that (1) cognitive abilities would correlate more strongly with performance-style dimensions than the interpersonal-style dimensions, and (2) some personality dimensions would relate more strongly to the assessment center's performance-style dimensions (such as scales related to conscientiousness), whereas some personality dimensions would relate more strongly to interpersonal-style dimensions (such as scales related to extraversion, agreeableness, and adjustment). On the whole, the MTMM evidence provided support for the rational hypothesis that assessment center ratings were driven by two underlying constructs (inference 6 in Figure 9.1).

Assessment centers have long relied on content-developed exercises and criterion studies showing strong relationships with various criteria. But studies using MTMM analyses have demonstrated a lack of evidence that assessment centers are actually measuring the underlying constructs that they purport to measure (Sackett & Dreher, 1982; Sackett & Harris, 1988). Assessment centers predict, but there is a lack of clear understanding as to why. Recent studies of construct validity have indicated areas for improvements in assessment center processes. The use of behavioral checklists for each assessment center exercise serves to improve MTMM results (Reilly, Henry, & Smither, 1990). Construct validity evidence is also stronger when overall ratings on dimensions are given only after all exercises are completed, following an integrative council discussion among assessors (Craik, Ware, Kamp, O'Reilly, Staw, and Zedeck, 2002). Thus, over time MTMM analyses have called into question the evidence for inference 6 in Figure 9.1 and then, as measurement procedures were changed, provided supportive evidence for it.

Another example of MTMM analysis involved an investigation of construct validity for rationally developed biodata scales (Killcullen, While, Mumford, and Mack, 1995). In this study, background data scales were constructed to measure the same constructs as the personality scales from Project A. An MTMM matrix of correlations demonstrated a pattern of convergent validities between the background data scales and their intended personality scales. However, the evidence for discriminant validity was weaker in some cases, as some background data scales correlated highly with personality scales that they were not intended to reflect. These data provided mixed evidence about whether the biodata scales constituted alternative measures of the same predictor constructs as the personality scales (inference 6 in Figure 9.1).

On the performance construct side, some time ago Campbell et al. (1973) used MTMM analysis of nine performance dimensions representing the performance domain for department managers of a retail store chain, as rated by two methods—behaviorally anchored scaled expectations and summated rating scales. The mono-trait, hetero-method correlations indicated strong convergent validity for the performance scales. Evidence for discriminant validity indicated that the behaviorally scaled expectations ratings were generally good at discriminating among the nine performance dimensions, although there were problems identified with two of the scales. However, the discriminant validity for the summated ratings was poor because of a strong method variance. If the scaled expectations ratings were used as criteria for personnel selection, this evidence would provide considerable support for inference 2 in Figure 9.1.

Experimental Methods for Testing Hypotheses about Constructs and Measures

Practitioners may have opportunities to use experimental and quasi-experimental methods for gathering evidence about constructs. Just as MTMM methods may help us understand the extent to which our constructs generalize across different measurement methods, experimental comparisons may help us understand the extent to which our constructs generalize across different subjects and settings. Experimental methods may prove useful for hypotheses about construct measures across subjects grouped according to characteristics such as age, culture, appearance, sex, or level of test anxiety. They may also prove useful for hypotheses about construct measures in different settings or conditions, such as high versus low levels of autonomy, high versus low problem-solving requirements, high-fidelity versus low-fidelity simulations, high-stakes versus low-stakes evaluations, or maximal versus typical performance conditions.

In organizations, a variety of natural experiments may be feasible, such as evaluating the effects of deploying a test to different locations over time or comparing effects on different subjective or objective criteria used in different settings.

Arvey, Strickland, Drauden, and Martin (1990) provided one example of using experimental designs to assess construct validity of a measure. In this study, an inventory was developed to assess various attitudes toward employment tests (the Test Attitude Survey, or TAS). The authors used three experiments to test hypotheses about the TAS constructs. In the first, they proposed that scores on this inventory would be sensitive to different employment test conditions, such as various cognitive tests that were perceived as difficult or easy. This hypothesis was tested by administering the TAS to introductory psychology students after they had completed either an easy or a difficult test. The second experiment evaluated TAS results for a sample of Army recruits taking both the computer adaptive testing version and the paper-and-pencil versions of the Armed Services Vocational Aptitude Battery (ASVAB). The third experiment examined TAS differences between incumbents and applicants for the job of highway maintenance worker. The fourth experiment involved examining the relationship between TAS factors and test scores on a perceptual speed test, an arithmetic test, and a work sample test, all administered to applicants for county financial worker positions. This experiment also allowed TAS effects to be compared by race, sex, and age. In all, the results from four experiments helped develop evidence supporting the construct validity of the TAS. Although the TAS is not intended for use as a selection test itself, it may prove useful as a moderator variable in selection contexts as well as for understanding the applicability of employment tests under varying conditions.

There is a substantial body of literature on experimental and quasi-experimental methods (for example, Campbell & Stanley, 1966; Cook, Campbell, & Peracchio, 1990) as well as on the intersection of experimental and correlational methods in psychology (Cronbach, 1957, 1975). These methods have not been widely used in personnel selection contexts, but we suggest that they hold potential for selection practitioners.

Conclusion

Why should a personnel selection practitioner consider using research methods to directly address the validity of constructs in an applied organizational construct? First, such methods engage multiple sources of evidence to support a mutually reinforcing network of inferences that together ultimately support the primary inference 4 from Figure 9.1—that the predictor measure is related to the performance domain. The heavy reliance on criterion and content validity "stamps" (Landy, 1986) often leaves organizations vulnerable in court to allegations of inadequate job analysis, poor test development, or limited criterion development, as well as technical problems inherent to criterion validation methods, such as poor criterion data, restriction of range, and test-taking motivation. In spite of the fact that the *Uniform Guidelines* discourage construct validation by pointing to its difficulty and its ambiguous and uncertain definition, the recent professional testing *Standards for Educational and Psychological Testing* (American Educational Research Association, American Psychological Association, & National Council on Measurement in Education, 1999) and *Principles for the Validation and Use of Personnel Selection Procedures* (Society for Industrial and Organizational Psychology, 2003) stress the need for hypotheses and substantive evidence to support the use of pre-employment tests (Mumford et al., 1996).

Second, in situations in which small samples or lack of time or resources could make criterion studies infeasible, some of the approaches we have discussed, such as generalization of validity from other sources or rational validity, may be viable options for gathering evidence to support the validity of a selection system.

Third, personnel psychologists, although interested in validation from a legal perspective, are also interested in advancing theoretical understanding of predictor and performance constructs. Mumford et al. (1996) stated that if a priori justifications and evidence for construct validity for predictors are not available, it is possible that any observed criterion relationship may be due to spurious, nonrelevant, causal influences. Attention to construct validation has grown with the recognition that content and criterion validations are not sufficient to advance understanding of theory or application (Hough & Oswald, 2000). One example of the importance of construct validation is in the research on assessment centers that was discussed earlier.

Still, there are clearly potential disadvantages to construct validation. The evidence and inferences involved are relatively multifaceted and complex, and they may be harder to interpret and explain to lay audiences, such as managers, attorneys, judges, and juries. Construct studies may also be more difficult and costly to plan and implement. Therefore, we suggest that the more complex and costly approaches to construct validation may be reserved for those situations in which there is (1) a high level of legal risk, such as potential for adverse impact, high visibility, and low face-validity, and (2) a high level of economic risk, such as situations in which there are greater risks to the organization due to employees' performance problems (police, pilots, air traffic controllers), or where there are high costs of training that make it expensive when an employee fails to perform.

In describing construct validity studies, the *Uniform Guidelines* in 1978 stated the following:

> Construct validity is a more complex strategy than either criterion-related or content validity. Construct validation is a relatively new and developing procedure in the employment field, and there is at present a lack of substantial literature extending the concept to employment practices. [14D(1)].

After almost thirty years, our understanding of construct validation for personnel selection has evolved. Personnel psychologists have embraced validation as a unitary concept, involving many approaches to gathering evidence for testing hypotheses about the inferences relating predictors and performance. We now have methodological strategies that do not clearly fall within the traditional categories of criterion, content, and construct validation. Perhaps we need to stop thinking of construct validation as new and complex, but rather begin seeing it as research that enhances our ability to advance scientific understanding while still providing defense against legal challenges to our selection methods.

For too long, validation for personnel selection has been constrained by the *Uniform Guidelines* and the "stamp collecting" mentality (Landy, 1986). Clearly, the newest *Principles* (Society for Industrial and Organizational Psychology, 2003) have codified validation as a unitary process of building and testing hypotheses and should help to broaden future validation efforts. We have the burden of precedents to overcome. But as we overcome them, Landy's (1986) call bears repeating:

> . . . psychologists should not aid and abet the stamp collectors who are determined to identify the right type of approach (or type of analysis) for every situation. Furthermore, psychologists should put

an end to the artificial distinction between *behavior* and *mental processes,* a distinction that the *Uniform Guidelines* seek to maintain. Instead, they should begin to apply the traditional standards for evaluating experimental design and hypothesis testing to all efforts, both conceptual and empirical, that seek to support inferences from test scores. In the most basic sense, psychologists must stop thinking of testing and the validation process as something different from traditional hypothesis testing. (p. 1191)

References

Ackerman, P. L., & Kanfer, R. (1993). Integrating laboratory and field study for improving selection: Development of a battery for predicting air traffic controller success. *Journal of Applied Psychology, 78,* 413–432.

American Educational Research Association, American Psychological Association, & National Council on Measurement in Education. (1999). *Standards for educational and psychological testing.* Washington, DC: American Education Research Association.

Arvey, R. D. (1992). Constructs and construct validation: Definitions and issues. *Human Performance, 5*(1 & 2), 59–69.

Arvey, R. D., Landon, T. E., Nutting, S. M., & Maxwell, S. E. (1992). Development of physical ability tests for police officers: A construct validation approach. *Journal of Applied Psychology, 77,* 996–1009.

Arvey, R. D., Strickland, W., Drauden, G., & Martin, C. (1990). Motivational components of test taking. *Personnel Psychology, 43,* 695–717.

Behling, O. (1998). Employee selection: Will intelligence and conscientiousness do the job? *Academy of Management Executive, 12,* 77–86.

Binning, J. F., & Barrett, G. V. (1989). Validity of personnel decisions: A conceptual analysis of the inferential and evidential bases. *Journal of Applied Psychology, 74*(3), 478–494.

Blakely, B. R., Quinones, M. A., Crawford, M. S., & Jago, I. A. (1994). The validity of isometric strength tests. *Personnel Psychology, 47,* 247–274.

Borman, W. C., Rosse, R. L., & Abrahams, N. M. (1980). An empirical construct validity approach to studying predictor-job performance links. *Journal of Applied Psychology, 65,* 665–671.

Campbell, D. T., & Fiske, D. W. (1959). Convergent and discriminant validation by the multitrait-multimethod matrix. *Psychological Bulletin, 56,* 81–105.

Campbell, D. T., & Stanley, J. C. (1966). *Experimental and quasi-experimental design for research.* Chicago: Rand McNally.

Campbell, J. P., Dunnette, M. D., Arvey, R. D., & Hellervik, L. V. (1973). The development and evaluation of behaviorally based rating scales. *Journal of Applied Psychology, 57,* 15–22.

Campbell, J. P., McHenry, J. J., & Wise, L. L. (1990). Modeling job performance in a population of jobs. *Personnel Psychology, 43,* 313–334.

Cook, T. D., Campbell, D. T., & Peracchio, L. (1990). Quasi experimentation. In M. D. Dunnette & L. M. Hough (Eds.), *Handbook of industrial and organizational psychology* (2nd ed., Vol. 1, pp. 491–576). Palo Alto, CA: Consulting Psychologists Press.

Craik, K. H., Ware, A. P., Kamp, J., O'Reilly, C., Staw, B., & Zedeck, S. (2002). Explorations of construct validity in a combined managerial and personality assessment programme. *Journal of Occupational and Organizational Psychology, 75,* 171–193.

Cronbach, L. J. (1957). The two disciplines of scientific psychology. *American Psychologist, 12,* 671–684.

Cronbach, L. J. (1975). Beyond the two disciplines of scientific psychology. *American Psychologist, 30,* 116–127.

Cronbach, L. J., & Meehl, P. E. (1955). Construct validity in psychological tests. *Psychological Bulletin, 52,* 281–302.

Equal Employment Opportunity Commission, Civil Service Commission, Department of Labor, & Department of Justice. (1978). *Uniform guidelines on employee selection procedures. Federal Register, 43*(166), 38290–38315.

Guion, R. M. (1980). On trinitarian doctrines of validity. *Professional Psychology, 11,* 385–398.

Hirsh, H. R., Schmidt, F. L., & Hunter, J. E. (1986). Estimation of employment validities by less experienced judges. *Personnel Psychology, 39,* 337–344.

Hoffman, C. C. (1999). Generalizing physical ability test validity: A case study using test transportability, validity generalization, and construct-related validation evidence. *Personnel Psychology, 52,* 1019–1041.

Hoffman, C. C., Holden, L. M., & Gale, K. (2000). So many jobs, so little "N": Applying expanded validation models to support generalization of cognitive test validity. *Personnel Psychology, 53,* 955–991.

Hoffman, C. C., & McPhail, S. M. (1998). Exploring options for supporting test use in situations precluding local validation. *Personnel Psychology, 51,* 987–1003.

Hough, L. R., & Oswald, F. L. (2000). Personnel selection: Looking toward the future—remembering the past. *Annual Review of Psychology, 51,* 631–664.

Jacobs, D. (1981). Toward a theory of mobility and behavior in organizations: An inquiry into the consequences of some relationships between individual performance and organizational success. *American Journal of Sociology, 87,* 684–707.

Kantrowitz, T. M. (2005). *Development and construct validation of a measure of soft skill performance.* Unpublished doctoral dissertation, Georgia Institute of Technology.

Killcullen, R. N., While, L. A., Mumford, M. D., & Mack, H. (1995). Assessing the construct validity of rational biodata scales. *Military Psychology, 7,* 17–28.

Landy, F. J. (1986). Stamp collecting versus science: Validation as hypothesis testing. *American Psychologist, 41,* 1183–1192.

McCormick, E. J., DeNisi, A. S., & Shaw, J. B. (1979). Use of the Position Analysis Questionnaire for establishing the job component validity of tests. *Journal of Applied Psychology, 64,* 51–56.

McCormick, E. J., Jeanneret, P. R., & Mecham, R. C. (1972). A study of job characteristics and job dimensions based on the Position Analysis Questionnaire (PAQ). *Journal of Applied Psychology, 56,* 347–368.

Mumford, M. D., Costanza, D. P., Connelly, M. S., & Johnson, J. F. (1996). Item generation procedures and background data scales: Implications for construct and criterion-related validity. *Personnel Psychology, 49,* 361–398.

Pearlman, K., Schmidt, F. L., & Hunter, J. E. (1980). Validity generalization results for tests used to predict job proficiency and training success in clerical occupations. *Journal of Applied Psychology, 65,* 373–406.

Reilly, R. R., Henry, S., & Smither, J. W. (1990). An examination of the effects of using behavior checklists on the construct validity of assessment center dimensions. *Personnel Psychology, 43,* 71–84.

Sackett, P. R., & Arvey, R. D. (1993). Selection in small *N* settings. In N. Schmitt & W. Borman (Eds.), *Personnel selection in organizations* (pp. 418–447). San Francisco: Jossey-Bass.

Sackett, P. R., & Dreher, G. F. (1982). Constructs and assessment center dimensions: Some troubling empirical findings. *Journal of Applied Psychology, 67,* 401–410.

Sackett, P. R., & Harris, M. J. (1988). A further examination of the constructs underlying assessment center ratings. *Journal of Applied Psychology, 3,* 214–229.

Salovey, P., & Grewal, D. (2005). The science of emotional intelligence. *Current Directions in Psychological Science, 14,* 281–285.

Schmidt, F. L., Hunter, J. E., Croll, P. R., & McKenzie, R. C. (1983). Estimation of employment test validities by expert judgment. *Journal of Applied Psychology, 68,* 590–601.

Schmidt, F. L., Hunter, J. E., & Pearlman, K. (1982). Progress in validity generalization: Comments on Callendar and Osburn and further developments. *Journal of Applied Psychology, 67,* 835–845.

Schmitt, N. (1989). Construct validity in personnel selection. In B. J. Fallon, H. P. Pfister, & J. Brebner (Eds.), *Advanced in industrial organizational psychology.* New York: Elsevier Science.

Schmitt, N., & Landy, F. J. (1993). The concept of validity. In N. Schmitt & W. Borman (Eds.), *Personnel selection in organizations* (pp. 275–309), San Francisco: Jossey-Bass.

Schneider, R. J., Kanfer, R., & Ackerman, P. L. (1996). To "act wisely in human relations": Exploring the dimensions of social competence. *Personality and Individual Differences, 21,* 469–481.

Shore, T. H., Thornton, G. C., & Shore, L. (1990). Construct validity of two categories of assessment center dimension ratings. *Personnel Psychology, 43,* 101–116.

Society for Industrial and Organizational Psychology. (2003). *Principles for the validation and use of personnel selection procedures* (4th ed.). Bowling Green, OH: Society for Industrial and Organizational Psychology.

Sternberg, R. (1997). Managerial intelligence: Why IQ is not enough. *Journal of Management, 23,* 475–493.

Streufert, S. Pogash, R., & Piasecki, M. (1988). Simulation-based assessment of managerial competence: Reliability and validity. *Personnel Psychology, 41,* 527–557.

Vance, R. J., Coovert, M. D., MacCallum, R. C., & Hedge, J. W. (1989). Construct models of job performance. *Journal of Applied Psychology, 74,* 447–455.

Wernimont, P. F., & Campbell, J. P. (1968). Signs, samples, and criteria. *Journal of Applied Psychology, 52,* 372–376.

PART 3

Implementation

Implementation Based on Alternate Validation Procedures: Ranking, Cut Scores, Banding, and Compensatory Models

Lorin Mueller, Dwayne Norris, and Scott Oppler

Implementation of a new selection procedure encompasses several steps that vary significantly depending on the nature and intended uses of the procedure: defining performance standards within the new procedure, determining how these performance standards will be applied, and integrating the application of those standards within the broader context of selecting candidates within a hiring or promotion system. Typically, selection procedures are implemented using a relative *ranking* of candidates based on their performance, comparing their performance against a minimal performance standard (that is, a *cut score* or *critical score*), grouping (or *banding*) candidates into two or more levels of performance within which there is little meaningful performance variance, or combining performance across multiple performance assessments into a single *compensatory* selection procedure. These implementation methods are not mutually exclusive. A complex personnel system may employ a combination of these methods to more validly inform the selection process.

Developing a sound implementation plan for a newly validated selection procedure is as important as any step in the validation process. A poorly implemented selection procedure has the potential to undermine the validity of personnel decisions based on the procedure. Consider the following scenario: a semi-structured interview designed to assess a candidate's job knowledge and skills is administered as a screen-out procedure prior to a less-structured (and possibly less valid) interview designed to assess person-organization fit. If performance standards on the screen-out assessment are too low, unqualified applicants passed on to the fit interview may eventually be selected. In contrast, if performance standards are too stringent on the screen-out interview, any gains in utility created by an increase in job performance may be offset by the increase in cost of recruiting a sufficient number of candidates who are able to pass the performance standard. In essence, implementation implies not only practicing sound scientific principles when determining performance standards, but also considering the practical and economic impact of those standards across the entire recruitment and selection process. Further, careful consideration of these issues and documentation of findings is ultimately the best defense to any legal challenges that may arise from the use of a selection procedure.

This chapter is organized in a manner slightly different from the previous chapters. In part, this is due to the fact that this chapter must be relevant to all validation approaches described in the previous chapters. Accordingly, the approach taken here is to describe a general model for implementation, rather than a step-by-step approach to applying a single model. This chapter begins with a review of professional and legal standards that apply to issues of implementation. The next section describes the general factors that must be taken into account when choosing among different methods of implementation (for example, ranking versus cut scores, multiple-hurdle versus compensatory models). The sections that follow describe in more detail the issues associated with using rankings, methods for defining performance standards for performance bands and cut scores, and methods for integrating or combining performance standards across multiple selection procedures. The final sections describe two examples of cases in which directly relevant information regarding potential candidate performance and criterion data were not available and explain how implementation issues were ultimately resolved using other relevant information. One case involves selecting mathematicians for a multiyear training program within a government agency; the other involves selecting police officers for a law-enforcement agency.

Professional and Legal Standards

The purpose of this section is to describe the general guidelines one must follow when developing a plan to implement a new selection procedure. As introduced in previous chapters, there are four primary sources of professional and legal guidance that apply to implementing selection procedures: Title VII of the Civil Rights Act of 1964, as amended by the Civil Rights Act of 1991; the *Uniform Guidelines on Employee Selection Procedures* (Equal Employment Opportunity Commission, Civil Service Commission, Department of Labor, & Department of Justice, 1978); the *Standards for Educational and Psychological Testing* (American Educational Research Association, American Psychological Association, & National Council on Measurement in Education, 1999); and the *Principles for the Validation and Use of Employee Selection Procedures* (Society for Industrial and Organizational Psychology, 2003). The last three of these have been discussed previously in relation to the validation of these procedures. There is a large and growing body of case law relevant to Title VII challenges of employment selection procedures that may also provide additional clarification to the process of implementing selection procedures; for more complete reviews of these guidelines and relevant case law, the reader is referred to Biddle (1993), Gutman (2000), Jeanneret (2005), and Kehoe and Olson (2005). The purpose of this review is to outline the general tenets set forth in these works, to better define the criteria for meeting professional and legal standards for selection procedure implementation.

Title VII of the Civil Rights Act

Title VII provides little specific guidance with respect to implementing selection procedures, despite being the primary legal basis for challenging employment selection procedures (that is, as of the writing of this work—see Kehoe and Olson, 2005; Zink and Gutman,

2005—however, Title I of the Americans with Disabilities Act of 1990 [ADA] may ultimately surpass Title VII in number, if not importance, of cases.) Title VII provides four very general stipulations with respect to implementing selection procedures. In the first and second stipulations, Title VII imposes a responsibility to ensure that any personnel selection procedure that results in adverse impact with respect to any protected subgroup is both job relevant *and* consistent with business necessity. This two-pronged test requires not only that one demonstrate the validity of the procedure for making inferences regarding one or more aspects of job performance, but also that the selection procedure provide some economic or strategic utility to the organization. Even when these standards are met, the third stipulation of Title VII states that a selection procedure may still be unlawful if alternative procedures exist that do not have adverse impact. The 1991 amendment to the Civil Rights Act added a fourth stipulation prohibiting the use of different selection procedures or standards on the basis of race, color, religion, sex, or national origin (for example, race-normed or group-adjusted scores, use of different cutoff scores across groups or quotas).

Taken together, these four stipulations (that is, that a technique be job-related, that it be consistent with business necessity, that there be no alternatives, and that within-group standards not be applied) have several implications for alternative validation techniques. Most important, in many cases reliable information about the adverse impact of the selection procedure will not be available as it is directly applied in a particular setting (namely, when a local adverse impact study is not feasible prior to implementation). When that is the case, indirect evidence of the potential for adverse impact must be examined by reviewing the professional literature, and the procedure should be reviewed for fairness by a diverse, knowledgeable group of stakeholders. If the potential for adverse impact exists, practitioners must determine whether equally useful alternatives exist that do not result in adverse impact. Moreover, any process to adjust or transform candidate performance on the selection procedure should be considered very carefully, and never for the main purpose of reducing adverse impact (or discriminating on the basis of protected group membership, although that should go without saying). Finally, regardless of the potential for adverse impact, this process should be thoroughly documented in the event that the procedure is ever challenged.

The Uniform Guidelines

Like Title VII, the *Uniform Guidelines* provide little direction to assist in developing a sound, legally defensible implementation plan. The *Uniform Guidelines* include two broad statements with respect to implementation issues. The first is a blanket statement that cutoff scores should be set to be reasonable and consistent with expectations of acceptable proficiency in the workforce. This statement seems to suggest that all candidates who would normally be expected to perform work at a minimally acceptable level merit further consideration. Of course, the term *acceptable proficiency* is subject to a wide range of interpretation, meaning the same selection procedure could be used with different cutoff scores across contexts. The second statement requires that selection procedures that rank candidates should be examined for their degree of adverse impact.

In terms of implementing a selection procedure on the basis of an alternative validation strategy, the implications of the *Uniform Guidelines* are similar to those of Title VII. First, the selection procedure should be reviewed for the potential for adverse impact, especially if the implementation plan calls for the rank-order selection of candidates. Second, the statement implies that any method used to set cutoff scores should be consistent with the concept of a minimally qualified candidate, rather than a higher standard.

The Standards

In comparison to Title VII and the *Uniform Guidelines,* the *Standards* provide a wealth of professional guidance about the process of developing an implementation plan for a new selection procedure. The *Standards* are organized into fifteen chapters across four broad sections that address nearly every important aspect of test development and implementation. Chapter Four of the *Standards,* "Scales, Norms, and Score Comparability," is probably the chapter most relevant to the development of a sound implementation plan, as it directly addresses issues such as setting guidelines for score interpretation and setting cut scores. Additionally, Chapter Six, "Supporting Documentation for Tests," includes significant guidance on aspects of the implementation plan that may need to be documented. Aside from these chapters, several individual standards contain important information to assist in implementing a new assessment.

The *Standards* include considerable professional guidance on the type and quality of the information that should be considered when making recommendations on performance standards for a given procedure. Specifically, the *Standards* state that empirical data associated with candidate performance on the selection procedure should be used as the basis for setting cut scores that define distinct interpretations of performance when it is feasible to do so (Standard 4.20). The *Standards* go on to note that this may be difficult to accomplish in employment settings, in which the relationship of performance on the selection procedure to the criterion of interest may be only one factor in the precise location of the cut score. The *Standards* also state a preference for expert judgment methods when criterion data are suspect, and they further clarify the use of expert judgments by stating that when these methods are used, the methods should be designed in such a way as to facilitate the application of the experts' knowledge and skills to the task of setting the cut score (Standard 4.21). In other words, the process should be simplified to the extent possible, experts should be trained in the judgmental task, and there should be an explicit correspondence between the judgmental task and the recommended performance standard.

Although the *Standards* state that misclassification rates should also be considered when developing a plan for implementing a new procedure (Standard 2.15), practitioners may want to be cautious about the extent to which and the manner in which they share information about the reliability of a procedure, errors in measurement, and resulting misclassification rates with judges in the process of standard setting. Content experts rarely possess the psychometric expertise required to adequately consider this information in their deliberations. This standard may be satisfied by ensuring that performance standards are not set outside the effective measurement range of the procedure, that standard setting experts are informed when they make a recommendation that is inconsistent with sound measurement, and that such recommendations are adjusted to be in line with reliable and valid use of the procedure.

Finally, if normative or field test data are to be used in informing standard setting recommendations, the data must be clearly documented with respect to their relevance to the candidate population to which the new procedure will be applied. That is, performance expectations should be based on a sample that is representative of the actual applicant population for the context in which the selection procedure is being applied. To the extent that a sample used to provide normative or field test data differs from the applicant pool, standard setting experts need to consider how those differences might affect performance on the assessment. For example, it is not uncommon for performance standards to be raised when a sample of job incumbents is used to provide background data on the assessment, in consideration of the likelihood that actual applicants will be more motivated to perform well.

Throughout the *Standards,* an emphasis is placed on the quality of criterion data used to provide evidence of the validity of a procedure, or to inform recommendations about performance standards on a procedure (such as Standards 1.5, 1.6, 4.2). These data should be reviewed for relevance and quality, to ensure that they are not overly influenced by such factors as measurement artifacts, contamination through knowledge of performance on the new procedure, and general deficiencies in the quality of measurement (for example, unreliability or nonrandom missing data). The general emphasis on criterion data suggests that it may be advisable to collect and review criterion data, if such an undertaking is feasible and the data are valid for illuminating the relationship between the selection procedure and work performance.

The *Standards* include several other points of emphasis relevant to implementing selection procedures, including maintaining standardized administration procedures and clear instructions as well as maintaining the security of test materials and individual scores. The *Standards* also recommend that the entire procedure used to set standards on a particular instrument should be documented (Standard 4.19), including the rationale behind the method chosen and the training provided to experts in the standard setting judgment task. The *Standards* also note that passing rates for credentialing should be based on the knowledge and skills required for acceptable performance in a profession, rather than adjusting passing rates to restrict or open entry into the field (Standard 14.17).

Chapter Ten of the *Standards,* "Testing Individuals with Disabilities," provides substantial professional guidance for ensuring assessments are valid for assessing individuals with disabilities. Evaluating the extent to which an assessment is valid for applicants with disabilities is advisable for several reasons, including compliance with the ADA and the potential for identifying applicants who may make positive organizational contributions with minimal accommodation. One specific standard to note is Standard 10.2, which states that individuals who make decisions about accommodations should have sufficient expertise to make such judgments. In cases in which testing accommodations may be an issue, practitioners are advised to consult with appropriate experts in areas such as a vocational rehabilitation or occupational therapy. These experts may be identified through such organizations as the American Occupational Therapy Association (http://aota.org) or the International Association of Rehabilitation Professionals (http://rehabpro.org).

In comparison with Title VII and the *Uniform Guidelines,* the *Standards* impose several additional responsibilities on practitioners using alternative validation techniques. The *Standards* emphasize providing a holistic rationale for developing performance standards (that is, cutoff scores) for selection procedures, including explicitly stating the need to document the process.

Finally, Chapters Three and Four of the *Standards* both reference the relevance of information on which expectations of candidate performance are to be based. In essence, these chapters suggest the practitioner should provide reasonable evidence that the data used to inform any recommendations relevant to implementing the procedure are based on a sample that is representative of the actual pool of candidates.

The Principles

Like the *Standards,* the *Principles* provide much more guidance with respect to implementing a selection procedure than do Title VII or the *Uniform Guidelines.* In contrast to the *Standards,* however, the *Principles* are more relevant to implementing procedures in an occupational context and are not intended to apply to educational or other psychological contexts. Much of the information relevant to developing a sound implementation plan is contained in the section of the *Principles* titled "Operational Considerations in Personnel Selection." The *Principles* provide guidance in four general areas related to implementing a new selection procedure: specifications for criterion data to be used for setting performance standards, the conditions under which cutoff scores and performance bands may be used, practical considerations that factor into defining cut scores, and alternate testing procedures for applicants with disabilities.

The *Principles* devote a considerable amount of attention to the type and quality of data that are appropriate for informing the process of implementing a new selection procedure. Much of this information is couched in terms of the appropriateness of criterion data for validity studies. These same standards apply to any criteria used to develop an implementation plan. For the most part, the *Principles* echo the *Standards,* in that they emphasize that criterion data should be relevant to the applicant population and should be collected only where it is feasible to collect high-quality data. The *Principles* specifically note the instances in which performance data gathered from incumbents may not be directly applicable to an applicant population: when the applicant pool has substantially lower qualifications than the incumbent pool (a good example of this case is when performance on the selection procedure may be substantially improved through on-the-job learning) or when the organization wishes to improve the qualifications of the workforce (p. 36).

The *Principles* give a significant amount of attention to the consideration of the conditions under which scores may be interpreted in a manner other than top-down selection. Cutoff scores, critical scores, and bands are specific methods cited by the *Principles* to use when top-down methods may not be the most ideal for use in a given selection situation. Cutoff scores, as described by the *Principles,* are score levels below which a candidate receives no further consideration. Cutoff scores may be used when top-down selection results in adverse impact or there is a desire to maintain a list of qualified applicants for a position. In contrast, a critical score is a score a candidate needs to achieve to be predicted to be successful on the job or to demonstrate minimum qualifications for entry, such as the minimum score required to pass a certification exam. Considerations for setting critical scores differ from those used to set cutoff scores. For cutoff scores, criterion performance is weighed alongside practical considerations, whereas meeting a minimum performance standard on the criterion is the sole consideration for setting critical scores. The *Principles* explicitly state that there is no single or best method for setting cut scores or, presumably, critical scores. Finally, bands are ranges of scores on a selection procedure within which all candidates are treated alike. The *Principles* state that bands may be used for a variety of practical considerations, including the desire to reduce adverse impact and to account for imprecision in measurement.

Practical considerations are a major point of emphasis in the *Principles*. For example, the *Principles* refer to issues relating to combining selection procedures, in the context of both selecting between multiple-hurdle and compensatory models and revising standards used when new selection procedures are introduced or existing procedures are reorganized. The *Principles* also discuss the need for documenting the rationale behind the use of selection procedures, including the expected utility of selection procedures and the rationale behind any cut score or banding procedures. The *Principles* include a section that provides guidance on the elements that should be included in a comprehensive technical report.

The final section of the *Principles,* titled "Candidates with Disabilities," addresses the topic of testing applicants with disabilities. In essence, the *Principles* stipulate that professional judgment should be used to minimize the impact of a disability and any accommodation for the disability on the validity of the selection procedure. The *Principles* admonish practitioners against noting when an assessment is administered with an accommodation, and urge documentation of any accommodations made, to ensure that they are consistent in future administrations. Finally, these accommodations should be made in a manner that will maintain the consistency of selection measures with those used throughout the organization.

Summary

There are several common themes among these sources of professional guidance for developing an implementation plan. One of the most commonly cited requirements is the need to continuously monitor and potentially revise selection procedures and any performance standards applied to applicants who may be subjected to those procedures. Revision can include, as noted by Title VII, replacement with alternative selection procedures that will reduce adverse impact.

Documentation is another common theme, and it may be especially important for alternative validation techniques. The *Standards* and the *Principles* provide excellent direction as to the elements of the implementation plan that should be documented. Specifically, all factors that go into decisions made about administration, cut scores, and departures from standard procedures must be documented.

In comparison with the *Standards* and *Principles,* Title VII and the *Uniform Guidelines* provide only very broad direction to the process of implementing a new selection procedure. In general, Title VII and the *Uniform Guidelines* require that selection procedures be job-relevant and implemented in a manner that is as fair as possible. The *Standards* and *Principles* go much further in their scope and are more focused on making recommendations on the implementation of selection procedures. Note that neither the *Standards* nor the *Principles* establish a preferred method for setting cutoff scores or bands, although the *Standards* recommend empirical methods where it is feasible to include reliable and valid data. Both sources suggest normative data should be used only when they are relevant to the applicant population. The *Standards* and *Principles* also recognize that a wide range of practical considerations may have a valid influence on the implementation of a selection procedure. Both sources also recommend taking proactive steps toward assessing applicants with disabilities in a manner that maximizes validity and consistency with other procedures used by the organization.

In the context of implementing a selection procedure based on alternative validation strategies, these sources have some interesting implications. First, when evidence of validity is gathered from a wide variety of sources (such as validity generalization and consortium studies), practitioners may need to be more selective in their use of these data for test implementation purposes. For example, to support validity generalization, studies may be used that are based on samples drawn from populations with different mean ability levels; these same studies would not be relevant for setting cutoff scores or performance bands, because they might give an inaccurate picture of what reasonable performance expectations might be. Practitioners should be especially careful when using normative data from other sources to provide an empirical basis for setting cut scores. Many alternative validation techniques provide better opportunities than traditional empirical validity studies to examine the possibilities for accommodating applicants with disabilities. Consortium studies, validity generalization, and techniques that rely on expert judgment allow researchers to collect data on aspects of the selection procedure that may attenuate its validity, some of which may be associated with types of accommodations.

As a final word regarding professional and legal guidance for implementation of selection procedures, one must bear in mind that these sources are not comprehensive in scope. A sound implementation plan requires reviewing local regulations and authorities—such as collective bargaining agreements, union policies, internal organizational policies, and perhaps even long-held organizational traditions—to ensure that the implementation plan does not conflict with management's or employees' expectations of how candidates will be treated in the selection process. This step is especially important with respect to promotions, for which a productive, ongoing relationship is desired among candidates who are not selected on the basis of a selection procedure.

General Issues Influencing Legal Defensibility

This section describes the general elements of an implementation plan that may influence the legal defensibility of a new procedure. The purpose is not to provide an exhaustive review of cases in which a court offered an opinion on the soundness of the cut score setting process. Readers are cautioned that using case law as a checklist for setting a legally defensible performance standard on a new selection procedure is akin to putting the cart before the horse. Cut scores should be set so as to meet the best possible professional standards while ensuring that the process does not contradict tenets set forth by the courts. Note that much of what is available on the topic is summarized by Cascio, Alexander, and Barrett (1988) and Biddle (1993), and more recently by Siskin and Trippi (2005). Cascio et al. concluded that plaintiffs typically attack the difficulty of the cut score, but that virtually any cut score is legally defensible as long as it is established using procedures consistent with professional standards. Biddle provided a thorough discussion of critical issues in setting valid cut scores, with court cases used to illustrate the importance of various decisions. Siskin and Trippi discussed the statistical issues associated with various methods of setting cut scores and how case law might inform the practitioner's choice of methods.

Two court cases are most frequently cited with respect to setting cut scores. The first, *National Education Association vs. South Carolina* (1978), involved using a standardized test to certify teachers. This case serves as a landmark in test implementation because it confirmed that a cut score may be legal despite the fact that it results in differential selection rates, so long as it was selected using procedures consistent with professional standards, grounded in job relevance, and consistent with business necessity. Second, it affirmed the organization's prerogative to adjust SME recommendations to take into account factors other than applicant qualifications, such as being able to fill positions and the relative costs of recruitment. In this case, the standard recommended by the SMEs using the Angoff method was lowered by one to three standard errors of measurement to adjust for staffing needs (that is, it was deemed more effective to select teachers with lesser qualifications than to overcrowd classrooms). Finally, the plaintiffs criticized the training of the SMEs, suggesting their lack of understanding of the process invalidated the process, but the court found that the process was sufficiently well-executed as to mitigate the effect of some poorly prepared SMEs.

A second case, which has received a great deal of attention due to ongoing legal proceedings, is *Lanning vs. Southeastern Pennsylvania Transportation Authority (SEPTA)* (1999, 2002). This case involved the use of a measure of aerobic capacity to select transit police officers and resulted in differential selection rates adversely affecting women applicants. At issue in the case was not whether the measure was generally valid for use in selecting officers, but whether the cut score set was too stringent so as to exclude many applicants who would be able to successfully perform the work (Gutman, 2003, 2004; Siskin & Trippi, 2005). The Appeals Court found that the cutoff was too stringent and that the statistical and scientific evidence provided to the court was not sufficient to justify its use. As evidence that the cut score was inappropriately high, the court also cited the fact that SEPTA's expert raised the cut score above what was recommended by an expert panel, based solely on his own professional judgment. This case serves as a warning that cut scores may need to be set in such a manner that they balance the need to select candidates who are likely to perform adequately on the job against the requirement that the cut score not exclude a high proportion of candidates who are likely to be able to perform adequately (false negatives) (Kehoe & Olson, 2005).

This section discusses four broad topics that may influence the legal defensibility of the implementation of a selection procedure: (1) the selection of an optimal procedure for setting a cut score, (2) selection and training of SMEs, (3) process and documentation of the procedure, and (4) periodic or ongoing monitoring of the effectiveness of the recommendations. For the sake of simplicity, we assume the selection procedure will be implemented using a cut score or performance bands, because a top-down implementation typically requires only focusing on psychometric issues as opposed to balancing psychometric issues with practical concerns, as is the case with cut scores. It should be noted that psychometric considerations are critical for both top-down and cut score selections when multiple predictors are used. For example, it is important to make sure multiple predictors are weighted appropriately (equally or as otherwise determined) by taking into account score variance on each predictor and standardizing scores prior to combining with other predictors. Failing to standardize scores will weight instruments with larger score variances more heavily.

Selection of an Optimal Procedure to Set a Cut Score

Selecting a procedure for setting cut scores (or performance bands) must be undertaken with reference to both the ultimate concern of setting a useful cut score and the practical constraints of the data available to inform the process. Practitioners are advised to develop a broad knowledge of standard setting methods to better inform this process. Note that we differentiate between general standard setting methods and standard setting procedures, which is the specific process a practitioner may use to determine an appropriate cut score and may vary somewhat from the general method. The key considerations in the selection of an optimal cut score setting procedure are (1) what types of information can be used in the standard setting process, (2) whether multiple methods may be used in the process, (3) whether multiple cut scores need to be set, and (4) the difficulty of the selection instrument. Each of these issues should be addressed with a clearly stated rationale for the decisions made, including the shortcomings of other options.

The primary consideration in selecting a cut score setting procedure is the type and quality of the information available for use in setting standards. If inadequate or potentially misleading data are used for informing the standard setting process, the credibility of the recommendations may be called into question. When inadequate data are used for setting standards, it is usually because the data are conveniently available, such as when cut scores are set based on national norms from a test publisher. Obviously, using information because it is convenient is not a sufficient rationale when setting standards, although the cost of data collection and the ultimate effect of that cost on the utility of the selection system is a reasonable consideration. Generally speaking, the best methods for setting cut scores balance the efficiency and feasibility of collecting the relevant data with the need for data that can be used to make valid inferences about the pool of candidates to which the selection instrument will be applied. In the third section of this chapter we discuss in more detail standard setting methods that may be useful for alternative validation strategies, based on the feasibility of obtaining the type of information needed in a typical application.

In many cases, multiple standard setting methods may be feasible, given the available data. However, there are competing viewpoints regarding the application of multiple standard setting methods to make cut score recommendations. One viewpoint holds that choosing a single optimal strategy is preferred. This viewpoint judges the reconciliation of various methods to be problematic in that each method is likely to result in a different recommendation. An alternative viewpoint does not consider the reconciliation of multiple methods as a problem per se. On the contrary, applying multiple methods allows for confirmation of one method with another. Different standard setting methods are expected to result in slightly different recommendations. Convergent but slightly different recommendations may be reconciled by choosing a cut score between those recommended by each method, or by choosing the superior method for situations in which professional standards and judgment dictate a clear advantage for one method. In cases in which each method results in divergent recommendations, it may be advisable to investigate alternative sources of data that may provide richer information relevant to the actual applicant pool, such as administering the instrument to all applicants for a period of time until a reasonable field test sample may be acquired. Divergent results might indicate that any single method may provide too little information to inform valid cut score recommendations. It may be valuable to confirm a preferred method with a complementary recommendation from an alternative feasible method, even when that method is not ideal, thereby demonstrating that the original was not overly influenced by the choice of standard setting method. In the case of divergent results, using multiple methods demonstrates that adequate precautions were taken to ensure the recommendations were valid for the applicant pool.

Setting multiple cut scores, such as when determining cut scores for each level of performance bands, poses additional challenges to the standard setting process (Berk, 1996). Some methods are more difficult to apply to multiple standards. For example, it may be difficult for SMEs to estimate Angoff probabilities for multiple performance levels, although other judgmental methods, such as the Bookmark method for setting standards (Mitzel, Lewis, Patz, & Green, 2001), may be well-suited for setting multiple cut scores. Empirical methods may be difficult to apply because there may not be enough representation in each performance band to reliably estimate scores that differentiate the bands. In light of these difficulties, it is critical to provide as much additional information to raters as possible. Specifically, to facilitate better judgments by the SMEs, performance level descriptions (PLDs) for each score band should be available, well-written, and precise.

In essence, a PLD is a concise document that describes elements of the desired level of performance and contrasts that with inadequate levels of performance, specifically in terms of the constructs measured by the selection procedure. The term *PLD* is typically associated with the Bookmark method. However, the documents have broad applicability to standard setting methods and are useful tools for facilitating SME judgments under most, if not all, methods. (For an example of how PLDs may be used to improve standard setting under the Angoff method, see Maurer and Alexander's 1992 discussion of the importance of describing the minimally competent person.) Good PLDs not only emphasize elements that typify performance at each level, but they also signal transitions from one performance level to the next. Behaviorally anchored rating scales (BARS) (Borman, Hough, & Dunnette, 1976) and behavior observation scales (BOS) (Borman, 1986) are excellent models for performance level descriptions and, in some cases, can be used as PLDs without modification. In sum, to maximize the defensibility of multiple recommendations, the criteria must be made as explicit as possible to facilitate SME judgments.

A final consideration when selecting an optimal cut score setting method is the anticipated difficulty of the selection instrument. Methods that are typically associated with lower standards (such as Nedelsky, 1954) may be poorly suited to setting standards for selection instruments for cases in which typical performance is expected to be relatively high. In contrast, methods that may result in higher standards (such as Angoff) are not recommended for exceptionally difficult assessments. The risk for legal defensibility occurs when cut scores are set so high that many qualified applicants are rejected; the risk for utility is that the cut score will be set so low that the instrument is not screening out unqualified applicants. When these methods are employed in cases for which they might not be ideal, it may be best to mitigate the potential for extreme cut scores by making SMEs aware of the tendency of these methods to set high or low standards.

Selection and Training of SMEs

Perhaps even more important than the selection of the cut score setting method itself is the selection of individuals to form an SME panel for making cut score recommendations. Two main issues are central to forming an SME panel: who is qualified to serve as an SME, and how many SMEs are required. Typically supervisors, trainers, or adequately experienced job-incumbents are considered for SME panels. In general, it is preferable to have job-incumbents, trainers, and supervisors who have participated in the hiring process and may be familiar with the applicant pool, as they may be better able to weigh the consequences of selection errors. Where incumbents, trainers, and supervisors are somewhat removed from the actual selection process, it may be wise to have human resources or other selection experts available to advise the process, even if they serve as "nonvoting" SMEs with respect to the content of the selection instrument. In extreme cases in which knowledgeable incumbents, trainers, and supervisors are in short supply, outside training providers or incumbents from other organizations may be able to serve adequately as SMEs as long as test security can be maintained.

An important consideration in the selection of SMEs involves discussing their general feelings about the use of the selection instrument. Nothing can derail a cut score setting process faster than an SME with a negative attitude toward the use of an assessment. In situations where there may be some controversy over the introduction of a new selection instrument, it may be wise to tactfully gauge potential SMEs' views on the introduction of an instrument before extending an invitation to serve on the SME panel. However, this evaluation must be done in a way that ensures that potential SMEs are not excluded in a way that decreases the gender or ethnic diversity of the panel. For example, a female firefighter may be opposed to the introduction of upper-body strength assessments to a selection battery; such a viewpoint may be valuable in setting standards that are both valid and reasonable for female applicants. Underrepresentation of protected group members from the standard setting process and negative SME evaluations of the standard setting process are particularly troublesome for the legal defensibility of the recommended standards.

In terms of the number of SMEs required for a panel, collecting data from SMEs about cut score recommendations is a psychometric process, and general data collection rules apply. Therefore, more SMEs are typically preferred, although there is certainly no minimum number to satisfy defensibility requirements. Biddle (1993) notes that cases have survived legal scrutiny with as few as seven to ten SMEs, although it is almost indubitable that cut scores have been set with fewer and survived legal challenges (but may not have been specifically mentioned by the court in its decision). Hurtz and Hertz (1999) suggest including ten to fifteen is sufficient for the Angoff method.

The psychometric issues of unreliability and sampling error may be partially addressed by limiting the reasonable range of scores within which a cut score may be placed, information sharing among SMEs, and multiple occasions of measurement. Additional SMEs should not be included if they would water down the expertise of the panel (Berk, 1996; Jaeger, 1991). In contrast to a purely psychometric endeavor, too many SMEs may be problematic.

From a practical perspective, SME panels over twenty-five members can be difficult to manage, especially during group discussions. It is advisable to break groups larger than ten into subgroups, each with an SME responsible for managing the discussion. Effective management of group deliberations ensures that all SMEs have an opportunity to provide input into the process and share any information they feel is important. Ultimately, managing the group process will affect the SMEs' evaluations of the procedure and improve the process by limiting error introduced by group dynamics. Test security becomes an issue with large groups of SMEs as well. The more SMEs included in the cut score setting process, the greater the likelihood that one SME or more may compromise some of the test content by providing it to potential test takers, either purposely or inadvertently.

Providing adequate training for SMEs is an important element of the defensibility of a cut score setting procedure. Training should spell out four elements of the cut score setting procedures: (1) the purpose and intended outcome of the procedure (that is, making a cut score recommendation for a new selection instrument), (2) the tools and information available to inform their judgments, (3) the precise judgmental task required of the SMEs, and (4) the general steps of the procedure (that is, training, discussion, rounds of evaluation, finalization, evaluation). Training should be thorough but should not belabor the issues. It may be reasonable to set aside some time during training to work one-on-one with SMEs who may not fully grasp what is required of them for the judgmental task. It follows that individuals who do not feel they understand the judgmental task should be given the opportunity to opt out of the procedure.

Process and Documentation of the Cut Score Setting Procedure

The general process of the cut score setting procedure has implications for legal defensibility. As such, it is important that all decisions associated with the procedures used are given careful consideration. It is generally advisable to set a tentative agenda for the procedure, acknowledging that the time required for adequate training and group discussions might alter the agenda. One process issue that is commonly debated among practitioners is how much SMEs should be allowed to discuss their ratings (Maurer & Alexander, 1992). Here we see general psychometric principles at odds with practical considerations. From a purely psychometric perspective, we would strive for complete independence among raters. However, from a practical perspective we want SMEs to share relevant information, and we realize that some social exchange may be necessary for SMEs to be confident in their judgments when the judgmental task is difficult. A sound compromise is to require SMEs to make an initial judgment (or judgments) before discussing their judgments with their peers. They may then be encouraged to consider any relevant information their peers may provide, while cautioning them not to be influenced by arguments unrelated to the content of the assessment.

Another issue that is often raised with respect to the cut score setting procedures is how many rounds of deliberation are required to make valid recommendations. In general, recommendations rarely change after two rounds of deliberations. When one cut score is being set, or when the first of several cut scores are set, a third round of deliberations may be included on the agenda and may be waived if the SMEs have reached near consensus. Later rounds should be limited to two rounds of deliberations, as SMEs often feel additional discussion is not an effective use of time.

A related issue is how recommendations should be combined across raters. In most cases, it is advisable to use the median rather than the mean of SME ratings. The median is preferred to the mean because it reduces the potential influence of an outlier SME. When scores are combined using the mean, savvy SMEs sometimes realize that they can influence the cut score by providing extreme ratings. Rather than explicitly removing such a rater from the score calculation, their ratings may be tempered by using the median rating.

Documentation is a critical aspect of the legal defensibility of a cut score setting procedure (Cizek, 1996). The greater the extent of the rationale supporting the decisions made, the easier it is to communicate to a court the validity of the inferences made based on the cut score recommendations. To maintain effective documentation of the procedure, it is best to have straightforward response documents and to retain those in their original form. It is also critical to document SME evaluations at several stages in the process. First, prior to making their initial ratings, it is a good idea to have them indicate whether they understand what the judgmental task requires and if they feel confident that they can make those judgments. SMEs may be able to provide this endorsement on the response document itself, if there is no need to make ratings anonymous. At the same time, there is an opportunity to ask SMEs to agree to maintain the confidentiality of deliberations as part of the procedure. This agreement serves the dual purposes of making SMEs feel more comfortable about sharing their true evaluations of the assessment while documenting steps taken to ensure that the SMEs felt confident in their abilities to perform the tasks. Prior to each subsequent rating, SMEs should again be asked to indicate whether they understand the judgmental task and feel confident in making their ratings. At the close of the procedure, SMEs should provide a general evaluation of the procedure, including whether they felt the training they received was adequate, whether the process was fair, whether they were given adequate opportunities to share all the information they felt was relevant to the process, and whether the final recommendation was reached in a valid manner regardless of what their personal recommendation would have been.

Periodic Monitoring

The recommendation that results from a cut score setting procedure should not be treated as etched in stone. To maximize the defensibility of the implementation of the new selection procedure, an ongoing monitoring process is required to collect data systematically on the usefulness of the decisions made with the new instrument. Livingston and Zieky (1989) emphasize that ongoing monitoring of the decisions made on the basis of an assessment is vitally important for any cut score set using a judgmental method. Hanser (1998) conceptualizes ongoing monitoring as a feedback loop that provides important information to revise, if necessary, both the standards chosen and the methods by which those standards are initially determined. When evaluating the effectiveness of decisions made using the assessment, the issues to consider are changes in the relative qualifications of the applicant pool, changes in the relative cost of making selection errors (such as rising recruiting costs increasing the cost of rejecting a qualified candidate), market changes, and the potential for adverse impact.

Common Methods for Setting Cut Scores

This section describes common methods used to set cut scores and performance bands, including both those commonly used for employment settings and some methods used more frequently in educational settings, but with applicability to employee selection. This section categorizes specific methods for setting cut scores into four groups: naïve methods, judgmental or rational methods, empirical methods, and methods used to combine performance standards across selection instruments. Naïve methods for setting cut scores are methods based on preconceived notions about how cut scores should be derived, without specific reference to the expected performance of the candidates on the selection instrument. Judgmental methods primarily rely on expert judgment to inform setting cut scores, although some techniques integrate statistical information about the items to aid expert judgment. In contrast, empirical techniques use data about the statistical relationship between the criterion and performance on the assessment as the primary basis for making decisions about cut scores (although these methods ultimately rely on human judgment as well). In some cases, standards must be combined into an integrated decision in situations in which multiple selection instruments are used concurrently to make selection decisions, and this process typically requires its own standard setting process.

Naïve Methods

Subject matter experts typically lack the expertise in testing that is required to make sound decisions about how scores on selection instruments should be interpreted and cut scores set. Beyond SMEs, many other individuals involved in testing—such as sales representatives of test publishers, test administrators, and human resources personnel—may be in positions to make recommendations about score interpretation without sufficient knowledge and training to do so. It is incumbent upon the selection expert to train SMEs and other personnel in the types of judgments that will be required in order to make sound recommendations about score interpretation. Too often, individuals who deal with test scores have preconceived notions about how scores may be interpreted. These preconceived notions are discussed here as "naïve methods" of setting cut scores; they are not appropriate for setting cut scores that are effective for identifying candidates who meet the desired performance standards on the assessment.

One common misperception about test scores is the "70 percent rule," which suggests that sufficient performance on a knowledge test corresponds to getting 70 percent or more of the items correct. This rule of thumb is common in many settings, largely because it is widely used as a criterion in educational settings. The use of the 70 percent rule in educational settings, in which the exact level of content knowledge required by a teacher or professor may be arbitrary, is very different from employee selection settings, in which the level of knowledge required to perform sufficiently on an assessment must be linked to the minimum requirements of the job. In addition to the obvious case in which cut scores are simply set at the 70 percent point on the total test score, the 70 percent rule can influence judgmental standard setting methods, such as when SMEs mistakenly assume that 70 percent of minimally qualified applicants should answer an item correctly, or that they should be able to reach the 70 percent mark when items are ordered by item difficulty.

Variations of the 70 percent rule may be encountered. For example, some SMEs will contend that for certain tests, such as safety tests, candidates must answer 100 percent of the items correctly. This could be thought of as a "100 percent rule" and is equally problematic, in that it ignores the possibility that test wording might be confusing, items might be open to some level of interpretation, or applicants might simply make a response transcription error. For tests with more than a few items, this rule of thumb can be troublesome, as it is reasonable that even qualified applicants may make a mistake unrelated to their actual level of knowledge.

False equating is another naïve method for setting cut scores that can result in improper cut score recommendations. False equating occurs when a test is assumed to be equated to a previously used test (or possibly one that is used in another context), and the cut score for the new test is set equal to the cut score used for the old test. Typically, false equating occurs when new content is developed to replace an outdated version of an employment test, and it is assumed that the new content is equal in difficulty to the content from the previous test, especially when the tests are developed to have a one-to-one correspondence with the content subdomains sampled from the old test. In reality, test equating can only be accomplished with extensive empirical data collection, and even when tests are perfectly correlated, different cut scores may be needed to account for differences in difficulty. False equating can affect other standard setting methods by providing an anchor point for judgmental and empirical methods from which SMEs might be reluctant to move very far.

National norms, although sometimes a good source of information on expected test performance, can be misused to set standards without appropriate contextual information. It is critical that national norms be relevant to the local applicant population if they are to be used to inform the cut score setting process. For some constructs, such as certain personality traits, national norms may not vary greatly across locations. Other constructs, such as job knowledge or culturally influenced aspects of personality, may vary enough to make national norms inappropriate for use in setting cut scores. Moreover, national norms for a U.S. population should rarely be assumed to be relevant for applicant groups outside the United States. Even when national norms are relevant, the practitioner should consider whether the range of scores on the instrument may be restricted by applicant self-selection or other elements of the selection system, and how that might influence the use of norms in setting cut scores.

The level of test performance in terms of national norms should be tied to the desired level of work performance, which is often not the case when national norms are used to set cut scores. There is one exception to this case, involving the use of personality tests (or other measures unrelated to cognitive ability or job knowledge) in situations in which alternative validation techniques must be employed. In these situations, the relationship between the latent construct measured by the selection device and job performance may be unclear to anyone but a psychologist with expert knowledge of the job. Thus, SMEs may not be able to adequately select reasonable cut scores on the selection procedure, and normative data may be the best source of provisional cut scores until adequate information about the predictor-criterion relationship can be collected.

Local norms, or fixed passing rates, are another method sometimes used for setting cut scores that can be problematic if not used carefully. Fixed passing rates are sometimes used as an alternative to top-down selection to ensure that candidates are treated consistently across applicant cohorts and that the costs are controlled during later stages of the selection process. Using this method, a cut score is interpolated from the desired percentage of applicants passing the selection instrument, based on a sample of applicant data. The cut score is then used to screen future applicants regardless of the number of applicants in the pool. This method has the obvious benefits of treating applicants consistently across applicant pools as well as restricting the number of applicants for cost effectiveness. The drawback is that the relative qualifications of the applicant pool may change over time, resulting in too few or too many applicants at the next stage. The consequences of altering the cut score to reflect these changes are unknown with respect to the desired level of job performance.

What these methods have in common is that they do not explicitly consider the relationship between the minimum or desired level of job performance and performance on the selection instrument. As such, they are not consistent with the need to consider expected levels of job proficiency noted in the *Uniform Guidelines* and *Standards*. The last two methods are "norm-referenced" methods, which may provide useful data as a "reality check" (Livingston & Zieky, 1989) to cut score setting procedures, or as a source of initial cut score information when no other method is viable.

An effective cut score setting procedure should address these naïve methods in training, including why these methods are inappropriate and how the information the SMEs may have access to can be used effectively. Despite the fact that these methods are described here as naïve methods, it is a mistake to assume that any cut score set using these methods is necessarily inappropriate or produces unacceptable personnel selection decisions. Many of these methods use information that would be relevant to other methods, so they may result in reasonable cut scores, although they lack strong defensibility in the face of employment litigation or evidence of selection errors.

Judgmental Methods

Judgmental methods for setting cut scores rely primarily on expert judgment as the basis for making decisions about the relationship of test performance to the desired level of job performance. These methods, sometimes called rational methods, are the best options when criterion data are not available or the relationship between the criterion and performance on the assessment is obscured by other elements of the selection system (such as direct or indirect restriction of range). Another way to think of these methods is as criterion-referenced methods, as they result in explicit inferences about performance on the test as it relates to an external performance criterion. Note that not all judgmental methods rely solely on expert judgment. Some methods incorporate empirical data about item difficulty to assist in guiding expert judgments, such as ordering test items by difficulty estimates from field test data. Four families of methods are discussed here as judgmental methods: the Angoff (1971) method and its modifications, the Nedelsky (1954) method, difficulty-importance methods, and item-ordering methods. Each of these families follows a general outline with various modifications for different types of response formats or other issues.

Angoff Method

The Angoff (1971) method essentially requires an expert judge to determine the probability that a minimally qualified candidate is able to answer a particular item correctly. These probabilities are then summed across items in the test to calculate the cut score, which is theoretically an estimate of the expected value of the mean of the distribution of scores for minimally qualified candidates. Occasionally this cut score is adjusted based on the standard error of measurement, up or down, to make the test more or less selective. Perhaps most commonly the Angoff cut score is adjusted downward to reduce the number of false negatives. Several modifications of the Angoff are in common use, and most vary the response format to facilitate expert judgments. The original Angoff method uses actual probability estimates from SMEs, whereas modifications reformat the question to ask the number of minimally qualified applicants who would answer the item correctly out of a group of ten (or another fixed group size), use a limited number of probability options (for example 5, 25, 50, 75, or 95 percent), or use forced choice response formats when there are a great number of SMEs available (for example "Should a minimally qualified applicant get this question correct? Yes/No").

These modifications were devised in large part to answer one of the main criticisms of the Angoff method: that SMEs often report difficulties estimating probabilities (Plake & Impara, 2001; National Research Council, 1999; Shepard, 1995; Impara & Plake, 1998; Livingston & Zieky, 1989). Practitioners should be aware of this issue, which may be exacerbated when a large number of test items are very easy or very difficult; raters may not be able to adjust their probabilities accordingly.

A second criticism of the Angoff technique is that it generally produces higher cut scores than other methods, and sometimes these cut scores can be unrealistic (Kramer, Muijtjens, Jansen, Dusman, Tan, & van der Vleuten, 2003). Despite these criticisms, several researchers have found that the Angoff method is both reliable and valid for deriving cut scores (Cizek, 1993; Hambleton et al., 2000; Plake & Impara, 2001), and it is one of the most widely used standard setting techniques in employee selection, professional certification, and educational settings. Note that because the Angoff technique requires only a few SMEs to rate the difficulty of items, it is well-suited to set cut scores for a selection instrument that has been validated using any alternative validation technique.

Nedelsky Method

The Nedelsky (1954) method for setting cut scores was one of the first proposed judgmental methods for setting cut scores. This method requires SMEs to examine each item on a multiple-choice test and estimate the number of response options for each item that would be implausible to a minimally qualified applicant. The reciprocal of the number of remaining response options becomes the estimated probability that a minimally qualified applicant would get the item right, and these probabilities are summed in the same way Angoff ratings are summed to calculate the cut score. Like the Angoff method, this cut score is often adjusted by a few points to make the assessment more or less selective. This method can be used only for tests composed entirely of multiple-choice items.

A major criticism of the Nedelsky method is that it is predicated on the assumption that once the candidate has eliminated as many implausible or clearly incorrect responses as possible, the minimally competent candidate is then constrained to guess randomly among the remaining options. This assumption is rarely tenable, however, because many candidates (even minimally competent ones) will have some information on which to base their final answer choice (Mills & Melican, 1988). Thus, the reciprocal of the remaining number of choices tends to underestimate the actual probability of a minimally competent candidate correctly answering the item. The result is that this method typically sets lower standards than other methods (Chang, 1999; Livingston and Zieky, 1989). This method is rarely used by itself but is very useful for setting the lower bound of acceptable cut scores (and minimal competence) when an assessment is very difficult, and there is some concern that SMEs might set a cut score below chance levels. Including distributional information of test scores around the cut point, such as simulated score distributions using the average correct response probability, may help judges move their recommendations from very low scores to more reasonable scores. Despite its shortcomings, the Nedelsky method is applicable for use in conjunction with any alternative validation technique.

Difficulty-Importance Methods

Difficulty-importance methods, as proposed by Cangelosi (1984) and Ebel (1979), essentially involve constructing a two-dimensional matrix of difficulty and importance ratings. Ebel (1979) originally suggested three levels of difficulty and four levels of importance, but the levels may be modified. Judges assign each item in the assessment to a cell in the matrix. A cell weight is derived by estimating the proportion of items within each cell that a minimally qualified applicant will answer correctly. The cut score is calculated by summing the number of items within each cell multiplied by the cell weight.

This method allows more important items to be weighted more heavily, making it desirable for assessments in which items vary substantially in their relevance to job performance. However, the method is complex and time consuming, and there is little evidence it produces more valid cut scores than other methods, because an unqualified applicant might achieve the same score as a qualified applicant by answering more of the less relevant items correctly. Other variants of this method allow importance weights to be assigned to individual items as opposed to groups of items. This method is rarely used in employee selection contexts, though it has the side benefit of collecting limited content validity evidence along with expected performance information. Therefore, it is occasionally employed when SME time is a particularly precious commodity. Despite the fact that it is rarely used, it is applicable to all alternative validation techniques.

Item-Ordering Methods

A fourth group of methods is the item-ordering methods, in which items are ordered in terms of their difficulty. SMEs are asked to identify the point in the ordered item set that differentiates the content to which a minimally qualified applicant is expected to be able to respond correctly (with some given probability) from the content that the applicant is not expected to answer correctly. Statistical information about the difficulty of the item is then used to interpolate a cut score based on the probability that an applicant at that performance level would answer the item correctly. Typically, the item location on a Rasch theta scale is used as the indicator of item difficulty, but nothing would prevent a savvy researcher from using classical item statistics and logistic regression on the raw score scale to accomplish the same result in lieu of using item response theory (IRT) methods.

The most common item-ordering method is the Bookmark method (Mitzel, Lewis, Patz, & Green, 2001), which asks SMEs to "bookmark" a page in a booklet of items ordered from easiest to most difficult. The bookmark should correspond to the item that differentiates the level expected to be reached by a minimally qualified applicant from the content level that more qualified applicants could be expected to answer correctly.

A newer technique, item-descriptor (ID) matching (Ferrara, Perie, & Johnson, 2002), asks SMEs to define the threshold region of items that correspond to minimum qualifications as opposed to higher performance levels. The threshold region is seen as preferable to a single item, because there may be substantial overlap in the difficulties of items that differentiate these levels of performance. The initial cut score for the ID matching procedure is typically interpolated from the midpoint of the threshold region, and further rounds of evaluation focus on refining this cut point.

The primary advantage to item-ordering methods for setting cut scores is that the cognitive task required of SMEs is much simpler than those required in other methods. Specifically, SMEs are not required to rate the absolute difficulty of the items, only the difficulty relative to the desired performance level. Of course, this simplification requires reliable item difficulty information, which may be difficult to collect. However, the item difficulty information does not necessarily have to be local, as the relationship between test performance and item difficulty may be somewhat consistent across applicant groups within reasonable variation in average performance, and there is no need to collect criterion information, which is often the barrier to performing a traditional validity study. The methods are also computationally intensive and may require psychometric expertise beyond the level of some practitioners. These methods are rarely used in employment settings, although they have been used extensively in educational and certification settings. Due to the need for item difficulty information, these methods may be impracticable in many cases in which alternative validation evidence is used, a notable exception being consortium studies.

Summary of Judgmental Methods

The Angoff method continues to be the most widely used standard setting technique and the most relevant to alternative validation contexts. The Nedelsky method is a viable option in concert with other methods and for cases in which there is a concern that the cut score may be set below reasonable guessing levels. Difficulty-importance methods are complex, but useful if there is a need to weight items by their importance. Item-ordering techniques address the main criticism of the Angoff method but require extensive psychometric information to be viable options. With all of these methods, cut scores may be set without reference to criterion data, which makes them well-suited to many alternative validation techniques.

Empirical Methods

Empirical methods rely primarily on the explicit relationship between performance on the selection instrument and performance on a given criterion to determine appropriate cut scores. Like judgmental methods, these methods are considered to be "criterion-referenced." In many cases, empirical methods are considered to be superior to methods that rely solely on expert judgment. When a selection instrument has been validated using alternative validation techniques, however, it is unlikely that strong evidence of a predictor-criterion relationship is available. Still, there are some cases in which empirical methods might be practicable and useful in alternative validation contexts. The four common empirical methods for setting cut scores are the contrasting groups method, the borderline group method, expectancy charts, and regression methods.

Contrasting Groups

The contrasting groups method (Livingston & Zieky, 1982) presents SMEs with distributions of scores from successful and unsuccessful incumbents. Generally, the initial cut score is set at the point where the two distributions intersect. SMEs then adjust the cut score to account for desired passing rates or the relative consequences of rejecting a qualified applicant compared to those for accepting an unqualified applicant. This method is simple and is typically well-received by SMEs (Berk, 1986). However, even when criterion data are available, if the relationship between performance on the selection instrument and performance on the job is not strong, the overlap between the groups will be large, which may undermine SME confidence in the method. As a result, this method may be difficult to apply in many selection contexts, especially those in which alternative methods of validation are required, despite the intuitive appeal of contrasting successful and unsuccessful performers.

Borderline Groups

The borderline groups method (Livingston & Zieky, 1982) uses a distribution of scores on the selection instrument from minimally qualified performers (that is, those on the borderline of being qualified). Under this method, the initial cut score is set at the median for the borderline group, and SMEs adjust the cut score using the same considerations as in the contrasting groups method. The advantage to this method is that it clearly identifies scores that are typical of minimally qualified applicants. The disadvantages are that it may be difficult to get a large enough sample of minimally qualified applicants to have a reasonable representation of the distribution of test scores associated with this population, and the definition of who fits the "borderline" definition may vary across SMEs. Also, as with the contrasting groups method, if the relationship between scores on the selection procedure and job performance is relatively weak, the distribution of scores may be very wide. This method is difficult to use in alternative validation contexts for those reasons.

Expectancy Charts

Expectancy charts are an alternate way of presenting information relating performance on the selection procedure to performance on the job. There are many ways to present this information. One way is essentially to transform the data from a contrasting groups procedure into a table displaying, for each score point, the expected percentages meeting or exceeding the desired level of job performance and the estimated percentage of those candidates who would not be selected despite being able to meet the job performance criterion (see Kehoe & Olson, 2005). This is essentially the same as using the contrasting groups procedure with a different presentation format. An alternative method is to present the expected level of job performance for each score point, which may be more applicable to situations in which the concept of "minimal" competence is not at issue. This method is generally easy for SMEs and other stakeholders to understand, but it is unlikely to be applicable in cases in which alternative validation techniques are employed—the notable exception being when validity information has been collected in another setting and the practitioner can be reasonably assured that there is a strong correspondence between performance across work contexts.

Regression Methods

Regression procedures are another way to set cut scores when criterion data are available. Although it is rare that sufficient data are available for successful use of regression as a method for setting cut scores, it may be possible in some cases in which validity evidence is gathered through meta-analysis or a consortium study. Using a regression method, the cut score is determined by the score associated with successful job performance on the criterion scale. The two variations of this technique, forward and reverse regression, produce slightly different results (Goldberger, 1984; Kehoe & Olson, 2005; Siskin & Trippi, 2005). Forward regression regresses the criterion scale on the test scale, whereas reverse regression regresses the test scale on the criterion scale. Unless the test scale and criterion scale are perfectly correlated, these methods produce slightly different cut scores. (Reverse regression results in more extreme cut scores than forward regression; that is, when the desired level of performance on the criterion is above the mean, reverse regression results in higher cut scores than forward regression. When the desired level of performance on the criterion is below the mean, the opposite is true.) The lower the correlation between the selection instrument and the criterion, the wider the variance in the recommendations derived from each technique. SMEs may be used to determine the point within this score range that is the most appropriate cut point. The drawback to this technique is that influential cases (that is, outliers with high leverage on the regression equation) may have a strong influence on the cut score chosen (Muijtjens, Kramer, Kaufman, and Van der Vleuten, 2003).

Summary of Empirical Methods

There may be few cases in which these methods will be available to a practitioner implementing a new selection measure based on alternative validation techniques. Even when criterion data are available, these methods are best suited to instances in which the criterion measure is strongly related to the selection instrument, and in these situations a criterion-related validity study is likely to be feasible. That is, if the selection instrument measures an aspect of job performance that is not the predominant determinant of the criterion measure, these methods may be less useful as cut score setting techniques than methods that make use of expert judgment.

Combining Performance Standards

It is often necessary to combine standards across measures for the purposes of implementation of a complete selection system. There are several methods for considering cut scores on multiple assessments serially or simultaneously. When multiple assessments are considered as individual components of a selection system, such as a multiple-hurdle selection system, the standards are called *conjunctive* standards. When performances on two or more selection instruments are combined for decision-making purposes, such as in a multiple regression approach, the standards are referred to as *compensatory* standards.

Conjunctive standards impose minimum performance standards on multiple assessments in order to be selected. The two major advantages of conjunctive standards are cost-effectiveness and simplicity of administration. Conjunctive standards are cost-effective because an applicant who does not achieve an acceptable level of performance on one selection measure does not need to go through the rest of the selection procedure. Conjunctive standards are also simpler from an administrative perspective because there is no need to combine scores to determine whether an applicant has performed sufficiently. The disadvantages of conjunctive standards are that (1) the reliability of the total selection system is lowered for each additional step in the selection process and (2) it may be difficult to determine the proportion of candidates that will pass the entire set of standards in advance. The reliability of the selection system is likely to be lowered because the reliability of the selection system is the product of the individual reliabilities of each element of the selection system (Haladyna & Hess, 1999). Unless steps in the selection process are perfectly reliable—which is unlikely, due to inevitable administrative errors and errors in measurement—

each additional step lowers the cumulative reliability of the system. Moreover, it may be difficult to estimate the proportion of applicants who will make it through the entire selection system if original cut scores for a selection instrument were based on information from the total applicant pool, as opposed to the restricted range of applicants who pass a previous step in the process (Ben-David, 2000). Adverse impact may be increased as well, as compensatory strategies allow differential selection rates in a single predictor to be offset by others, whereas conjunctive standards maintain differential selection rates. Note that conjunctive standards do not necessarily need to be administered sequentially. In some cases, the order of administration may be varied for administrative efficiency (such as in an assessment center where one candidate is interviewed while another participates in a role-play), and others may be considered concurrently (such as education and experience on a résumé).

Compensatory standards allow for good performance on one selection procedure to compensate for poorer performance on another. An advantage of a compensatory standard system is that the overall decisions will always be more reliable than those made by a conjunctive system of standards (Haldyna & Hess, 1999). Furthermore, performance tradeoffs and job analysis findings can be considered through weighting each of the selection procedures in deriving the final selection decisions. Disadvantages include the fact that it may be difficult to determine appropriate tradeoffs among selection procedures, especially when more than two selection procedures are involved, and in some cases performance tradeoffs may be completely inappropriate. For example, consider a certification exam for medical personnel that requires a sufficient grade point average in a core curriculum at an accredited institution, acceptable performance on a written examination, and successful completion of a one-year practicum. In this case, it might be dangerous to patients' safety to certify someone who performed very poorly on the written exam despite how well the candidate performed on the other elements of the process.

Haladyna and Hess (1999) discuss hybrid approaches, sometimes called "disjunctive standards," that allow for compensatory standards to be used within a restricted set of conjunctive standards. To return to the medical certification example, a hybrid approach would allow for exceptional performance on the practicum and coursework to compensate for poorer performance on the written test, provided the candidate achieves some minimally acceptable level of performance on each component of the system.

One method for combining multiple standards in a compensatory or hybrid approach is the "body of work" method of setting standards (Kingston, Kahl, Sweeney, and Bay, 2001). This method requires SMEs to sort exemplar applicants into qualified and unqualified categories by examining all the information on selection procedures to be considered at one time. There are many variations of the body of work method. Another way to combine multiple selection procedures is to create performance bands for each procedure, then construct a matrix of the performance bands. SMEs could determine whether each combination of performance bands connotes that applicants with those performance levels meet the desired performance level. Combining educational background and previous work experience is a case in which a body of work matrix may be useful. Table 10.1 shows an example of a qualifications grading matrix for administrative and management positions from the U.S. Office of Personnel Management's *Operating Manual for Qualification Standards* (n.d.) that closely resembles the result of a body of work method of compensatory standards.

Summary of Common Methods for Setting Cut Scores

Judgmental methods for setting cut scores are generally more applicable to the implementation of employment selection procedures that have been validated using alternative techniques than are empirical techniques. In many cases, these methods make use of the same expert judgments used to provide evidence for the validity of the selection procedures for making employment decisions. As such, judgmental methods make use of the close tie between the experts' knowledge of the relationship of the selection procedure to work performance, and the level of performance required on the selection procedure to produce the desired level of work performance. Consistent with the comment in the *Standards,* empirical methods are typically not preferred for selection procedures validated through alternative techniques. As acknowledged in the

Table 10.1. U.S. Office of Personnel Management Qualification Standards for Administrative and Management Positions.

Grade	Education	Experience General	Specialized
		Experience	
		General	Specialized
GS-5	4-year course of study leading to a bachelor's degree	3 years, 1 year of which was equivalent to at least GS-4	None
GS-7	1 full year of graduate level education *or* superior academic achievement	None	1 year equivalent to at least GS-5
GS-9	master's or equivalent graduate degree *or* 2 full years of progressively higher level graduate education leading to such a degree *or* LL.B. or J.D., if related	None	1 year equivalent to at least GS-7
GS-11	Ph.D. or equivalent doctoral degree *or* 3 full years of progressively higher level graduate education leading to such a degree *or* LL.M., if related	None	1 year equivalent to at least GS-9
GS-12 and above	None	None	1 year equivalent to at least next lower grade level

Note: Equivalent combinations of education and experience are qualifying for all grade levels for which both education and experience are acceptable.

Source: U.S. Office of Personnel Management (n.d.).

Standards, in many cases empirical methods may not be feasible, may impose an unrealistic economic burden on the practitioner, or may simply be misleading due to the complex nature of job performance. Empirical methods should be used only when practitioners are reasonably confident that they can meet all the necessary conditions for their sound application without incurring high data collection costs that will undermine the utility of the selection procedure. In many cases, these analyses can be part of the ongoing monitoring of the selection procedure.

Table 10.2 summarizes recommended cut score setting techniques on the basis of the general availability of data for each alternative validation technique. Note that these are general recommendations and that the specifics of a particular application may restrict the use of particular methods and benefit others.

Exemplar Scenarios

This section presents two exemplar scenarios for dealing with the complex issues of implementing a new selection procedure that had been validated using alternative techniques. These scenarios describe the context in which the new selection procedure would be introduced, including the technique used to validate the procedure, the available applicant pool, and the overall goals of the selection system into which the procedure was to be integrated. The scenarios also describe the alternative implementation methods considered and why they were ultimately rejected. The first scenario describes the development of an implementation plan for a test of advanced mathematics to select candidates for a training program within a large government agency, in a case in which the source of validity evidence is primarily job analytic. The second scenario describes the implementation of a test battery that was validated using a concurrent, criterion-related validation strategy.

Scenario One: Implementation of a Test of Advanced Mathematics

This scenario describes the implementation of a test of advanced mathematics knowledge that was validated primarily through job analytic methods. The test was intended for use in screening applicants

Table 10.2. Optimal and Possible Cut Score Setting Methods for Alternative Validation Techniques.

Validation Technique	Judgmental Methods				Empirical Methods			
	Angoff	Nedelsky	Difficulty-Importance	Item Ordering	Contrasting Groups	Borderline Groups	Expectancy Charts	Regression
Transportation	Acceptable	Possible	Possible	Possible	Possible	Possible	Possible	Possible
Consortia Studies	Acceptable	Possible	Possible	Optimal	Possible	Possible	Possible	Possible
Job-Component Validation	Acceptable	Possible	Possible	—	—	—	—	—
Synthetic	Acceptable	Possible	Possible	—	—	—	—	—
Meta-Analysis/VG	Acceptable	Possible	Possible	Possible	Possible	Possible	Possible	Optimal
Job Analytic[a]	—	—	—	—	Possible	Possible	Possible	Possible
Construct	Acceptable	Possible	Possible	—	—	—	—	—
Content	Acceptable	Possible	Possible	—	—	—	—	—

[a]Provisional cut scores may be set using normative data for job analytic techniques, but it may be advisable to collect data to support other techniques through ongoing monitoring, to the extent feasible.

for technical positions in a large government agency. This test was designed to replace an earlier test of similar information. The new test was desired to replace the old test because the validity information available for the previous test was dated, and there were concerns about test security because the previous exam had been used for several years. Moreover, little was known about how the cut score was set for the previous test. Creating a new test afforded the agency an opportunity to update the content of the assessment and scoring procedures and to revisit how the test was used in the decision-making process.

Background

The purpose of the previous assessment was to ensure that individuals selected into the agency's training program had adequate mathematical knowledge to be able to comprehend the material presented, complete the training curriculum, and ultimately apply what they learned. This agency's training program lasts for approximately two years, during which a trainee's contribution to organizational objectives is minimal. Thus, ensuring that candidates have the minimum knowledge required to be successful in training is especially critical. The previous assessment had been used by the agency for over thirty years, and although there were few concerns regarding the test key itself, there were concerns that some of the content of the assessment might have become public knowledge over the years, thereby reducing its validity as a predictor (that is, some applicants may have been better prepared than others). The new assessment was designed to provide the same basic function, although there was a desire to consider revision of how test scores were used to screen candidates and how information about the test was shared with applicants. Candidates not achieving the cut score on the previous assessment were not considered in later parts of the selection process.

The typical applicant pool for this training program varies widely in the individual applicants' levels of mathematical knowledge. Applicants span the bachelor's, master's, and doctoral levels of training in mathematics. This broad span of educational levels in the applicant population makes it diverse with respect to what acceptable applicants know and are able to do. Further, those with higher levels of mathematical training may have more specialized knowledge, making it difficult to assume that applicants with higher levels of training necessarily will achieve higher scores on the test.

In addition to the complexities created by the various levels among applicants, there are a limited number of colleges and universities that provided a separate curriculum in mathematics, as in many schools mathematics has been subsumed by other academic departments. This situation creates a diverse applicant population in another sense. Because mathematics is not a common major field of study, such as business, economics, or engineering, there may be wide variance in what students have been trained to know and do.

Together, these factors suggest there might be many different ways a candidate could demonstrate the mathematical knowledge required to succeed in the training program, which has several implications for determining the most appropriate cut score for the new test.

Cut Score Setting Method

Several methods were considered for determining the cut score, taking into account the applicant pool characteristics, availability of criterion data, relationship to the previous test, and availability of SMEs. Empirical approaches, such as the contrasting group method or regression methods, were not feasible, because complete criterion data for success in training would not be available for two years. Moreover, due to the successful use of the previous test and additional selection measures, the rate at which selected candidates do not complete training was relatively low. Not surprisingly, this reasoning also led to the conclusion that a criterion-related validity study was not feasible.

Typically, a judgmental method, such as the Angoff method, would be appropriate for a case in which job analytic information was used to provide evidence of validity based on the test content. However, in this case the Angoff (1971) method was ruled out due to the educational diversity of the applicant population; that is, the development team was concerned that SMEs could not validly estimate the percentage of minimally qualified applicants who would correctly answer a particular question, because there was not a shared concept of the knowledge and skills of a minimally qualified applicant. Methods that relied on information about applicant performance on the test were rejected because the test had never been administered to potential applicants in its final form. Item analyses were based on several administrations of pilot test forms, and the samples were not similar enough to support an equating study. Finally, because the test was difficult (that is, to pass the previous version of the test applicants had only had to correctly answer approximately 35 percent of the questions), there was some concern that the panelists would set the cut score at or near the average score an applicant could achieve by guessing.

These factors ruled out the feasibility of any of the traditional approaches to setting cut scores described in the previous sections. The development team decided to build a hybrid approach, using elements of cut score setting procedures based on the relevant information and resources on hand. The relevant information available to the development team consisted of item analyses from multiple pilot test samples and test scores from a small set of new incumbent trainees. Other resources available included the cut score from the previous test and a set of SMEs who served as trainers and participated in the selection process for new trainees. The cut score from the previous test was useful in the sense that the content of the new test was similar in difficulty to that of the previous test, suggesting the level of the new cut score should not be greatly different. The SMEs were very knowledgeable in both the content of the assessment, the expected pass rates of the applicants, and the context in which data from the incumbent sample could be interpreted as applicable to actual applicants.

Using these resources, the development team derived a new method for setting cut scores, which we referred to as the simulated contrasting groups method. This method was based on simulating two distributions of scores from unqualified candidates. The first distribution was a distribution of scores from applicants who were guessing at random. The development team felt it was important to use the *distribution* of scores rather than simply inform the SME panel of the average score for guessing, to emphasize that a proportion of unqualified applicants might score well above chance levels purely by chance. (It is a common misperception among SMEs that guessing can be countered by setting the cut score two or three points above the mean chance score.) The second distribution was a distribution of simulated scores for *educated guessers*—applicants who did not know any correct answers but knew enough to eliminate implausible response options. Implausible response options were defined as response options that were endorsed by fewer than 5 percent of the pilot test sample. On average, approximately one in five response options was eliminated, thereby both raising the average score of the educated guesser distribution slightly above that of the pure guesser distribution and marginally increasing the standard deviation.

The distribution of test scores provided by incumbent trainees was also provided to the SME panel. All of the incumbent trainees who took the assessment were presumed to be qualified, having passed the previous test as well as a rigorous set of interviews and other qualifications screens. However, the incumbent trainees had little motivation (other than pride) to perform well on the assessment, as was evidenced by the high proportion of items for which the incumbents did not guess at the correct answer. In contrast, the pilot test participants were provided moderate financial incentives to perform well on the test, and the nonresponse rate was very low. Taking this result into consideration, incumbent scores were adjusted upward for "nonguessing." (Specifically, points were added to each incumbent's score equal to the number of omitted items times the reciprocal of the number of plausible response options on omitted items.) The final distributions used are represented in Figure 10.1.

This method was derived as a combination of the Nedelsky (1954) method and the contrasting groups method (Livingston & Zieky, 1982). The Nedelsky method was the source for using the mean score for guessing as a starting point for setting the cut score. The contrasting groups method was the source of using distributions rather than discrete scores and for providing a comparison group of incumbent trainees who were presumed to have the minimum requirements to be successful.

Cut Score Setting Procedure

The contrasting distributions were presented in two ways. First, the distributions were presented as histograms on transparent paper so that they could be overlaid on each other. Second, a table showing the passing rate for each group at each cut point on the test was distributed to the SMEs. These tables also served as

Figure 10.1. Distributions of Test Performance from Simulated Contrasting Groups Procedure.

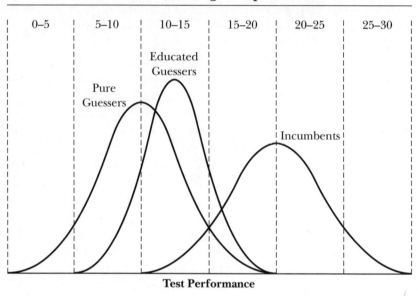

| 0–5 | 5–10 | 10–15 | 15–20 | 20–25 | 25–30 |

Educated
Guessers

Pure
Guessers

Incumbents

Test Performance

the response documents for the SMEs. Training for the SMEs consisted of an opening presentation on the importance of setting valid cut scores, the legal and practical implications, the process being used to set the cut score, and the materials and resources available for informing their judgments. During this presentation, it was noted that the role of the SMEs was to make recommendations on the cut score, and that those recommendation might need to be revised based on applicant flow issues, changes in applicant performance, or other unforeseen circumstances. In addition to the score distributions, copies of the final test form and item analyses from the pilot and field administrations were made available. Following training presentation, SMEs were encouraged to discuss the general goals for the implementation of the new test, agree on its intended use, and ask any final questions of the development team. As a final step in the process, SMEs were asked to sign a document stating that they understood the training and the judgmental tasks and agreeing to keep deliberations confidential.

The actual process of setting the cut score was accomplished over two rounds of deliberations. During the first round, SMEs were asked to go through the resources provided on their own, to discuss the materials with their peers, and to make an independent initial judgment of where they thought the cut score should be set. Following this initial judgment, SMEs were again encouraged to discuss the rationales underlying various recommendations. The discussion started with the extreme scores, then worked toward the rationales for the scores near the median. Once this discussion had run its course, a second round of independent recommendations was gathered from the SMEs, again followed by a discussion. As expected, there was some convergence nearer to the median of the initial recommendation, although the median changed slightly. Complete consensus was not achieved, but based on the feedback from the panel, all SMEs judged that the cut score was set appropriately, and there was no need for further deliberations. The resulting cut score was very close, but not identical, to the cut score from the previous test. In a post-panel survey, SMEs reported satisfaction with the process and felt it was an effective way to set the cut score.

Other Implementation Issues

At the close of the cut score panel meeting, the SMEs were asked to discuss additional options for implementing the new test. Panelists concluded that there was no need to administer the previous test alongside the new test. Panelists judged that the new test was appropriate for use and that there was no need to do any kind of equating to the previous test. Panelists were asked if the new test should be used without a strict cut score for the first year of operational administration, but they again endorsed the new assessment and concluded it was ready for full operational use. Finally, the panel agreed that the cut score should be reexamined after the first year of operational administration, when better data about applicant performance and the utility of the test in the selection process would be available.

Scenario Two: Implementation of a Test Battery for Selection of Law Enforcement Personnel.

This scenario describes the implementation of a test battery that was validated using a concurrent, criterion-related validation strategy. The test battery was composed of both cognitive and noncognitive measures and was originally intended for use in screening a large number of applicants for existing law enforcement positions in a government agency. This new test battery was being developed to replace an old test battery that had become the focus of ongoing litigation because of disparate impact. However, what was more unique to this situation—and the reason why a test battery that was validated using a concurrent, criterion-related validation approach is addressed in this chapter on implementation of selection procedures based on alternative validation strategies—is that the test battery was ultimately used to select law enforcement personnel into a newly developed job classification. Specifically, at the onset of this project, the agency decided to create a new classification of law enforcement officer that would handle a subset of the duties currently being handled by individuals in the existing classification of law enforcement officers. Thus, the position of focus did not exist at the time of the study, and therefore there were no true job incumbents on which to base a concurrent, criterion-related validation study. Yet despite this circumstance, the legal issues surrounding the previous test battery used for law enforcement personnel at this agency compelled the decision-makers to conduct a concurrent, criterion-related validation study anyway.

Background

Aside from selecting applicants into a newly created job classification, there were multiple stated objectives to this study. Primary among these objectives was the desire to develop a selection process that was job-related and would result in minimal adverse impact. (This project actually called for the development of a selection process composed of a written test battery and a structured interview; in this chapter we discuss only the work associated with implementation of the written test battery.) In addition, this selection process was specified to include a written test battery that would be used as the first hurdle in a multiple-hurdle selection process. The agency had expected that this test battery would be administered to approximately twenty thousand applicants and that administration of the test battery could take no longer than three hours to complete in order to allow for two administrations per day. Additionally, the agency expressed concern with the security of the test battery, during both test development and administration.

The purpose of the written test battery was to ensure that selected candidates had the requisite skills and abilities to complete an extensive multiyear training program, as well as to perform the entry-level job requirements. Because a new job classification was being created, the project began with a future-oriented job analysis to identify the projected requirements of the target positions, particularly the knowledge, skills, abilities, and other characteristics (KSAOs) that could appropriately be assessed during selection. The preliminary test development activities consisted of reviewing the research literature to identify the types of measures used for assessing the KSAOs targeted by the written test battery, including an examination of the reliability and validity of various types of measures as well as the research supporting how these measures might affect the level of adverse impact and perceptions of fairness with the selection process. The literature review also considered other organizational concerns, such as handling a large number of candidates and maintaining the security of the selection process. Based on the literature review, a number of different types of selection measures were developed for inclusion in the experimental written test battery, including custom-designed cognitive ability tests, biodata measures, and low-fidelity work simulations. Also included in the experimental written test battery was a commonly used off-the-shelf personality measure. The custom-designed tests were pilot tested and refined prior to conducting the validation study.

A major challenge in the criterion-related validation study was the identification of a validation sample. Although the focal job did not exist at the time of the project, the duty, task, and KSAO requirements defined for the future job incumbents were currently being performed by incumbents in a different job classification. Thus, there did exist a population of highly similar law enforcement officers whose responsibilities included, in part, the responsibilities being assigned to the new job classification. Although these individuals provided a population from which to sample, their use presented several major obstacles in the validation study. First, the available job incumbents were performing many duties in addition to those that were defined for the new job classification. Thus, there was a known source of potential contamination in criterion scores (that is, job performance ratings). Second, there had been a hiring freeze in the years prior to this project, thereby rendering any sample of the existing law enforcement officers a severely restricted one, because at the time of this project most of them had already undergone significant training and been on the job performing for several years. Given these concerns, careful attention was given to the design of the data collection instruments, the choice of a sample of incumbents to participate in the study, and the types of analyses that were conducted throughout the study. For example, dimension-level job performance ratings were obtained in addition to overall, holistic ratings, and tenure data were gathered and used as a covariate in the validity analyses.

The experimental test battery was administered to a sample of current law enforcement officers who had been on the job for ten years or less. For these individuals, supervisory ratings of job performance were also obtained. The criterion measures were designed to ensure that information that was specific to the requirements of the new job classification was obtained. These criterion measures were developed and collected specifically for the validation study.

In analyzing the relationship between test scores on the experimental test battery and job performance criteria, several a priori models were developed by using a combination of tests and test-weighting strategies. These a priori models were hypothesized based on their anticipated ability to meet the requirements of the written test battery. By positing these models prior to analyzing the data, it was possible to preclude models that would not be supported by research and practice to achieve both of the two main objectives—demonstrating job relatedness and minimizing adverse impact.

The results of the analyses supported two models for implementing the written test battery. However, given the issues with the sample used in the validation study, it was decided to administer all of the tests used to create these two models to applicants prior to implementing the final test battery and scoring procedures. This approach was feasible because the plan called for the administration of the written test battery during a very short testing window. Thus, the written test battery most supported by the validity study was eventually administered to approximately twelve thousand applicants across multiple U.S. locations over a period of several weeks.

Implementation Methodology

The plan for choosing a final model for using the written test battery comprised three steps: specifying the selection procedures, conducting item analyses and scoring applicant data, and conducting validity and impact analyses.

The first step involved specifying the selection procedures to be evaluated in the postadministration analyses. There were two decision points in this step—specification of test score composites and determination of the likely selection ratio or ratios needed to achieve hiring objectives.

A maximum of six possible test score composites could be created by following the strategy used in the validation study. These test score composites were created by crossing two of the a priori models from which validity evidence was found in the criterion-related validity study with three weighting schemes that gave equal or greater weight to the cognitive component of the test battery relative to the noncognitive component. These three weighting schemes also were supported in the criterion-related validity study.

In addition to the specification of the test score composites, the possible selection ratios for achieving the hiring objectives were identified. One possible selection ratio was that associated with a top-down selection model. This selection ratio was directly determined once the hiring needs were fully specified by the agency. The other possible selection ratios were those that assumed that applicants who score above a given score cut point were to be randomly selected from an eligibility list. These latter selection ratios all were greater than the selection ratio based on top-down selection.

The specific selection procedures to be evaluated were established by specifying the test score composites and selection ratios. However, additional constraints (such as time and money) made it necessary to focus on only the most promising test battery and the three weighting schemes that resulted in the best validity evidence. Thus, there were three test score composites to evaluate. Furthermore, the selection ratios under the random selection model were set at two, three, and four times the calculated selection ratio under the top-down selection model. This resulted in a total of twelve selection procedures to evaluate—three test score composites crossed with four selection ratios.

Once the specification of selection procedures to evaluate was complete, item analyses were conducted using the applicant data, and test composites scores were produced. Item analyses were conducted in a manner similar to item analyses during the validation study and allowed the identification of problematic items and the assessment of potential differences in the applicant and validation context. For example, given the severe level of range restriction in the validation sample, many items that appeared easy in the validation study were retained under the expectation that these items would function differently in the applicant population. The primary objectives of the item analyses were to ensure that the item characteristics based on the applicant population met expectations and that they were appropriate for use in calculating test scores. Once item analyses were complete, the test score composites being evaluated were computed. In doing so, the test score means and standard deviations from the applicant population were used to appropriately weight the components in the test score composites.

In the final step, validity and impact analyses were conducted to provide a foundation for evaluating each of the selection procedures under evaluation. To do this, it was first necessary to recalculate the validity estimates from the criterion-related validation study when assuming the use of a top-down selection model. The validity estimates were recalculated for each of the test score composites that were being evaluated. In recalculating all validity estimates, the applicant test results were used to make the appropriate statistical corrections for range restriction in the validation sample.

The validity estimates, assuming the cut points associated with each of the selection ratios under a random selection model, were then calculated. This activity was necessary because validity estimates that assume top-down selection will overestimate test score composite validities associated with the random selection model. Again, in calculating these estimates, the applicant test results were used to make the appropriate statistical corrections for range restriction, as was done in recalculating the validity estimates for the top-down selection model.

Finally, gender and ethnic subgroup differences (that is, effect sizes) among the applicant population were calculated for each of the test score composites. In addition, the selection ratio for each gender and ethnic subgroup was determined, assuming top-down selection. These subgroup ratios were used to evaluate the level of adverse impact associated with each of the test score composites. Selection eligibility rates were calculated for each of the selection ratios that were evaluated under the random selection model. These selection eligibility rates were used to evaluate the level of adverse impact in defining the pool of applicants from which random selection would occur.

After completing all the postadministration analyses, the results from both the validation study and the postadministration analyses were compiled and evaluated against the stated objectives of the project. In compiling these results, a specific recommendation for using the results to make hiring decisions was also developed. As discussed in earlier sections of this chapter, all the project activities associated with the development and implementation of the written test battery were documented in a series of technical reports and briefings.

Summary of Exemplar Scenarios

These scenarios demonstrate two applications of appropriate cut score setting strategies under circumstances in which traditional criterion validation was not possible or was significantly restricted. Scenario One demonstrated the use of a judgmental method combined with an empirical method that made efficient use of limited data. The selection procedure in Scenario One was implemented in a relatively low-risk environment; there was strong evidence of content validity for the selection procedure, and it was used to screen a relatively small number of applicants. In contrast, Scenario Two illustrated a higher-risk selection procedure with a high number of applicants in a historically litigious employment sector (that is, law enforcement). In this scenario, it was determined that an empirical method for setting cut scores was needed to support the strongest possible legal defense of the selection instrument. Scenario Two details the complex considerations and statistical processes required to provide maximally valid cut score recommendations when the sample and performance criteria do not meet the ideal standards of a criterion validity study.

Conclusions

Implementing a new selection procedure entails making numerous decisions that often require balancing scientific concerns, such as maximizing reliability and validity of selection decisions, with practical concerns, such as being able to fill positions at reasonable levels and maximizing the utility of a selection procedure. Good decision making on these issues is even more challenging when validity evidence for the new selection procedure is based on an alternative validation technique. It is not enough, however, to simply make good decisions. Throughout the sources of professional guidance, case law, and scientific literature relating to the implementation of a new selection procedure is the recurring theme that documentation of these decisions is as important as the decisions themselves. The process of documenting decisions is critical to establishing that the selection procedure is used in a manner based on its job relevance and is consistent with business necessity.

Title VII, the *Uniform Guidelines,* the *Standards,* and the *Principles* all provide solid professional guidance on matters related to implementing a new selection procedure, including general guidelines for using empirical data to inform implementation decisions, which aspects of the decision-making process are most important to carefully document, and factors that influence the quality and defensibility of implementation decisions. The *Standards* and *Principles* provide the most guidance, but stop well short of being prescriptive when it comes to endorsing methods for setting cut scores or how selection procedures should be combined in the selection process.

It is generally assumed that selection procedures can be used in a top-down manner to rank order applicants. When rank-ordering of applicants is neither feasible, appropriate, nor desirable, some method must be selected for determining which applicants merit further consideration. Performance bands and cut scores are two methods for grouping applicants into categories for further consideration. There are several methods for setting cut scores, each of which has particular advantages and applicability to contexts in which various alternative validation techniques have been employed. The Angoff (1971) method and its various modifications generally have the most widespread applicability to setting cut scores for cases in which alternative techniques are employed to validate a new selection procedure. Other techniques may be practicable based on the availability of data, the nature of the selection procedure, and the relationship of performance on the selection procedure to the criterion of interest.

Choosing an appropriate cut score setting method is only one aspect of setting the cut score that influences the validity and defensibility of the procedure. Selection and training of SMEs is also critically important. Judges must understand the standard setting task, how to bring their expertise to bear on the judgment task, and the practical considerations that may influence them to adjust their recommendations, such as the relative costs of false positive and false negative selections. Finally, implementation requires careful consideration of how the selection measure will be used in concert with other selection procedures. Conjunctive, or multiple-hurdle, approaches tend to lower the reliability of the overall selection system and may maximize the potential for adverse impact, but they are often administratively efficient when some selection procedures are costly or time-consuming. Compensatory standards are generally more reliable, but they may impose a risk if applicants can compensate for poor performance on a critical element of a selection battery with a high level of performance on a less-important selection procedure.

It is often said that there is no best method for setting cut scores. Likewise, there is no single best answer for addressing broader selection procedure implementation issues. Practitioners are advised that making sound decisions on test implementation in a context in which validity evidence is gathered through alternative techniques often requires being resourceful, flexible, and creative. The scenarios presented in this chapter are good examples of ways that many sources of information can be combined to result in effective test implementation decisions.

References

American Educational Research Association, American Psychological Association, & National Council on Measurement in Education. (1999). *Standards for educational and psychological testing.* Washington, DC: American Educational Research Association.

Americans with Disabilities Act of 1990, 42 U.S.C. § 12101 *et seq.* 1993.

Angoff, W. H. (1971). Scales, norms, and equivalent scores. In R. L. Thorndike (Ed.), *Educational measurement* (2nd ed.). Washington, DC: American Council on Education.

Ben-David, M. F. (2000). AMEE guide no. 18: Standard setting in student assessment. *Medical Teacher, 22*(2), 120–130.

Berk, R. A. (1986). A consumer's guide to setting performance standards on criterion-referenced tests. *Review of Educational Research, 56*(1), 137–172.

Berk, R. A. (1996). Standard setting: The next generation (where few psychometricians have gone before!). *Applied Measurement in Education, 9*(3), 215–235.

Biddle, R. E. (1993). How to set cutoff scores for knowledge tests used in promotion, training, certification, and licensing. *Public Personnel Management, 22*(1), 63–79.

Borman, W. C. (1986). Behavior-based rating scales. In R. A. Berk (Ed.), *Performance assessment: Methods & applications* (pp. 100–120). Baltimore, MD: Johns Hopkins University Press.

Borman, W. C., Hough, L. M., & Dunnette, M. D. (1976). *Development of behaviorally based rating scales for evaluating the performance of U.S. Navy recruiters* (Institute Report #6). (NPRDC TR-76–31). Navy Personnel Research and Development Center.

Cangelosi, J. S. (1984). Another answer to the cut-off score question. *Educational Measurement: Issues and Practice, 3*(4), 23–25.

Cascio, W. F., Alexander, R. A., & Barrett, G. V. (1988). Setting cutoff scores: Legal, psychometric, and professional issues and guidelines. *Personnel Psychology, 41,* 1–24.

Chang, L. (1999). Judgmental item analysis of the Nedelsky and Angoff standard setting methods. *Applied Measurement in Education, 12*(2), 151–165.

Civil Rights Act of 1964, 42 U.S.C.

Civil Rights Act of 1991, 42 U.S.C.

Cizek, G. J. (1993). *Reaction to National Academy of Education report, "Setting performance standards for student achievement."* Washington, DC: National Assessment Governing Board.

Cizek, G. J. (1996). Standard setting guidelines. *Educational Measurement: Issues and Practice, 15*(1), 13–21.

Ebel, R. L. (1979). *Essentials of educational measurement* (3rd ed.). Englewood Cliffs, NJ: Prentice-Hall.

Equal Employment Opportunity Commission, Civil Service Commission, Department of Labor, & Department of Justice. (1978). *Uniform guidelines on employee selection procedures. Federal Register, 43*(166), 38290–38315.

Ferrara, S., Perie, M., & Johnson, E. (2002, September). *Matching the judgmental task with standard setting panelist expertise: The item-descriptor (ID) matching procedure.* Invited colloquium for the Board on Testing and Assessment of the National Research Council, Washington, DC.

Goldberger, A. S. (1984). Reverse regression and salary discrimination. *Journal of Human Resources, 19*(3), 293–318.

Gutman, A. (2000). *EEO law and personnel practices* (2nd ed.). Thousand Oaks, CA: Sage.

Gutman, A. (2003). On the legal front: Adverse impact: Why is it so hard to understand? *The Industrial Psychologist, 40*(3), 42–50.

Gutman, A. (2004). On the legal front: Ground rules for adverse impact. *The Industrial Psychologist, 41*(3), 109–119.

Haladyna, T., & Hess, R. (1999). An evaluation of conjunctive and compensatory standard-setting strategies for test decisions. *Educational Assessment, 6*(2), 129–153.

Hambleton, R. K., Brennan, R. L., Brown, W., Dodd, B., Forsyth, R. A., Mehrens, W. A., Nellhaus, J., Reckase, M., Rindone, D., van der Linden, W. J., & Zwick, R. (2000). A response to "Setting reasonable and useful performance standards" in the National Academy of Sciences' Grading the Nation's Report Card. *Educational Measurement: Issues and Practice, 19*(2), 5–14.

Hanser, L. M. (1998). Lessons for the National Assessment of Educational Progress from military standard setting. *Applied Measurement in Education, 11*(1), 81–95.

Hurtz, G. M., & Hertz, N. R. (1999). How many raters should be used for establishing cutoff scores with the Angoff method? A generalizability theory study. *Educational and Psychological Measurement, 59*(6), 885–897.

Impara, J. C., & Plake, B. S. (1998). Teachers' ability to estimate item difficulty: A test of the assumptions of the Angoff standard setting method. *Journal of Educational Measurement, 35,* 69–81.

Jaeger, R. M. (1991). Selection of judges for standard-setting. *Educational Measurement: Issues and Practice, 10*(2), 3–6.

Jeanneret, R. (2005). Professional and technical authorities and guidelines. In F. J. Landy (Ed.), *Employment discrimination litigation: Behavioral, quantitative, and legal perspectives* (pp. 47–100). San Francisco: Jossey-Bass.

Kehoe, J. F., & Olson, A. (2005). Cut scores and employment discrimination litigation. In F. J. Landy (Ed.), *Employment discrimination litigation:*

Behavioral, quantitative, and legal perspectives (pp. 410–449). San Francisco: Jossey-Bass.

Kingston, N., Kahl, S. R., Sweeney, K., & Bay, L. (2001) Setting performance standards using the body of work method. In G. J. Cizek (ed.), *Setting performance standards: Concepts, methods, and perspectives.* Mahwah, NJ: Erlbaum.

Kramer, A., Muijtjens, A., Jansen, K., Dusman, H., Tan, L., & van der Vleuten, C. (2003). Comparison of a rational and an empirical standard setting procedure for an OSCE. *Medical Education, 37,* 132–139.

Lanning v. Southeastern Pennsylvania Transportation Authority (SEPTA) (CA3 1999), 181 F. 3d 478.

Lanning v. Southeastern Pennsylvania Transportation Authority (SEPTA) (2002), U.S. App Lexis 21506 (2002).

Livingston, S. A., & Zieky, M. J. (1982). *Passing scores: A manual for setting standards of performance on educational and occupational tests.* Princeton, NJ: Educational Testing Service.

Livingston, S. A., & Zieky, M. J. (1989). A comparative study of standard-setting methods. *Applied Measurement in Education, 2,* 121–141.

Maurer, T. J., & Alexander, R. A. (1992). Methods of improving employment test critical scores derived by judging test content: A review and critique. *Personnel Psychology, 45,* 727–762.

Mills, C. N., & Melican, G. J. (1988). Estimating and adjusting cutoff scores: Features of selected methods. *Applied Measurement in Education, 1*(3), 261–275.

Mitzel, H. C., Lewis, D. M., Patz, R. J., & Green, D. R. (2001). The Bookmark procedure: Psychological perspectives. In G. J. Cizek (Ed.), *Setting performance standards: Concepts, methods, and perspectives.* Mahwah, NJ: Erlbaum.

Muijtjens, A.M.M., Kramer, A.W.M., Kaufman, D. M., & Van der Vleuten, C.P.M. (2003). Using resampling to estimate the precision of an empirical standard setting method. *Applied Measurement in Education, 16*(3), 245–256.

National Education Association v. South Carolina, 43 U.S. 1026 (1978).

National Research Council. (1999). Setting reasonable and useful performance standards. In J. W. Pelligrino, L. R. Jones, & K. J. Mitchell (Eds.), *Grading the nation's report card: Evaluating NAEP and transforming the assessment of educational progress* (pp. 162–184). Washington, DC: National Academy Press.

Nedelsky, L. (1954). Absolute grading for objective tests. *Educational and Psychological Measurement, 14,* 3–19.

Plake, B. S., & Impara, J. C. (2001). Ability of panelists to estimate item performance for a target group of candidates: An issue in judgmental standard setting. *Educational Assessment, 7,* 87–97.

Shepard, L. A. (1995). Implications for standard setting of the National Academy of Education evaluation of National Assessment of Educational Progress achievement levels. In *Proceedings of the Joint Conference on Standard Setting for Large-Scale Assessments* (Vol. 2, pp. 143–160). Washington, DC: U.S. Government Printing Office.

Siskin, B. R., & Trippi, J. (2005). Statistical issues in litigation. In Landy, F. J. (Ed.), *Employment discrimination litigation: Behavioral, quantitative, and legal perspectives* (pp. 132–166). San Francisco: Jossey-Bass.

Society for Industrial and Organizational Psychology. (2003). *Principles for the validation and use of personnel selection procedures* (4th ed.). Bowling Green, OH: Society for Industrial and Organizational Psychology.

U.S. Office of Personnel Management. (n.d.). *Operating manual for qualification standards.* Retrieved from http://www.opm.gov/qualifications/index.asp

Zink, D. L., & Gutman, A. (2005). Statistical trends in private sector employment discrimination suits. In F. J. Landy (Ed.), *Employment discrimination litigation: Behavioral, quantitative, and legal perspectives* (pp. 101–131). San Francisco: Jossey-Bass.

PART 4

Where Do We Go from Here?

CHAPTER 11

The Validation of Personnel Decisions in the Twenty-First Century: Back to the Future

Frank J. Landy

I have been thinking about the concept of validation for an un-healthy period of time. It can make your head hurt after a while. My head has been hurting for about forty years—ever since I was exposed to Bob Guion's first personnel testing book (Guion, 1965). So validation has always been a part of my view of the world of work, whether the issue was the validity of inferences made from test scores, training programs, or stress interventions. I have made that argument several times before and won't repeat it here (Landy, 1986; Schmitt & Landy, 1992). In this chapter, I will limit my observations to the traditional areas of the validity of selection, promotion, and licensing or certification decisions and how changes in both scientific thinking and research and the nature of work have presented new challenges to the concept of establishing the validity of inferences. You note that I refer to my "observations." My "observations" emerge from a complex web of consultation, research, expert testimony, textbook writing, and semistuporous late-night debates at SIOP conferences with some very smart people in dark bars with lots of smoke. In short, I am simply giving the reader the benefit of my thoughts, having survived forty years of the psychometric wars. These observations are meant to be representative of the issues we face in applied psychometrics; they are far from comprehensive or exhaustive.

Some History

The years leading up to the establishment of the EEOC and the issuance of the first set of "guidelines" for test validation were volatile ones, during which I/O and psychometrics were dragged into the spotlight and asked to answer for the wretched excesses of the dust-bowl empiricism eras of the '40s and '50s. There was good news and bad news in the history of personnel psychology. The good news was that we had convinced most lay people (including the courts) that empiricism (meaning criterion-related validity) was the only path to truth. The bad news was that we had convinced most lay people (including the courts) that empiricism was the only path to truth.

In the early days of regulatory guidelines, we were hoisted with our own empirical petard and asked to demonstrate, in each instance of a personnel decision, that the particular decision was valid. This was the doctrine of "situational specificity." If I were a cynic, I would be tempted to speculate that the regulatory agencies were more aware of the tragic insufficiency of criterion measures than were the psychometricians and knew that the requirement to demonstrate criterion-related validity was an invitation to lunch on the *Titanic* for I/O psychologists. In fact, though, the early regulatory views of validity were the views of troglodytes.

Fortunately, the cave-dwellers were forced to abandon the darkness by two related movements—one was conceptual and the second was empirical. The conceptual argument was that there were many ways to demonstrate validity and that criterion relationships represented only one of those ways (Cronbach & Meehl, 1955; Landy, 1986; Binning & Barrett, 1989). The empirical argument was presented by Schmidt and Hunter (2002) in their refutation of the doctrine of situational specificity and the introduction of the concept of validity generalization (and the supporting tool of meta-analysis). Thus, the "final" policy and regulatory view of the validation world—the *Uniform Guidelines on Employee Selection Procedures* (Equal Employment Opportunity Commission, Civil Service Commission, Department of Labor, & Department of Justice, 1978)— churlishly accepted the notion that validation evidence could come from many different sources (although the *Uniform Guidelines* were and often still are interpreted to mean that one must choose *the* validation model for defending personnel inferences—so it would appear that the authors traveled to the mouth of the cave, but were reluctant to come out completely). And of course, the *Uniform Guidelines* predated the validity generalization (VG) explosion, so the absence of any extended discussion of VG in the *Uniform Guidelines* is to be expected.

Some Future

The *Uniform Guidelines* were issued in 1978, and in the almost thirty years since they were published, they have become neither better nor worse than they were then. They remain a psychometric Rorschach test, open to the interpretation of interested parties (or worse, they form an Alice-in-Wonderland glossary that allows a word to mean whatever the interested party wants it to mean!). Fortunately, SIOP has tried to fill that epistemological void with various editions of the *Principles for the Validation and Use of Employee Selection Procedures* (Society for Industrial and Organizational Psychology, 2003) and has been largely successful in that endeavor. There is a continuing debate about whether the *Uniform Guidelines* should be revised. To channel Rhett Butler in *Gone with the Wind*, "Frankly, my dear, I don't give a damn." Neither the *Uniform Guidelines* nor the *Principles* will help us out of the current dilemma of validation posed by the changed and changing nature of work that I outline in this chapter. The publications both represent retrospective views and are not expected to anticipate, in any practical way, what the future will bring. That anticipation appears to be the goal of this book. And I am pleased to join in that anticipation. I will present my observations about the challenges to validation posed by twenty-first-century work in several categories. These include changes in the nature of work, predictor issues, criterion issues, the validation continuum, and emerging practical issues.

Changes in the Nature of Work

Several years ago, in the process of preparing a textbook in industrial and organizational psychology (Landy & Conte, 2004), Jeff
Conte and I took notice of the dramatic changes that had occurred
in the nature of work during the period 1980 to 2000. We observed
that these changes were so profound and so rapid that they outran
existing theory and research. In a recent revision of that text
(Landy & Conte, 2007), we see no reason to change that view. If
anything, the nature of work is changing even *more* rapidly than it
did during that earlier twenty-year period. In the following passages
I will identify the major changes and then indicate some implications of each of those changes for the way we validate personnel
decisions.

Team Work

From the beginnings of the industrial revolution until the onslaught
of downsizing in the early 1980s, work (at least in the United States)
could be characterized as solitary. To be assigned to a team was seen
as a punishment or a sign of distrust. To be sure, the experiments
in Yugoslavia and Sweden in self-managed groups received some attention but were largely seen as unsuitable for the United States. At
its most mechanical level, downsizing radically increased the span
of control in most organizations by reducing the number of first-
and middle-level managers. This dilution of supervision meant that
workers were expected to make decisions, collectively and individ-
ually, that had been made before by supervisors and managers. Solitary work largely became a thing of the past. Simultaneously,
manufacturing models—such as TQM, quality circles, and, more
recently, Six Sigma environments—required teamlike behavior. To
be sure, there has been an increasing recognition of the importance of understanding the team behavior that has always existed,
such as in cockpit crews, medical teams, and nuclear power control room teams (see Hackman, 1987, 1990; Salas and Cannon-
Bowers, 2001). The point is that team behavior and job-imposed
requirements for team behavior are more common now than ever
before and unlikely to diminish.

Implications: The nature of modern work requires interaction. Nevertheless, I/O psychology, at least in the context of assessment, clings to the individual differences model. As a result, our empirical validation efforts also correspond to the individual differences model, with single predictor scores associated with individual criterion scores. Our content-related validation designs seem more forgiving in that respect. It is common for job analyses to identify team-related behavior as an important part of a job and interpersonal competencies (such as personality, communication, values) as critical for these behaviors. There is, however, a substantial validation void in predicting successful team performance.

Virtual Work

Thirty years ago, with the exception of sales positions, it was the uncommon white-collar employee who was not "at work," in the literal sense, for a forty-hour week. Today, a substantial amount of non-sales, white-collar work is performed in places other than "at work." These places include frequent-traveler lounges, home offices, and second homes. This type of work has been labeled "virtual work" and is an increasingly common mechanism for achieving a more reasonable work-life balance, particularly in dual wage-earning families. It is fair to speculate that the context (as defined in the O*NET architecture) of virtual work is different from the context of nonvirtual work.

Implications: The context in which a task is performed may be an important element for understanding the nature of that task performance. The knowledge, skills, abilities, and other characteristics (KSAOs) and the competencies for performing virtual work are likely to be different in some important respects from the KSAOs and competencies for performing the same work in an office. When coupled with the concept of *teams* addressed earlier, the work of *virtual teams* becomes even more challenging to understand. In turn, this complexity means that in the context of any traditional validation strategies, the parsing of both predictor and criterion space becomes more crucial. As virtual work continues to expand, it is likely that competency models of this type of work will emerge and make the validation process more efficient, but until they do, job analysis platforms need to recognize the differences between virtual and nonvirtual work.

Contingent and Temporary Work

The advent of the Japanese model of manufacturing in the '80s introduced the concept of just-in-time (JIT) production. JIT thinking led to reductions in both inventory and workforce. Organizations adopted a lean-and-mean posture, which meant that headcount was kept at a bare minimum. There was no full-time labor pool to act as a safety net for absences, terminations, or unanticipated increases in workload. To provide that manpower safety net at the lowest cost, organizations turned to temporary or contingency workers who would be available or on call but who were not paid benefits or guaranteed full-time work. Often, these contingent workers are recruited and selected using more primitive selection systems (and sometimes with no selection at all) than those systems used to recruit and hire regular, full-time workers.

Implications: If contingent and permanent part-time workers are regularly and satisfactorily performing tasks that are identical to those of regular, full-time workers, and they undergo no or little assessment, the business necessity and job-relatedness of the system used to select regular full-time workers are subject to serious question. There is little conceptual difference between performing duties on a regular rather than part-time basis (excluding, of course, the issue of retention).

Technical and Nontechnical Work

The last decade has seen an explosion of interest in what might be labeled nontechnical work performance. Nontechnical aspects of work include both counterproductive work behaviors (CWB) and organization citizenship behaviors (OCB). There is some evidence that these two types of nontechnical work behavior are ends of a single continuum (see Landy & Conte, 2007). It is also generally acknowledged that work in the twenty-first century requires protection against CWBs and enhanced prediction of OCBs. Work has become more interpersonal (such as team, customer, and service orientation), more stressful (providing a rich soil for CWB), and more competitive (requiring greater extra-role investment by employees). Validation studies that specifically include the prediction of OCB and CWB are still few and far between.

Implications: Most of the studies that currently find their way into meta-analyses of predictor variables give little or no attention to the performance domain. The criteria are combinations of overall performance, composite performance, a mishmash of individual technical and nontechnical performance dimensions, employee rankings on some broad notion of merit, and the like. This criterion mélange means that any absolute inference about the validity of an assessment device or practice based on work done thirty or forty years ago cannot be interpreted in the current context. In other words, a lot of what we took as gospel twenty years ago (such as the validity of tests of "g") must be revisited in terms of twenty-first-century work. In particular, we must acknowledge that work and job performance is both technical and nontechnical, and it is no longer sufficient to concentrate on predicting only technical performance. The changing nature of work reminds us of the dynamic nature of validity data.

Volatile Technical Work

Even with respect to technical work, things are changing. The tasks that defined a job thirty years ago were relatively stable, particularly in skilled and semiskilled blue-collar work. That is no longer the case. In lean production and TQM environments, it is not unheard of for tasks to change literally overnight. When the worker appears for his or her next shift, the work procedures card on a work station may have been rewritten, the subassemblies may have changed, and the worker may be part of a different team or report to a different supervisor. The worker may even be told to report to a different production line or department.

Implications: In Chapter One of this volume, the editor implies that the "death of the job" may be more hyperbole than fact. He may be right. But if he were to extend this to mean that the "death of the task" is overstated, he could be wrong. Tasks are much more volatile than they have been in the past. For that reason, for many jobs, traditional task-based job analyses are less useful as a foundation for validation than has been the case in the past. Instead, it is more valuable to consider general work areas or duties such as those suggested by the generalized work behaviors of the O*NET architecture. Alternatively, competency modeling (that is, the identification of task clusters that represent behaviors that are strategically important to the organization) provides a level of magnification more in keeping with the nature of work (that is, less temporally volatile). On the attribute side of the job analysis equation, there is considerable debate regarding competencies versus KSAOs. The debate is of greater commercial value (that is, for the branding of competencies by dueling consultants) than scientific or psychometric value. As Lincoln is said to have wryly noted, calling a horse's tail a leg does not mean the horse has five legs or can run any faster.

Work Has Become More Cognitive

Economists and social observers assert that work is becoming simpler or less complex. The implication is that cognitive ability may be less critical for successful work performance than may have been the case in earlier decades. In fact, work is becoming less complex and more complex simultaneously. Semiskilled jobs are becoming *either* unskilled or skilled, some becoming less complex and some becoming more complex. Increasing complexity, in turn, emphasizes specific mental abilities such as inductive and deductive reasoning, problem solving, and creativity.

Implications: Our view of the unity and predominance of "g" is, in part, the product of a combination of a method (factor analysis), a person (Spearman), a zeitgeist (behaviorism), and an earlier world of work (which was, on average, less complex). Today, we have at our disposal tools—particularly cognitive task analysis—that will help us unpack the mental black box of the behaviorists. Just 'cause we can't see it, don't mean we can't infer it. Using tools such as cognitive task analysis to more finely parse criterion space and an increasingly sophisticated view of cognitive abilities (see Ackerman, 1992; Carroll, 1993), we need to reopen the discussion about "g" and "s" and their relative contributions to work performance.

Global Work

In 1980, most industrialized nations (largely Western) included some form of *foreign worker* or *guest worker* in their lexicon. As of 2006 those terms have become largely meaningless. As an example, at an auto assembly plant outside of Melbourne, Australia, fifty-seven first languages could be heard on the production floor. The point is not differences of language, but that the languages represent profound variations in national culture. At higher levels in the organization, cross-border mergers and acquisitions have a similar effect on cultural variations in work performance. As a result of various sociopolitical changes (for example, the end of the Warsaw Pact, the evolution of the EU, the introduction of NAFTA), the cultural diversity of most workforces has expanded dramatically. Most cross-national meta-analyses of validity ignore the systematic variations of national culture by aggregating studies from culturally similar nations (such as the United States, Australia, New Zealand, the U.K., Canada, and South Africa, or Sweden, Norway, Denmark, and Finland) and then claiming that predictors are robust to cultural variation.

A simple example might help illustrate the issue of cross-national validation (Cole, Gay, Glick, & Sharpe, 1971). Researchers were examining the construct of concept formation in Liberia. They presented the experimental subjects with a series of objects. These objects were designed to represent four categories: food, things to use in eating food, things to use in preparing food, and things to use in storing food. The experimenters presented these objects to the subjects as a random collection, hoping for four clean categories of objects. Instead, they received anywhere from two to eight categories completely unrelated to their intended groups. After hours of "unrewarding" stimulus presentation, they finally asked the subjects how they defined their categories. One respondent answered that he had done it "as a wise man" would do it. He said he had placed things together that would be used to prepare, serve, eat, and store a typical meal. Then the experimenters asked the respondent how a fool would do it—and the respondent promptly reproduced the categories that the experimenters had hoped for! My point is that assessment responses are often culturally influenced. It is not about translations—it is about meaning.

Implications: Claims of cross-border transportability of validity findings must be made cautiously—and only when there has been evidence of cultural similarity. I realize that this may be seen as simply the global variation of the situational specificity argument, but until studies appear across a wide variety of cultures, claims of transportability or generalizability are premature. This consideration becomes particularly important for multinational organizations that seek to roll out a "global" assessment program for various job families in the organization.

Predictor Issues

It is axiomatic that when validity is being discussed, there must be a consideration of predictors. In this section, I will consider predictor issues.

Attributes

To some extent, I have anticipated the discussion of predictors in several sections above, particularly with respect to cognitive abilities, but I will revisit this issue briefly. In 1920, E. L. Thorndike, in his brief and infamous discussion of emotional intelligence, decried the fact that virtually all attempts to measure intelligence involved paper and pencil tests (Thorndike, 1920). It was his belief that using such a narrow medium begged some important questions about the manifestation of human abilities in the real (nonpaper) world. A perfect example of something new under the sun is the emergence of situational judgment tests (Chan & Schmitt, 2002). Situational judgment tests represent a conflation of process and content. They ask the assessee to solve problems of a practical nature, and they can be administered in paper-and-pencil or electronic (such as web or PC) format. Recent research (Chan & Schmitt, in press) suggests that these tests assess a combination of "g," tacit knowledge, and adaptability (Pulakos, Arad, Donovan, & Plamandon, 2000). Initial evaluations of situational judgment tests are promising. They seem to represent psychometric alchemy (adverse impact is down, validity is up), they seem to assess practically important KSAOs, and assessees like them.

Implications: As is the case with the periodic chart of elements in physics, I don't think there is much likelihood of discovering any new human attributes that account for more than trivial amounts of variance in practical situations. Nevertheless, I think that new methods of stimulus presentation and assessment can illuminate many corners of predictor space. Situational judgment is an example of such illumination. Among other things, the twenty-first century presents a greatly enhanced menu of assessment processes. Many of these processes present opportunities for dynamic and interactive assessment that will require a reevaluation of the accepted wisdom regarding the role of attributes in successful work performance. By exploring these new assessment methods, it is likely that the grand specification equation for predicting the "ultimate" performance criterion will change. Instead of having only "g" and personality on the predictor side of the equation, we might profitably add experience, declarative knowledge, situational judgment, values, interests, and motivation, thus providing a fuller specification of the prediction equation. Thorndike would be delirious to be given today's possibilities for assessment.

Ipsative Scoring

Historically, the dominant mode of scoring for psychometric devices has been normative or between-subjects scoring, i.e., an individual response (and subscale score) is understood in the context of the responses (and subscale scores) of other assessees. Recently, and particularly in personality testing, ipsative scoring or within-subjects scoring has been offered as an alternative; that is, an individual score is understood in the context of the other responses (and subscale scores) of the *same* assessee. As examples, two popular personality tests used in industry (the OPQ, offered by SHL, and the WAVE, offered by Saville Consulting) require the respondent to order choices or endorsements relative to each other—for example, choosing the most-like-me and the least-like-me from three alternatives—thus setting up a within-individual or ipsative comparison. At least in part, the impetus for ipsative scoring in personality tests has been to combat the social desirability

tendencies of assessees. Nevertheless, the creation of both normative and ipsative scale scores presents an opportunity to understand
how and why certain attributes predict work performance. The
most obvious example would be the Big Five scored both norma-
tively and ipsatively. To the extent to which concerns about "faking"
or social acceptance influences distort personality measurements,
ipsative scoring can reduce those fears.

Implications: There are rumblings in the applied psychometric
community that personality dimensions such as conscientiousness,
extraversion, and emotional stability should be brought under the
protective VG umbrella. Until there is a concerted effort to understand the implications of ipsative versus normative scoring for
personality measures, declaring VG-hood for personality attributes
is premature. I suspect that the validity patterns for these two different methods of scoring will vary substantially from each other,
particularly when the criterion space is appropriately parsed into
technical and nontechnical space. I suspect that some of the validity coefficients for ipsative personality scores will be higher than
their normative counterparts, if for no other reason than that of
the enforced "variance" of ipsative scoring compared to the potential suppressing effect on variance as a result of social desirability influences.

Process versus Substance

I/O psychologists continue to confuse substance and process in
discussions of predictors. A paper-and-pencil or web-based standardized multiple choice test can assess any of a number of attributes, including "g," "s," personality, motives and values, procedural
knowledge, and tacit knowledge. Each of these can also be assessed
by an interview or a work sample. Considering issues of the validity of measures of "g" versus an interview is a classic apples-and-
oranges problem. If the measure of "g" is a standardized multiple
choice test and the interview or work sample has a technical work
focus (for example, problem solving, inductive reasoning), there
is no reason to suspect that one or the other assessment will represent much incremental value. Nevertheless, it is common for
studies to compare exactly these two predictors and conclude that
the interview or the work sample has no incremental validity. Had

the interview been directed at attributes such as personality, motives, interpersonal skills, or values, and had the criterion space been sufficiently deconstructed into technical and nontechnical components, incremental validity would have been a much more likely outcome.

Implications: In many of the early studies included in VG and related meta-analyses (circa 1950 to 1980), there was little concern for (and often little possibility of) determining the exact content of predictors other than standardized multiple choice tests. This problem is compounded by the fact there is even less concern for (and, again, little possibility of) determining exactly what criterion space (technical or nontechnical) is being addressed in the research. In some instances, our inferences regarding the "population values" produced through meta-analysis might need to be qualified in terms of what we know about both the predictor and criterion spaces. As the studies we depend on for meta-analyses provide more and more information regarding both predictors and criteria, it will be possible to include some of these nuanced variables (such as nature of the criterion space, method of assessment within attribute) as moderator variables. Until that is possible, modesty in inference may be appropriate.

Criterion Issues

I have injected criterion issues into several of the earlier sections, so I will simply repeat the suggestion that until and unless we are clear in our description of criterion space (that is, technical versus nontechnical), we remain in the dust bowl.

Implications: Criterion-related validity studies are often "given a walk" with respect to the content of the criterion measure. To be sure, we are required to demonstrate that the criterion is relevant, but that is a pretty low bar for a psychometrician. Certainly, most nonpsychometricians would accept a measure of overall performance as relevant, but in the more demanding context of inference, what does that correlation coefficient really tell us? Does it tell us we will have good extra-role performers, or good problem solvers, or producers of high-quality goods or services, or people who will come to work on time and not leave before they should? The criterion theme is an old one. Progress has certainly been made in the conceptualization and measurement of criteria. Less progress has been made in integrating criterion issues with predictor issues in the context of validation.

The Validation Continuum

One can think of a validity continuum that runs from the concrete to the abstract. At the concrete end we have orthodox criterion-related validation and at the other end VG. In between, we have validity transport, meta-analysis of predictor data, synthetic and component validity, content-oriented validity, and construct validity.

It doesn't get more concrete than a good old local criterion-related validity study. We have an observed predictor score and an observed criterion score. A supporting and only slightly less concrete analysis might include a meta-analysis of the same predictor with varying criteria in other settings. Similarly, validity transport is one more step removed from the bedrock concrete, as there is no local criterion.

The next step on the path to abstraction is the content-related validation strategy, as we have no direct connection between an observed predictor score and an observed criterion score. Instead, we have the conceptual connection between attributes necessary to perform well on the test and attributes necessary to perform well on the job. Nevertheless, content-related validation is concrete in

Figure 11.1 The Validation Continuum.

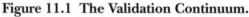

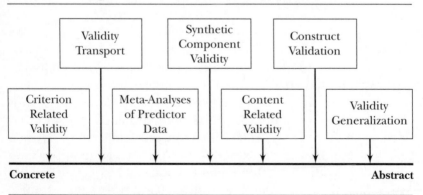

Note: I am grateful to Kylie M. Harper for the production of Figure 11.1.

the sense that it addresses "real" job duties and "real" attributes—and the inferences drawn are about specific positions or job families.

Somewhat less concrete are the notions of synthetic and component validity. These strategies deal with parts of jobs and, as such, are aggregating pieces of information about specific jobs into a "hypothetical" job of sorts. Although synthetic and component validity have historically embraced empirical criterion-related arguments, there is no reason why these approaches could not embrace content-related principles as well.

The next most abstract point on the continuum is what I will refer to as *local construct validity,* which uses a network of predictor-predictor and predictor-criterion relationships related to a specific job or job family to address the proposed test-score or criterion relationship. *General construct validity* is not tied to any specific job or job family, but it is tied to a specific predictor or subset of predictors.

Finally, at the most abstract end of the continuum we have VG. VG addresses a very broad range of predictors and criteria and seeks to generalize across a wide variety of jobs or job families.

Implications: As the nature of work changes from the stable to the volatile, the luxury of orthodox criterion- and content-related studies is often no longer available. The same is true of the evolution from solitary to team-based work. This emergence of twenty-first-century work will require us to move further toward the abstract end of the validation continuum. To be sure, there will always be opportunities for traditional criterion- and content-related investigations, but there will also be an increasing need to explore the more abstract end of the continuum. And, of course, without empirical studies, VG dies of its own weight. VG (and more specifically meta-analysis) really can make a silk purse out of a sow's ear. But you need the ears to start with.

Supporting Inferences

You can never be too thin or too rich, or have too many sources of support for test score inferences. Although this text advances a number of novel approaches to providing validation evidence, the fact remains that inference is about confidence. The more sources of validation information are available, the more confident we can be in making inferences from test scores.

Implications: Not much new here. Examine the validation continuum in Figure 11.1. Three sources of support are better than two, and two are better than one—at least from the psychometric perspective. The die-hard positivists (that is, most regulatory agencies) will continue to argue that evidence from the concrete end of the continuum is somehow better than evidence from the abstract end. Psychometricians will (should!!) respond that well-designed research anywhere on the continuum contributes to this evidentiary base for inference.

Comprehensive Validation

As Maslow famously noted, when your only tool is a hammer, everything is treated as a nail. In the twenty-first century, we are both burdened and liberated. We are burdened with the studies of the '50s, '60s, and '70s that viewed the world through "g" and O(verall performance) lenses. We know better now. We know that there are many attributes in the predictor space, and we know that the criterion space can be parsed more finely. That is our liberation.

Implications: Validation research can no longer hide behind the troglodytic language of the *Uniform Guidelines*. In I/O psychology, the issue has always been the prediction of job performance in its most expansive version. Validation can no longer be about the smallest predictable part of a job. It must be about the feasibly predictable part of the job. Twenty-first-century validation designs should acknowledge that we know more about work and about attributes than we did in 1964.

Summary

To summarize my observations, for better or worse, the changing nature of work has introduced many new wrinkles to the validation architecture. Many things that we, as a profession and as a science, might have thought (or wished to be) settled, are now unsettled. Much of what we know resembles a photo album with pictures of adolescence, young adulthood, and so on. But a photo captures a static reality. Our reality is changing rapidly, more rapidly than it has in any similar period since we have been a science. That does not mean we reject what we have known; it means that we have to accept that what we "know" sits on shifting sands. Donald Rumsfeld has been famously quoted on epistemology: "There are things we know, there are things we don't know, there are things we know we don't know . . ." We might add to his wit and wisdom, "and there are things we knew but may not know anymore."

References

Ackerman, P. L. (1992). Predicting individual differences in complex skill acquisition: Dynamics of ability determinants. *Journal of Applied Psychology, 77,* 598–614.

Binning, J. E., & Barrett, G. V. (1989). Validity of personnel decisions: A conceptual analysis of the inferential and evidential bases. *Journal of Applied Psychology, 74,* 478–494.

Carroll, J. B. (1993). *Human cognitive abilities: A survey of factor-analytic studies.* Cambridge, England: Cambridge University Press.

Chan, D., & Schmitt, N. (2002). Situational judgment and job performance. *Human Performance, 15*(3), 233–254.

Chan, D., & Schmitt, N. (In press). Situational judgment tests. In N. Anderson, A. Evers, & O. Voskuijil (Eds.), *Blackwell handbook of selection* (n.p.). Oxford, England: Blackwell.

Cole, M., Gay, J., Glick, J., & Sharpe, D. W. (1971). *The cultural context of learning and thinking.* New York: Basic Books.

Cronbach, L. J., & Meehl, P. E. (1955) Construct validity in psychological tests. *Psychological Bulletin, 52,* 281–302.

Equal Employment Opportunity Commission, Civil Service Commission, Department of Labor, & Department of Justice. (1978). *Uniform guidelines on employee selection procedures. Federal Register, 43*(166), 38290–38315.

Guion, R. M. (1965). *Personnel testing.* New York: McGraw-Hill.

Hackman, J. R. (1987). The design of work teams. In J. W. Lorsch (Ed.), *Handbook of organizational behavior* (pp. 315–342). Englewood Cliffs, NJ: Prentice Hall.

Hackman, J. R. (1990). *Groups that work (and those that don't).* San Francisco: Jossey-Bass.

Landy, F. J. (1986). Stamp collecting versus science: Validation as hypothesis testing. *American Psychologist, 41*(11), 1183–1192.

Landy, F. J. (2005). The long, frustrating, and fruitless search for social intelligence. In K. R. Murphy (Ed.), *The emotional intelligence bandwagon: The struggle between science and marketing for the soul of EI.* Mahwah, NJ: Erlbaum.

Landy, F. J., & Conte, J. M. (2004). *Work in the 21st century.* New York: McGraw-Hill.

Landy, F. J., & Conte, J. M. (2007). *Work in the 21st century* (2nd ed.). Boston: Blackwell.

Pulakos, E. D., Arad, S., Donovan, M. A., & Plamandon, K. E. (2000, August). Adaptability in the workplace: Development of a taxonomy of adaptive performance. *Journal of Applied Psychology, 85*(4), 612–624.

Salas, E., & Cannon-Bowers, J. A. (2001). The science of training: A decade of progress. *Annual Review of Psychology, 52,* 471–499.

Schmidt, F. L., & Hunter, J. E. (2002). History, development and impact of validity generalization and meta-analysis methods. In K. R. Murphy (Ed.), *Validity Generalization: A Critical Review.* Mahwah, NJ: Erlbaum.

Schmitt, N., & Landy, F. J. (1992) The concept of validity. In N. Schmitt and W. Borman (Eds.), *Frontiers of industrial and organizational psychology: Volume 4—Personnel selection in organizations.* (pp. 275–309). San Francisco: Jossey-Bass.

Society for Industrial and Organizational Psychology. (2003). *Principles for the validation and use of personnel selection procedures.* (4th Ed). Bowling Green, OH: Society for Industrial and Organizational Psychology.

Thorndike, E. L. (1920). Intelligence and its use. *Harper's, 140,* 227–235.

Name Index

Subject Index

consortium studies and security issues of, 243; construct validation hypotheses, 338–339; content validation and procedures of, 261, 306–308; differential predication of job performance, 161–162; distributions of performance from simulated contrasting groups procedure, 392fig; Employment Aptitude Series, 99; fairness issue of, 41–43; Guidelines on Employee Testing Procedures (EEOC), 4; linking KSAOs and work behaviors, 308–309; linking work behavior and KSAOs to, 295–300; O*NET (Occupational Information Network) predicting results of, 100t; PAT (physical ability test), 95–97, 98t; racial differences in employment test scores, 161–163; 70 percent rule of, 371–372; Specific Aptitude Test Battery, 113; Technical Recommendations for Psychological Tests and Diagnostic Techniques (APA), 3; Test Attitude Survey (TAS), 339; transportability, 111; validity generalization to support validity of, 169–174; Workplace Literacy Tests, 99. See also Cut scores; General Aptitude Test Battery (GATB); Standards for Educational and Psychological Tests

Theory: advancing, 321; consortium studies, 247–249; content validation, 253–263; transportable validation, 29–35; validation strategies building, 11–12

Title I (Americans with Disabilities Act), 352

Title VII (Civil Rights Act), 279, 280, 351–353, 356, 400

TQM environments, 415

Transportable validation: comparing traditional approaches to, 35–37;

conditions required for, 29–35, 217–219; constraints and risks of, 76–79; construct validation using, 332, 333; described, 35–37, 332, 333; JCV PAQ testing, 111; job similarity indices using, 34, 74–75, 206; legal implications of, 39–51; practical development of, 54–74; professional guides on, 108–109, 205; professional implications of, 51–54; research base of, 37–39; researching transportability from personality predictors, 204–209; synthetic validation application of, 150, 152; Uniform Guidelines regarding, 35–37, 108–109, 205, 333

Transportable validation legal issues: Albemarle Paper v. Moody, 40–41, 49t, 50, 87; Bernard v. Gulf Oil Corporation, 46–47, 49t, 50, 168; Dickerson v. United States Steel Corp., 41–43, 49t, 51; Friend v. Leidinger, 45–46, 50, 51, 166; Pegues v. Mississippi State Employment Service, 47, 49t, 50, 51, 167; Vanguard Justice Society v. Hughes, 43–45, 49t, 50

Transportable validation steps: 1: review job information/develop preliminary project plan, 55–58; 2: review source study, 58–61; 3: develop procedures, plan analyses, gather data to examine job similarity, 61–68t; 4: complete analyses of job similarity/document study results, 68–74; overview of, 54–55

U

Uniform Guidelines on Employee Selection Procedures (EEOC): addressing validity generalization in context of, 163–164, 336, 411; choice of settings permitted by, 109; codification of tripartite